Guide to Housing Benefit and Council Tax Benefit 2009-10

John Zebedee, Martin Ward and Sam Lister

Shelter

[redacted]

Shelter

We are one of the richest countries in the world, and yet millions of people in Britain wake up every day in housing that is run-down, overcrowded or dangerous. Many others have lost their homes altogether. Bad housing robs us of security, health, and a fair chance in life.

Shelter helps more than 170,000 people a year fight for their rights, get back on their feet, and find and keep a home. We also tackle the root causes of Britain's housing crisis by campaigning for new laws, policies and solutions. Our website gets more than 100,000 visits a month; visit *shelter.org.uk* to join our campaign, find housing advice, or make a donation.

For more information about Shelter, please contact:

88 Old Street
London
EC1V 9HU

Tel: 0845 458 4590

shelter.org.uk

For help with your housing problems, phone Shelter's free housing advice helpline on 0808 800 4444 (open seven days a week from 8am to 8pm; charges may apply to mobile phone calls) or visit *shelter.org.uk/getadvice*

Chartered Institute of Housing

The Chartered Institute of Housing (CIH) is the professional body for people involved in housing and communities. We are a registered charity and not-for-profit organisation. We have a diverse and growing membership of over 22,000 people – both in the public and private sectors – living and working in more than 20 countries on five continents. We exist to maximise the contribution that housing professionals make to the wellbeing of communities.

Chartered Institute of Housing
Octavia House
Westwood Way
Coventry
CV4 8JP

Telephone: 024 7685 1700
E-mail: *customer.services@cih.org*
Web site: *www.cih.org*

Guide to Housing Benefit
Peter McGurk and Nick Raynsford, 1982-88
Martin Ward and John Zebedee, 1988-90

Guide to Housing Benefit and Community Charge Benefit
Martin Ward and John Zebedee, 1990-93

Guide to Housing Benefit and Council Tax Benefit
John Zebedee and Martin Ward, 1993-2003
John Zebedee, Martin Ward and Sam Lister, 2003-10

John Zebedee is an independent benefits trainer and consultant. He has taught more than 2,000 HB/CTB courses for local authorities, housing associations, advice organisations and others; and also advises and represents claimants and others at first-tier and upper tribunal hearings (email: *johnzebedee@hotmail.com*).

Martin Ward is an independent benefits consultant and trainer (e-mail: *mward@info-training.co.uk*). He maintains a web-site which gives convenient access to relevant legislation and other useful sources – *www.info-training.co.uk*

Sam Lister is policy and practice officer at the Chartered Institute of Housing (email: *sam.lister@cih.org*) and a founding director of Worcester Citizens Advice Bureau and Whabac.

John Zebedee and Martin Ward have specialised in housing benefit and council tax benefit since the schemes were introduced.

ISBN 978 1 903595 86 2

Production by Davies Communications *(www.daviescomms.com)*

Printed in the UK by CPI William Clowes Beccles NR34 7TL

Preface

This Guide explains the rules about housing benefit and council tax benefit as they apply from April 2009. It uses the information available on 1st April 2009.

We welcome comments and criticisms on the contents of our guide and make every effort to ensure it is accurate. However, the only statement of the law is found in the relevant Acts, regulations, orders and rules (chapter 1).

This guide has been written with the help and encouragement of many other people. This year we thank the following in particular:

Denise Blake, Mary Connolly, Lynn Hambleton, Colin Hull (chapter 11), Michael Iyekekpolor, James Kelly, Phillip J. Miall, Sean O'Sullivan, Jonathan Reid, Mark Rodgers, Ben See, Andrew Waugh, Linda Davies and Peter Singer (editing and production) as well as staff from the Department for Work and Pensions and the Rent Service. Their help has been essential to the production of this guide.

John Zebedee, Martin Ward and Sam Lister

April 2009

Contents

Contents

Abbreviations

The principal abbreviations used in the guide are given below. A key to the footnotes can be found in chapter 1 in table 1.4.

CTB	Council tax benefit
CTC	Child tax credit
DSD	The Department for Social Development in Northern Ireland
DWP	The Department for Work and Pensions in Great Britain
EP	Extended payment
ESA	Employment and support allowance (including ESA(C) and ESA (IR))
ESA(C)	Contributory employment and support allowance
ESA(IR)	Income-based employment and support allowance
GLHA	The DWP guidance local housing allowance
GM	The DWP HB/CTB Guidance Manual
HB	Housing benefit
HMRC	Her Majesty's Revenue and Customs
HRA	Housing revenue account
IB	Incapacity benefit
IS	Income support
JSA	Jobseeker's allowance (including JSA(C) & JSA(IB))
JSA(C)	Contribution-based jobseeker's allowance
JSA(IB)	Income-based jobseeker's allowance
NI	Northern Ireland
NIHE	The Northern Ireland Housing Executive
OG	The DWP HB/CTB Overpayments Guide
SDA	Severe disablement allowance
SI	Statutory instrument
SR	Statutory rules (Northern Ireland)
UK	England, Scotland, Wales and Northern Ireland
WTC	Working tax credit

Abbreviations

1 Introduction

1.1 Welcome to this guide, which describes housing benefit (HB) and council tax benefit (CTB) throughout the UK from April 2009. The guide helps administrators, advisers, claimants, landlords and appeal tribunals.

1.2 HB helps people pay their rent (or rates) and CTB helps people pay their council tax. They are an important source of help for many households: some basic statistics are given in table 1.1.

1.3 This chapter contains:

- a summary of the HB/CTB schemes;
- the benefit figures, terminology and references used in this guide;
- the administration of the HB/CTB schemes;
- HB/CTB law and guidance and how to get hold of it; and
- the rules about proper decision-making.

Please turn back a page to find the main abbreviations used in this guide.

Summary of the HB and CTB schemes

Who gets HB and CTB?

1.4 In broad terms, the main rules about who can get HB and CTB are:

- nearly everyone with low or lowish income and capital can get HB (if they pay rent, and/or in Northern Ireland rates) or CTB (if they pay council tax) or both (chapter 6);
- to get HB or CTB the claimant has to make a claim – and keep the claim going by providing details of changes in their circumstances (chapters 5 and 17);
- HB and CTB are only payable on the claimant's normal home, but there are rules for people who are temporarily absent or are liable for rent on two dwellings (chapter 3);
- because rents can be expensive, there are limitations on how much rent can be met by HB (chapters 8 to 10);
- some groups of people cannot get HB or CTB no matter how low their income is; for example, many care leavers, most full-time students and certain migrants (chapters 2, 20 and 21 respectively).

Table 1.1: Key HB and CTB statistics

HB claims in Great Britain as at 30 September 2007*	
Number of cases	3.39 million
Average weekly payment	£73.15
Main CTB claims in Great Britain as at 30 September 2007*	
Number of cases	4.29 million
Average weekly payment	£15.27
Take up of HB/CTB in Great Britain 2006-07*	
HB by caseload	between 81 and 87%
HB by expenditure	between 86 and 92%
CTB by caseload (social rented tenants)	between 87 and 93%
CTB by caseload (owner occupiers)	between 38 and 43%
Annual expenditure in Great Britain in 2008-09*	
HB planned expenditure	£16.614 billion
CTB planned expenditure	£4.253 billion
NIHE tenants in Northern Ireland in receipt of HB 2007-08**	
Number of claimants	67,269 (77%)
Receiving full rebate	56,769 (84%)
Average weekly payment	£55.69

* Source: DWP, Information and Analysis Directorate

** Source: DSD Statistics and Research Agency

HB, CTB and the 'passport benefits'

1.5 The state 'safety net' of benefits is designed to make sure citizens have enough money to live on. It has the following two halves.

1.6 Four benefits – often called the 'passport benefits' – can help meet basic living needs (such as food and heating – but not rent, rates or council tax):

- income-based jobseekers' allowance (JSA(IB));
- income support (IS);
- guarantee credit (part of state pension credit); and
- income-related employment and support allowance (ESA(IR)).

1.7 Help with rent, rates and council tax can be met by HB and CTB. People on one of the passport benefits get maximum help, but many other people qualify for some help.

How much HB and CTB?

1.8 HB for rent is usually worked out on either the rent the claimant actually pays, apart from any charges included in the rent for services which HB cannot meet (chapter 8); or a fixed 'local housing allowance' figure depending on where the claimant lives and the size of accommodation needed (chapter 9). CTB is worked out on the amount of council tax payable on the claimant's dwelling and HB for rates on the amount of rates payable on the dwelling (chapter 11).

1.9 The amount of HB/CTB a claimant qualifies for depends on the following main things (chapter 6):

- whether the claimant (or partner) is on one of the 'passport benefits' (para. 1.6);
- if they are not on one of the passport benefits, how much income and capital the claimant (and partner) have (chapters 13 to 15);
- if they are not on one of the passport benefits, how much they (and their family) are treated as needing to live on, known as their 'applicable amount' (chapters 4 and 12);
- the circumstances of other adults in their home, known as 'non-dependants' (para. 1.10).

1.10 HB and CTB can be reduced because a non-dependant is expected to contribute towards the rent, rates or council tax (chapter 6). However, there is also a less common type of CTB known as second adult rebate that depends not on the claimant's circumstances but on those of a non-dependant (chapter 10).

Awards and appeals

1.11 HB and CTB are administered mainly by local councils (which are largely reimbursed for this by the government: chapter 23) or in Northern Ireland by executive agencies of government. Once they have assessed HB/CTB, they must notify the decision (and any later changes to it) to the claimant and sometimes others (chapter 16).

1.12 There is a right to obtain further information about matters relating to an award of HB or CTB, to ask the council to reconsider, and to appeal to an independent tribunal (chapter 19). This covers decisions about how much HB and CTB is awarded, how it was calculated, when HB and CTB starts including decisions about backdating (chapter 5), and what happens when HB or CTB is overpaid (chapter 18).

Table 1.2: Summary of changes since April 2008

SI 2008/698 NISR 2008/112 14th April 2008	Various recasting and tidying up of the main regulations which do not affect the operation of the law but remove redundant paragraphs and obsolete references including defunct historic social security benefits (e.g. 'supplementary benefit').
SI 2008/1042 NISR 2008/179 19th May 2008	Further consolidation to delete references in the working age regulations to the pensioner and higher pension premiums and various other consequential amendments. Various other amendments to update incorrect or otherwise obsolete references and to correct some errors which occurred when the regulations were consolidated in 2006.
SI 2008/1599 NISR 2008/262 August/ September 2008	Up-rating of figures used in assessing student cases. Clarification of the rules about the treatment of student loans which are paid other than on a quarterly basis where the student abandons their course.
SI 2008/2112 SI 2008/2114 NISR 2008/342 NISR 2008/343 1st September 2008	Enhanced data sharing arrangements between DWP and between the local authority teams who administer HB/CTB and the Supporting People programme. Tenants who apply for help under the Supporting People programme will not have to provide the same information twice and the Supporting People team will not have to seek informed consent from the tenants to obtain details of their social security benefits.
SI 2008/2299 NISR 2008/371 1st October 2008	A claim can now be made for HB/CTB by telephone direct to the DWP where that person is also making a claim for a passport benefit, incapacity benefit or any kind of JSA or ESA. Obsolete references in regulations to gateway offices and ONE pilots deleted.
SI 2008/959 NISR 2008/285 6th October 2008	A claimant who qualifies for an extended payment of HB/CTB is no longer required to make a claim when they start work; instead the authority must consider entitlement to an extended payment as part of the change of circumstances procedure. Claimants are no longer required to make a fresh claim in order to continue to qualify for HB/CTB after that.

SI 2008/2424 SI 2008/2824 NISR 2008/410 NISR 2008/504 6th October 2008	Time limit for claiming HB/CTB by pension credit age (60+) claimants' reduced from 12 months to three months (effectively limiting the award for a past period to a maximum of three months). The maximum period for which HB/CTB can be backdated for working age claimants is reduced from 52 weeks to six months.
SI 2008/1082 SI 2008/2428 NISR 2008/378 27th October 2008	Introduction of employment and support allowance (ESA) to replace incapacity benefit and income support for all new claims where the claimant is currently unable to work due to sickness or disability. The new benefit has two elements: contribution-based (ESA(C)) which is dependent on the claimant's national insurance record; and income related ESA(IR) which replaces income support paid on grounds of incapacity and which is a new passport benefit for HB/CTB. In non ESA(IR) claims ESA(C) will count in full as income. ESA also affects the calculation of the applicable amount. The disability premium is abolished for new claimants entitled to ESA. Instead claimants may be entitled to additional components in their ESA once they reach the 'main phase' stage after 13 weeks. There are two components a 'work-related activity' component and a 'support component' for the most disabled claimants. If awarded the component is included in their HB/CTB applicable amount. Single claimants aged under 25 are entitled to higher rate personal allowance once they reach the main phase of ESA.
SI 2008/1042 NISR 2008/179 27th October 2008	Child maintenance to be disregarded in full in the assessment of income for HB/CTB
SI 2008/2667 NISR 2008/417 30th October 2008	Clarification of the rules concerning suspensions so as to allow the authority to suspend HB/CTB where they are waiting to receive the decision of a tribunal, upper tribunal or court. Clarification as to when the date of change of circumstances takes effect with respect to a payment for a former home so that the change takes place on the day after last day that they are treated as occupying it.

SI 2008/2683 SI 2008/2685 SI 2008/2698 3rd November 2008	The following changes under the Tribunals, Courts and Enforcement Act 2007: Social security appeal tribunals renamed 'First-tier Tribunals'; Commissioner hearings renamed 'Upper Tribunals'. Commissioners (renamed tribunal judges) are now able to exercise a limited judicial review function. Rules do not apply in Northern Ireland where for the time being the old rules remain in force.
SI 2008/2767 NISR 2008/428 17th November 2008	Further consolidation of the regulations to remove obsolete references to the independent living fund and related trusts; youth training schemes; community charge benefit; and miscellaneous legislation.
SI 2008/3140 NISR 2008/497 5th January 2009	The whole of the increase in child benefit which takes effect from this date is disregarded (£1.20 for the first child and £0.65 for each subsequent child). This is a temporary disregard until the normal up-rating takes effect.
SI 2008/3157 NISR 2008/498 5th January 2009	Income and capital disregards are aligned with other means-tested social security benefits. A new disregard is introduced to enable the statutory £10 war pension disregard (in Northern Ireland full disregard) to continue to apply when the war pension has been abated by an Armed Forces Pension Scheme payment. Other minor technical amendments, update of some outdated references and revoke some redundant provisions.
SI 2008/3156 NISR 2008/506 5th January 2009	Changes made to rules concerning how rent officers determine the extent of the broad rental market areas (BRMAs) which effectively reverses the House of Lords decision on the 30/07/08 of R (Heffernan) v The Rent Service. BRMAs can now be set over a wide area encompassing an entire city. Except in Northern Ireland BRMAs also now apply to local reference rents – replacing localities.

SI 2009/362 NISR 2009/68 18 March 2009	Nationals of Zimbabwe made an offer of settlement by the UK Government at any time between 28/2/2009 and 17/3/2011 are exempt from the habitual residence test.
1st April 2009	In England the Rent Service is abolished and its functions (and the work of rent officers) transferred to the Valuation Office Agency an executive agency within the HMRC.
SI 2009/497 NISR 2009/89 1st/6th April 2009	Annual up-rating of HB/CTB figures.
SI 2009/471 NISR 2009/90 6th April 2009	A person who is an ineligible foreign national is no longer required to have a national insurance number if their eligible partner makes a claim
SI 2008/2824 6th April 2009	In Great Britain, where the claimant rents their mobile home site from the authority but pays rent for the home to another landlord, HB on both is paid as a rent allowance and the claim is assessed as a standard case. Law clarified so that claims relating to county council gypsy or traveller sites are not normally referred to the rent officer.
SI 2008/2824 NISR 2008/504 6th April 2009	Overpayment rules are clarified Overpayments, other than those caused by a failure to notify are recoverable from the claimant and the payee. Overpayments caused by a failure to notify are recoverable from anyone who failed to notify. Recovery from a partner is only to be used where the overpayment is being recovered from ongoing HB. The new rules are not intended to reflect a change in policy from CH/4234/2004.
SI 2009/614 6th April 2009	In Great Britain, the LHA is restricted to five bedroom properties. Transitional rules apply for existing claims for properties with six or more bedrooms.
October 2009	Child benefit will be fully disregarded as announced in the 2008 budget.

Using this guide

1.13 The HB and CTB rules in this guide are the ones applying from April 2009. The rules change frequently. The main changes since the last edition of this guide are given in table 1.2 (which also gives future changes where they are known).

HB/CTB and other benefit figures

1.14 The various figures used in calculating HB and CTB are up-rated each April together with other social security benefits and tax credits, usually in line with inflation. For the exact dates this year, see table 1.3. For the main figures for HB/CTB and other benefits this year, see appendices 4 and 5.

Table 1.3: April 2009 up-rating dates

For HB for rent if the rent is due weekly or in multiples of weeks	Monday 6th April 2009
For HB for rent in all other cases, and for HB for rates and CTB in all cases	Wednesday 1st April 2009
Most other state benefits	Week commencing 6th April 2009 *
Tax credits	Monday 6th April 2009 *

* These changes are taken into account for HB/CTB on 1st/6th April 2009 but see also para. 13.47.

Terminology used in this guide

1.15 In this guide, the following terms are used:

- 'authority' means any of the public authorities which administers HB/CTB (para. 1.18);
- 'tenant' is used to describe any kind of rent-payer (including, for example, licensees);
- 'housing benefit' (HB) means any form of HB for rent or (in Northern Ireland) rates;
- 'rent rebate' means HB for rent for a council tenant;
- 'rent allowance' means HB for rent for anyone else;
- 'council tax benefit' (CTB) means any form of CTB including the less common kind called 'second adult rebate' (referred to in the law as 'alternative maximum CTB');

- 'state pension credit' refers to either type of pension credit – 'guarantee credit' and 'savings credit';
- 'guarantee credit' is used to refer to any award of pension credit which includes an amount of guarantee credit – whether it is paid with or without the savings credit;
- 'savings credit' is used to refer to awards of pension credit which consist solely of an award of the savings credit.

Abbreviations and references

1.16 A list of abbreviations used in the text is given at the front of this guide, following the contents page. The references in the footnotes throughout this guide refer to the law governing HB and CTB. Table 1.4 provides a key to these. All the references are to the law as amended (para. 1.29).

1.17 For example, the footnote for this paragraph (which is actually about overpayments which cannot be recovered: para. 18.10) refers to regulation 100(2) of the Housing Benefit Regulations 2006, regulation 81(2) of the Housing Benefit (Persons who have attained the qualifying age for state pension credit) Regulations 2006, the two Northern Ireland equivalents, and the two CTB equivalents, all six of which say exactly the same thing.

Administering the HB/CTB schemes

Who administers the HB and CTB schemes?

1.18 HB was first introduced throughout the UK in 1982-83, and CTB in 1992-93 with the introduction of council tax. There are different arrangements for administering HB/CTB in different parts of the UK:

- in areas in England with two layers of local government (county and district/borough), HB/CTB are administered by the district/borough councils;
- in the rest of Great Britain (areas with one layer of local government), HB/CTB are administered by English unitary authorities and London boroughs (including the Common Council of the City of London), Welsh county and county borough councils, and Scottish local councils;
- in Northern Ireland, HB for rent and rates for tenants is administered for tenants by the Northern Ireland Housing Executive (NIHE) and for owners by the Land and Property Services. More details and exceptions are in table 1.5.

1.17 HB 100(2); HB60+ 81(2); NIHB 97(2); NIHB60+ 78(2); CTB 83(2); CTB60+ 68(2)

1.18 AA 134(1),(1A),(1B),(2), 139(1),(2), 191; NIAA 126(2),(3)

Table 1.4: Key to footnotes

Each reference applies to Great Britain only unless otherwise stated or prefixed by 'NI' (e.g. NIAA) in which case it applies to Northern Ireland only.

AA	The Social Security Administration Act 1992, followed by section number.
Art	Article number.
CBA	The Social Security Contributions and Benefits Act 1992, followed by section number.
CPR	The Housing Benefit and Council Tax Benefit (Consequential Provisions) Regulations 2006, SI No. 217, followed by the regulation number.
CTB	The Council Tax Benefit Regulations 2006 (as amended), SI No. 215 followed by regulation number.
CTB60+	The Council Tax Benefit (Persons who have attained the age for state pension credit) Regulations 2006 (as amended), SI No. 216, followed by regulation number.
CPSA	The Child Support, Pensions and Social Security Act, followed by the section number.
DAR	The Housing Benefit and Council Tax Benefit (Decisions and Appeals) Regulations 2001, SI No. 1002, (as amended), followed by the regulation number.
DAR99	The Social Security and Child Support (Decisions and Appeals) Regulations 1999, SI No. 991, (as amended), followed by the regulation number.
EEA	The Immigration (European Economic Area) Regulations 2006, SI No. 1003, followed by regulation number (UK reference).
FTPR	The Tribunal Procedure (First-tier Tribunal)(Social Entitlement Chamber) Rules 2008, SI No. 2685 (as amended) followed by rule number.
HB	The Housing Benefit Regulations 2006, SI No. 213, (as amended), followed by the regulation number.
HB60+	The Housing Benefit (Persons who have attained the age for state pension credit) Regulations 2006, SI No. 214 (as amended), followed by regulation number.
IAA99	The Immigration and Asylum Act 1999, followed by the section number (UK reference).

NIAA	The Social Security Administration (Northern Ireland) Act 1992, followed by the section number.
NICBA	The Social Security Contributions and Benefits (Northern Ireland) Act 1992, followed by the section number.
NICPR	The Housing Benefit and Council Tax Benefit (Consequential Provisions) Regulations (Northern Ireland) 2006, SR No. 407, followed by the regulation number.
NICPSA	The Child Support, Pensions and Social Security Act (Northern Ireland) 2000, followed by the section number.
NIDAR	The Housing Benefit (Decisions and Appeals) Regulations (Northern Ireland) 2001 SR No. 213 (as amended), followed by regulation number.
NIDAR99	The Social Security and Child Support (Decisions and Appeals) Regulations (Northern Ireland) 1999 SR No. 162 (as amended), followed by regulation number.
NIED	The Housing Benefit (Executive Determinations) Regulations (Northern Ireland) 2008 SR No. 100.
NIHB	The Housing Benefit Regulations (Northern Ireland) 2006, SR No. 405 (as amended) followed by regulation number.
NIHB60+	The Housing Benefit (Persons who have attained the age for state pension credit) Regulations (Northern Ireland) 2006, SR No. 406 (as amended) followed by the regulation number.
NISR	Statutory Rules of Northern Ireland (equivalent to Statutory Instruments in GB).
NISSCPR	The Social Security Commissioners (Procedure) Regulations (Northern Ireland) 1999, SR No. 225 (as amended), followed by the regulation number.
Reg	Regulation, followed by regulation number.
ROO	In England and Wales, The Rent Officers (Housing Benefit Functions) Order 1997, SI 1984; in Scotland, The Rent Officers (Housing Benefit Functions) (Scotland) Order 1997, SI 1985; in both cases followed by article number or schedule and paragraph number.
sch	Schedule.
SI	Statutory instrument, followed by year and reference number.
SR	Statutory rules, followed by year and reference number (apply to NI only).
UTPR	The Tribunal Procedure (Upper Tribunal) Rules 2008, SI No. 2698 (as amended) followed by rule number.

Table 1.5: Where to claim rate rebates, rate relief and lone pensioner allowance

Land and Property Services	Northern Ireland Housing Executive (NIHE)
Owner occupiers	NIHE tenants
Partners of sole owners	Housing association tenants
Former partners of sole owners	Tenants of private landlords
Former non-dependants of sole owners	People with a life interest
	People in co-ownership schemes
	People in rental purchase schemes

Arranging for someone else to administer HB/CTB

1.19 Authorities in Great Britain (but not Northern Ireland) may arrange for HB (but not CTB) to be administered on their behalf by another authority or by a number of authorities jointly. This does not apply to HB for claimants who are council tenants renting from the authority which administers their HB. So if an authority has properties in another area, the tenants there claim HB from their landlord authority, but CTB from the authority for the area they live in.

1.20 Authorities can contract out the administration of HB and CTB to private companies (in other words, pay them to do part or all of their work). They do this under the Deregulation and Contracting Out Act 1994 and the Contracting Out (Functions of Local Authorities: Income-related Benefits) Regulations 2002/1888. When contractors make decisions on claims, they must submit a daily 10% random sample of claims for the authority to check. The claimant does not lose their right of appeal about any contracted out decisions.

Good administration

1.21 Under the Local Government Act 1999 authorities in England and Wales are required to do what a good authority would do anyway – such as to provide the best value they can, achieve continuous improvement (until the service is completely perfect), publish their plans for how they will perform, and check up on themselves from time to time.

1.22 The DWP sets authorities 'performance indicators' (checks on how well they do their work). The key indicators for 2009-10 are:

1.19 AA 134 (1A),(5), 191

1.22 AA 139A-139H

- a new 'right time' indicator – which is the average time to process claims and changes to entitlement; and
- a new 'right benefit' indicator – which is the number of changes to entitlement in a year.

The DWP can ask the Audit Commission/Welsh Audit Office to study how well authorities are doing and to inspect and report on their administration generally and on the prevention and detection of fraud. The Performance Guide, which provides good practice guidance to help authorities manage their services efficiently, is available at *www.dwp.gov.uk/housingbenefit/performance-value-for-money/perf-stands/*. The DWP can then require an authority to take action on its failings and (if it then fails to improve) can make it give HB/CTB administration work to someone else (typically a contractor).

Maladministration

1.23 In individual cases of bad authority administration, the claimant (or someone else) can complain to the Local Government Ombudsman. For guidance on how to complain, what constitutes maladministration, and recent Ombudsman's reports on HB/CTB, see *www.lgo.org.uk* (England), *www.ombudsman-wales.org.uk* (Wales), *www.spso.org.uk* (Scotland) and *www.ni-ombudsman.org.uk* (Northern Ireland).

HB and CTB law

Acts of Parliament

1.24 The Acts which give the basic rules of the HB/CTB schemes are the Social Security Contributions and Benefits Act 1992, the Social Security Administration Act 1992 and their Northern Ireland equivalents, and also (as regards decision-making and appeals) the Child Support, Pensions and Social Security Act 2000.

1.25 The Data Protection Act 1998 controls the use of, and access to, information about an individual held on a computer or any other retrievable filing system. This Act does not stop disclosure when other law requires it (section 35 of the Act) but authorities are under a duty to protect personal information (GM chapter D3).

1.26 Other Acts affecting HB and CTB include section 115 of the Immigration and Asylum Act 1999 (about migrants), section 87 of the Northern Ireland Act 1998 (requiring the social security system to be UK-wide), the Human Rights Act 1998, various anti-discrimination laws, the Local Government Finance Act 1982, the Deregulation and Contracting Out Act 1994, the Local Government Act 1999, the Audit Commission Act 1998 and the Public Audit (Wales) Act 2004.

Regulations, orders and rules

1.27 The regulations, orders and rules giving the detail of the HB/CTB schemes are all passed under the Acts mentioned above and are listed in Appendix 1. They are known technically as Statutory Instruments (SIs) and in Northern Ireland as Statutory Rules (SRs). The main regulations became law in 2006, when they 'consolidated' hundreds of earlier ones (wrote them out again). Although there are separate regulations for (a) HB vs CTB, (b) Great Britain vs Northern Ireland and (c) claimants aged 60+ (i.e. 'persons who have attained the qualifying age for state pension credit') vs those under 60, the law in each of these six cases is largely the same.

Obtaining the law

1.28 Members of the public have a right to see copies of the relevant legal material (plus details of any local scheme: para. 22.12) at an authority's principal office.

1.29 The Acts, regulations, orders and rules are available at *www.opsi.gov.uk.* For the consolidated legislation, see the DWP's *The Law Relating to Social Security,* volume 8 parts 1 and 2 (also called 'the blue volumes') available for Great Britain at *www.dwp.gov.uk/advisers/docs/ lawvols/bluevol/index.asp* and for Northern Ireland at *www.dsdni.gov.uk/ law_relating_to_social_security.* The Child Poverty Action Group's (CPAG's) annual publication, *Housing Benefit and Council Tax Benefit Legislation,* also contains all the law relevant in Great Britain at the point of publication plus a detailed commentary including references to case law.

Proper decision-making

1.30 This part of the guide explains how an authority should go about making decisions on HB/CTB by working through the following steps:

- identifying what the relevant facts are in any particular case;
- properly considering the evidence that does exist, if the facts are in doubt or in dispute;
- establishing the facts 'on the balance of probability' if this is necessary;
- correctly interpreting the relevant law and applying it to the facts of the case; and
- arriving at decisions that can be understood in terms of the relevant facts and law.

Relevant facts

1.31 The only facts which are relevant to the authority are those which affect the HB/CTB schemes:

- sometimes the facts are clear and not in dispute. For example, it may be agreed by the claimant and the authority that the claimant has a grown-up son living with him;
- sometimes facts are unclear or are in dispute. For example, the claimant may say the son is not living with him (but other things suggest he is);
- sometimes there is no evidence of the facts at all. For example, the claimant may have left all of the 'your household' section of his HB/CTB application form blank.

1.32 The law uses two ideas to deal with uncertainty about the facts: 'burden of proof' and 'balance of probability'. Lawyers argue about what these mean, and which applies when, but it is possible to distinguish them in a general way.

Burden of proof

1.33 The 'burden of proof' is the idea that it is up to someone to prove their side of a dispute. It is used when there is something that has to be shown to be the case in order for HB/CTB law to apply at all. Two examples are:

- when a claimant first makes a claim for HB/CTB, there is at the outset no evidence – and so it is for the claimant to support the claim by supplying the authority with all the evidence it reasonably requires (para. 5.17);
- when the authority says that a recoverable overpayment has occurred, the authority must have evidence to support this (para. 18.11).

1.34 The 'burden of proof' is also used when a decision cannot be made by the 'balance of probability' because there is no evidence either way, or the evidence that does exist is exactly balanced. In these cases the side with the burden loses unless they can supply evidence that adjusts the balance of probability in their favour.

Balance of probability

1.35 The 'balance of probability' is the idea that in the end a decision has to be made or nothing would ever get done. It is used when there is a disagreement about the facts. In such a case, the authority must consider the available evidence to decide what the true position is. The evidence each way must be weighed up and the 'facts' of the case are those supported by the greater weight of evidence. There does not have to be absolute certainty. It is because HB/CTB decisions are civil matters that the appropriate test is the 'balance of probability' (not 'beyond reasonable doubt', which is a test used in criminal law).

Examples: Relevant facts and balance of probability

1. The claimant and the authority agree that the claimant's grown-up son is living with him.

   The facts are not in dispute, so the facts are that the son does live there.

2. The authority receives reports from its HB/CTB visiting officer that a claimant's grown-up son is living with him and has been there on four consecutive visits, on one occasion coming down from his bedroom when the visiting officer arrived. The claimant says his son is not living there, but it is his correspondence address. He also says he does not know where the son is living.

   The facts are in dispute, but it is suggested here that, weighing up the evidence, it is more likely than not that the son is living there. So the facts are (on the balance of probability) that he is.

3. Following on from 2, six months later, the son makes his own claim for HB from another address and the authority accepts that he is living at that other address.

   Following this change of circumstances, the facts are no longer in dispute, so the facts are that the son is not (any longer) living with his father.

Applying the law

1.36 The HB and CTB schemes are governed by law passed by Parliament (paras. 1.24-29). The starting point for applying the law is that it means exactly what it says – though many words have special meanings in HB/CTB (as described throughout this guide) and precedents can affect how the law is interpreted (para. 1.38).

1.37 Having worked out which piece of law applies (and what it means), it must then be applied to the case in hand. For example, the question of whether or not a claimant's son counts as a non-dependant for HB/CTB purposes can only be answered by considering the legal definition of 'non-dependant' and applying it to the relevant facts. Part of the legal definition of a 'non-dependant' is that the person must 'normally reside' with the claimant. So if the facts of the case are that the son normally resides somewhere else but merely visits the claimant from time to time, then as a matter of law he cannot be a non-dependant.

Precedents from courts and upper tribunals

1.38 When there are 'precedents' (also called 'case law'), these should be followed. A 'precedent' is a binding decision by a court or an upper tribunal (para. 19.71) on a case which is relevant to the case in hand. For example, in deciding whether a person 'normally resides' with a claimant (in order to decide whether they count as a 'non-dependant') there is a precedent in the decision

Kadhim v Brent LBC (para. 4.45) which may well have a bearing on other individual cases. Generally speaking, precedents from one part of the UK are regarded as binding in other parts of the UK (for example GB precedent is taken into account in Northern Ireland: *C001/03-04(HB)*), and precedents from other parts of the social security system may be binding on similar decisions in HB/CTB (for example on backdating: para. 5.58).

1.39 Case law from the courts is given throughout this guide, and a list is given in appendix 2 (which also gives details of how to find the case law online). Most upper tribunal decisions are available for Great Britain at *www.administrativeappeals.tribunals.gov.uk* and for Northern Ireland at *www.dsdni.gov.uk/index/ law_and_legislation/nidoc_database.htm.*

Judgment and discretion

1.40 Sometimes a decision about HB/CTB requires the authority to use its judgment. The law uses terms like 'reasonable', 'appropriate', 'good cause' or 'special circumstances' to show that the authority has a judgment to make. Examples of judgments are:

- whether it is 'reasonable' for the authority to award HB on two homes in the case of person who has fled violence (para. 3.12);
- how much it is 'appropriate' to restrict a claimant's eligible rent in an old case (para. 8.63);
- whether a claimant has 'good cause' for their delay in claiming HB/CTB (para. 5.58);
- whether a claimant has 'special circumstances' for their delay in notifying an advantageous change in circumstances (para. 17.40).

1.41 And sometimes a decision about HB/CTB allows the authority to use its discretion. A discretion differs from a judgment in the sense that an authority may simply choose what to do. The law usually says that an authority 'may' do something to show that it has a discretion. Examples of discretion are:

- whether to award a discretionary housing payment (para. 22.2);
- whether to recover a recoverable overpayment of HB/CTB (para. 18.25);
- the appropriate assessment period for estimating earnings (para. 14.7).

Judicial review

1.42 When using judgment or discretion, authorities are bound by the principles of administrative law evolved by the courts. If they ignore these they can be challenged by applying to the High Court (or in Scotland the Court of Session) for 'judicial review'. Examples of when a challenge may be successful are if the authority:

- fails to consider each case on its merits, instead applying predetermined rules;
- takes into account matters which it ought not to consider;

- does not consider matters which it ought to take into account; or
- reaches a conclusion that no reasonable authority could have come to (what is reasonable here means rational rather than what is the best decision).

1.43 For more on judicial review, see *Judicial Review Proceedings,* Jonathan Manning, Legal Action Group; or *Judicial Review in Scotland,* Tom Mullen & Tony Prosser, Wiley.

DWP guidance

1.44 The DWP (Department for Work and Pensions) is the central government department responsible for HB/CTB policy. It publishes guidance on the schemes which is often very useful and is referred to throughout this guide. But (like this guide itself) it is guidance not law: *CH/3853/2001.*

1.45 DWP guidance includes the following:

- *Housing Benefit and Council Tax Benefit Guidance Manual* (GM);
- *Subsidy Guidance Manual;*
- *HB/CTB Overpayments Guide* (OG);
- *Guidance on Discretionary Housing Payments;*
- circulars in the 'A' series (about adjudication and operations);
- circulars in the 'F' series (about fraud);
- circulars in the 'S' series (about statistics and subsidy);
- circulars in the 'G' series (about general matters); and
- circulars in the 'U' series (about urgent matters).

1.46 The manuals are at *www.dwp.gov.uk/housingbenefit/claims-processing/operational-manuals/.* The 'A', 'S', 'G' and 'U' circulars are at *www.dwp.gov.uk/housingbenefit/user-communications/.* The 'F' circulars are not available to the public. Strictly speaking, DWP circulars do not apply to Northern Ireland although the authorities there generally accept the validity of 'A' circulars (unless the law in Northern Ireland is different).

2 Who is eligible for HB/CTB?

2.1 This chapter explains who can get HB and/or CTB. It describes:

- the basic conditions for getting HB/CTB;
- who is eligible for HB/CTB;
- who is excluded from HB/CTB;
- what payments HB can meet; and
- non-commercial, 'contrived', and other lettings where HB cannot be paid.

Basic conditions for getting HB/CTB

2.2 To get HB, the claimant must satisfy all the conditions in paragraph 2.3. To get CTB the claimant must satisfy all the conditions in paragraph 2.4. Once an award of HB/CTB is made, it continues until the claimant no longer satisfies all those conditions, at which point it ends (para. 17.21).

Housing benefit

2.3 The basic conditions for HB are:

- the claimant is liable to pay rent (or certain other items) for a dwelling in the UK (para. 2.27);
- the claimant occupies that dwelling as their normal home (chapter 3);
- the claimant (or someone on their behalf) makes a valid claim and provides relevant information and evidence (chapter 5);
- the claimant is not a member of an excluded group (paras. 1.4 and 2.8);
- the claimant's capital does not exceed £16,000 (para. 13.13) – but this does not apply if the claimant is on guarantee credit;
- any deductions for non-dependants (para. 6.17) do not exceed the claimant's eligible rent (or in Northern Ireland rates);
- the claimant's income is not too high (para. 2.5); and
- the result of the calculation of HB is at least 50p per week (para. 6.12) – but in Northern Ireland this does not apply to HB for rates.

There are also rules about when a person is treated as not being liable to make payments even though they are (para. 2.34).

2.3 AA 1(1),(1A),(1B); CBA 130(1),(4),134(1)(4); NIAA 1(1),(1A),(1B); NICBA 129(1), 130(1),(3)

Council tax benefit

2.4 The basic conditions for CTB are:

- the claimant is liable to pay council tax in respect of a dwelling (para. 11.7);
- the claimant has their sole or main residence in that dwelling (para. 11.7);
- the claimant (or someone on their behalf) makes a valid claim and provides relevant information and evidence (chapter 5);
- the claimant is not a member of an excluded group (paras. 1.4 and 2.7);
- the claimant's capital does not exceed £16,000 (para. 13.13) – but this does not apply if the claimant is on guarantee credit, and nor does it apply to second adult rebate;
- any deductions for non-dependants (para. 6.17) do not exceed the claimant's eligible council tax; and
- the claimant's income is not too high (para. 2.5) – but this does not apply to second adult rebate.

The first two rules above are very similar in their effect to the first two rules relating to HB (para. 2.3), but the law uses different words.

How low must the claimant's income be?

2.5 A claimant's income is low enough for them to get HB/CTB if any of the following applies:

- they are in receipt of JSA(IB), ESA(IR), income support or guarantee credit, or treated as being in receipt of those benefits (paras. 6.5-6);
- they have no income (para. 6.9);
- their income is less than or equal to their applicable amount (para. 6.9); or
- their income is greater than their applicable amount but the 'taper' calculation (paras. 6.10-11) still leaves an entitlement to HB/CTB.

Examples and types of HB and CTB

2.6 Examples of the cases in which a claimant can get HB or CTB or both are in table 2.1. HB is awarded as a rent rebate (para. 16.14) to people renting from a council or the Northern Ireland Housing Executive. HB is awarded as a rent allowance (para. 16.15) to people renting from a private landlord, housing association, co-op or hostel. CTB (and in Northern Ireland HB for rates) is awarded (as a rebate: para. 16.26) to home owners, leaseholders, tenants, and anyone else who is liable for council tax (or rates).

2.4 AA 1(1),(1A),(1B); CBA 131(1),(3)-(6), 134(1),(4)

Table 2.1: Straightforward examples of who can get HB/CTB

People who own their home	Not eligible for HB (because not liable for rent) Eligible for CTB
People in shared ownership schemes	Eligible for HB (on their rent) Eligible for CTB
People renting self-contained accommodation	Eligible for HB Eligible for CTB
People renting non-self-contained accommodation	Eligible for HB Not eligible for CTB (because not liable for council tax)

Exclusions from HB/CTB

Exclusions from CTB

2.7 The following people cannot get CTB:

- full-time students who are not liable for council tax (paras. 11.10-11);
- most other full-time students (para. 21.23 – but the rules for second adult rebate are different: chapter 6);
- some recent migrants (chapter 20);
- all under-18-year-olds (because they cannot be liable for council tax: para. 11.11);
- people who are severely mentally impaired (unless they are liable for council tax, which is unusual: paras. 11.10-11);
- owners and other landlords of unoccupied dwellings (para. 11.8);
- owners and other landlords of houses in multiple occupation (para. 11.8).

Exclusions from HB

2.8 The following people cannot get HB:

- most full-time students (para. 21.23);
- some recent migrants (chapter 20);
- many under-18-year-old care leavers (para. 2.9); and
- many members of religious orders (para. 2.13).

Care leavers aged under 18

2.9 The following rules apply, under section 6 of the Children (Leaving Care) Act 2000 (in Northern Ireland, section 6 of the Children (Leaving Care) Act (Northern Ireland) 2002), to 16-year-olds and 17-year-olds who have left local authority care. In such cases the responsibility for maintenance and accommodation falls on the social services authority. There is no equivalent rule for CTB as persons aged under 18 years cannot be liable for council tax.

2.10 Except where the circumstances in paragraph 2.12 apply, a person is not eligible for HB if he or she is aged 16 or 17 and:

- has been looked after (in Scotland only, looked after and 'accommodated') by the social services authority for a period or periods amounting to at least 13 weeks beginning after they reached the age of 14 and ending after they reached the age of 16; or
- in England, Wales and Northern Ireland only, was not subject to a care order at the time they became 16 because of being in hospital or being detained in a remand centre, a young offenders institution or a secure training centre or any other institution as the result of a court order; and immediately beforehand they had been looked after by a local authority for a period or periods amounting to at least 13 weeks which began after they reached the age of 14.

2.11 In calculating the 13 week periods (in all four countries), no account should be taken of any time during which the child was looked after by social services in certain pre-planned short-term placements (respite care). To qualify, each such placement must not exceed four weeks and at the end of it the child must be returned to the care of his or her parent (or the person who has parental responsibility). In Scotland only, whether a person has been 'accommodated' includes instances where the person has been placed under a supervision requirement following a children's hearing.

2.12 The above exclusion from HB does not apply, however, if the following circumstances apply:

- in England, Wales and Northern Ireland to anyone who lived with someone under a family placement for a continuous period of six months or more unless the family placement broke down and the child ceased to live with the person concerned. This rule applies whether the period of six months commenced before or after the child ceased to be looked after by the local authority;
- in Scotland when the authorities have placed the young person with their family. Family in this instance includes any person aged at least 18 or who was looking after them before they went into care;

2.9 SI 2001 No 2189; SI 2001 No 2874; SI 2004 No 747; SI 2004 No 1732; NISR 2005 No 221

2.12 SI 2004 No 747 Reg (2)(2)(c); NISR 2005 No 324 Reg 2(2)

- in Scotland to a care leaver who left care before 1st April 2004. These persons are entitled to HB in the normal way; or
- in Northern Ireland to a care leaver who left care before 1st September 2005. These persons are entitled to HB in the normal way.

Members of certain religious orders

2.13 Members of a religious order are not eligible for HB if they are maintained fully by that order. Monks and nuns in enclosed orders are excluded under this provision. The DWP (GM A3.257) points out that members of religious communities (as opposed to religious orders) are often eligible for HB since they frequently do paid work or retain their own possessions. In such cases, the residents are not eligible for CTB as the council tax bill goes to the owner.

Which housing costs can HB meet?

2.14 HB is available towards a claimant's 'eligible rent'. As explained in chapter 7, this typically includes all or part of a claimant's rent in the day-to-day sense of the word. This section describes the several special types of accommodation in relation to which there are extra rules.

Care homes and independent hospitals

2.15 Residents of 'care homes' and 'independent hospitals' are not eligible for HB. In Scotland the equivalent institutions are known as the 'care home service' and 'independent healthcare service' and in Northern Ireland 'residential care homes', 'nursing homes' and 'independent hospitals'. See paragraphs 3.21-22 and 3.32-34 where residence is unlikely to be permanent.

2.16 There are rare exceptions to the rule in the previous paragraph, but only for accommodation provided by social services and only in the case of residents who have been in the accommodation since before 1990 or, in some cases, 1993 (GM A8.150).

Housing costs met through IS/JSA(IB)/ESA(IR)

2.17 Claimants whose accommodation costs are included in their income support, JSA(IB) or ESA(IR) are excluded from help through the HB scheme. The main examples are home owners (para. 2.18), Crown tenants (para. 2.25) and payments for a tent and its pitch. If a person on HB becomes eligible for help with their housing costs through IS/JSA(IB) for the first time (e.g. if they buy their home) then HB can continue for a further four weeks following the IS/JSA(IB)/ESA(IR) award. This is in practice unheard of.

2.13 HB 9(1)(j); HB60+ 9(1)(j); NIHB 9(1)(j); NIHB60+ 9(1)(j)

2.15 HB 2(1), 9(1)(k),(4); HB60+ 9(1)(k),(4); NIHB 2(1), 9(1)(k),(4); NIHB60+ 9(1)(k),(4)

2.16 CPR sch 3 para 9; NICPR sch 3 para 9

2.17 HB 11(2),(4); NIHB 11(2),(4)

Owner-occupiers and long leaseholders

2.18 A person who owns their home, or whose partner does, is not eligible for HB. The same applies to someone with the right to sell the freehold only with the consent of other joint owners. It also apples to a long leaseholder. A long leaseholder (or 'long tenant') means someone who has a lease on their home which was for more than 21 years when it was first granted, and complies with the legal formalities of being a lease: *R(H) 3/07.* (However, mortgage interest, ground rent and service charges can be met through IS, JSA(IB), ESA(IR) or guarantee credit.)

Shared owners

2.19 A shared ownership scheme (also called equity sharing) means that the person is part-buying and part-renting their home – which can be from a social landlord or (nowadays) from a private firm. A shared owner is eligible for HB on their rent (and their mortgage interest can be met through IS, JSA(IB), ESA(IR) or guarantee credit).

Co-owners

2.20 Payments under a co-ownership scheme are not eligible for HB. A co-ownership scheme is one in which the tenant is a member of the association, who on ceasing to be a member of the association will be entitled to a payment related to the value of the home.

Co-op tenants

2.21 Co-operative tenants are eligible for HB for their rent provided they have no more than a nominal equity share in the property.

Hire purchase, credit sale and conditional sale agreements

2.22 The following payments are not eligible for help under the HB scheme:

- a hire purchase agreement (for example to buy a mobile home);
- a credit sale agreement; or
- a conditional sale agreement unless it is for land. Conditional sale agreements are agreements for the sale of goods or land under which the purchase price is payable by instalments and the goods or land remain the seller's until the instalments are paid.

2.18 HB 2(1), 12(2)(a),(c),(f); HB60+ 2(1), 12(2)(a),(c),(f); NIHB 2(1), 13(2)(a); NIHB60+ 2(1), 13(2)(a)

2.19 HB 2(1), 12(2)(a); HB60+ 2(1), 12(2)(a)

2.20 HB 2(1), 12(2)(b); HB60+ 2(1), 12(2)(b)

2.21 HB 12(1); HB60+ 12(1); NIHB 13(1); NIHB60+ 13(1)

2.22 HB 12(2)(d); HB60+ 12(2)(d); IHB 13(2)(b); NIHB60+ 13(2)(b)

Rental purchase agreements

2.23 Payments under a rental purchase scheme are eligible for HB. A rental purchase agreement is one in which the whole or part of the purchase price is paid in instalments over a specified period of time and completion of the sale is deferred until the final instalment of a specified amount of the purchase price has been paid (GM A4.140).

Bail and probation hostels

2.24 Payments on a bail or probation hostel are not eligible for HB. See table 3.1 for HB towards the normal home of someone currently in a bail or probation hostel.

Crown tenants and former Crown tenants

2.25 A Crown tenant is someone renting their home from the Crown or a government department. In Great Britain, all Crown tenants are excluded from HB, except for those renting from the Duchies of Cornwall and Lancaster or whose property is managed by the Crown Estate Commissioners. In Northern Ireland, only tenants of the Ministry of Defence are excluded from HB. Those excluded from HB can get IS, JSA(IB), ESA(IR) or guarantee credit towards their rent. If they do not qualify for that, they may get a rent rebate under voluntary schemes run by their landlords. Even if such a scheme is administered by an authority (on behalf of the landlord) it is separate from HB itself.

Former Crown tenants (and licensees) are eligible for HB. This applies when their agreement to occupy a Crown property has been terminated but they are continuing to occupy against the wishes of their landlord and liable to pay mesne or violent profits. (See GM A3.213.)

Houseboats, mobile homes and caravans

2.26 Houseboat mooring charges and berthing fees, and caravan and mobile home site charges are eligible for HB. So is the rent on such accommodation if it is rented out. For these purposes a 'houseboat' can include a canal narrow boat *(CH/4250/2007).* Also, from 6th April 2009, 'caravans and mobile homes' always includes those of people with a nomadic or caravanning cultural tradition (regardless of their race or origin) – including travellers, travelling show people and circus people, and also those who no longer travel for reasons of health or age. For them there are also new rules about their eligible rent (para. 7.7) and about how HB is paid when they are on local authority or county council sites (para. 16.14).

2.23 HB 12(1)(i); HB60+ 12(1)(i); NIHB 13(1)(h); NIHB60+ 13(1)(h)

2.24 HB 7(5); HB60+ 7(5); NIHB 7(5); NIHB60+ 7(5)

2.25 HB 2(1) 12(2)(e); HB60+ 2(1) 12(2)(e); NIHB 2(1) 13(2)(c); NIHB60+ 2(1) 13(2)(c)
HB 2(1); HB60+ 2(1); NIHB 2(1); NIHB60+ 2(1)

2.26 HB sch 2 para 3; HB60+ sch 2 para 3.

Liability to pay rent

2.27 The general rule is that a claimant is eligible for HB only if he or she is liable (has a legal obligation or duty) to pay rent for the home.

The nature of liability for rent

2.28 Liability for rent typically arises under a tenancy or licence, but rent has a wider meaning for HB purposes (paras. 7.3-4 and table 7.1). It can arise whether or not there is a written agreement (GM A3.50) and can arise by word of mouth alone: *R v Poole Borough Council ex p Ross.* The landlord must normally have a sufficient interest in the dwelling in order to be able to grant the letting, but exceptions can arise: *CH/2959/2006.* Most landlords would also expect to end the letting if the claimant does not pay rent. Very large 'rent arrears' may be an indication that there is no liability for rent: *CH/1849/2007.*

2.29 It is not possible in law to grant a tenancy to oneself, nor can liability arise under a tenancy 'granted' to someone who already has the right to occupy the property in question. In the second case, for example, if a couple are joint owners of a property and one leaves, the other has the right to occupy all of it, so the absent one cannot 'grant' a tenancy to the present one.

2.30 A claimant who is unable to act typically has someone appointed to act for them, such as a receiver appointed by the Court of Protection. But even if someone is wholly incapacitated and cannot appreciate the nature of the agreement they are entering, this does not mean the letting agreement is void: *CH/2121/2006.* And according to the common law a person aged under 18 can enter into a legally binding contract for goods and services which are 'necessities' (e.g. food, clothing, shelter) and so can have a legal liability to pay rent.

Treating a claimant as liable even when he or she is not

2.31 Any of the following, even if not liable to pay rent, are treated by law as liable, and are therefore eligible for HB:

(a) the partner of the liable person (including the partner of a full-time student who is not eligible for HB: para. 21.24);

(b) a former partner of the liable person who has to make the payments in order to continue to live in the home because the liable person is not doing so;

(c) anyone who has to make the payments if he or she is to continue to live in the home because the liable person is not making the payments and the authority considers it reasonable to treat him or her as liable to make those payments;

2.27 CBA 130(1)(a); NICBA 129(1)(a); HB 8(1)(a); NIHB 8(1)(a); NIHB60+ 8(1)(a)

2.31 HB 8(1)(b)-(e),(2); HB60+ 8(1)(b)-(e),(2); NIHB 8(1)(b)-(e),(2); NIHB60+ 8(1)(b)-(e),(2)

(d) a person whose liability is waived by the landlord as reasonable compensation for repairs or redecoration work actually carried out by the tenant – but only up to a maximum of eight benefit weeks in respect of any one waiver;

(e) someone who has actually met his or her liability before claiming.

2.32 The objective of the rule in paragraph 2.31(b) and (c) is that HB is there to keep the roof over the head of someone who could perhaps arrange to become the tenant in the property but who has not (yet) done so. The rule is typically used when a tenant has gone away for too long to continue to get HB (para. 3.31), or has left permanently, and a partner or other person remains in the dwelling. The rule can also be used when the liable person is a firm or other body rather than a human being *(R(H) 5/05).* As regards what is reasonable (in relation to (c)), if the only reason the liable person is not paying the rent is that they are barred from HB (because of the rules in the next section), it may not be reasonable to award HB to someone else *(CH/606/2005).*

2.33 Where the rent is varied either during an award or retrospectively, the claimant is treated as liable for the revised amount due.

Examples: Treated as liable to pay rent

A claimant has been deserted by her partner. Although she is not the tenant, the landlord will allow her to remain in the property if she continues to pay the rent. She should be treated as liable if her former partner is not paying the rent.

A claimant is the son of a council tenant. He takes over responsibility for paying rent while his father is working abroad for two years. The son should be treated as liable if it is reasonable to do so.

'Contrived' lettings and other exclusions from HB

2.34 The remainder of this chapter describes the circumstances in which a claimant cannot get HB, even though he or she is in fact liable for rent. The law does this by saying the claimant is treated as not liable to make the payments.

Landlord a close relative residing in the dwelling

2.35 If the claimant's landlord is a 'close relative' (para. 2.36) of the claimant, or of the claimant's partner, and the landlord also resides in the dwelling (para. 2.38), the claimant is not eligible for HB.

2.35 HB 9(1)(b); HB60+ 9(1)(b); NIHB 9(1)(b); NIHB60+ 9(1)(b)

Who counts as a close relative?

2.36 A 'close relative' is:

- a parent, step-parent or parent-in-law; or
- brother or sister; or
- son, son-in-law, daughter, daughter-in-law, step-son, step-daughter; or
- the partner of any of the above.

2.37 Arguably the term 'brother' and 'sister' should be taken to include 'half-brothers' and 'half-sisters' (GM paras. A3.240-241 and R(SB) 22/87), but not 'step-brothers' or 'step-sisters'.

What does 'resides in' mean?

2.38 For the landlord to count as 'residing in' the same dwelling as the claimant (para. 2.35), it is not necessary to share all the accommodation, merely some essential living accommodation: *CH/542/2006.* Similarly, if the tenant has exclusive possession of one room in a house, this does not mean that the landlord is not residing with him or her: *CH/3656/204.* Despite the slight difference of wording, the definition of 'residing with' (para. 4.45) also applies here (GM A3.238).

Non-commercial agreements

2.39 A claimant is not eligible for HB if the agreement under which he or she occupies the dwelling is not on a commercial basis. What constitutes a 'commercial basis' is not defined in the regulations but the authority must have regard to whether the agreement contains terms which are not enforceable at law.

2.40 Whether an arrangement is or is not on a commercial basis is a question of fact and judgment: *R(H) 1/03;* and is a 'notoriously imprecise and difficult concept': *CH/2491/2007* (a case involving a religious charity providing accommodation for those suffering 'substance-based and emotional abuse', in which the lettings were held not to be commercial). A letting is not commercial if, on the balance of possibilities, the principal basis on which the arrangement was made was not a commercial one (and this can be the case even if the original purpose was commercial, so long as the reasons why it changed can be identified): *CH/3497/2005.*

2.41 What is commercial is not necessarily limited to the financial relationship: *R v Sutton London Borough Council ex parte Partridge.* It takes into account all the terms of the agreement, the important factor being whether the arrangements are at 'arm's length' or more like the arrangements that would exist between close relatives who generally only make contributions to their keep or household running costs: *R v Sheffield CC HBRB ex parte Smith and others.* Friendliness

---

2.36 HB 2(1); HB60+ 2(1); NIHB 2(1); NIHB60+ 2(1)

2.39 HB 9(1)(a),(2); HB60+ 9(1)(a),(2); NIHB 9(1)(a),(2); NIHB60+ 9(1)(a),(2)

between the parties cannot change a commercial agreement into a non-commercial one: *R v Poole Borough Council ex parte Ross* and *CH/4854/2003* (but see *CH/3286/2006* for an example of a non-commercial letting which was 'a truly personal arrangement... merely clothed in the garments of a legal liability'). Similarly, religious reasons cannot change a non-commercial arrangement into a commercial one: *Campbell and Others v South Northamptonshire District Council and Another* (reported as *R(H) 8/04*) – a case which decided that it was not an infringement of the right to freedom of religion to take into account claimants' manifestations of their religious belief when determining the factual question of whether their tenancy was on a commercial basis.

Former foster children

2.42 More specifically, the DWP has advised that an arrangement that involves a former foster child remaining in his or her foster accommodation and paying rent once the fostering allowance ceases, for example where the foster child reaches the age of 18, should not normally be treated as a non-commercial arrangement (circular HB/CTB A30/95 para. 17 iv).

Disability-related lettings

2.43 Similar considerations can apply to disability-related lettings. In *CH/296/2004,* the landlord was the father of the tenant who lived at the same address in a self-contained flat, and suffered from Asperger's syndrome and autism, and could live independently with support. The commissioner held that, while a family arrangement may be indicative that an arrangement is not commercial, it is one factor and is not decisive. The fact that the landlord might not evict but might accept a lower rent if HB was not awarded, was not evidence of non-commerciality. It might be bowing to the inevitable. The tribunal did not place enough weight on items such as these but overemphasised the care and support aspects of the arrangements. The commissioner made his own finding of fact that the letting was not non-commercial.

More recent decisions, however, note that the legislation 'seems very ill-suited to providing humane outcomes in these cases' and have sometimes found these arrangements to be non-commercial: *CH/1096/2008.*

Contrived liabilities

2.44 A claimant is not eligible for HB if the authority is satisfied that his or her liability was created to take advantage of the HB scheme. This is commonly referred to as a 'contrived' letting. General DWP guidance on this is in GM paragraphs A3.310-319.

2.44 HB 9(1)(l); HB60+ 9(1)(l); NIHB 9(1)(l); NIHB60+ 9(1)(l)

2.45 In *R v Solihull MBC HBRB ex parte Simpson* the court considered that while the ability to attract HB could never realistically be the sole purpose of a tenancy, equally, and importantly, anyone eligible for HB must, by definition, have entered into an agreement to pay a rent which he could not afford. The mere fact of having done so could not of itself, except perhaps in extreme cases, be evidence of an arrangement entered in order to take advantage of the scheme. A similar point was made in *R v Sutton LBC HBRB ex parte Keegan.* The judge quashed the review board's decision not to award HB because 'it had attached a wholly disproportionate weight to the fact that the claimant could not meet her liability to pay rent'.

2.46 In the *Sutton* case the judge considered that before an agreement could be said to be 'contrived' the means, circumstances and intentions of the claimant and the landlord must be considered. In particular, consideration should be given to the consequences if HB is not to be paid. If it seems likely that the landlord will have to ask the claimant to leave the dwelling so that it can be re-let or sold, this is evidence that the liability has not been created to take advantage of the scheme.

2.47 In the *Solihull* case it was held that 'an arrangement whereby persons, who would in any event be eligible for HB, were provided with accommodation by a parent or relation who was then to receive rent generated from HB was not of itself an arrangement created to take advantage of the HB scheme'.

2.48 *R v Manchester CC ex parte Baragrove Properties* was an early example of the sort of extreme case envisaged in the Solihull judgment. Manchester had acted correctly in excluding the claimants from HB entitlement because the landlords were specifically charging higher rents to vulnerable tenants whose eligible rent could not be restricted (para. 8.59). Much more recently, the commissioners have agreed that relatively complicated arrangements involving companies were created to take advantage of the HB scheme (or were at least non-commercial): *CH/3933/2006* and *CH/136/2007.* This type of case is expected to continue, in conjunction with cases about whether accommodation is 'exempt' (paras. 7.23-24).

2.49 In *CSHB/718/2002,* the commissioner emphasised the need for clarity in deciding why someone is not eligible for HB. There is a difference between not being liable for rent at all (paras. 2.27-29) and being liable in a way that was created to take advantage of the scheme. The claimant rented from his mother who was for all or part of the time in a nursing home. He did not pay any of the HB he received to his mother. The council said his tenancy was created to take advantage of the scheme. The commissioner quashed this decision and directed a rehearing because the authority had failed to consider whether the claimant was disentitled by not being liable in the first place, and also failed to look at whether the intention to abuse the scheme existed at the time the agreement was created (he did not claim HB for the first three years of the tenancy).

Renting a former joint home from an ex-partner

2.50 If a couple separate and the one remaining in the home, or a new partner, makes payments to the one who has left, the person making the payments is not eligible for HB.

2.51 In *R (Painter) v Carmarthenshire County Council HBRB,* Mr Painter had originally been a lodger renting a bedroom and with the right to use the common parts. He subsequently formed a relationship with his landlady and moved into her room and jointly occupied the accommodation. The relationship ended and Mr Painter reverted back to being a tenant and was liable to pay rent. The authority decided that Mr Painter was not eligible for HB because he was renting a former joint home from an ex-partner. It was argued that this rule only applied if the dwelling in respect of which the payments were due was the same dwelling which had been occupied during the relationship. Mr Painter submitted that the dwelling was in fact different. It no longer included the landlady's room. Additionally it was argued that if the regulation was applicable, it was incompatible with the Human Rights Act 1998. The court held that the informal arrangements to occupy separate rooms did not affect the reality of the situation that the dwelling remained the same. It also held that there had been no breach of the Convention rights. Any discrimination was justifiable as a precaution against potential abuse of the HB scheme.

Responsibility for the landlord's child

2.52 A claimant is not eligible for HB if he or she is responsible, or a partner is responsible, for the landlord's child (i.e. someone under the age of 16). The DWP (GM A3.269) emphasises that 'responsibility for a child' means more than 'cares for'.

2.53 This is a difficult rule to interpret as it blurs certain established concepts so far as means-tested benefits are concerned. It would appear to apply where the 'landlord' is the biological mother or father of a child, or has adopted a child, but where the child is nevertheless considered to be part of the claimant's family for JSA(IB), IS or HB purposes. The legality of this rule and the argument that it offended the Human Rights Convention was argued in *R v Secretary of State for Social Security, ex parte Tucker.* The court held that the rule was not *ultra vires* nor contrary to the European Convention on Human Rights.

Trusts

2.54 A trust is an arrangement under which property is transferred to one or more people known as trustees. Trustees are required to look after the property or deal with it for the benefit of someone else, 'the beneficiary', or for some other purpose such as that of a charity.

2.50 HB 9(1)(c); HB60+ 9(1)(c); NIHB 9(1)(c); NIHB60+ 9(1)(c)

2.52 HB 9(1)(d); HB60+9(1)(d); NIHB 9(1)(d); NIHB60+ 9(1)(d)

Renting from a trust of which one is a trustee or beneficiary

2.55 A claimant is not eligible for HB if his or her landlord is a trustee of a trust of which one of the following is a trustee or a beneficiary:

- the claimant or partner; or
- the claimant's or partner's close relative (para. 2.36) if the close relative 'resides with' (para. 4.45) the claimant; or
- the claimant's, or partner's, former partner,

unless in each case the claimant satisfies the authority that the liability was not intended to take advantage of the HB scheme.

Renting from a trust of which one's child is a beneficiary

2.56 A claimant is not eligible for HB if his or her landlord is a trustee of a trust of which the claimant's or partner's child is a beneficiary. Unlike in the previous paragraph, this rule has no exception.

Renting from a company of which one is a director or an employee

2.57 A claimant is not eligible for HB if his or her landlord is a company of which one of the following is a director or an employee:

- the claimant or partner; or
- the claimant's or partner's close relative (para. 2.36) if the close relative 'resides with' (para. 4.45) the claimant; or
- the claimant's, or partner's, former partner;

unless in each case the claimant satisfies the authority that the liability was not intended to take advantage of the HB scheme. Note also that this rule does not apply if a claimant is employed by a company and rents from a director of the company (since a director is not the company itself).

2.58 The DWP advises (GM para. A3.271) that a 'company' means a registered company. This can be checked with Companies House and, if the company is registered in England, Scotland or Wales, this can be done on-line at *www.companies-house.gov.uk* for a small fee (normally £1.00).

2.55 HB 9(1)(e),(3); HB60+ 9(1)(e),(3); NIHB 9(1)(e),(3); NIHB60+ 9(1)(e),(3)

2.56 HB 9(1)(f); HB60+ 9(1)(f); NIHB 9(1)(f); NIHB60+ 9(1)(f)

2.57 HB 9(1)(e),(3); HB60+ 9(1)(e),(3); NIHB 9(1)(e),(3); NIHB60+ 9(1)(e),(3)

Former non-dependants

2.59 A claimant is not eligible for HB if:

- he or she was, at any time prior to the creation of the rent liability, a non-dependant of someone who resided in the dwelling; and
- that person continues to reside in the dwelling,

unless the claimant satisfies the authority that the liability was not intended to take advantage of the HB scheme.

Former owners

2.60 A claimant is not eligible for HB if:

- he or she, or a partner, previously owned the dwelling (including owning it on a long lease: para. 2.18); and
- owned it within the last five years (even if the claimant subsequently moved out and then back in: *CH/1353/2007*),

unless the claimant is able to satisfy the authority that he or she or a partner could not have continued to live in the dwelling without letting go of ownership. Good advice on this is given in DWP circular HB/CTB A5/2009 in the light of the increasing number of these cases, also known as 'sale and rent back' cases.

2.61 Whether the claimant could have remained in the dwelling is a practical test based on fact – and in exceptional cases this can include the claimant's perceptions if the stress of the situation they were in forced a quick sale: *R(H) 6/07.* Authorities are entitled to examine why the claimant gave up ownership and what other options they might have had, such as getting work to finance the mortgage, taking in a tenant, etc: *CH/1586/2004.* The claimant is not expected to act irresponsibly (e.g. using a credit card to pay mortgage arrears): *CH/2340/2008.* The claimant may have had no real choice if a mortgage lender would have sought possession and a housing association used a mortgage rescue scheme to buy the property and rent back to them (GM A3.282-286).

Tied accommodation

2.62 A claimant is not eligible for HB if his or her, or a partner's, occupation of the dwelling is a condition of employment by the landlord. The DWP advises (GM A3.291) that this test should not be taken to mean 'as a result of the employment'. A retired employee, for example, may continue to live in previously tied accommodation but this would no longer be as a condition of employment by the landlord, and so this rule would not prevent eligibility for HB.

2.59 HB 9(1)(g),(3); HB60+ 9(1)(g),(3); NIHB 9(1)(g),(3); NIHB60+ 9(1)(g),(3)

2.60 HB 9(1)(h),(ha); HB60+ 9(1)(h),(ha); NIHB 9(1)(h),(ha); NIHB60+ 9(1)(h),(ha)

2.62 HB 9(1)(i); HB60+ 9(1)(i); NIHB 9(1)(i); NIHB60+ 9(1)(i)

Illegal and unlawful tenancies and sub-tenancies

2.63 Sub-tenancies which are created in breach of a clause in the head lease not to sublet or assign the tenancy do not prevent the assignment or sub-letting from being valid between the head tenant and sub-tenant: *Governors of Peabody Donation Fund v Higgins* (not a HB case). Such lettings are unlawful rather than illegal and expose the head tenant to eviction for breach of the agreement. Given that there is a legal liability for rent it seems that these lettings are eligible for HB, unless it is also a letting to which paragraphs 2.34-62 above apply.

2.64 An illegal letting is one in which its creation would necessarily involve committing a criminal offence. An example would be where a landlord lets a dwelling which he or she knows is in contravention of a Housing Act prohibition order. In contrast to unlawful contracts, illegal contracts are generally not binding (see *A Casebook on Contract,* Ninth Edition, J.C. Smith) and so would not be eligible for HB. Where a letting was not illegal at the time it was created (e.g. prior to a prohibition order) it seems likely it would remain binding until the end of the next rental period, or if let on a fixed term at the end of the fixed term.

3 Occupying the home

3.1 One of the main conditions for getting HB is that the claimant must be occupying the accommodation in question as his or her home. This chapter explains this, and covers

- what it means to occupy somewhere as a home for HB purposes;
- when HB can be awarded on two homes;
- when a claimant can get HB before moving in;
- when a claimant can get HB on a former home when they have no current liability on which they may claim HB;
- how HB and CTB work when the claimant is temporarily absent.

3.2 This chapter does not apply to CTB – except for the rules about temporary absence (para. 3.31). Instead, the equivalent condition for getting CTB is that the claimant must be resident in his or her dwelling (para. 2.4). In practice this usually means the same thing as the HB condition mentioned above. There are no rules about two homes and moving home in CTB. CTB can be awarded on only one home at a time (but see para. 3.25).

HB: occupation as a home

3.3 HB can only be awarded on accommodation that the claimant is occupying as a home. Accommodation occupied only for a holiday or business purposes is not a home and therefore is not eligible. Except as described later in this chapter, HB is usually only payable on one home – the home the claimant 'normally occupies' or if a member of a family 'normally occupies' with their family *(CH/2521/2002).* This is not restricted to considering where their 'centre of interests' is: it is a question of fact to be decided in each case *(CH/1786/2005).* In certain specific circumstances however, such as where statutory overcrowding would arise, the 'dwelling occupied as the home' might comprise more than one building (*Secretary of State for Work and Pensions v Miah R(JSA)9/03* – see para. 3.25). The rules in this section do not apply to CTB (para. 3.2).

3.4 The general rule is that 'occupying' a home means more than simply being liable for rent: it means being physically present. A commissioner has made an exception *(RH 9/05).* In that case the claimant, aged 87, had terminated her former tenancy and her family had moved her furniture and possessions into her new home, but the claimant was unable to move in because she was taken ill at the last minute. The commissioner held that in these circumstances the claimant should be treated as 'normally occupying' the new home.

3.3 CBA 130(1)(a); NICBA 129(1)(a); HB 7(1); HB60+ 7(1); NIHB 7(1); NIHB60+ 7(1)

Doubts about a claimant's occupation of the dwelling can often arise as a result of residency checks by an authority's visiting/fraud officers. If there is any doubt as to whether or not the claimant occupies the dwelling, the authority should consider all the relevant evidence before determining this matter.

3.5 In considering which home the claimant normally occupies, the authority must have regard to any other dwelling occupied by the claimant or family, no matter whether it is here or abroad. The DWP advises (GM para. A3.356) that this requirement is not intended to exclude from eligibility someone who has set up home in this country but whose family, no longer being part of his or her household, remain abroad. Further specific rules are given in the remainder of this chapter.

HB: moving home and having two homes

3.6 There are several different rules about what happens when someone moves home or has two homes; in only some of these cases is the claimant eligible for HB on two homes at a time. The rules are very specific. This section does not apply at all to CTB (para. 3.2). It is never possible to get CTB on more than one dwelling at a time.

Claimants who have moved but remain liable for rent at their old home

3.7 A claimant moving from one rented dwelling to another rented dwelling is eligible for HB on both of them – but only if all three of the following conditions are met:

- only for the period after he or she has moved into the new dwelling;
- only if his or her liability for rent on both dwellings could not reasonably have been avoided; and
- only for up to four weeks from the date of the move.

This is the 'two homes' version of the rule (for the 'one home' version, see para. 3.9). It is often called the overlapping HB rule. For how HB is calculated in such cases, see paragraph 3.29. Note that the rule does not apply when a claimant moves out for repairs to be done (para. 3.23).

3.8 This 'two homes' version of the rule often applies when a claimant in private rented accommodation is offered social housing at short notice, and has to take up the new letting before notice on the old one has run out. Note that, to get HB on both properties, the claimant must actually have moved into the new one (para. 3.4). If the claimant is in a family, then the other members of the family must have moved in too, and the family must be occupying it as a home rather than preparing it for occupation *(CH/1911/2006)*.

3.5 HB 7(2); HB60+ 7(2); NIHB 7(2); HB60+ 7(2)

3.7 HB 7(6)(d); HB60+ 7(6)(d); NIHB 7(6)(d); NIHB60+ 7(6)(d)

3.9 Similarly, a claimant moving from a rented dwelling to a non-rented dwelling is eligible for HB on the one he or she has left – but only if all three of the following conditions are met:

- only for the period after he or she has moved into the new dwelling;
- only if his or her liability for rent on that former dwelling could not reasonably have been avoided; and
- only for up to four weeks from the date of the move.

This is the 'one home' version of the rule (for the 'two homes' version, see para. 3.7). It could apply when the claimant moves from a rented home to one he or she owns, or to a care home, or to live with parents, or to a prison following sentencing, and so on. In particular, in the case of moving to a care home, this rule can apply following an award of HB during a trial period (paras. 3.31-33 and the example following them): *Secretary of State for Work and Pensions v Selby DC* reported as *R(H) 4/06.*

3.10 For many years, the DWP has suggested (in relation to the 'two homes' version of the rule) that it should only be used in 'exceptional circumstances' (GM A3.670). There is no such test in the law. The question of whether something is '(un)exceptional' is obviously different from the question of whether something is '(un)reasonable', and it is surprising to find such questionable guidance persisting for so long. Though in considering whether liability for rent could reasonably have been avoided the authority may look at what alternatives were open to the claimant *(CH/4546/2002),* that does not change the test of what is reasonable into what is exceptional.

3.11 For both versions of the rule, there is no legal requirement for a separate claim to be made for HB for the period in question. That said, the authority does, of course, need information and evidence that enable it to identify that the conditions of the rules are met (for example, that there remains a liability at the old address, and that it could not reasonably have been avoided).

Claimants who have moved because of fear of violence

3.12 A claimant is eligible for HB on two rented homes for up to 52 weeks if he or she:

- has left and remains absent from the former home through fear of violence
  - in the home, or
  - by a person who was formerly a member of the claimant's family; and
- has an intention to return to it; and
- is liable for rent on both that home and where he or she is now living; and
- it is reasonable to meet the rent on both homes.

3.9 HB 7(7),79(9); HB60+ 7(7),59(9); NIHB 7(7); NIHB60+ 7(7)

3.12 HB 7(6)(a); HB60+ 7(6)(a); NIHB 7(6)(a); NIHB60+ 7(6)(a)

3.13 For how HB is calculated in such cases see paragraph 3.29. If the claimant does not intend to return to the old dwelling, the previous rule applies instead (allowing HB to be paid on both for only four weeks: para. 3.7). If he or she is liable for rent on the old dwelling but not the new one, the rule about absences from home – described in paragraphs 3.32-34 and table 3.1 – applies instead. If the claimant is liable for rent on the new dwelling but not the old one (e.g. is fleeing from an owner-occupied dwelling), there is nothing to stop the claimant from getting HB on the new home (assuming it counts as his or her normal home), and the capital value of the old home is very likely to be disregarded (para. 13.74).

3.14 Actual violence need not have occurred for the rule to apply. The claimant has only to be afraid of violence occurring. If the authority considers, however, that the fear of violence is one that is not reasonably held *(CH/1237/2004, para. 18)* or that the claimant brought it upon himself or herself, it may consider it unreasonable that HB should be paid in respect of both homes.

3.15 The feared violence in the home need not be related to a family or former family member. It could be related to anyone, e.g. a neighbour, so long as it is feared that violence could occur in the home. Where the fear is of violence outside the home it must be a former member of the claimant's family who poses the threat of violence. This would include not only an ex-partner but also an adult child. On the other hand, it is of course the case that someone who is afraid of violence outside the home may well be afraid of it coming into the home.

3.16 Authorities are advised to check regularly that the claimant intends to return to the previous home (GM A3.631). If the claimant subsequently decides not to return, HB on the former home stops. The HB paid on the former home while the claimant had the intention to return will have been properly paid and is not an overpayment (GM A3.632).

Claimants waiting for adaptations for a disability

3.17 If a claimant becomes liable for rent on a new dwelling, but does not move into it straight away because they are necessarily waiting for it to be adapted to meet their disablement needs or those of a family member (para. 4.11), the claimant is eligible for HB for up to four weeks before moving in, so long as the delay in moving is reasonable. To qualify under this rule, the adaptation must involve a change to the fabric or structure of the dwelling; furnishing, carpeting or decorating are not enough: *CSH/149/2006.*

3.18 In this case, if the claimant is also liable for rent on their old home, they are eligible for HB on both homes during those four weeks. For how HB is calculated in such cases, see paragraph 3.29. Whether in the case of HB for one home or two, HB can be awarded only after the claimant has moved in and the claim, or notice of the move, must be made promptly: paragraph 3.30.

3.13 HB 7(10); HB60+ 7(10); NIHB 7(10); NIHB60+ 7(10)

3.17 HB 7(6)(e); HB60+ 7(6)(e); NIHB 7(6)(e); NIHB60+ 7(6)(e)

3.18 HB 7(8)(b)(ii),(c)(i); HB60+ 7(8)(b)(ii),(c)(i); NIHB 7(8)(c)(i); NIHB60+ 7(8)(c)(i)

Claimants waiting for a social fund payment

3.19 If a claimant becomes liable for rent on a new dwelling, but does not move into it straight away because he or she:

- has applied for a social fund payment to help with the move or with setting up home; and
- is aged 60 or more, or has a child aged under 6, or someone in the family is disabled in one of the ways relevant to a disability premium or disabled child premium,

the claimant is eligible for HB for up to four weeks before moving in, so long as the delay in moving is reasonable.

3.20 In this case, the claimant is not eligible for HB on his or her old home as well – a feature of the rule that has been criticised frequently over the years as discriminating against someone moving from a furnished rented home to his or her first unfurnished rented home. HB can be awarded only after the claimant has moved in and the claim must be made promptly: paragraph 3.30.

Claimants waiting to leave hospital or a care home

3.21 If a claimant becomes liable for rent on a new dwelling, but does not move into it straight away because they are waiting to leave a hospital, care home or independent hospital (para. 2.15), they are eligible for HB for up to four weeks before moving in, so long as the delay in moving is reasonable.

3.22 This might well arise if someone's discharge from hospital is delayed, or someone cannot immediately manage to leave a care home. HB can be awarded only after the claimant has moved in and the claim must be made promptly: paragraph 3.30.

Moving out for repairs to be done

3.23 A claimant who has had to leave his or her normal home while it is having essential repairs, and who has to make payments (rent or mortgage payments) on one but not both the normal home and the temporary accommodation, is treated as occupying the home for which payments are made. If the payments due on that home are mortgage payments, the claimant is not eligible for HB. The other rules about moving home (above) and absences from home (below) do not apply to such claimants.

Large families

3.24 Where the claimant's family (para. 4.11) is so large they have been housed by a housing authority (in Northern Ireland, the NIHE) in two separate

---

3.19 HB 7(8)(c)(ii); HB60+ 7(8)(c)(ii); NIHB 7(8)(c)(ii); NIHB60+ 7(8)(c)(ii)

3.21 HB 7(8)(c)(iii); HB60+ 7(8)(c)(iii); NIHB 7(8)(c)(iii); NIHB60+ 7(8)(c)(iii)

3.23 HB 7(4); HB60+ 7(4); NIHB 7(4); NIHB60+ 7(4)

dwellings, the claimant is eligible for HB on both homes. The DWP (GM para. A3.660) advises that both homes should be provided, but not necessarily owned, by the local authority. There is no time limit in this case.

What is 'one' home?

3.25 The Court of Appeal has held that a claimant (in uncommon circumstances) can occupy two nearby houses as 'one home' for JSA(IB) purposes and this is persuasive for HB: *Secretary of State for Work and Pensions v Miah, R(JSA)9/03.* Also, two flats knocked together, though renterd from two landlords, might constitute 'one home': *CH/1895/2008.* As regards CTB, it has been held that two nearby flats in a block, used by a single family as one home (with bedrooms in one flat and living areas in the other), could be a single 'sole or main residence' (for council tax purposes) and so CTB should be awarded on the combined amount of council tax for the two of them.

Single and lone parent students and trainees

3.26 A single claimant or lone parent who is a student or on a government training course, and who has two homes but pays rent on only one, is treated as normally occupying that one (and is thus eligible for HB on it), even if he or she in fact normally lives in the other one.

3.27 The training courses referred to are those provided by or via the Secretary of State, Scottish Enterprise, or Highlands and Islands Enterprise; or by a local authority on behalf of one of those bodies, either direct or via another organisation.

Example: Occupation as a home

The claimant normally lives with her parents but rents accommodation while on a government training course. So she is treated as normally occupying the rented accommodation during the period she is liable to pay housing costs.

Student couples

3.28 A couple (para. 4.13) are eligible for HB on two homes if one is a student who personally fulfils the criteria for student eligibility for HB and the other is not a student, or if both are students each of whom personally fulfils the criteria for student eligibility for HB (table 21.1). But occupying two homes must be unavoidable and it must be reasonable to pay HB on two homes (table 21.2). There is no time limit in this case.

3.24 HB 7(6)(c); HB60+ 7(6)(c); NIHB 7(6)(c); NIHB60+ 7(6)(c)

3.26 HB 7(3); HB60+ 7(3); NIHB 7(3); NIHB60+ 7(3)

3.27 HB 7(18); HB60+ 7(18); NIHB 7(18); NIHB60+ 7(18)

3.28 HB 7(6)(b); HB60+ 7(6)(b); NIHB 7(6)(b); NIHB60+ 7(6)(b)

Calculation of benefit on two homes

3.29 In the cases above in which HB is awarded on two homes (paras. 3.7, 3.12, 3.18, 3.24 and 3.28), there is one HB calculation based on the aggregated eligible rent of the two properties (but only one non-dependant and only one 65% taper adjustment per claim: GM A5.800-801). Where the dwellings are in different areas, authorities need to liaise and/or establish agency arrangements (para. 1.19).

Entitlement prior to moving in: prompt claims

3.30 In the cases above in which HB is awarded before someone moves in (paras. 3.17, 3.19 and 3.21), it is necessary to claim (or notify the move) promptly (i.e. before or in the first week of the new liability for rent – unless the claimant requests and is awarded backdated benefit: paras. 5.53-54, or the claimant or any partner is aged 60+: paras. 5.51-52). If the claim is then refused (perhaps because at that time the authority is not sure that the claimant will in fact move in), and the claimant reapplies within four weeks, the reapplication should be treated as having been made at the same time as the refused claim. And the award of HB cannot start until the claimant actually does move in.

HB and CTB: temporary absence

3.31 Claimants can, in the circumstances described in the remainder of this chapter, get HB and/or CTB even while temporarily absent from their home. In practice, the rules for HB and CTB are the same.

3.32 There are three specific rules about temporary absences. During an absence from their home, a claimant remains eligible:

- for up to 13 weeks during a trial period in a care home (or immediately following that: *Secretary of State for Work and Pensions v Selby District Council* reported as *R(H) 4/06*) – so long as the claimant intends to return to their normal home if the care home is unsuitable (but if the claimant was absent from home for another reason before this, their total absence from home must not exceed 52 weeks); or
- for up to 52 weeks if they are absent (in the UK or abroad) for one of the reasons in table 3.1 – so long as the claimant intends to return to their normal home within 52 weeks or, in exceptional circumstances, not substantially later; or
- for up to 13 weeks during an absence (in the UK or abroad) for any other reason – so long as the claimant intends to return to their normal home within a strict 13 weeks.

3.29 HB 80(10); HB60+ 61(11); NIHB 78(10); NIHB 60+ 59(10)

3.30 HB 7(9); HB60+ 7(9); NIHB 7(9); NIHB60+ 7(9)

3.32 HB 7(11)-(18); HB60+ 7(11)-(18); NIHB 7(11)-(18); NIHB60+ 7(11)-(18); CTB 8; CTB60+ 8

The intention to return

3.33 Each of the above rules requires the claimant to intend to return to their normal home. It is the claimant's intention which is relevant (not, say, the intention of a relative or official) but that intention must be capable of being realised. In one case a claimant desired to return from his nursing home to his housing association property, but the commissioner held that to desire is not the same as to intend. It had been found as a fact that it was objectively impossible for the claimant to return, so the absence from home provisions could not apply to him *(CSHB/405/2005)*.

Example: Trying out a care home and then deciding to stay there

A woman who rents her home has been on HB and CTB for a while. She then goes into a care home for a six-week trial period to see if it suits her.

- She remains eligible for HB and CTB.

In the fourth week of her trial period, she decides that this is the care home for her. She gives four weeks' notice to her former landlord, and informs the authority of these matters promptly. The authority is satisfied that she could not reasonably have avoided the liability at her old address.

- She remains eligible for HB and CTB for the additional four-week period.

Absences: additional conditions

3.34 In each of the above three cases (para. 3.32), there are three further conditions which must be met in order for HB/CTB to be granted during the absence:

- the claimant must still be liable for rent/council tax on their normal home; and
- the part of the home the claimant normally occupies must not be let or sub-let; and
- the claimant must provide the authority with the information and evidence needed for the claim to continue (para. 3.43 and chapter 17).

Counting the length of the absence

3.35 In *R v Penwith DC HBRB ex parte Burt* it was held that the 13-week and 52-week time limits refer to absences which are continuous. So if the claimant (with the exception of prisoners on temporary release: para. 3.40) returns to, and occupies the dwelling as a home, even for a short time, the allowable period of temporary absence starts again. The DWP suggests (GM A3.460) that a stay at home lasting, for example, only a few hours may not break the absence but one that lasts at least 24 hours may do so.

3.34 HB 7(11)-(17); HB60+ 7(11)-(17); NIHB 7(11)-(17); NIHB60+ 7(11)-(17); CTB 8(2)-(6); CTB60+ 8(2)-(6)

Table 3.1: People who can get HB/CTB during an absence of up to 52 weeks

Claimants in prison etc, who have not yet been sentenced (e.g. on remand).

Claimants in a probation hostel, or a bail hostel, or bailed to live away from their normal home.

Claimants in a care home or independent hospital (para. 2.15) who are not just trying it out (e.g. during periods of respite care).

Claimants in hospital, or receiving medically approved* care.

Claimants undergoing medical treatment or medically approved* convalescence or who are absent because their partner or child is undergoing this.

Claimants undertaking medically approved* care of someone else.

Claimants caring for a child whose parent or guardian is absent from home in order to receive medical treatment or medically approved* care.

Claimants following a government training course (as defined in para. 3.27).

Students who are eligible for HB/CTB (e.g. if they have to study abroad for part of their course).

Claimants absent because of fear of violence in their normal home (regardless of who it would be from) or fear of violence from a former member of their family (whether this would occur in the normal home or elsewhere). This would apply to people other than those mentioned in paragraph 3.12 because, for example, they are staying with relatives and are not liable to pay rent on two homes but intend to return to occupy their original homes.

* 'Medically approved' means approved in writing by a GP, nurse or similar – but this need not be in a formal certificate (GM A3.541).

3.36 Depending upon the facts of the case, however, the authority may decide that the claimant's normal home is elsewhere for HB purposes (paras. 3.3-5). If another person occupying the dwelling starts paying rent in the absence of the claimant, the authority should consider treating that other person as liable and therefore eligible for HB (para. 2.31).

3.37 The assessment of whether or not the period of temporary absence is likely to exceed 13/52 weeks has to be made by reference to the date at which the claimant left the dwelling in question (*CH/1237/2004,* para. 12). Continued entitlement has to be judged on a week by week basis. If at any date it becomes likely that the 13/52 weeks will be exceeded, then that is a relevant change of

T 3.1 HB 7(16)(c); HB60+ 7(16)(c); NIHB 7(16)(c); NIHB60+ 7(16)(c); CTB 8(4); CTB60+ 8(4)

circumstances, allowing a re-consideration of the entitlement (*CH/1237/2004*, para. 12). Once it becomes clear that the claimant is going to be away for more than 13 or 52 weeks, HB/CTB entitlement ends under the temporary absence rule (but see para. 3.9 for the circumstances in which the claimant may be entitled to up to four weeks additional entitlement). Also note that in the case of the absences in table 3.1 if the absence is unlikely to substantially exceed the 52-week period, and if there are exceptional circumstances, the authority must pay up to the end of the 52nd week of absence. DWP guidance (GM A3.532) suggests that the term 'substantially exceed' relates to periods of absence greater than 15 months. It is, however, for the individual authority to interpret the term. The GM illustrates the concept of exceptional circumstances with the examples of someone prevented from returning home by an unanticipated event, and a discharge from hospital being delayed by a relapse. Other circumstances may also be considered.

Absences in prison, etc

3.38 As indicated in table 3.1, until they are sentenced, a claimant in prison, etc, can get HB for up to 52 weeks. This means that (almost) all prisoners on remand can get HB.

3.39 If and when the claimant is sentenced to prison, etc, this counts as a change of circumstances. The relevant question is then: 'Will they return home within 13 weeks of when they left home?' Only if the answer is 'yes' can the claimant continue to get HB under the temporary absence rule *(CH/499/2006)*. However, in deciding this, account must be taken of any remission the prisoner may get for good behaviour, so prisoners with a sentence of up to six months (or up to ten months if they are on Home Detention Curfew) are likely to be entitled. And in predicting the length of the absence, the prisoner's own prediction is irrelevant if release could be considered earlier (*CH/2638/2006*, in which the parole hearing should have occurred earlier than the prisoner believed). For further guidance see GM A3.512-518.

Prisoners on temporary release

3.40 Prisoners on temporary release (home leave) are counted as still being in prison, unless they were already eligible for HB immediately beforehand under the above rules (paras. 3.38-39).

Absences on bail

3.41 As indicated in table 3.1, a person on bail can get HB for up to 52 weeks. This applies whether the person is in a bail hostel or bailed to live anywhere other than his or her normal home (e.g. at a relative's).

3.40 HB 7(14)-(15); HB60+ 7(14)-(15); NIHB 7(14)-(15); CTB60+ 8(5)-(6)

3.41 HB 7(16)(c); HB60+ 7(16)(c); NIHB 7(16)(c); NIHB60+ 7(16)(c); CTB 8(4)(a); CTB60+ 8(4)(a)

Example: Remand and conviction

A man has been receiving HB for a while. He is then arrested and detained on remand pending his trial.

- The authority should assume that he will be absent for no more than 52 weeks. He therefore remains eligible for HB.

Fifteen weeks later he is tried, found guilty, and sentenced to a term of one year's imprisonment.

- Although he may well serve only six months in prison (after remission), and although the 15 weeks he has been on remand will count towards this, his total absence from home will now exceed 13 weeks. So his eligibility for HB under the temporary absence rule ceases, because the fact that he has been sentenced is a change in his circumstances (chapter 17). (But the HB he was awarded for his 15 weeks on remand was nonetheless correctly paid.) If, however, the necessary conditions are met (para. 3.9) the claimant may be entitled to a further four weeks of HB.

Death of claimant

3.42 There is no provision to award HB/CTB following the death of the claimant. HB must cease at the end of the benefit week containing the date of the death (paras. 2.3, 2.4 and 17.21) and CTB ceases on the day before the date of the death (because there is no liability for council tax from the date of death onwards). If the claimant has a surviving partner, he or she may make their own claim, but is not 'covered' by their deceased partner's claim. Also, the fact that the estate of the deceased may be required to pay for a notice period on the property does not mean that the deceased (or the estate) is somehow still entitled to HB.

Notifying a temporary absence

3.43 If the claimant or any partner is aged 60+ there is a specific duty to notify the authority of an absence exceeding or likely to exceed 13 weeks. Apart from that, it has been held that there is no requirement in law to notify the authority in advance of a temporary absence *(CH/996/2004).* On the other hand, it makes sense for a claimant (of any age) to notify any absence that is longer than (say) a couple of weeks – to avoid any difficulties that might arise if they were visited during the absence.

3.43 HB60+ 69(6)(c); NIHB60+ 65(4)(c); CTB60+ 59(7)(b)

4 The claimant's household

4.1 This chapter describes:

- the different categories of claimant and the people who may live in the claimant's household;
- the circumstances in which the claimant is considered to be responsible for a child or young person for HB and CTB;
- the circumstances in which partners and children or young people are treated as members of the claimant's household; and
- other people who may reside with the claimant or live in the same accommodation.

4.2 Authorities need to identify and correctly categorise the people who live with the claimant to work out HB/CTB entitlement since:

- only one family member counts as the claimant for benefit purposes and can claim HB/CTB;
- in the case of second adult rebate, partners and/or jointly liable persons can affect entitlement;
- fixed deductions are made from HB/CTB in certain cases in respect of other people who live in the claimant's household who are classified as 'non-dependants';
- second adult rebate is worked out on the basis of the gross income of certain people who reside with the claimant known as 'second adults';
- where the claimant is not in receipt of JSA(IB), ESA(IR), IS or pension credit the amount of HB/CTB is worked out on the basis of the combined needs of the claimant's family (in the form of the applicable amount) and the income and capital of the claimant and any partner;
- money from (sub-) tenants and boarders is taken into account in the assessment of the claimant's income for HB/CTB where the claimant is not in receipt of JSA(IB), ESA(IR), IS or pension credit.

Household composition

Membership of a household

4.3 The concept of the household is important for HB/CTB as well as other passport benefits. The term is not defined in HB/CTB legislation. Therefore it should be given its common sense meaning as being a domestic arrangement involving two (or more) people who live together as a unit *(R(IS) 1/99).* To be considered a unit implies a reasonable level of independence and self sufficiency *(R(SB) 8/85).* Household is a broader concept than the 'family' (para. 4.11) (which is defined) and can include other people who are part of the same unit (paras. 4.8-9).

4.4 Whether two people are considered to be part of the same household will depend very much upon the particular facts in each case. In the majority of claims deciding who is a member of a household will be fairly straightforward. However, there are a number of fairly common circumstances in which it is much more difficult to determine, for example where two people are in the process of starting or ending a relationship or where a person maintains two separate addresses and spends roughly equal amounts of time in both. These kinds of cases can only be decided by a careful examination of all the facts.

4.5 For a person to be considered to be living as part of the same household requires more than their transitory presence: it requires a settled course of daily living *(R(F) 2/81).* A friend or relative making a short visit is not a member of the household.

4.6 A person cannot be a member of more than one household at once *(R(SB) 8/85).* Where two people are maintaining separate homes they cannot be part of the same household *(R(SB) 4/83).* A person can only be part of a household if that is where they spend the major part of their time.

4.7 A house may contain a number of households but if one person has exclusive occupation of separate accommodation he or she cannot be considered to be part of the same household. Two or more people living in the same dwelling may constitute separate households if:

- they have independent arrangements for cooking and storage of food;
- they have separate eating arrangements;
- there is no evidence of family life;
- they arrange their financial affairs independently;
- they have their own obligations for housing costs, even if their liability is to someone at the same address.

4.8 The claimant's household may consist of:

- the claimant;
- the claimant's family;
- any other person who lives in the dwelling and who is classified as a 'non-dependant'.

4.9 In addition to the above, certain other people such as joint occupiers, (sub-)tenants, boarders, carers and au pairs may live in the same accommodation as the claimant.

The claimant

4.10 The claimant may be:

- single – i.e. a claimant who does not have a partner and is not responsible for a child/young person; or
- a lone parent – i.e. someone who does not have a partner but who is responsible for and is a member of the same household as a child/young person; or
- a member of a couple or polygamous marriage.

The family

4.11 The claimant's family for benefit purposes consists of:

- the claimant's partner(s), if a member of the same household; and
- any child(ren) or young person(s) the claimant is responsible for (not just sons and daughters) and who are treated as members of the household.

Partners

4.12 A partner means:

- where a claimant is a member of a couple, the other member of that couple; or
- where a claimant is polygamously married to two or more members of the household, any such member.

4.13 Either member of a couple but not both may claim (para. 5.4). The term 'couple' refers to:

- a man and woman who are married to each other and are members of the same household;
- a man and woman who are not married to each other but are living together as husband and wife;
- two people of the same sex who are civil partners of each other and are members of the same household (para. 4.15); or
- two people of the same sex who are not civil partners of each other but are living together as if they were civil partners (see para. 4.15).

4.14 The partner must be a member of the same household as the claimant. It is possible, for example for a married couple or civil partners to live in the same dwelling but live separate lives and thus not constitute a household *(CIS/072/1994)*. In such a case one would not be the partner of the other.

4.10 HB 2(1); HB60+ 2(1); NIHB 2(1); NIHB60+ 2(1); CTB 2(1); CTB60+ 2(1)

4.11 CBA 137(1); NICBA 133(1)

4.12 CBA 137(1); NICBA 133(1); HB 2(1); HB60+ 2(1); NIHB 2(1); NIHB60+ 2(1); CTB 2(1); CTB60+ 2(1)

Living together as husband and wife or as civil partners

4.15 A man and woman who are married to each other and same sex civil partners are treated as one unit as long as they are members of the same household (paras. 4.3-7). The same rules apply to a man and woman who are not married to each other but are 'living together as husband and wife' and to two people of the same sex who are not civil partners but who are living together as if they were.

4.16 Neither the Act nor regulations define the phrase 'living together as husband and wife'. DWP guidance on the matter notes that it is important to consider the changing nature of modern-day relationships (GM C1 annex A para. A1.03).

4.17 The first consideration is the purpose of the parties in living together *(Crake and Butterworth v the Supplementary Benefit Commission).* The HB/CTB schemes recognise many different ways in which two people could live together in the same dwelling, e.g. joint occupiers, landlady/lodger, etc.

4.18 If the purpose of the parties is unclear, the question of whether a couple are living together can only be decided by looking at their relationship and living arrangements and asking whether they can reasonably be said to be those of a married couple. A body of case law developed. This is considered in detail in vol. 3, chapter 11, paras. 11039-11069 of the DWP *Decision Maker's Guide (www.dwp.gov.uk/publications/dwp/dmg/index.asp).*

4.19 The case law (see *Crake* para. 4.19) suggests that the following factors need to be considered before deciding that two people are a couple:

- whether or not they share the same household;
- the stability of the relationship;
- the financial arrangements;
- the presence or absence of a sexual relationship;
- shared responsibility for a child;
- public acknowledgment that they are a couple.

4.20 While all the above factors should be considered, none individually is conclusive (*GM C1 Annex A para. A1.02).* What matters is the general relationship as a whole *(R(SB)17/81).* The GM *(C1, Annex A paras. A1.07-10)* provides authorities with advice regarding the information they should gather and the questions they should ask when considering whether two people are living together as husband and wife or as civil partners.

4.21 Even where two people are part of the same household they may not be a couple: what matters is the reason why they live together. For example, two people who lived together for reasons of 'care, companionship and mutual convenience' were held not to be a couple *(R(SB) 35/85).* A couple whose

---

4.15 HB 2(1); HB60+ 2(1); NIHB 2(1); NIHB60+ 2(1); CTB 2(1); CTB60+ 2(1)

relationship has ended should not be treated as partners if they maintain separate households (paras. 4.6-7). When a relationship comes to an end, a shared understanding that it has ended and the actual living arrangements are more important than shared responsibilities and financial arrangements *(CIS/72/1994).* But a shared understanding may not be sufficient to show that they form separate households in the case of a married couple *(CIS/2900/1998).*

4.22 If the DWP has treated two people as a couple for JSA(IB), ESA(IR), IS or pension credit awards it does not mean that the authority must do so *(R(H)9/04).* Although the authority may regard the DWP decision as satisfactory in the absence of any contrary evidence, if the claimant asserts that the DWP's decision is wrong the authority has to reach its own conclusion *(R(H)9/04 para. 37).* Conversely, if the DWP has awarded a passport benefit on the basis that someone is not part of a couple then the authority is not normally entitled to take a different view. The exception would be if the authority has evidence of fraud which the DWP is unaware of and has not considered *(CH/4014/2007).*

Polygamous marriage

4.23 A polygamous marriage is one in which a party to it is married to more than one person. The ceremony of marriage must have taken place under the law of a country which permits polygamy. No marriage that takes place in the UK is valid if one of the partners is already married. When a polygamous marriage is formed in the UK, a second or subsequent partner should be treated as a non-dependant *(GM C1 1.42).*

Absence and membership of the same household

4.24 The claimant and/or any partner is normally treated as a member of the household even if temporarily living away from the other members of the family. Temporary absence is not defined for CTB but for HB the claimant or partner will no longer be counted as a member of the household if they are living away from the other family members and:

- they do not intend to resume living with them; or
- the absence is likely to exceed 52 weeks, unless there are exceptional circumstances where the person has no control over the length of the absence (e.g. in hospital) and the absence is unlikely to be substantially more than 52 weeks.

4.25 Where someone is no longer counted as a member of the household their needs, income and capital should not be taken into account when calculating HB/CTB. Any money received from an absent partner should be treated as maintenance (para. 13.121).

4.23 HB 2(1); HB60+ 2(1); NIHB 2(1); NIHB60+ 2(1); CTB 2(1); CTB60+ 2(1)

4.24 HB 21(1),(2); HB60+ 21(1),(2); NIHB 19(1),(2); NIHB60+ 19(1),(2); CTB 11(1); CTB60+ 11(1)

Children and young persons

4.26 A child is defined as someone under the age of 16. A young person is defined as someone aged 16 or over who meets the definition of a qualifying young person for child benefit purposes and who is not on JSA(IB), ESA(IR) or IS nor a person aged 16 or 17 who would be excluded from HB if they made a claim as a result of the Children Leaving Care Act (paras. 2.9-12).

4.27 A qualifying young person for child benefit purposes is:

- a person aged 16, from the date they attain that age up to and including the 31st August that next follows that date; or
- a person aged 16 years and over but under 20 who is undertaking a course of full-time, non-advanced education started before reaching the age of 19; or
- a person aged 16 years or over but under 20 who is undertaking approved training that is not provided through a contract of employment and that was started before reaching the age of 19.

4.28 An education course counts as full-time where the average time spent during the term time in tuition, practical work, supervised study, or taking examinations exceeds 12 hours per week. A person is treated as undertaking a course during the period between the end of one course and the start of another where they are enrolled on and start the latter course. Non-advanced education is education up to and including the following and equivalents: GCE (A Level), advanced GNVQ or equivalent, Scottish certificate of education (higher level) or Scottish certificate of sixth year studies.

4.29 Approved training means the training provided:

- in England – under 'Entry to Employment' or 'Programme Led Pathways';
- in Wales – under 'Skillbuild', 'Skillbuild Plus' or 'Foundation Modern Apprenticeships';
- in Scotland – under 'Get Ready for Work', 'Skillseekers' or 'Modern Apprenticeships'; or
- in Northern Ireland – under 'Access' or 'Jobskills Traineeships'.

4.30 A person remains a qualifying young person for child benefit purposes where they have left education or training up to and including the week including the terminal date; or if they attain the age of 20 on or before that date, the week including the last Monday before they were 20. The terminal date is whichever of the following dates occurs first after they have ceased education or training:

- the last day in February;
- the last day in May;

4.26 HB 2(1),19; HB60+ 2(1),19; NIHB 2(1),17; NIHB60+ 2(1),17; CTB 2(1),9; CTB60+ 2(1),9

- the last day in August;
- the last day in November.

4.31 Child benefit is extended for 16 and 17 year olds where they:

- have ceased to be in education or training;
- are registered for work, education or training with the Careers or Connexions Service;
- are not engaged in remunerative work; and
- an application for payment of child benefit during the extension period has been made within three months of the date education or training ended.

The child benefit extension period begins on the first day of the week after the week in which education or training stopped and ends 20 weeks later.

4.32 Once the young person is no longer counted for child benefit purposes they become a non-dependant for HB/CTB purposes. HB and CTB claims should be re-assessed to exclude the young person's personal allowance and, where appropriate, the family premium. No non-dependant deduction is made for anyone under 18 (table 6.2).

Responsibility for a child or young person

4.33 The claimant is considered responsible for any child or young person they normally live with and this is not dependent upon the receipt of child benefit. Deciding responsibility is usually straightforward but where the child or young person spends equal amounts of time in different households (e.g. where the parents have separated), or where there is doubt over which household they are living in, the child or young person is treated as normally living with the person who gets the child benefit. If no-one gets child benefit, the child or young person is considered the responsibility of:

- the person who has claimed child benefit; or
- the person the authority considers has 'primary responsibility' if more than one person has made a claim for the child benefit or no claim has been made.

4.34 A child or young person can only be the responsibility of one person in any one benefit week (GM C1.91). If the claimant has a child or young person who lives with them and that child or young person has a child of their own, the authority must decide whether the claimant's child is dependent on them or forms a family of their own. If the claimant's child receives JSA(IB) or IS for themself and their child, they should not be considered part of the claimant's family (GM C1.70).

4.35 Where the claimant is treated as not responsible for a child or young person because that child spends more time in another household, then arguably they should not be treated as occupying the claimant's dwelling for rent referral

4.33 HB 20(1),(2); HB60+ 20(1),(2); NIHB 18(1),(2); NIHB60+ 18(1),(2); CTB 10(1),(2); CTB60+ 10(1),(2)

4.34 HB 20(3); HB60+ 20(3); NIHB 18(3); NIHB60+ 18(3); CTB 10(3); CTB60+ 10(3)

and LHA cases (paras. 9.17 and 10.36) *(R v Swale BC HBRB ex p Marchant).* It is also arguable that in some circumstances a child should be included in more than one household, as a result of *Hockenjos v Secretary of State for Social Security (No. 2)* reported as R(JSA) 2/05. This was a JSA case where former partners were both held to be entitled to a personal allowance for each of their children, because the linking of allowances for dependent children in JSA to the payment of child benefit discriminates against men, contrary to EC Directive 79/7. The DWP considers that HB/CTB are not within the scope of the directive (circular G1/2007, para. 42).

Child/young person's membership of the same household

4.36 Where the claimant is treated as responsible for a child or young person, that child or young person is counted as a member of the claimant's household (with the exceptions identified in para. 4.38). This is the case even where the child or young person is temporarily living away.

4.37 Temporary absence is not defined for CTB, but for HB the same considerations apply to a child or young person who is absent as to adult dependants (para. 4.24).

4.38 A child or young person is not counted as a member of the claimant's household where they are:

- absent from the claimant's home and being looked after by a local authority, or in Scotland or Northern Ireland are in the care of a local authority or the Department;
- a foster child placed with the claimant or partner by a local authority or voluntary organisation, or in Scotland and Northern Ireland boarded out with the claimant or partner; or
- placed for adoption or custodianship with the claimant or partner or elsewhere (though once adopted, they become a member of the household).

4.39 A child or young person in local authority care who lives with the claimant under supervision must be treated as a member of the household (GM C1.120). So must a child or young person in care who returns to live with the claimant for part or all of a benefit week if, given the nature and frequency of the visits, it is reasonable to do so (GM C1.150).

4.40 A child or young person who is absent in any other circumstance, e.g. attending boarding school, should be regarded as temporarily absent and treated as a member of the family (GM C1.140).

4.36 HB 21(1),(2); HB60+ 21(1),(2); NIHB 19(1),(2); NIHB60+ 19(1),(2); CTB 11(1); CTB60+ 11(1)

4.38 HB 21(3),(4); HB60+ 21(3),(4); NIHB 19(3),(4); NIHB60+ 19(3),(4); CTB 11(2),(3); CTB60+ 11(2),(3)

4.39 HB 21(5); HB60+ 21(5); NIHB 19(5); NIHB60+ 19(5); CTB 11(4); CTB60+ 11(4)

Non-dependants

4.41 A non-dependant is someone who normally resides with the claimant on a non-commercial basis such as an adult son or daughter, or other relative. Consequently someone who is staying with the claimant but normally resides elsewhere is not a non-dependant. Someone who resides with the claimant and who has a legal liability to make payments to the claimant but who is treated as not liable for HB purposes (paras. 2.34-62) will be a non-dependant (GM C1.184).

4.42 The definition of a non-dependant specifically excludes:

- members of the claimant's benefit family (para. 4.11);
- a child or young person who lives with the claimant but who is not a member of the claimant's household, e.g. foster children (para. 4.38);
- the persons identified in paras. 4.48-51 and para 4.53.

4.43 Where the claimant resides with the landlord, neither the landlord nor a member of the landlord's family, e.g. a landlady's adult daughter, are treated as non-dependants of the claimant.

4.44 Except where paragraph 2.31 (item (c)) applies, non-dependants cannot claim HB/CTB for any payments they may make for their keep. Payments made by the non-dependant to the claimant are disregarded from the claimant's income (table 13.2) – instead a fixed deduction may be made from the claimant's HB/CTB (para. 6.17).

Residing with

4.45 There is no definition of 'residing with' in the CTB rules. For HB purposes a person does not count as normally residing with the claimant if they only share a bathroom, lavatory and/or communal area (e.g. halls, passageways and rooms in common use in sheltered accommodation). Thus people in self-contained accommodation within the same building as the claimant do not count as non-dependants even if they share a bathroom and lavatory with the claimant. A finding that someone shares more of the accommodation than a bathroom, lavatory and/or communal area with the claimant is a necessary but not a sufficient condition for deciding that they reside with the claimant *(Kadhim v Brent LBC)*. That person must also have the sort of relationship that could be described as residing with in an ordinary sense. This is more than simply sharing parts of the accommodation.

4.46 The question of who counts as a non-dependant is not always straightforward. In one case the claimant's cousin came to live with her for ten weeks after being deported from the USA. She took him in rather than see him living on the streets as he had no source of income while waiting for his JSA claim.

4.41 HB 3(1),(2); HB60+ 3(1),(2); NIHB 3(1),(2); NIHB60+ 3(1),(2); CTB 2(1); CTB60+ 2(1)

4.45 HB 3(4) sch 1 para 8; HB60+ 3(4) sch 1 para 8; NIHB 3(4) sch 1 para 8; NIHB60+ 3(4) sch 1 para 8

He slept on the sofa. The tribunal failed to consider whether he was normally residing with the claimant. The commissioner decided that he was not so a non-dependant deduction did not apply *(CH/4004/2004)*. Likewise, in *CH/3935/2007* the claimant's mentally ill daughter had been evicted and moved in with her. The tribunal decided that she was not normally residing with the claimant during the first six months of her stay but that there was sufficient evidence to justify superseding that decision after that date and treating her as a non-dependant.

4.47 However, in the same case the commissioner pointed out that if the authority had decided to supersede the decision (as opposed to the tribunal) then 'the legal burden would be on [them] to prove any change' and that 'no deduction can be applied if the evidence available is insufficient to show when circumstances changed'. Further, once the authority supersedes its previous decisions on entitlement and substitutes then with fresh ones all aspects of those decisions (fact and the law) can be appealed and this right is not dependent on satisfying the requirements for an 'anytime review' (para. 19.21) *(CH/3691/2007)*.

Other people who may live in the claimant's dwelling

Boarders

4.48 A boarder is someone who lives in board and lodging accommodation. This is accommodation that is provided for a charge which includes the provision of some cooked or prepared meals. The meals must be either cooked or prepared by someone other than the claimant or a member of their family. They must also be consumed in the premises. A person whose payment does not include an amount for meals should be treated as a tenant or sub-tenant (para. 4.50). Income from a boarder or sub-tenant is taken into account in the assessment of HB/CTB (table 13.2). Boarders can claim HB but not CTB in their own right.

Joint occupiers

4.49 For HB purposes a joint occupier is someone other than the claimant's partner who is jointly liable with the claimant to make payments in order to occupy the dwelling (paras. 2.27-64), e.g. joint tenants. For CTB purposes a joint occupier is someone other than the claimant's partner who is jointly and severally liable for the council tax, except where that liability is in question as defined by paragraphs 2.35, 2.39, 2.44 or 2.59. Joint occupiers may be eligible for HB/CTB in their own right. In such cases any tax/rates and/or rent is apportioned between them (paras. 8.9-10, 11.26-29, 11.46).

4.46 HB sch 5 para 42; HB60+ 2(1) sch 5 para 9; NIHB sch 6 para 45; NIHB60+ 2(1) sch 6 para 10; CTB sch 4 para 23; CTB60+ 2(1) sch 3 para 9

4.47 HB 3(2)(d),(3); HB60+ 3(2)(d),(3); NIHB 3(2)(d),(3); NIHB60+ 3(2)(d),(3); CTB 3(2)(d),(e),(3); CTB60+ 3(2)(d),(e),(3)

4.48 HB sch 5 para 22; HB60+ sch 5 para 10; NIHB sch 6 para 23; NIHB60+ sch 6 para 11; CTB sch 4 para 22; CTB60+ sch 3 para 10

Tenants and sub-tenants

4.50 A tenant or sub-tenant is someone who is contractually liable to pay the claimant for the right to occupy part of the claimant's accommodation, but who is not:

- a member of the claimant's family;
- a non-dependant;
- a joint tenant/owner;
- a boarder.

4.51 Where the payment includes something for meals, the person should be treated as a boarder (para. 4.48). A formal tenancy or sub-tenancy does not have to exist for someone to be treated as a tenant or sub-tenant for HB/CTB purposes, but equally an award of HB/CTB does not create or imply the existence of a legal tenancy or sub-tenancy. In this respect the HB/CTB regulations and the landlord/tenant provisions of the Housing and Rent Acts do not match each other. A tenant or sub-tenant is able to claim HB in their own right except where the authority decides the tenancy or sub-tenancy is contrived (para. 2.59). For the treatment of income from a tenant or sub-tenant, see table 13.2.

Au pairs

4.52 Au pairs are usually young people who are expected to do light housework such as cleaning, dusting, taking care of children and shopping in return for lodgings, board and pocket money. The treatment of an au pair in the claimant's household is ambiguous but the DWP advises that au pairs should not be treated as non-dependants provided a genuine commercial arrangement exists (GM C1.185).

Carers

4.53 A carer who lives with the claimant does not count as a non-dependant (or boarder) if they are looking after the claimant or partner and engaged by a charitable or voluntary organisation (not a public or local authority) which makes a charge to the claimant or partner for the services provided.

Second adults

4.54 Non-dependants, au pairs and carers, if they are aged 18 or over and not disregarded for the purpose of council tax discounts (para. 11.16-17), count as second adults for the purpose of second adult rebate (paras. 6.42-43).

4.51 HB 3(2)(f); HB60+ 3(2)(f); NIHB 3(2)(f); NIHB60+ 3(2)(f); CTB 3(2)(f); CTB60+ 3(2)(f)

5 Making a claim

5.1 This chapter describes how to claim HB and CTB and when awards start. It explains:

- who makes the claim;
- how and where to claim (by telephone, by internet or in writing);
- the information and evidence needed;
- how incomplete claims are dealt with;
- when awards start (date of claim and first day of entitlement);
- awards for past periods for 60+s; and
- backdating for 'good cause'.

5.2 This chapter does not apply when someone already on HB/CTB moves from one address to another within an authority's area, as this is a change in circumstances (para. 17.29) and does not require a claim for HB/CTB.

Who makes the claim

5.3 The general rule is that the claimant is responsible for making the claim – and the claimant can ask anyone they like to help with filling in the application form. There are further rules for couples (and polygamous marriages) and people who are unable to act.

Couples

5.4 In the case of a couple or polygamous marriage (paras. 4.15, 4.23) one partner makes the claim (though in practice both may be asked to sign the claim form). They may choose between them which partner this is to be. If they cannot agree, the authority must choose. In some cases a couple are better off if one partner rather than the other is the claimant. These are identified in this guide as they arise (e.g. paras. 12.24-25, 12.33).

People unable to act

5.5 A claim may be made by a third party if the claimant is unable, for the time being, to act. In such cases, that person takes over all rights and responsibilities in relation to the HB/CTB claim.

5.3 AA 1,5; NIAA 1,5

5.4 HB 82(1); HB60+ 63(1); NIHB 80(1); NIHB60+ 61(1); CTB 68(1); CTB60+ 52(1)

5.5 HB 82(6); HB60+ 63(6); NIHB 80(6); NIHB60+ 61(6); CTB 68(6); CTB60+ 52(6)

5.6 Where one of the following has been appointed to act for the claimant, the authority must accept a claim from him or her:

- a receiver or deputy appointed by the Court of Protection;
- an attorney;
- in Scotland, a judicial factor or other guardian;
- in Northern Ireland, a controller appointed by the High Court; or
- a person appointed by the DWP to act on the claimant's behalf in connection with some other benefit.

5.7 In any other case, the authority may accept a written request from an individual over 18, or a firm or organisation, to be an appointee, for example, a friend or relative, a social worker or solicitor. In doing this the authority should take account of any conflict of interests between the claimant and appointee. Either the authority or the appointee can terminate the appointment by giving four weeks' written notice.

How and where to claim

5.8 This section describes where and how to claim HB/CTB, and how claims may be amended and withdrawn. The two commonest methods of claiming are:

- in writing to the authority which administers HB/CTB (para. 1.18);
- by telephone to the DWP in conjunction with a claim for, or an award of, JSA, ESA, incapacity benefit, income support or pension credit.

In the above and all cases, claims must be supplemented by appropriate information and evidence (para. 5.17). Even if a claimant cannot complete a claim by the methods mentioned here, they may notify their intention to do so (para. 5.34).

Telephone claims

5.9 A claim for HB/CTB may be made wholly by telephone to:

- the authority if the authority permits telephone claims – but only to the telephone number they have chosen for that purpose;
- the DWP if they permit this – in conjunction with a claim for, or an award of, pension credit (already possible); ESA (expected soon); or (perhaps later) JSA, incapacity benefit or income support.

In either type of telephone claim, the authority can require the claimant to approve a written statement of their claim.

5.6 HB 82(2); HB60+ 63(2); NIHB 80(2); NIHB60+ 61(2); CTB 68(2); CTB60+ 52(2)

5.7 HB 82(3)-(5); HB60+ 63(3)-(5); NIHB 80(3)-(5); NIHB60+ 61(3)-(5); CTB 68(3)-(5); CTB60+ 52(3)-(5)

5.9 HB 83(4A)-(4BA); HB60+ 64(5A)-(5CA); NIHB 81(4A)-(4BA); NIHB60+ 62(5A)-(5CA); CTB 69(4A)-(4BA); CTB60+ 53(4A)-(4CA)

Internet claims

5.10 An authority may choose to allow claims for HB/CTB to be made wholly by internet – but only with the approval of the authority's Chief Executive (in Northern Ireland, the authority), who must also approve the internet claim form and communication and authentication procedures. Authorities may use an intermediary (e.g. a private firm) for this purpose, and can require internet claims to be made via an intermediary. They may also require claimants to keep written and/or electronic records. No similar provisions apply to claims for HB/CTB via the DWP.

Written claims

5.11 Any claim not made wholly by telephone or internet must be made in writing (though even a written claim can be started over the phone or internet: para. 5.34). Written claims are made to the authority itself (para. 5.12), or to the DWP (though this is uncommon because such claims are normally by telephone: paras. 5.13-14). Authorities must provide forms free of charge at their offices, and may make them available via others (such as advice agencies and social landlords). A sample form is at www.dwp.gov.uk.

Claims to an authority

5.12 A claim for HB and/or CTB may always be made to the authority administering that benefit. Written claims must be delivered to an office designated by the authority for that purpose, including the authority's benefit office, the offices of the county council (where different), or any office the authority selects (such as a hostel or social landlord). This is often known as a 'designated office', and the postal address of each designated office must be included on every HB/CTB claim form (along with the authority's email address if it wishes). For telephone and internet claims see above (paras. 5.9-10).

Claims via the DWP

5.13 A claim for HB and/or CTB may be made via the DWP whenever a claimant is making a claim for, or dealing with an award of, JSA, ESA, incapacity benefit, income support or pension credit. Such claims are normally by telephone (para. 5.9) to an 'authorised office' (in effect a call centre) but can be in writing to an 'appropriate DWP office' (any office open to the public and dealing with claims for the DWP benefits mentioned).

5.10 HB 83A, sch 11 paras 1-3; HB60+ 64A; sch 10 paras 1-3; NIHB 81A, sch 11 paras 1-3; NIHB60+ 62A; sch 10 paras 1-3; CTB 69A; sch 9 paras 1-3; CTB60+ 53A; sch 8 paras 1-3

5.11 HB 83(1),(2); HB60+ 64(2),(3); NIHB 81(1),(2); NIHB60+ 62(2),(3); CTB 69(1),(2); CTB60+ 53(1),(2)

5.12 HB 2(1), 83(4); HB60+ 2(1), 64(5); NIHB 2(1), 81(4); NIHB60+ 2(1), 62(5); CTB 2(1), 69(4); CTB60+ 2(1), 53(4)

5.13 HB 2(1), 83(4); HB60+ 2(1), 64(5); NIHB 2(1), 81(4); NIHB60+ 2(1), 62(5); CTB 2(1), 69(4); CTB60+ 2(1), 53(4)

5.14 Part of the claim procedure for the DWP benefits mentioned is that the person is asked if they also wish to claim HB/CTB. The DWP sends the authority details of the information they have gathered, and should do this within two working days (GM para. DW1.304). The forms they use for this are called either a 'Local Authority Input Document' (LAID) or 'Local Authority Claims Input document' (LACI). Authorities also have electronic access to relevant details. For more on the exchange of information between authorities and the DWP see paragraph 5.21.

HB/CTB claims when there are DWP delays

5.15 Even people claiming JSA, ESA, incapacity benefit, income support or pension credit are entitled to claim HB/CTB direct from the authority (para. 5.12) and this can be advisable when there are DWP delays. The authority's power to require information and evidence involves a test of reasonableness (para. 5.17), and if there is evidence of what the claimant's actual circumstances are, it is not reasonable to delay assessing HB/CTB in order to wait for the DWP to make a decision. If the claimant has no income, he or she qualifies for maximum HB/CTB (para. 6.9) regardless of what the DWP decides. This would include a claimant living off voluntary payments from friends or relatives, or payments in kind such as food, which are in each case disregarded; or living entirely off savings.

Amending or withdrawing a claim

5.16 Before a decision is made on a claim, the claimant may:

- amend the claim: the amendment is treated as having been made from the outset;
- withdraw the claim: the authority is then under no duty to decide it.

A claim which was made wholly by telephone (para. 5.9) may be amended or withdrawn by telephone or in writing. Amendments and withdrawals of other claims must be in writing. If the telephone claim was to the authority, any telephone amendment must be to them; if it was to the DWP, any amendment may be to them or the DWP.

Information and evidence

5.17 When a claimant makes a claim for HB/CTB, it is for them to support their claim by supplying the authority (or DWP: para. 5.13) with the information and evidence it reasonably requires. The authority (or DWP) may ask the claimant to provide 'certificates, documents, information and evidence' if they are 'reasonably required... in order to determine... entitlement'. This applies in deciding whether a claim is complete (para. 5.25), and also during the course of

---

5.14 HB 111; HB60+ 64(5B), 92; NIHB60+ 62(5B); CTB 94; CTB60+ 53(4B), 79

5.16 HB 87; HB60+ 68; NIHB 83; NIHB60+ 64; CTB 73; CTB60+ 58

5.17 AA 5(1); NIAA 5(1); HB 83(1),86(1),(1A); HB60+ 64(2),67(1),(1A); NIHB 81(1),82(1),(1A); NIHB60+ 62(2),63(1),(1A); CTB 69(1),72(1),(1A); CTB60+ 53(1),57(1),(1A)

an award (para. 17.43). The authority (or DWP) must request the claimant to provide these (para. 5.26). The authority may additionally request the claimant to attend an interview, but may not insist on this: *R v Liverpool CC ex parte Johnson No. 2.* Evidence should be obtained direct from a third party only with the claimant's written agreement (GM para. D3.400) – which is sometimes given by signing the declaration on the application form.

Signatures

5.18 It has often been assumed that a signature by the claimant (or someone acting for them: paras. 5.5-7) is an absolute requirement for a claim to be valid, and that a signature by a partner (if any) is highly desirable too. The law does not specifically require this, but in practice a signature by the claimant is normally a reasonable requirement (para. 5.17) – at least in the case of a paper claim. In relation to telephone claims the DWP has confirmed that a signature is not required (DWP circular G20/2008).

Information the claimant need not disclose

5.19 An authority may not require any information or evidence whatsoever about the following types of payment, whether they are made to a claimant, partner, child, young person, non-dependant or second adult. These payments are in any case always disregarded in the assessment of HB and CTB:

- payments from the Macfarlane Trusts, the Eileen Trust, the Skipton Fund, the Fund or the London Bombing Charitable Relief Fund, and in certain cases payments of money which originally derived from those sources (para. 13.108);
- payments in kind of capital from a charity or from the above sources;
- payments in kind of income from any source.

A 'payment in kind' is a payment made in goods (e.g. food, fuel) rather than in money (e.g. cash, cheques).

National Insurance numbers

5.20 In HB and CTB (except for claims for HB made in respect of a hostel: para. 10.21) the claimant must either provide their National Insurance (NI) number and the NI number of their partner, along with information or evidence establishing this; or provide information or evidence enabling it to be ascertained; or make an application for an NI number and give information or evidence to assist with this – even if it is highly improbable that one will be granted: *CH/4085/2007.* Matters relating to the provision of an NI number are appealable, including the question of what information or evidence is needed to ascertain one: *CH/1231/2004.*

However, since 6th April 2009, the claimant's partner is not required to have an

---

5.19 HB 86(2),(4); HB60+ 67(2),(4); NIHB 82(2),(4); NIHB60+ 63(2),(4); CTB 72(2),(4); CTB60+ 57(2),(4)

5.20 AA1(1A); NIAA 1(1A); HB 4; HB60+ 4; NIHB 4; NIHB 60+ 4; CTB 4; CTB 60+ 4

NI number if that partner has no right to enter the UK and is not entitled to social security benefits. (*Secretary of State for Work and Pensions v Wilson,* reported as *R(H) 7/06,* therefore no longer applies.)

Information and evidence provided by (or to) the DWP

5.21 There are three rules about information and evidence provided by (or to) the DWP:

- For all claimants, there are rules about when evidence from the DWP must be accepted by the authority (and vice versa): table 5.1.
- Also, for claimants who have been (lawfully) awarded JSA(IB), IS or guarantee credit, this award is binding as proof that (at the relevant dates) the claimant therefore fulfils the income-related conditions for receiving maximum HB/CTB (paras. 6.5 and 13.4): *R v Penwith District Council ex parte Menear* and *R v South Ribble Council Housing Benefit Review Board.*
- And for claimants who have been (lawfully) awarded savings credit, then certain figures are binding on the authority (para.13.158).

Proof and the DWP's security guidance

5.22 The law does not (except as described above and in table 5.1) specify what proof the authority should require about any particular matter (though a forged document does not prove anything, even if its contents are true: *R v Winston*). Almost all authorities follow the DWP's Security Guidance (June 2006). This gives general advice about proof, and advises that claimants should provide the original of a document rather than a copy. The Security Guidance is guidance, not law. It does not apply if it conflicts with the legal test of what the authority can lawfully require (para 5.17): *CH/2323/2002;* and does not apply to tribunals: *CH/5088/2002.* The Security Guidance itself specifies that it does not apply to hostel claimants (para. 10.21) for the first 13 weeks of their claim.

Table 5.1: Verification done by the DWP for the authority (and vice versa)

Evidence provided by the DWP to the authority

The authority must use information in connection with a claim for or award of HB/CTB, without verifying its accuracy, if it is relevant and was used by the DWP in connection with a claim for or an award of any of the following benefits:

- jobseeker's allowance
- employment and support allowance
- incapacity benefit
- income support
- disability living allowance
- attendance allowance
- carer's allowance
- retirement pension
- state pension credit
- winter fuel payment
- bereavement allowance
- bereavement payment
- widowed parent's allowance.

However, authorities retain the duty to decide whether information is to be used or not, because the rule then goes on to say that the above requirement on the authority does not apply if:

- the information is supplied more than 12 months after it was used as above – or the date it was used cannot be ascertained; or
- although it is provided within 12 months, the authority has reason to believe that the information has changed since then.

Evidence provided by the authority to the DWP

The reverse of the above rule (including the exceptions) applies to information used by the authority in connection with a claim for HB/CTB and provided to the DWP in connection with one of its benefits.

Additionally, other information the authority has verified and forwarded to the DWP (even if it wasn't used in connection with HB/CTB) must also be used by the DWP in connection with one of its benefits unless:

- it has reasonable grounds for believing the information is inaccurate; or
- the information is received more than four weeks after it was verified by the authority.

5.21 SI 2007/2911; NISR 2007/467

T 5.1 SI 2007/2911 regs 1-4; SI 2007/467 regs 1-4; SI 2007/2911 regs 3,4

Incomplete claims

Claims not received

5.23 An HB/CTB claim which does not reach the authority (or DWP if appropriate) has not been made and so the authority has no duty to decide it or act on it in any way. This applies to:

(a) a written claim which is not received by the authority (or DWP);

(b) a telephone claim if the authority (or DWP) does not answer the phone;

(c) a telephone claim if the claimant does not answer all the questions;

(d) a telephone claim if the authority requests the claimant to approve a written statement as a result of the telephone call (para. 5.9) and the claimant fails to do so;

(e) an internet claim which the authority's computer does not accept;

(f) an internet claim which is not in the form approved by the authority's Chief Executive.

In case (d), the law treats the (attempted) claim as not a 'valid' claim. In case (f), the law treats the (attempted) claim as not having been submitted. In each case, this seems intended to be different from the incomplete ('defective') claims described below. In all the above cases, if the claimant claims again there may be good cause for a late claim (para. 5.53, and see para. 5.51 if the claimant or any partner is aged 60+).

Incomplete claims

5.24 If a claim is received by the authority (or DWP if appropriate) but is incomplete in some way, the authority (or DWP) must give the claimant the chance to complete it – as described in this section. (In the law, an incomplete claim is also described as being 'defective'.)

What is a complete claim

5.25 A claim is complete if it is made:

- in writing or by internet (paras. 5.10-11) and is on an application form approved by the authority and completed in accordance with the instructions on the form – including any instructions to provide information and evidence;
- in some other written form which the authority accepts as sufficient in the

---

5.23 HB 83(4),(4B),(4C) sch 11 paras 2(7),4; HB60+ 64(5),(5C),(5D) sch 10 paras 2(7),4; NIHB 81(4),(4B),(4C) sch 11 paras 2(7),4; NIHB60+ 62(5),(5C),(5D) sch 10 paras 2(7),4; CTB 69(4),(4B),(4C) sch 9 paras 2(7),4; CTB60+ 53(4),(4C),(4D) sch 8 paras 2(7),4

5.25 AA 1,5,6; NIAA 1,5; HB 83(1),(4C),(9); HB60+ 64(2),(5D),(10); NIHB 81(1),(4C),(9); NIHB60+ 62(2),(5D),(10); CTB 69(1),(4C),(9); CTB60+ 53(1),(4D),(9)

circumstances of a particular case or class of cases, having regard to whether the information and evidence provided with it is sufficient;

- by telephone (para. 5.9) and the claimant provides the information and evidence required to decide the claim.

Dealing with incomplete claims

5.26 If the above conditions are not met, the authority must give the claimant the opportunity of doing whatever is needed to make it complete. In the case of a claim via the DWP, however, the DWP may do this (but if it does not, the authority must). Depending on the circumstances, this could mean:

- the authority sending the claimant an application form;
- the authority returning an application form to the claimant for completion; or
- the authority or the DWP requesting information and evidence (or further information and evidence) from the claimant.

In all cases, the authority must also inform the claimant of the duty to notify relevant changes of circumstances which occur, and say what these are likely to be.

5.27 The claimant must be allowed at least one month to provide what is required (para. 5.31), and must be allowed longer if it is reasonable to do so. In the case of telephone claims, the law specifically permits more than one reminder, and the month is counted from the last such reminder. In the case of written and internet claims, some authorities send a reminder, allowing a further period for the reply. In all these cases, if the claimant does what is required within the time limit, the claim is treated as having been complete from the outset.

Deciding incomplete claims

5.28 A telephone claim in which the claimant does not answer all the questions may nonetheless be decided by the authority. Any other claim must be decided even if the claimant does not complete it. In such cases, the authority might (as appropriate):

- decide that the claimant is not entitled to HB/CTB because they do not satisfy the conditions of entitlement, as they have not provided the necessary information or evidence; or
- draw a negative inference (which means 'assume the worst') in order to make its decision. For example, if a claimant's bank statement shows that he withdrew £20,000 three weeks ago, and the claimant refuses to explain this, it might be reasonable to decide that he does not qualify for HB/CTB because his capital remains £20,000.

5.26 HB 83(4D)-(4E); (6)-(9), 86(1)(2); HB60+ 64(5E)-(5F) (7)-(9), 67(1),(2); NIHB 81(4D)-(4E), (6)-(9), 82(1),(2); NIHB60+ 62(4D)-(4E), (7)-(9),63(1),(2); CTB 69(4D)-(4E) (7)-(9),72(1),(2); CTB60+ 53(4E)-(4F) (6)-(9),57(1),(2)

5.28 HB 83(4F),89; HB60+ 64(5G),70; NIHB 85; NIHB60+ 66; CTB 69(4F),75; CTB60+ 53(4G),60

In each of the above cases, the claimant may appeal against the decision to a tribunal (chapter 19).

When HB/CTB starts

5.29 HB and CTB start on the Monday following the claimant's 'date of claim', unless the 'week-one-yes rule' applies, in which case they start on a date up to two weeks earlier. The details are in the remainder of this chapter. The main rules are:

- the 'date of claim' usually means the date the claimant first notified their intention (to one of the relevant offices) to claim HB/CTB – but it can be earlier (para. 5.33);
- the 'week-one-yes rule' applies if the claimant becomes liable for rent/council tax, and moves in, and claims HB/CTB, all in the same benefit week (para. 5.49).

Duration of award

5.30 There is no fixed limit to an award of HB/CTB. Entitlement may change if there is a change in circumstances (chapter 17). Otherwise it simply continues until the claimant:

- stops being entitled – for example, gains too much capital or income, dies or becomes an ineligible student (para. 17.21); or
- fails to respond to a request for information or evidence and then the award of HB/CTB is terminated (para. 17.51).

Definition of 'month'

5.31 Many of the rules in this guide refer to allowing someone a 'month' to do something in connection with a claim, etc. This means a calendar month, and the month is counted as follows *(R(IB) 4/02):*

- if the authority issues a letter on 26th June inviting the claimant to provide something, the claimant has provided it within a month if he or she gets it to the authority by the end of 26th July;
- if the authority issues a letter on 31st January inviting a claimant to provide something, the claimant has provided it within a month if he or she gets it to the authority by the end of 28th or 29th February (depending on whether it is a leap year).

Things sent out by the authority (such as requests for information or evidence, decision letters) are counted in the law as being sent out on the date of posting. Things received by the authority (such as claims, information and evidence) are

5.31 HB sch 11 para 4; HB60+ ; sch 10 para 4; NIHB sch 11 para 4; NIHB60 sch 10 para 4; CTB sch 9 para 4; CTB60+ sch 8 para 4; DAR 2; NIDAR 2

counted in the law as being received on the date of receipt. In the case of internet communications, this means the date recorded by the computer as the date of sending or receipt unless the authority reasonably directs otherwise.

Definition of 'benefit week'

5.32 Many of the rules in this guide refer to a 'benefit week'. A benefit week (for HB/CTB) is defined as beginning on a Monday and ending on the following Sunday.

Date of claim

5.33 The rules about what counts as the claimant's 'date of claim' are summarised in table 5.2 (and were confirmed in *R(H) 9/07*). Further details follow.

Notifying an intention to claim

5.34 This rule applies if:

- the claimant notified their intention to claim HB/CTB to the authority or DWP;
- it sent the claimant an application form; and
- the claimant returned the form within one month of when it was sent out, or longer if reasonable.

5.35 In this case, the date of claim is the day the claimant notified their intention to claim to the office in question. The claimant can do this 'by any means' (which includes telephoning, emailing, writing, texting, visiting or sending a friend: *CIS/2726/2005*).

Claims following death or separation

5.36 This rule applies if:

- the claimant claims HB/CTB within one month of their partner's death or of their separation from their partner; and
- that partner was on HB/CTB at the time of the death or separation.

5.37 In this case, the date of claim is the date of the separation or death in question, the intention being that there should be no gap in entitlement to HB/CTB. The one month time limit cannot be extended, but if the claimant is aged 60+ another rule applies instead (para. 5.51) and if they are under 60 they may have good cause for backdating (para. 5.53).

5.32 HB 2(1); HB60+ 2(1); NIHB 2(1); NIHB60+ 2(1); CTB 2(1); CTB60+ 2(1)

5.33 HB 83(5); HB60+ 64(6); NIHB 81(5); NIHB60+ 62(6); CTB 69(5); CTB60+ 53(5)

5.34 HB 83(5)(d); HB60+ 64(6)(d); NIHB 81(5)(d); NIHB60+ 62(6)(d); CTB 69(5)(d); CTB60+ 53(5)(d)

5.36 HB 83(5)(c); HB60+ 64(6)(c); NIHB 81(5)(c); NIHB60+ 62(6)(c); CTB 69(5)(c); CTB60+ 53(5)(c)

Passport benefit claimants who claim HB/CTB within one month

5.38 This rule applies if:

- the claimant or a partner claims and is awarded a passport benefit (JSA(IB), ESA(IR), IS or guarantee credit); and
- the claimant's HB/CTB claim is received by the authority or the DWP no more than one month after the passport benefit claim was received by the DWP.

Table 5.2: Date of claim for HB/CTB: summary

Situation	Date of claim
The claimant asked for a form (or notified an intention to claim) and returns it, properly completed, within one month of when it was sent out (or longer if reasonable)	The day the claimant asked for it (or notified the intention to claim)
The claim is made within one month of the claimant's partner's death or the claimant's and partner's separation, and the partner was on HB/CTB at the time	The day of the death or separation
The claimant or a partner was awarded JSA(IB), ESA(IR), IS or guarantee credit, and the claim for HB/CTB is received within one month of when the claim for that benefit was received	The first day of their entitlement to JSA(IB), ESA(IR), IS or guarantee credit
The claimant or a partner is on JSA(IB), ESA(IR), IS or guarantee credit, and the claim for HB/CTB is received within a month of them first becoming liable for rent/council tax	The first day of their liability for rent/council tax
In any other case	The day the HB/CTB claim is received
But if the claimant or any partner is aged 60+ (regardless of whether they have 'good cause')	Up to 3 months before the day the claim was received
And if the claimant and any partner are under 60 and have 'good cause'	Up to 6 months before the day the claimant requested backdating

- Detailed rules are in para. 5.34 onwards.

Example: Date of claim following notice of an intention to claim

On Thursday 28th May 2009, a claimant realises she might qualify for HB/CTB and telephones the authority to ask to claim. The authority sends an application form out that very day. She posts it back and it reaches the authority on Friday 12th June 2009.

Her date of claim is Thursday 28th May 2009 and (unless the week-one-yes rule applies: para. 5.49) the first day of her entitlement to HB/CTB is the following Monday, 1st June 2009.

5.39 In this case, the date of claim for HB/CTB is the date of first entitlement to the passport benefit (and in the case of JSA(IB) and ESA(IR) this means the first 'waiting day'). The one month time limit cannot be extended.

Passport benefit claimants who become liable for rent, rates or council tax

5.40 This rule applies if:

- the claimant or a partner is receiving a passport benefit (JSA(IB), ESA(IR), IS or guarantee credit); and
- the claimant becomes liable for rent, rates or council tax for the first time; and
- the claimant's HB/CTB claim is received by the authority or the DWP no more than one month after the new liability begins.

5.41 In this case, the date of claim for HB is the first day of their new liability for rent or rates; the date of claim for CTB is the first day of their new liability for council tax. The one month time limit cannot be extended.

Other claims

5.42 This rule applies if none of the earlier rules applies (but see also paras. 5.51 and 5.53 for past periods).

5.43 In this case, the date of claim is the day the claim is received by the benefit authority or the county council (if authorised) or the DWP (paras. 5.12-14).

Advance claims

5.44 This rule applies if a claimant claims:

- HB/CTB up to 17 weeks before their 60th birthday; or
- if aged 60+, HB/CTB up to 17 weeks before an event which makes them entitled to HB/CTB; or

---

5.38 HB 83(5)(a); HB60+ 64(6)(a); NIHB 81(5)(a); NIHB60+ 62(6)(c); CTB 69(5)(a); CTB60+ 53(5)(a)

5.40 HB 83(5)(b); HB60+ 64(6)(b); NIHB 81(5)(b); NIHB60+ 62(6)(b); CTB 69(5)(b); CTB60+ 53(5)(b)

5.42 HB 83(5)(e); HB60+ 64(6)(e); NIHB 81(5)(e); NIHB 62(6)(e); CTB 69(5)(e); CTB60+ 53(5)(e)

- If under 60, HB/CTB up to 13 weeks before an event which makes them entitled to HB/CTB; or
- CTB, or HB for rates, up to eight weeks before they become liable for council tax/rates;
- HB for a period of up to four weeks before moving into their home if they meet the conditions in paragraph 3.30.

The third and fourth rules do not, however, apply to someone who counts as a migrant or new arrival (para. 20.2).

5.45 In these cases, the date of claim is:

- in the first three cases above, any date in the week before the benefit week (para. 5.32) containing the birthday or event in question;
- in the fourth case above, the date of first liability for council tax/rates;
- in the fifth case above, the day the claim was received (para. 5.43), or if later, the date the claimant actually moves in.

Delays in setting council taxes

5.46 This rule applies if:

- an authority delays setting its council taxes until after 31st March in any year; and
- a CTB claim is received within four weeks after the setting of the council taxes.

5.47 In this case, the date of claim is set so that the claimant's entitlement begins on 1st April in that year (or the benefit week in which the person's entitlement begins if this falls between 1st April and the date the claim is received).

5.44 HB 7(7),83(10),(11); HB60+ 7(7); 64(11),(12); NIHB 7(7); 81(10),(11); NIHB60+ 7(7); 62(11),(12); CTB 69(10); (12),(13); CTB60+ 53(10),(12)

5.46 CTB 69(11); CTB60+ 53(11)

First day of entitlement

The general rule

5.48 The general rule is the claimant's first day of entitlement to HB/CTB is the Monday following their 'date of claim' (paras. 5.33-47). Even if their date of claim is a Monday, their first day of entitlement is the following Monday. The exceptions follow.

The week-one-yes rule

5.49 The week-one-yes rule applies only if the claimant or partner becomes liable for rent/council tax, and moves in, in the benefit week (para. 5.32) containing their 'date of claim'. In such cases, their first day of entitlement to HB/CTB is the day their liability for rent or council tax begins. (DWP circular HB/CTB A8/2006 appears to give different advice on this point.) In Northern Ireland the week-one-yes rule also applies to HB for rates if the rates are included in the rent.

If the result of the above is that the first day of entitlement is not a Monday, in the first benefit week the claimant's HB/CTB is calculated and awarded on a daily basis (the daily amount of HB/CTB being one-seventh of the weekly rent.)

The rule for certain dwellings with daily rents

5.50 This rule applies only to residents who are liable to pay their rent on a daily basis to:

- a hostel (para. 10.21); or
- any other accommodation in which they have been placed as a homeless person and which is board and lodging accommodation, accommodation licensed to the authority, or short-term leased accommodation (with a lease of no more than 10 years) outside the authority's housing revenue account.

In such cases, there is no time limit on when the residents may claim, and their HB is always awarded back to when they moved into the accommodation. In other words, their first day of entitlement to HB is always the day they moved in. In practice, this rule is likely to be needed only for short periods (as leaving it any longer may mean the claimant is no longer available to provide the information and evidence necessary for their claim).

5.48 HB 76(1); HB60+ 57(1); NIHB 74(1); NIHB60+ 55(1); CTB 64(1); CTB60+ 48(1)

5.49 HB 76(2),80(4)(a); HB60+ 57(2); 61(4)(a); NIHB 74(2),78(4)(a); NIHB60+ 55(2); 59(4)(a); CTB 64(2),(5),57(1); CTB60+ 48(2)(5),40(1)

5.50 HB 76(3)-(5); HB60+ 57(2)-(4); NIHB 74(3)-(5); NIHB60+ 55(2)-(4)

Examples: First day of entitlement

The general rule

A man claims HB/CTB because his income has reduced. His date of claim is Thursday 23rd July 2009.

His first day of entitlement to HB/CTB is the Monday following his date of claim, which is Monday 27th July 2009.

The week-one-yes rule: whole weeks

A woman moves into her flat on Monday 1st February 2010, and is liable for rent and council tax from that very day. Her date of claim is Thursday 4th February 2010.

Her first day of entitlement to HB/CTB is the day her liability for rent/council tax begins, which is Monday 1st February 2010. (The answer is the same whether the rent is due weekly, monthly or on any other basis.)

The week-one-yes rule: part weeks

A woman moves into her flat on Saturday 1st August 2009, and is liable for rent and council tax from that very day. Her date of claim is Friday 31st July 2009.

Her first day of entitlement to HB/CTB is the day her liability for rent/council tax begins, which is Saturday 1st August 2009. In her first week she gets two-sevenths of a week's HB and CTB (for the Saturday and the Sunday). (The answer is the same whether the rent is due weekly, monthly or on any other basis.)

Awards for past periods for 60+s

5.51 If the claimant or any partner is aged 60+, a claim covers any period in the three months before the day the claim is actually received – but only back to their 60th birthday, or the day they became liable for rent or council tax, if these are later. (The time limit used to be 12 months before October 2008.)

5.52 The claimant does not have to ask for this rule to apply: it applies automatically in all cases. It is not the same as 'backdating' (para. 5.53), and entitlement in the past need not have been continuous or even at the same address.

5.51 HB60+ 64(1); NIHB60+ 62(1); CTB60+ 53(1ZA),56

Example: Awards for past periods for 60+s

A claimant aged 92 sends in his first ever claim for HB/CTB. It reaches the authority on Friday 18th September 2009. He would have qualified for several years for a small amount of HB/CTB had he applied.

His date of claim is Thursday 18th June 2009 and (unless the week-one-yes rule applies: para. 5.49) the first day of his entitlement to HB/CTB is the following Monday, 22nd June 2009.

Backdating for 'good cause'

Backdating HB/CTB

5.53 The rules about backdating HB/CTB apply only if the claimant and any partner are under 60. They are as follows:

- HB/CTB must be backdated if the claimant requests benefit for an earlier period in writing, and 'had continuous good cause for [his or her] failure to make a claim' (para. 5.58).
- HB/CTB cannot be backdated more than six months before the date on which the authority received the claimant's written request (even if this is later than when the claimant made his or her claim for HB/CTB).
- It is the date of claim which is backdated. So even if the claimant is not currently entitled to any HB/CTB, a claim is backdated (if the above conditions are met) to a period when they were entitled;
- HB/CTB during any backdated period is calculated using the figures and rules which applied at that time.

(The six months time limit used to be 52 weeks before 6th October 2008; and the government is currently considering further reducing it to three months: circular HB/CTB G4/2009.)

5.54 Backdating does not apply if the claimant or any partner is aged 60+, because for them there is an automatic equivalent to backdating (para. 5.51).

What is and is not 'backdating'?

5.55 The question of backdating only arises when HB/CTB is requested for a past period for which the claimant has not already claimed HB/CTB. Basing a claim on an application form which was (on the balance of probability) received by the authority or the DWP, but was then mislaid, does not count as backdating (because in fact a claim was made).

5.53 HB 83(12); NIHB 81(12); CTB 69(14)

How to claim backdated HB/CTB

5.56 Many authorities include a question on their HB/CTB application forms about whether the claimant wishes to claim backdating, but it is also possible to write a letter (at the time of claiming or later) to request backdating. The claimant does not have to use particular words (e.g. 'backdating'): it is enough if it is clear that they are asking for HB/CTB for a past period: *CH/3402/2005.*

Backdating is obligatory if there is 'good cause'

5.57 Backdating is obligatory once the authority determines that the claimant had good cause for failure to make the claim earlier and that his or her good cause lasted throughout the period in question (whether for the same reason throughout, or for different reasons).

'Good cause'

5.58 Good cause has been explained (in relation to various social security benefits) by commissioners and courts right back to the late 1940s, and this case law is binding in HB/CTB: *CH/5221/2001.* DWP guidance (GM chapter A2, annex A) gives a good summary of the case law up to April 2002, and cases since then are summarised in table 5.3. The following are the main principles.

5.59 Good cause includes 'any fact that would probably have caused a reasonable person to act as the claimant did', but it is for the claimant to establish they have good cause. A claimant is expected to take reasonable steps to ascertain what his or her rights may be, but 'claimants cannot always be assumed to have an understanding of public administration' (this paragraph: *CS/371/1949,* quoted with approval in *CH/450/2004*).

5.60 The case law shows that the circumstances in which a claimant has good cause usually fall into four broad categories:

- the claimant was so ill (physically or mentally) or otherwise unable to act that they could not claim and could not ask someone to claim for them;
- someone the claimant should have been able to rely on (such as the authority, the DWP, an advice agency and possibly others) advised them they could not get HB/CTB when in fact they could;
- there were good reasons for the claimant not believing they could claim, amounting to more than just not thinking or not caring;
- some external factor prevented the claimant from making a claim (e.g. failure of the postal services, imprisonment).

The above are the commonest categories. Other situations may also amount to good cause. Whether a claimant has good cause is appealable to a tribunal – and also to a commissioner, particularly because at that level questions of good cause are regarded as questions of law *(R(SB) 39/91)* as well as fact.

Example: Backdating for good cause

A single claimant under 60 sends in his first ever claim for HB/CTB. It reaches the authority on Friday 18th September 2009. He would have qualified for several years for a small amount of HB/CTB had he applied. With his claim he writes asking for his HB/CTB to be backdated to Monday 6th July 2009 when he was admitted to hospital in an emergency. He was so ill that it was impossible for him to communicate throughout his time in hospital. He came home from hospital on Tuesday 8th September 2009, but took a few days to start thinking about his finances. He has a grown-up daughter living with him (and who remained in his house throughout).

Although his daughter could perhaps have decided to claim for him, this has no effect on his backdating request: *CH/3817/2004.* Whilst in hospital and unable to communicate he could not claim and could not ask someone to claim for him, so he had good cause. Taking eight days to claim, after such a bad illness, is how a reasonable person would act, so during those eight days he also had good cause.

Because he had continuous good cause, his HB/CTB must be backdated to Monday 6th July 2009, the day he went into hospital. His HB/CTB therefore start on Monday 13th July 2009.

Note that in any backdating case, it is often possible to think of some other fact that might alter the answer. In this case for example, was he so ill before he went into hospital that his HB/CTB should be backdated to an earlier date? We do not know.

Table 5.3: Backdating case law

This table summarises case law about backdating HB/CTB since 2002, when commissioners started issuing decisions on this. Case law before then is summarised in DWP guidance (para. 5.58) and see also paragraph 5.60.

- *Case law on other benefits:* Case law about other DWP benefits is binding on HB/CTB *(CH/5135/2001, CH/5221/2001).*
- *What constitutes a request for backdating:* A request for backdating does not have to be expressed as such: it needs merely to be a claim for HB/CTB for a past period. In this case a late claim was capable of being a claim for the period since the last award of HB/CTB ended *(CH/3402/2005).*
- *Backdating if claimant does not qualify during the period:* The question of backdating does not arise if the other conditions of entitlement are not satisfied in the backdated period *(CH/996/2004).*

- *Backdating if claimant qualifies for only part of the period:* So long as there is good cause, there is nothing to stop HB/CTB from being backdated for a period in the past (within the 52 weeks) but then to cease in the past because entitlement ceased *(CH/1237/2004).*
- *Good cause and illness:* If a claimant was ill, the test of good cause related not to the severity or seriousness of the illness but to the resulting incapability of the claimant to claim *(CH/5135/2001).*
- *Good cause and mental incapacity:* In deciding good cause, a mentally disabled person is treated as having their mental age not their chronological age. So a person with the mental age of an infant had good cause *(CH/393/2003).*
- *Good cause and inability to speak English:* Not speaking English is not in itself good cause, particularly if there is evidence of a growing community with good facilities speaking the claimant's first language *(CH/3579/2003).*
- *Good cause in the case of a couple:* When considering good cause in the case of a claimant in a couple, it is only the claimant's circumstances that are relevant and not the other partner's. Specifically the other partner does not have to show good cause *(CH/3817/2004).*
- *Good cause and a mistaken belief reasonably held:* The claimant (who had mental health problems) had believed he did not have to pay council tax, when in fact he was liable but needed to claim full CTB because he was on income support. He had good cause because he had not been careless or sought to obtain something to which he was not entitled. He had a firmly held misunderstanding which amounted to a mistaken belief reasonably held (*CH/450/2004* and see para. 5.59). Similarly, a reasonably held belief that one cannot get HB if one has not paid national insurance contributions might amount to good cause *(CH/2198/2008).*
- *Good cause and imprisonment:* The claimant had thought he could not qualify for HB because there were delays with his parole hearing which would also make his absence greater than 13 weeks. Due to the particular complications in this case, the claimant had good cause *(CH/2639/2006).*
- *Good cause and failure to receive documents from the authority:* A failure to receive a document from the authority is not to be dismissed as possible good cause. In all three cases cited here, the document was a renewal claim form *(CSHC/352/2002, CH/3009/2004, CH/3402/2005).*

6 Calculating HB and CTB

6.1 This chapter explains:

- the main calculation of HB and CTB
- how non-dependant deductions affect HB and CTB;
- who is eligible for second adult rebate and how to calculate it; and
- converting figures to weekly amounts and rounding.

6.2 HB (for rent or rates) is always based on the income and other details of the claimant and any partner (para. 6.3). CTB is calculated in two ways. The main calculation is based on the income and other details of the claimant and any partner (para. 6.3). The other calculation of CTB is called second adult rebate (known in the law as alternative maximum CTB) and is based on the income and other details of a non-dependant in the home (para. 6.36). If the claimant qualifies for both types of CTB they get only the one that is worth the most (para. 6.64).

How much HB and CTB

6.3 This section describes the main calculation of HB and CTB. Table 6.1 summarises the rules.

Maximum benefit

6.4 The starting point for all calculations of HB and CTB is the claimant's 'maximum benefit'. On a weekly basis, this is:

- in calculating HB:
  - the whole of the claimant's weekly eligible rent (chapter 7) and/or rates in Northern Ireland (chapter 11),
  - minus any non-dependant deductions which apply;
- in calculating CTB:
  - the whole of the claimant's weekly eligible council tax (chapter 11),
  - minus any non-dependant deductions which apply.

6.4 CBA 130(1),(3)(a),130A,131(1),(3); NICBA 129(1),(3)(a),129A; HB 70; HB60+ 50; NIHB 68; NIHB 60+ 48; CTB 57; CTB60+ 40

Claimants on JSA(IB), ESA(IR), IS or guarantee credit

6.5 A claimant qualifies for maximum benefit (para. 6.4) while he or she (or any partner) is:

- on income-based jobseeker's allowance (JSA(IB)); or
- on income-related employment and support allowance (ESA(IR)); or
- on income support (IS); or
- on guarantee credit; or
- treated as receiving JSA(IB) or IS (para. 6.6).

Claimants treated as being on JSA(IB), ESA(IR) or IS

6.6 A claimant also qualifies for maximum benefit (para. 6.4) while he or she (or any partner) is:

- entitled to JSA(IB) or ESA(IR) but not receiving it because of a sanction; or
- in the 'waiting days' before his or her JSA(IB) or ESA(IR) starts – or would start apart from a sanction; or
- subject to a restriction in his or her JSA(IB) or IS as a result of breaching a community order.

6.7 In these cases, the law works by treating the claimant as though he or she was actually on JSA(IB), ESA(IR) or IS.

Claimants not on JSA(IB), ESA(IR), IS or guarantee credit

6.8 In any case other than those described above (paras. 6.5-7), if the claimant's capital (assessed as in chapters 13 to 15) is over £16,000, then he or she does not qualify for any HB or CTB at all (but see para. 6.49 about second adult rebate). Otherwise, the claimant's weekly income (chapters 13 to 15) is compared with his or her applicable amount (chapter 12).

6.9 If the claimant has no income, or has income which is less than (or equal to) his or her applicable amount, the claimant qualifies for maximum benefit (para. 6.4).

6.10 If the claimant's weekly income is more than his or her applicable amount, the difference between the two is known as 'excess income'. The claimant qualifies for:

- maximum benefit (para. 6.4);
- minus a percentage of this excess income (para. 6.11).

6.5 CBA 130(1),(3)(a),130A,131(5),(6); NICBA 129(1),(3)(a),129A; HB 2(3), sch 5 paras 4,5, sch 6 paras 5,6; HB60+ 2(3),26; NIHB 2(3) sch 6 paras 4,5, sch 7 paras 5,6; NIHB60+ 2(3),24; CTB 2(4) sch 4 paras 4,5, sch 5 paras 5,6; CTB60+ 2(4),16

6.6 HB 2(1),(3); NIHB 2(1),(3); CTB 2(1),(4)

6.9 CBA 130(1),(3),130A; NICBA 129(1),(3),129A

6.10 CBA 130(1),(3),130A,131(5),(8); NICBA 129(1),(3),129A

6.11 The percentage, also known as a 'taper', is as follows:

- 65 per cent in calculating HB (for rent);
- 20 per cent in calculating CTB;
- 20 per cent in calculating HB for rates in Northern Ireland.

Table 6.1: Amount of HB and CTB: summary

Housing benefit	Council tax benefit
Weekly eligible rent	Weekly eligible council tax
MINUS	**MINUS**
Any non-dependant deductions which apply	Any non-dependant deductions which apply
MINUS	**MINUS**
65% of excess income (if claimant is not on JSA(IB), ESA(IR), IS or guarantee credit)	20% of excess income (if claimant is not on JSA(IB), ESA(IR), IS or guarantee credit)
EQUALS	**EQUALS**
Weekly entitlement to HB	Weekly entitlement to CTB

- The right hand column applies also to HB for rates in Northern Ireland

6.11 HB 71; HB60+ 51; NIHB 69; NIHB60+ 49; CTB 59; CTB60+ 43

Examples: Calculating HB and CTB

Claimant on JSA(IB), ESA(IR), IS or guarantee credit

A claimant has no non-dependants: she lives alone. Her eligible rent is £105.00 per week. The council tax on her home would be £20.00 per week apart from the fact that she qualifies for a 25% council tax discount, which reduces her liability to £15.00 per week.

Claimants on JSA(IB), ESA(IR), IS or guarantee credit get maximum benefit – which equals their eligible rent and eligible council tax.

HB:	Eligible rent	
	equals weekly HB	£105.00
CTB:	Eligible council tax	
	equals weekly CTB	£15.00

Claimant not on JSA(IB), ESA(IR), IS or guarantee credit

A couple have no non-dependants. They are not on JSA(IB), IS or guarantee credit. Their joint weekly income exceeds their applicable amount by £20.00. Their eligible rent is £130.00 per week. Their eligible council tax liability is £22.56 per week.

Claimants with excess income get maximum benefit minus a percentage of their excess income.

HB:	Eligible rent	£130.00
	minus 65% of excess income (65% x £20.00)	£13.00
	equals weekly HB	£117.00
CTB:	Eligible council tax	£22.56
	minus 20% of excess income (20% x £20.00)	£4.00
	equals weekly CTB	£18.56

Minimum benefit

6.12 If the weekly amount of HB (in Northern Ireland, HB for rent) calculated as above is less than 50p, then it is not awarded. There is no equivalent rule in CTB (in Northern Ireland, HB for rates), where an award can be less than one penny.

CTB and the 'better buy'

6.13 If the amount of a claimant's CTB calculated as above is lower than his or her entitlement to second adult rebate, he or she will not get CTB, but will get second adult rebate instead. This is because of the 'better buy' comparison, described in paragraphs 6.64 onwards.

6.12 HB 75; HB60+ 56; NIHB 73; NIHB60+ 54

6.13 CBA 131(9)

HB and rent-free or rate-free periods

6.14 The following additional rules apply if a claimant has weeks or other periods in which no rent or rates are due. They do not apply in cases where a landlord has waived the rent or rates in return for works carried out by the tenant (para. 2.31). No HB is awarded during rent-free periods, including in Northern Ireland rate-free periods where rates are paid with the rent. HB is awarded only for periods in which rent is due (and if a rent-free or rate-free period begins or ends part way through a benefit week, the eligible rent and rates that week are calculated on a daily basis: para. 6.38).

6.15 During the periods in which rent is due, the calculation factors (i.e. applicable amount, income and any non-dependant deductions) are adjusted as follows:

- if rent is expressed on a weekly basis: multiply the calculation factors by 52 or 53, then divide by the number of weeks when rent is due in that year;
- if rent is not expressed on a weekly basis: multiply the calculation factors by 365 or 366, then divide by the number of days when rent is due in that year.

Other reasons HB/CTB may be lower

6.16 A claimant's HB/CTB can also be reduced to recover a recoverable overpayment (para. 18.11-12) or an administrative penalty (para. 18.63); or to apply a punishment for bad behaviour (para. 22.18).

Non-dependant deductions

6.17 HB and CTB are normally reduced for each non-dependant living in the claimant's home. The next paragraphs explain when a deduction is or is not made, and the amounts involved. If the claimant or any partner is aged 65 or over, the deductions are delayed (paras. 6.34-35).

6.18 Non-dependants are usually adult sons, daughters, other relatives or friends who live in the claimant's household on a non-commercial basis (paras. 4.41-43). Some claimants receive money from their non-dependants to pay towards their costs. This may include a contribution towards rent, council tax, food or household expenses. This money is not treated as the claimants' income (table 13.2). Instead deductions are made from the claimant's HB and CTB. However, these deductions are not related to what the non-dependant actually pays. They are fixed sums which apply even if the non-dependant pays the claimant nothing at all. The level of deductions (table 6.3) is high in some cases, and may cause claimants hardship.

6.14 HB 81(1),(2); HB60+ 62(1),(2); NIHB 79(1),(2); NIHB60+ 60(1),(2)

6.15 HB 81(3); HB60+ 62(3); NIHB 79(3); NIHB60+ 60(3)

6.18 HB 3; HB60+ 3; NIHB 3; NIHB60+ 3; CTB 3; CTB60+ 3

Cases in which no deduction is made

6.19 There are no non-dependant deductions in either HB or CTB (no matter how many non-dependants there are in the household) if the claimant or any partner:

- is blind or has recently regained their sight (paras.12.45-47); or
- receives the care component of disability living allowance payable at any rate; or
- receives attendance allowance payable at any rate or any of the related benefits in paragraph 12.44.

The second and third cases cease to apply when disability living allowance or attendance allowance themselves cease – for example, when the claimant or partner have been in hospital for four weeks.

6.20 No deduction applies for anyone in the groups in table 6.2. And no deduction applies for anyone who is not a non-dependant (such as a sub-tenant or boarder, an under-20-year-old for whom the claimant or partner are responsible, or certain carers: chapter 4). Appendix 6 lists all the rules about whether a non-dependant deduction applies in HB and CTB.

Cases in which a deduction is made

6.21 The amounts of the non-dependant deductions are in table 6.3. They depend on whether the non-dependant is in 'remunerative work' and, if so, on the level of their gross income. The details are in the following paragraphs.

6.22 There are no rules saying how the gross amount is to be assessed, though none of the disregards in chapters 13 to 15 applies. For non-dependants with savings, the actual interest received should be included here (not tariff income).

Non-dependants in remunerative work

6.23 For non-dependants in remunerative work (para. 6.27), there are various levels of deduction in HB and CTB (table 6.3), depending on the level of the non-dependant's gross income. This means income from all sources before the deduction of any tax or national insurance. But the following types of income are always disregarded:

- disability living allowance (either or both components);
- attendance allowance and the related benefits in paragraph 12.44;

6.19 HB 2(1),74(6), HB60+ 2(1),55(6); NIHB 2(1),72(6); NIHB60+ 2(1),53(6); CTB 2(1),58(6); CTB60+ 2(1),42(6)

6.20 HB 3(2),74(7),(8),(10); HB60+ 3(2),55(7)-(9); NIHB 3(2),72(7),(8),(10); NIHB60+ 3(2),53(7)-(9); CTB 3(2),58(7),(8); CTB60+ 3(2),42(7),(8)

6.21 HB 74(1),(2); HB60+ 55(1),(2); NIHB 72(1),(2); NIHB60+ 53(1),(2); CTB 58(1),(2); CTB60+ 42(1),(2)

- payments from (or which originally derived from) the Macfarlane Trusts, the Eileen Trust, the Skipton Fund, the Fund, the Independent Living Funds (para.13.108);
- payments from the London Bombing Charitable Relief Fund (para. 13.110).

6.24 Gross income of a non-dependant in remunerative work is averaged over any recognisable cycle. If there is none, the authority should take into account the expected hours of work and (unless the non-dependant is just starting work) the average in the period before the claim for HB/CTB – which should be five weeks unless some other period would give a more accurate estimation.

Table 6.2: Non-dependants for whom no deduction applies

- Non-dependants aged under 18.
- Non-dependants aged under 25 who are on JSA(IB) or IS.
- Non-dependants aged under 25 who are in the assessment phase (first 13 weeks) of ESA(IR).
- Non-dependants on either kind of pension credit.
- In CTB (or in Northern Ireland, HB for rates only), non-dependants aged 25+ who are on JSA(IB) or IS. In HB for rent there is a deduction in such cases. For ESA, see table 6.3.
- Non-dependants who are students (but in HB only, and only if the claimant and any partner are under 65, there is a deduction in the summer vacation if they take up remunerative work).
- Non-dependants who are youth trainees.
- Non-dependants in prison or similar forms of detention.
- Non-dependants who have been in hospital for 52 weeks or more.
- Non-dependants whose normal home is elsewhere.
- In CTB only, non-dependants who fall within any of the groups who are 'disregarded persons' for council tax purposes.

Note:

Appendix 6 gives full information about all the above.

6.23 HB 74(1),(2),(9); HB60+ 55(1),(2),(10); NIHB 72(1),(2),(9); NIHB60+ 53(1),(2),(10); CTB 58(1),(2),(9); CTB60+ 42(1),(2),(9)

6.24 HB 6(2),(4),(5); HB60+ 6(2),(4),(5); NIHB 6(2),(4)-(5); NIHB60+ 6(2),(4),(5); CTB 6(2)-(5); CTB 60+ 6(2),(4)-(6)

Table 6.3: Weekly non-dependant deductions

	HB	CTB
If claimant/partner is registered blind or was in the last 28 weeks, or claimant/partner gets DLA (care component) or AA		
◆ every non-dependant in their household	£0.00	£0.00
If non-dependant is under 18/ a youth trainee/full-time student:	£0.00	£0.00
If non-dependant is in hospital (52 weeks-plus)/prison:	£0.00	£0.00
If non-dependant is on pension credit (guarantee or savings):	£0.00	£0.00
If non-dependant is on income support:		
◆ aged 25+	£7.40	£0.00
◆ aged under 25	£0.00	£0.00
If non-dependant is on JSA (jobseeker's allowance):		
◆ on JSA(C) any age	£7.40	£2.30
◆ on JSA(IB) aged 25+	£7.40	£0.00
◆ on JSA(IB) aged under 25	£0.00	£0.00
If non-dependant is on ESA (employment and support allowance):		
◆ on ESA(C) any age: main phase or assessment phase	£7.40	£2.30
◆ on ESA(IR) aged 25+: main phase or assessment phase	£7.40	£0.00
◆ on ESA(IR) aged under 25: main phase	£7.40	£0.00
◆ on ESA(IR) aged under 25: assessment phase	£0.00	£0.00
If non-dependant works less than 16 hrs/wk, or is on maternity, paternity, adoption or sick leave	£7.40	£2.30

If non-dependant works 16+ hrs/wk (and is not on leave as described above) and has gross income of:		
◆ £382.00 or more per week	£47.75	£6.95
◆ £306.00 to £381.99 per week	£43.50	£5.80
◆ £231.00 to £305.99 per week	£38.20	£4.60
◆ £178.00 to £230.99 per week	£23.35	£4.60
◆ £120.00 to £177.99 per week	£17.00	£2.30
◆ under £120.00 per week	£7.40	£2.30
Any other non-dependant:	£7.40	£2.30

Notes.

For references to 16 hrs/wk or more, see the description of 'remunerative work' (para. 6.27-29). CTB figures also apply for HB for rates in Northern Ireland.

In CTB only, there is also no deduction for people who are disregarded for the purposes of a council tax discount (table 6.5).

6.25 If the recognisable cycle of work is one year (e.g. in a school), weekly hours are averaged only during the periods the non-dependant works (e.g. term-times). The result applies during both those periods and the periods they do not work (e.g. holidays). But changes in income are taken into account. So a non-dependant who is a school assistant could count as being in remunerative work throughout the year, but changes in their income may mean different levels of non-dependant deduction in term-times and holidays.

Non-dependants not in remunerative work

6.26 For non-dependants not in remunerative work (para. 6.27), the lowest deduction applies (table 6.3) regardless of the amount if any of the non-dependant's income.

Remunerative work

6.27 Remunerative work is work for which payment is made, or expected to be made; and which averages 16 hours or more per week. It must be work, as opposed to education or training, and does not include voluntary work.

6.25 HB 6(3); HB60+ 6(3); NIHB 6(3); NIHB60+ 6(3); CTB 6(3); CTB 60+ 6(3)

6.26 HB 74(1); HB60+ 55(1); NIHB 72(1); NIHB60+ 53(1); CTB 58(1); CTB60+ 42(1)

6.27 HB 6(1); HB60+ 6(1); NIHB 6(1); NIHB60+ 6(1); CTB 6(1); CTB 60+ 6(1)

6.28 A non-dependant continues to count as being in remunerative work during:

- any recognised, customary or other holiday;
- a period of absence without good cause.

6.29 A non-dependant does not count as being in remunerative work during:

- any benefit week they receive JSA(IB), ESA(IR), IS or pension credit for four days or more;
- maternity, paternity or adoption leave (with the right to return to work under their contract or employment law);
- absence from work because of illness (whether or not receiving statutory sick pay and regardless of whether the employer is making up his or her wages);
- periods during which they are laid off;
- periods when their only income is from a Sports Council sports award.

Assuming the highest rate of non-dependant deduction

6.30 If there is no evidence of a non-dependant's income (and the non-dependant is in remunerative work), the law permits the authority to apply the highest deduction (table 6.3). If evidence is provided later showing that a lower deduction should have been made, this means that the claimant has been awarded too little benefit: the claimant must be awarded the arrears – if he or she provides the evidence within one month of the notice of the decision on his or her claim (though the time limit can be extended in certain circumstances: para. 17.40).

6.31 The above should not be done if it would not reflect the non-dependant's likely circumstances: *CH/48/2006*. In this case, it was accepted that the non-dependant was working 20 hours per week in poorly paid work. The authority was not given evidence of her income, and so assumed the highest non-dependant deduction. The commissioner held it was inherently improbable that she was earning enough for the highest deduction to apply. It was probable that she was earning something in the region of £150 per week including overtime, and the authority should take such matters into account.

Non-dependant couples

6.32 In the case of a non-dependant couple (or a polygamous marriage), only one deduction applies, being the higher (or highest) of any that would have applied to the individuals if they were single claimants. In appropriate cases,

6.28 HB 6(5); HB60+ 6(5); NIHB 6(5); NIHB60+ 6(5); CTB 6(5); CTB 60+ 6(5)

6.29 HB 2(1),6(6)-(8); HB60+ 2(1),6(6)-(8); NIHB 2(1),6(6)-(8); NIHB60+ 2(1),6(6)-(8); CTB 2(1),6(3)-(8); CTB 60+ 2(1),6(3)-(8)

there is no deduction (e.g. if they are both under 18). For the purpose of the various gross income limits in table 6.3, each non-dependant partner is treated as possessing the gross income of both of them.

Examples: Calculating HB and CTB

Claimant on income support with working non-dependant

A lone parent is on income support. Her eligible rent is £85.00 per week. Her eligible council tax liability is £19.00 per week. Her 26-year-old son lives with her. He earns £400 per week gross for a 35-hour week.

Claimants on income support get maximum benefit, which in this case involves a non-dependant deduction. The son is in remunerative work with gross income of at least £382 per week, so the highest level of deduction applies in both HB and main CTB (table 6.3).

HB:	Eligible rent	£85.00
	minus non-dependant deduction, which in this case is	£47.75
	equals weekly HB	£37.25
CTB:	Eligible council tax	£19.00
	minus non-dependant deduction, which in this case is	£6.95
	equals weekly CTB	£12.05

Claimant on income support with non-dependant on income support

The son in the previous example loses his job and starts receiving income support.

The calculation is as above, except that now there is no non-dependant deduction in main CTB and the lowest deduction applies in HB (table 6.3).

HB:	Eligible rent	£85.00
	minus non-dependant deduction, which in this case is	£7.40
	equals weekly HB	£77.60
CTB:	Eligible council tax	£19.00
	no non-dependant deduction applies	
	equals weekly CTB	£19.00

6.32 HB 74(3),(4); HB60+ 55(3),(4); NIHB 72(3),(4); NIHB60+ 53(3),(4); CTB 58(3),(4); CTB60+ 42(3),(4)

Non-dependants of joint occupiers

6.33 The following rules apply when a claimant is jointly liable for the rent or council tax on his or her home with one or more other persons who are not his or her partner, and there is also a non-dependant living there. They would arise, for example, if a brother and sister are joint occupiers and have a non-dependant living with them. The law is slightly unclear in some of these cases but the key question is 'whose household is the non-dependant part of?' Having decided that, the rules work as follows:

- If the non-dependant is part of the household of only one of them, then the whole non-dependant deduction is made in any claim for benefit made by that one, and no deduction is made in any claim for benefit made by the others.
- If the non-dependant is part of the household of more than one of them, the amount of the non-dependant deduction is shared between them. Any of them claiming benefit gets his or her resulting share of the non-dependant deduction.
  - In CTB, the share must be equal between the joint occupiers (but only between the ones who are jointly liable for the council tax on the home: para. 11.27).
  - In HB, the share need not be equal: the authority should take into account the number of joint occupiers concerned and the proportion of rent each pays (para. 8.9).

Delayed effect of non-dependant changes for people aged 65 or more

6.34 The following rule applies when:

- the claimant or any partner is aged 65 or more; and
- a non-dependant moves in, or there is any change in a non-dependant's circumstances which causes an increase in the amount of the deduction.

6.35 In such cases the change in entitlement to HB or CTB is not implemented until the day 26 weeks after the change actually occurred or, if that is not a Monday, the following Monday.

6.33 HB 74(5); HB60+ 55(5); NIHB 72(5); NIHB60+ 53(5); CTB 58(5); CTB60+ 42(5)

6.34 HB60+ 59(10)-(13); NIHB60+ 57(12)-(15); CTB60+ 50(10)-(13)

Second adult rebate

6.36 This section, which applies only in England, Wales and Scotland, explains the type of CTB known as 'second adult rebate' (also sometimes called 'alternative maximum CTB'). It covers:

- who is eligible for the 'student only' type of second adult rebate;
- who is eligible for the general type of second adult;
- who is a 'second adult';
- how to calculate second adult rebate; and
- the 'better buy' comparison.

6.37 Both types of second adult rebate are awarded to the claimant (the council tax payer) but based on the circumstances of a 'second adult' (para. 6.41). The level of the claimant's own income and capital (and that of any partner) is irrelevant. But because of the 'better buy' comparison (para. 6.64), second adult rebate is only awarded if the claimant is better off on second adult rebate than they would be on CTB calculated using the main rules.

'Student only' second adult rebate

6.38 The 'student only' type of second adult rebate compensates the claimant (council tax payer) for the loss of council tax exemption caused by the presence of the 'second adult' in their home. The claimant qualifies if:

- the dwelling is wholly occupied by students who are not in the eligible groups;
- but for the presence of one or more second adults on JSA(IB), ESA(IR), IS or pension credit.

6.39 The amount is always 100% of the council tax liability on the dwelling (so there is nothing to pay at all by way of council tax while it is awarded). For this purpose, 'student' is defined using HB/CTB law (paras. 21.4-5); and the 'eligible groups' means the groups who are eligible to claim HB/CTB as listed in table 21.1.

General second adult rebate

6.40 The general type of second adult rebate compensates the claimant (council tax payer) for the loss of council tax discount caused by the presence of the 'second adult'. It is worth up to 25% of the council tax liability on the dwelling. Table 6.4 shows who qualifies and is followed by further details.

6.38 CBA 131(1) (3),(6),(7),(9); CTB 62(1) sch 2 para 1(c); CTB60+ 46(1)sch 6 para 1(c)

6.40 CBA 131(1),(3),(6),(7),(9); CTB 62(1) sch 2 para 1(a),(b); CTB60+ 46(1) sch 6 para 1(a),(b)

Table 6.4: Eligibility for general second adult rebate

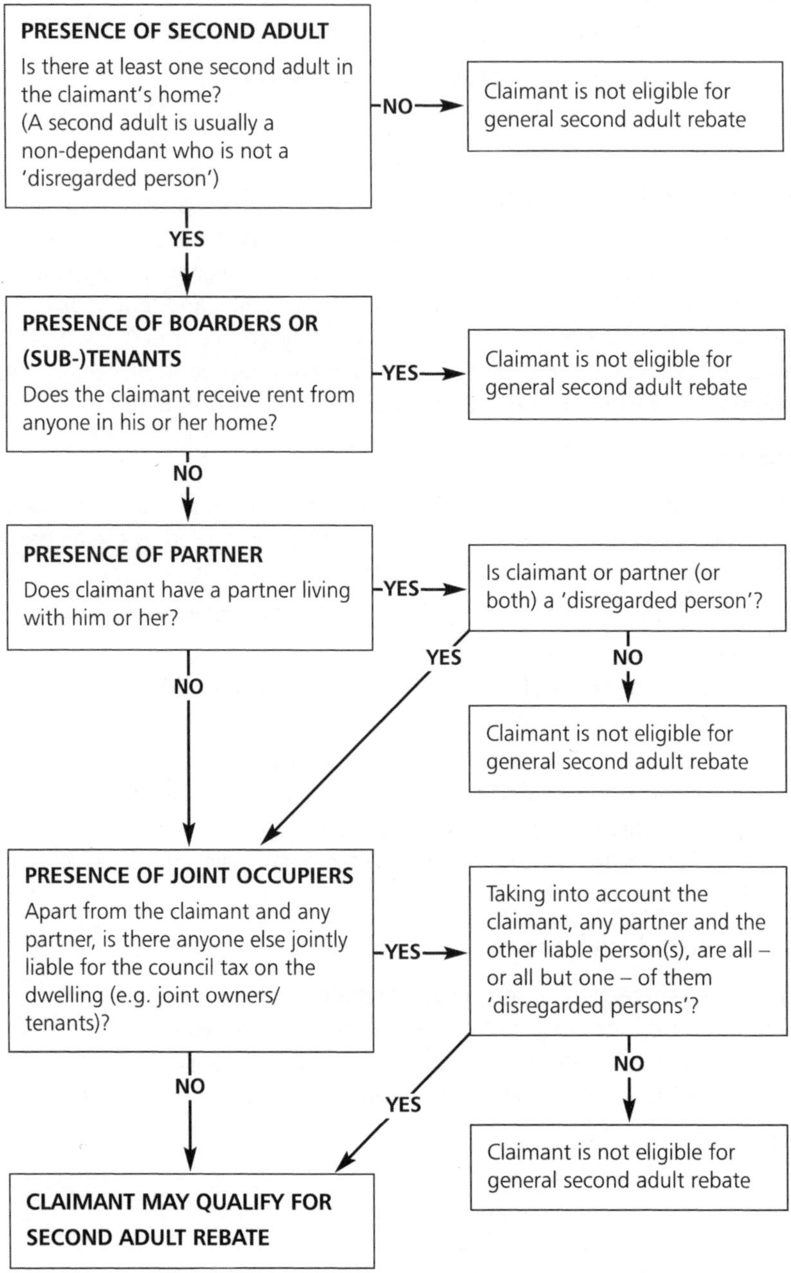

Who is a 'second adult'?

6.41 A claimant can only qualify for second adult rebate (of either type) if there is at least one 'second adult' in his or her home. A person is a 'second adult' if he or she:

- is a non-dependant or in certain circumstances someone else (paras. 6.42-43); and
- is not a 'disregarded person' (para. 6.44).

There may be two or more 'second adults' in the claimant's home: the claimant can still qualify for second adult rebate.

6.42 A non-dependant is by far the most common kind of second adult so long as he or she is not a 'disregarded person'. Typical non-dependants are adult sons, daughters, other relatives or friends who live in the claimant's household on a non-commercial basis (paras. 4.41-43).

6.43 A person can also be a second adult if he or she is the type of carer who is defined in law as not being a non-dependant (para. 4.53), so long as he or she is not a 'disregarded person'. This is not common because many carers are 'disregarded persons' (categories 10 to 12 in appendix 6). There may be other categories who count as a second adult, such as paid companions or live-in employees of the claimant or partner – so long as they are not a 'disregarded person' (and do not pay rent: para. 6.45).

6.44 A 'disregarded person' cannot be a second adult. This means a person who falls within any of the groups which are disregarded for council tax discount purposes (para. 10.17). The main groups are summarised in table 6.5. Appendix 6 defines all the relevant categories of people and gives the detailed rules about whether they are 'disregarded persons'.

Presence of boarders or (sub-)tenants

6.45 A claimant who receives rent from any resident in his or her home is not eligible for second adult rebate (even if all the other conditions are fulfilled). Typically, this means that home-owner claimants with boarders or tenants, and tenant claimants with boarders or sub-tenants, cannot get second adult rebate.

6.46 The exclusion from entitlement applies only if the person paying rent is 'resident' in the claimant's dwelling. A 'resident' means a person aged 18 or more who has 'sole or main residence' there. Therefore, rent received from an under-18-year-old or a holiday-maker does not prevent entitlement.

6.47 The exclusion appears in the Act of Parliament rather than the regulations. The Act does not, however, define 'rent'. The regulations give a definition of 'rent' for other purposes as being (in broad terms) a payment which could be met by HB, and this definition seems appropriate here.

6.41 CBA 131(6)(b),(7)(a),(11); CTB 63(a),(c); CTB60+ 47(a),(c)

6.45 CBA 131(6)(a),(11); CTB 2(1); CTB60+ 2(1)

Table 6.5: 'Disregarded persons': summary

See appendix 6 for more detailed definitions.

- People under 18, or aged 18 or 19 if child benefit is payable.
- Education leavers under 20.
- Most full-time students, student nurses and foreign language assistants.
- Youth trainees under 25.
- Apprentices on NCVQ/SVEC courses.
- People who are severely mentally impaired.
- Many carers.
- People in prison or other forms of detention.
- People who normally live elsewhere.
- Members of religious communities.
- Diplomats and members of international bodies or of visiting forces.

6.48 The exclusion is worded in such a way that it applies only if someone is liable to pay rent to the claimant. It does not apply if someone is liable to pay rent to the claimant's partner (or any other resident).

Claimant's income and capital

6.49 None of the rules about eligibility for second adult rebate takes into account the amount of a claimant's (or partner's) income or capital in any way. In particular, the £16,000 capital limit (which applies for HB and main CTB) does not apply when second adult rebate is being considered. Millionaires can get second adult rebate (so long as they fulfil the appropriate conditions).

Claimant's and partner's other circumstances

6.50 If the conditions mentioned earlier are satisfied, the final condition about eligibility for second adult rebate, which applies for general second adult rebate only (para. 6.40), depends on whether the claim is made by:

- a single claimant or a lone parent (with no joint occupiers);
- a couple (with no joint occupiers); or
- a claimant who has joint occupiers.

6.50 CBA 131(7)(b)

Single claimants and lone parents

6.51 There is no further condition if the claimant is single or a lone parent. It does not matter whether he or she is or is not a 'disregarded person' (para. 6.44). But if the claimant is jointly liable for council tax, see paragraph 6.54.

Couples

6.52 There is a further condition for general second adult rebate (para. 6.40) if the claimant is in a couple. Couples are eligible for second adult rebate only if at least one partner is a 'disregarded person' (para. 6.44). It does not matter whether this is the claimant or the partner – and so long as one of them is a 'disregarded person' it does not matter whether the other one is or is not a 'disregarded person'. But if the couple are jointly liable for council tax with some other person, see paragraph 6.53. A polygamous marriage is eligible for general second adult rebate if all – or all but one – of the partners are 'disregarded persons'.

Examples: Second adult rebate

Single claimant

A single claimant is liable for council tax on her home. The level of her income means she cannot qualify for main CTB. Only her son lives with her. He is on ESA(IR).

The claimant's son is her second adult. The claimant qualifies for second adult rebate of 25% of her council tax liability.

Couple

A couple are jointly liable for council tax on their home. Only their daughter lives with them. The woman in the couple is a student nurse (and is thus a 'disregarded person'). The couple's income is too great for them to qualify for main CTB. The daughter works part-time for a gross income of £100 per week.

The couple's daughter is their second adult. They qualify for second adult rebate of 15% of their council tax liability.

Students

A full-time student is liable for council tax on his home. His parents live with him; they are on pension credit.

If his parents did not live with him, his home would be exempt from council tax. But because they do live with him, they are his second adults. Because they are on pension credit, the student qualifies for second adult rebate of 100% of his council tax liability.

6.52 CTB 63(b); CTB60+ 47(b)

Joint occupiers

6.53 There is also a further condition for general second adult rebate (para. 6.46) if the claimant is jointly liable for the council tax on his or her home with at least one other person (other than just his or her partner). In such cases, information is needed about all of these joint occupiers. Each one who makes a claim is eligible for general second adult rebate so long as either:

- all the joint occupiers are 'disregarded persons'; or
- all but one of the joint occupiers are 'disregarded persons'.

6.54 This rule typically applies to joint owners and joint tenants. For example, if two sisters jointly own their home (and they have a second adult), each of them is eligible for general second adult rebate so long as at least one of them is a 'disregarded person' (para. 6.44). Or if three single people jointly rent their home (and they have a second adult), each of them is eligible for general second adult rebate so long as at least two of them are 'disregarded persons'.

6.55 In all such cases, each joint occupier who makes a claim qualifies for his or her share of the total amount of second adult rebate. This share must always be equal between all the joint occupiers.

Amount of second adult rebate

6.56 Having established that the claimant is eligible for second adult rebate, the authority needs the following information in order to calculate the amount on a weekly basis:

- the claimant's weekly eligible council tax liability (para. 6.58); and
- for general second adult rebate only (para. 6.40) details of the second adult's income or, if the claimant has more than one second adult, details of all the second adults' incomes (paras. 6.59 onwards).

6.57 'Student only' second adult rebate (para 6.38) is always 100% of the claimant's weekly eligible council tax. As shown in table 6.6, the amount of general second adult rebate (para. 6.40) may be 25%, 15% or 7½% of the claimant's weekly eligible council tax – depending on the income of the second adult(s). No matter how many second adults a claimant has, the claimant can only get one amount of second adult rebate.

6.58 The amount of a claimant's eligible council tax liability is described in chapter 11. Paragraph 6.69 explains how to convert council tax figures to a weekly amount. Examples of the calculations of general second adult rebate follow.

6.53 CTB 63(d); CTB60+ 47(d)

6.55 CTB 62(2),(3); CTB60+ 46(2),(3)

Table 6.6: Amount of general second adult rebate

For claimants with one second adult

If the second adult is on JSA(IB)*, ESA(IR)*, IS or pension credit	25%
If the second adult is not on those benefits and his or her gross income** is:	
under £175.00 per week	15%
between £175.00 and £227.99 per week	7½%
£228.00 per week or more	nil

For claimants with two or more second adults

If all the second adults are on JSA(IB)*, ESA(IR)*, IS or pension credit	25%
If at least one of the second adults is not on those benefits and the combined gross income of all the second adults*** is:	
under £175.00 per week	15%
between £175.00 and £227.99 per week	7½%
£228.00 per week or more	nil

Notes

* This includes a person entitled to JSA(IB) or ESA(IR) but not receiving it because of a sanction, or in the 'waiting days' before JSA(IB) or ESA(IR) starts (or would start apart from a sanction).

** This includes any partner's gross income.

*** This includes any partner's gross income. But if any of the second adults is on JSA(IB), ESA(IR), IS or pension credit (or has a partner who is), then his or her income (and any partner's) is disregarded.

Assessing second adults' gross income

6.59 To calculate the amount of general second adult rebate (para. 6.40 and table 6.6), it is necessary to assess the gross income of any second adult who is not on JSA(IB), ESA(IR), IS or pension credit (or treated as receiving JSA(IB) or ESA(IR): table 6.6). If the second adult has a partner, the partner's income is added in with the second adult's income (even if the partner is a 'disregarded person' and so could not be a second adult in his or her own right).

T 6.6 CTB 2(4),62(1), sch 2 para 1; CTB60+ 2(4),46(1), sch 6 para 1

6.59 CTB sch 2 paras 2,3; CTB60+ sch 6 paras 2,3

6.60 If a claimant has more than one second adult, it is necessary to combine the income of all of them, apart from any who are on JSA(IB), ESA(IR), income support or pension credit (or treated as receiving JSA(IB) or ESA(IR): table 6.6) – adding in the income of the partner of each second adult.

6.61 It is gross, not net, income which is relevant, and it is calculated in exactly the same way as a non-dependant's income is calculated for the purposes of main CTB, as outlined in paragraphs 6.23-25. The authority is entitled to require the same level of evidence, proof, etc, as when it assesses a claimant's income (paras. 5.17-19 and 5.22).

6.62 Providing details of second adults' income (and that of their partners) can pose several difficulties for claimants. They may not be able to obtain these details, or may not wish to ask. However, if the authority does not know how much the gross income is, it cannot award a general second adult rebate.

Discretionary housing payments

6.63 If a claimant qualifies for second adult rebate only, no discretionary housing payment (para. 22.5) may be awarded.

The 'better buy'

6.64 A claimant cannot be awarded both main CTB and second adult rebate at the same time. Deciding which one the claimant is actually awarded is often called a 'better buy' comparison:

- a claimant who only qualifies for main CTB is awarded that;
- a claimant who only qualifies for second adult rebate is awarded that;
- a claimant who qualifies for both is awarded whichever of the two is higher or, if the two are the same, main CTB.

Some examples of the better buy comparison are given below.

Joint occupiers and the better buy

6.65 If a dwelling has two or more joint occupiers and one or more of them claims CTB, each joint occupier's entitlement to main CTB and second adult rebate is assessed separately, and the better buy comparison is done separately for each joint occupier. This can mean that one joint occupier is awarded main CTB, another second adult rebate. The second of the examples at the end of this chapter illustrates this.

6.64 CBA 131(9)

6.65 CBA 131(9); CTB 62(2),(3); CTB60+ 46(2),(3)

Conversion to weekly amounts and rounding

6.66 HB and CTB are assessed on a weekly basis (though for technical reasons some of the CTB regulations are expressed on a daily basis).

6.67 The following paragraphs explain the rules that apply whenever figures involved in the calculation of HB and CTB (including second adult rebate) have to be converted to weekly amounts. The final paragraph describes rounding.

Rent and rates

6.68 Whenever a weekly figure is needed for rent (and any rates payable with it), the following rules apply (and the same rules apply to service charges):

- for rent due in multiples of weeks, divide the rent (and any rates) by the number of weeks it covers;
- for rent due calendar monthly (or in multiples of calendar months), divide by the number of months (if necessary) to find the monthly figure, then multiply by 12 to find the annual figure, then divide by 52 to find the weekly figure. Dividing by 52 (a figure which cannot be varied) intentionally gives a slightly generous weekly figure;
- for rent due daily (or, in any case other than above, in multiples of days), divide by the number of days (if necessary) to find the daily figure, then multiply by seven to find the weekly figure.

Council tax

6.69 Whenever a weekly figure is needed for council tax liability, the following rules apply:

- for annual figures, divide the council tax by 365 (366 in financial years ending in a leap year) to find the daily figure, and then multiply the daily figure by seven;
- for figures which do not relate to a whole year, divide the council tax by the number of days it covers to find the daily figure, and then multiply the daily figure by seven.

Income

6.70 Whenever a weekly income figure is needed, the following rules apply:

- for an amount relating to a whole multiple of weeks, divide the amount by the number of weeks it covers;
- for an amount relating to a calendar month, multiply the amount by 12 to find the annual figure, then divide the annual figure by 52;

6.68 HB 80; HB60+ 61; NIHB 78; NIHB60+ 59

6.69 CTB 57(1)(b); CTB60+ 40(1)(b)

- for an amount relating to a year, divide the annual amount by 365 or 366 as appropriate to find the daily figure, and then multiply the daily figure by seven. (The law for 60+s gives a different rule: simply divide the annual amount by 52);
- for an amount relating to any other period, divide the amount by the number of days it covers to find the daily figure, then multiply the daily figure by seven.

Rounding

6.71 In HB, the authority may 'if appropriate' round any amount involved in the calculation to the nearest penny, halfpennies being rounded upwards. In CTB, there is no similar rule: indeed the DWP recommends that entitlement should be calculated to at least six decimal places (GM para. A5.902). This is to avoid reconciliation errors at the end of the financial year. Decision notices sent to claimants about their HB/CTB entitlement may be rounded to the nearest penny.

6.70 HB 33(1); HB60+ 33(1); NIHB 30(1); NIHB60+ 31(1); CTB 23(1); CTB60+ 23(1)

6.71 HB 80(8); HB60+ 61(7); NIHB 78(8); NIHB60+ 59(7)

Examples: Calculating second adult rebate

Single claimant with second adult on JSA(IB)

A single claimant is the only person liable for council tax on his home. The only person living with him is his adult daughter, who is on JSA(IB). Neither the claimant nor his daughter is a 'disregarded person'. His eligible council tax liability is £20.00 per week.

Eligible for second adult rebate?

As a single claimant, he is eligible for second adult rebate because:

- he has a second adult living with him (his daughter); and
- he does not receive rent from a boarder or (sub-)tenant.

Amount of second adult rebate

His daughter is on JSA(IB) so the weekly amount is:

25% of weekly eligible council tax (25% x £20.00)	£5.00

Couple with two second adults

A couple are the only people liable for council tax on their home. The only people living with them are their two adult sons. One son is on JSA(IB). The other son is working and his gross pay is £133 per week. He also has savings which generate a weekly gross interest of £5 per week. One partner in the couple is a full-time mature university student. The other partner and the sons are not 'disregarded persons'. The couple's eligible council tax liability is £24.00 per week.

Eligible for second adult rebate?

As a couple, they are eligible for second adult rebate because:

- they have at least one second adult living with them. In fact they have two second adults (the sons); and
- they do not receive rent from a boarder or (sub-)tenant; and
- at least one of the couple is a 'disregarded person' (the student).

Amount of second adult rebate

If there is more than one second adult, their gross incomes are combined. But in this case the income of the son on JSA(IB) is disregarded. So only the other son's income counts. That son's gross weekly income is £133 (from the job) plus £5 (interest), which amounts to £138, so the weekly amount of second adult rebate is:

15% of weekly eligible council tax (15% x £24.00)	£3.60

Discount plus second adult rebate

A single woman is the only person liable for council tax on her home. The only other person living with her is her father, who is on pension credit. The woman is a carer who counts as a 'disregarded person'. Her father is not a 'disregarded person'. The council tax for the dwelling (before any discount is granted) is £730 per year – which is £14 per week.

Discount

When calculating council tax discounts, 'disregarded persons' are ignored (appendix 6). So for discount purposes, this dwelling has one resident. The woman qualifies for a 25% discount which, on a weekly basis, is:

25% of the weekly amount for the dwelling (25% x £14.00)	£3.50

Eligible for second adult rebate?

As a single claimant her own circumstances are immaterial. She is eligible for second adult rebate because:

- she has a second adult living with her (her father); and
- she does not receive rent from a boarder or (sub-)tenant.

Amount of second adult rebate

Her father is on pension credit so she qualifies for second adult rebate of 25% of her weekly eligible council tax. This means 25% of liability for council tax before the discount is subtracted, which is:

25% of weekly eligible council tax (25% x £14.00)	£3.50

She qualifies for both the discount and the second adult rebate, the total of the two being £7.00 per week.

Better buy

It turns out in this particular case that, because of her own low income, the woman qualifies for main CTB of £4.00 per week. Since her main CTB is greater than her second adult rebate, she gets only her main CTB. The final result is that she qualifies for main CTB of £4.00 plus the discount of £3.50, so in total her council tax bill is reduced by £7.50 per week.

Example: Better buy

Lone parent with one non-dependant/second adult

A lone parent is the only person liable for the council tax on her home. She is not on income support and has excess income for main CTB purposes of £25.00. The only people living with her are her daughter of 15 and her son of 21. The son works 12 hours per week for a gross pay of £180 per week (and has no other income). Only the daughter (because of being under 18) is a 'disregarded person'. The lone parent's eligible council tax liability is £16.00 per week. Her circumstances means that she is eligible for second adult rebate (the son is her second adult) as well as main CTB (taking the son into account as a non-dependant).

Main CTB

Weekly eligible council tax	£16.00
minus non-dependant deduction for son (he is not in remunerative work, so the lowest deduction applies: table 6.3)	£2.30
minus 20% of excess income (20% x £25.00)	£5.00
equals weekly main CTB	£8.70

Second adult rebate

The level of the son's gross income means that the claimant qualifies for a 7½% second adult rebate:	
weekly second adult rebate (7½% x £16.00)	£1.20

Better buy comparison

Her entitlement to main CTB is greater than her entitlement to second adult rebate, so she is awarded main CTB only.

Example: Better buy for joint occupiers

Joint home-owners with a non-dependant/second adult

Three sisters live together. Elsie and Lacie jointly own their home, and are jointly liable for the council tax there. Tillie lives there rent-free as their non-dependant. The council tax for the dwelling is £20.00 a week.

Elsie is a full-time student and is therefore a 'disregarded person'. She has capital of £20,000.

Lacie is working and is not a 'disregarded person'. She has excess income of £30.00 (and no capital).

Tillie is on income support and is not a 'disregarded person'. She is therefore a second adult.

Elsie's claim for CTB

Elsie is not eligible for main CTB – she has too much capital (and, in any case, most full-time students are not eligible for main CTB).

Elsie is eligible for second adult rebate (para. 6.53). Tillie is on income support, so the second adult rebate for the whole dwelling is 25 per cent of the council tax. Elsie qualifies for half of this, which is

(½ of 25% x £20.00)	£2.50

Lacie's claim for CTB

Lacie is eligible for main CTB with no non-dependant deduction for Tillie because she is on income support (and under 25), which is:

weekly eligible council tax (½ x £20.00)	£10.00
minus 20% of excess income (20% x £30.00)	£6.00
which equals	£4.00

Lacie's entitlement to second adult rebate is the same as Elsie's,

which is (½ of 25% x £20.00)	£2.50

Better buy comparisons

Elsie: No better buy comparison is required.	
She is awarded second adult rebate of	£2.50
Lacie: A better buy comparison is required.	
Her main CTB (£4.00) is greater than her	
second adult rebate (£2.50).	
So she is awarded main CTB of	£4.00
The total weekly CTB awarded on the dwelling is therefore	£6.50

7 Eligible rent

7.1 HB is worked out by reference to the claimant's 'eligible rent'. This chapter explains this term, and directs the reader to the appropriate chapter (i.e. chapter 8, 9 or 10) to work out the 'eligible rent' according to the type of case. It covers:

- what counts as 'rent' for HB purposes and how this differs from 'eligible rent';
- the four different methods for assessing the eligible rent;
- how to identify which eligible rent rules apply for all types of claim (i.e. chapter 8, 9 or 10);
- the terms and definitions used in this chapter and in chapters 8, 9 and 10.

Note that in this guide the term 'standard case' is used to describe the method for assessing the eligible rent in the majority of claims and not (in earlier versions of the HB scheme) to refer to claims where the claimant does not receive a passport benefit (such as income support) (para. 7.33).

'Rent' and 'eligible rent'

'Rent'

7.2 The term 'rent' has various meanings in different branches of the law. As far as HB is concerned, all the types of payment shown in table 7.1 count as rent. In this chapter, the term 'actual rent' is used to mean the total of all the payments shown in that table which a claimant is liable to pay on his or her home.

7.3 Charges for services are also included in the legal definition of 'rent' for HB purposes. This does not mean that HB will necessarily pay for them (paras. 8.12-44). Also, note that certain categories of claimant and certain types of dwelling are not eligible for HB even where the claimant is liable for rent (paras. 2.14 onwards); that some housing costs which do not count as rent for HB purposes can be met through JSA(IB), ESA(IR), income support or guarantee credit (paras. 2.17-18); and that further rules apply in relation to increases to cover arrears of rent; to garages and land; and to business premises (paras. 8.11 and 8.43-44).

'Eligible rent'

7.4 A claimant's 'eligible rent' is the figure used in calculating his or her entitlement to HB (para. 6.4). It could be exactly equal to his or her actual rent (this happens in the majority of council tenant cases, for example), but often it is different. The main reasons for this are:

7.2 HB 11(1),12(1); HB60+ 11(1),12(1); NIHB 11(1),13(1); NIHB60+ 11(1),13(1)

- in standard, old and rent referral cases, many types of service charges cannot be met by HB: for example charges for water, meals or fuel and in Northern Ireland any element included for the rates;
- for most not-for-profit landlords (for example local authority and registered housing association) the eligible rent can be restricted if the authority considers it to be unreasonable;
- for certain types of specialist accommodation, such as mobile homes, hostels and claims where there is board and attendance, the eligible rent is based on the rent officer's figures instead of the actual rent;
- in the case of private rented or other accommodation not included above, the eligible rent is based on the LHA instead of the actual rent and any service charges charged by the landlord (chapter 9).

7.5 There are four different methods of calculating the eligible rent as follows:

- where the eligible rent is based on the actual rent minus any ineligible service charges. This is the standard method of assessment for council/NIHE tenancies and the vast majority of housing association tenancies (table 7.4) and so applies to the majority of claims (standard cases)(chapter 8);
- where the eligible rent is determined by reference to the old case rules (chapter 8);
- where the eligible rent is determined by the rent officer (chapter 10);
- where the eligible rent is determined by reference to the LHA. This method of assessment applies to the majority of private sector claims (chapter 9).

Table 7.1: Payments counted as rent for HB purposes

- Rent in its ordinary sense, whether under a tenancy or licence, including board and lodging payments and payments for 'use and occupation'.
- 'Mesne profits' in England, Wales and Northern Ireland or 'violent profits' in Scotland (paid after a tenancy or right to occupy is terminated).
- Houseboat mooring charges and berthing fees and caravan and mobile home site charges (even if owned by the claimant, and in addition to rental if not owned).
- Payments made by residents of charitable almshouses.
- Payments under rental purchase agreements.
- Payments for crofts and croft land in Scotland.

7.5 HB 11(1),12B(2),12C(2),12D(2); HB60+ 11(1),12B(2),12C(2),12D(2); CPR sch 3 para 5(1); NIHB 11(1),13A(2),13B(2),13C(2); NIHB60+ 11(1),13A(2),13B(2),13C(2); NICPR sch 3 para 5(1)

How to identify which eligible rent rules apply

7.6 It is essential to identify the correct method which applies to a particular case because, for example, different rules apply about the treatment of service charges. Table 7.2 provides a summary of how to identify which method applies to a particular case according to landlord or tenancy type. Table 7.3 provides a summary of the appropriate method of assessment for tenants of private landlords and table 7.4 where the landlord is a housing association or stock transfer body. The detailed rules which determine the correct method are set out in paragraphs 7.7-14. Paragraphs 7.15-33 define in detail the terms used in this section and the remainder of the chapter (e.g. registered housing association, protected tenancy).

7.7 The following types of claim are dealt with as standard cases (paras. 7.33 and 8.3-6):

- rent rebate cases (i.e. council, council ALMO and NIHE tenants);
- where the dwelling is let on a protected tenancy (e.g. where the rent is registered) (paras. 7.27-30);
- the landlord is a housing action trust;
- the landlord is a registered housing association (para. 7.26 and table 7.4);
- the tenancy relates to a (former public sector) stock transfer property (table 7.4);
- a caravan, mobile home or houseboat sited on the authority's land (para. 16.14);
- gypsies' and travellers' caravan or mobile home sites, and the caravans and mobile homes themselves, on a site where payments are to the county council.

In theory at least, each of the items above can be dealt with either as a standard case or as an old case although in practice this distinction has no effect (para. 8.4). In the case of the last four items, if the authority considers that either the home is too large or the rent too expensive then they will be treated as a rent referral case (chapter 10).

7.8 Regardless of whether the authority considers the claim to be reasonable, if the home is let by a registered housing association on a shared ownership tenancy (para. 2.19) the claim will be dealt with as a standard case.

7.9 Where the home is let by a registered housing association and the authority considers the claim to be unreasonable and is able to refer it (table

---

7.7 HB 13C(5)(a)-(c),14(1),(2), sch 2; HB60+ 13C(5)(a)-(c),14(1),(2), sch 2; NIHB 14C(5)(a)-(c),14(1),(3), sch 3; NIHB60+ 14C(5)(a)-(c),14(1),(3), sch 3

7.8 HB 13C(5)(a),14(1), sch 2 para 12; HB60+ 13C(5)(a),14(1), sch 2 para 12

7.9 HB 13C(5)(a),14(1); HB60+ 13C(5)(a),14(1); NIHB 14C(5)(a), 15(1); NIHB60+ 14C(5)(a), 15(1); NIDAR 7A(3)

7.4), the claim will be treated as a rent referral case (chapter 9), unless it is also an old case (paras. 7.15-17 and table 7.4).

7.10 Any case not covered by paragraphs 7.7-9 which relates to:

- a caravan, houseboat or mobile home (see para. 7.7 for exceptions);
- a hostel (para. 10.21);
- a tenancy where a substantial amount of the rent is attributable to board and attendance (para. 9.48);

will be a rent referral case (chapter 9) unless it is also an old case (paras. 7.15-17).

7.11 In old cases to which paragraphs 7.8 or 7.9 apply, the claim will still be referred to the rent officer but their figures are advisory and it is the authority which must decide the eligible rent (including any restriction) (para. 8.7).

7.12 Any case not covered by paragraphs 7.7-11 which relates to 'exempt accommodation' (para. 7.22) will be treated as an old case (paras. 7.15-17).

7.13 Any case not covered by paragraphs 7.7-12 above will be treated as a rent referral case if the claimant has been on HB continuously at the same address since before 7th April 2008 or as an old case if they have been on HB at the same address since before 2nd January 1996 (1st April 1996 in Northern Ireland) (paras. 7.18-21). In rent referral cases the rules are those that applied immediately before 7th April 2008. The pre-April 2008 rules are broadly the same as current rules (chapter 10) but there are some small differences; see the 2007-08 edition of this guide for details. It could be argued that if 52 weeks have passed since the last referral took place, but none of the changes described in table 10.2 have occurred, then the claim should now be treated as a standard case.

7.14 All other kinds of claim not covered by paragraphs 7.7-13 above will be treated under the LHA rules (chapter 9). This will include cases where:

- the dwelling is let by a private landlord;
- the tenancy is managed by a registered housing association under a management agreement with a private landlord;
- the dwelling to which the claim relates is a (former public sector) stock transfer property where the landlord is not a registered housing association and the authority considers that the rent or dwelling size is unreasonably

---

7.10 HB 13C(5)(d),(e),14(1); HB60+ 13C(5)(d),(e),14(1); NIHB 14C(5)(d),(e),15(1); NIHB60+ 14C(5)(d),(e),15(1); NIDAR 7A(3)

7.12 HB 12B(1),13C(5)(b),14(2)(b); HB60+ 12B(1),13C(5)(b),14(2)(b); NIHB 13A(1),14C(5)(b),15(3)(b); NIHB60+ 13A(1),14C(5)(b),15(3)(b)

7.13 HB 13(1),13C(2)(a)-(c),14(1)(c),(f),(g)(8); HB60+ 13(1),13C(2)(a)-(c),14(1)(c),(f),(g)(8); NIHB 14(1),14C(2)(a)-(c),15(1); NIHB60+ 14(1),14C(2)(a)-(c), 15(1); SI 2007/2868 reg 1; SI 2007/2869 reg 1; NISR 2008/101 reg 1; NISR 2008/102 reg 1.

T7.2 HB 12B(1),13C(5),14(1),(2), sch 2; HB60+ 12B(1),13C(5),14(1),(2), sch 2; CPR sch 3 para 4; NIHB 13A(1),14C(5),15(1),(3), sch 3; HB60+ 13A(1),14C(5),15(1),(3), sch 3; NICPR sch 3 para 4

7.14 HB 12B(1),13(1),13C(1)-(3),14(1); HB60+ 12B(1),13(1),13C(1)-(3),14(1); NIHB 13A(1),14(1),14C(1)-(3),15(1); NIHB60+ 13A(1),14(1),14C(1)-(3),15(1)

Table 7.2: Which eligible rent rules apply – all new claims starting after 6th April 2008

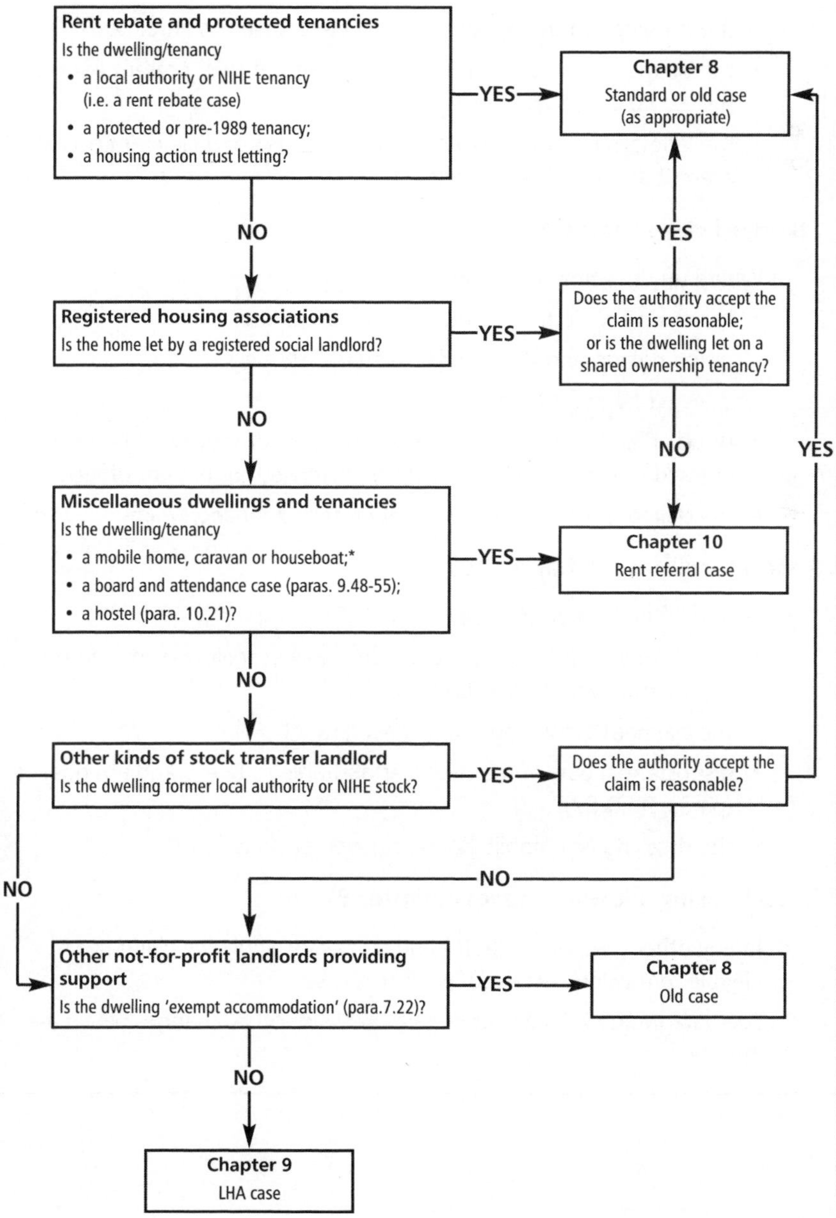
Rent rebate and protected tenancies
Is the dwelling/tenancy
• a local authority or NIHE tenancy (i.e. a rent rebate case)
• a protected or pre-1989 tenancy;
• a housing action trust letting?
YES
Chapter 8
Standard or old case (as appropriate)
NO
YES
Registered housing associations
Is the home let by a registered social landlord?
YES
Does the authority accept the claim is reasonable; or is the dwelling let on a shared ownership tenancy?
NO
NO
YES
Miscellaneous dwellings and tenancies
Is the dwelling/tenancy
• a mobile home, caravan or houseboat;*
• a board and attendance case (paras. 9.48-55);
• a hostel (para. 10.21)?
YES
Chapter 10
Rent referral case
NO
Other kinds of stock transfer landlord
Is the dwelling former local authority or NIHE stock?
YES
Does the authority accept the claim is reasonable?
NO
NO
Other not-for-profit landlords providing support
Is the dwelling 'exempt accommodation' (para.7.22)?
YES
Chapter 8
Old case
NO
Chapter 9
LHA case

* see paragraph 7.7 for exceptions

Table 7.3: Assessing the eligible rent for private sector and other independent landlords

Old cases (para. 8.7)

(a) Without exception the eligible rent will be assessed as an old case if

- the claimant has been on HB continuously* at their present address since before 2nd January 1996; or
- the landlord operates on a not-for-profit basis and claimant occupies exempt accommodation (para. 7.22).

Standard cases (paras. 8.5-6)

(b) Where (a) does not apply and

- the claimant's letting agreement began before:
  - in England and Wales, 15th January 1989; or
  - in Scotland 2nd January; or
- the claimant's tenancy has a registered rent or they would be entitled to have one registered if they applied to the rent officer;
- the claimant has any other kind of protected tenancy (paras. 7.27-30).

Rent referral cases (chapter 10)

(c) Where (a) and (b) do not apply and

- the claimant has been on HB continuously at their present address since before 7th April 2008;
- the claimant's dwelling is a hostel (para. 10.21);
- a substantial part of the rent is attributable to board and attendance (paras. 9.50-52);
- the dwelling is a mobile home, caravan or houseboat.

Local housing allowance cases (chapter 9)

(d) In any other case where (a),(b) and (c) do not apply the claim the eligible rent will be assessed as an LHA case.

* See paragraphs 7.18-21 for certain breaks or other changes which are ignored.

T7.4 HB 13C(5), sch 2 paras 1,3-8,11,12; HB60+ 13C(5), sch 2 paras 1,3-8,11,12; CPR sch 3 para 4; NIHB 14C(5), sch 2 paras 1,3-5; NIHB60+ 14C(5), sch 2 paras 1,3-5; NICPR sch 3 para 4

Table 7.4: Assessing the eligible rent for housing association and stock transfer landlords

Old cases (para. 8.7)

(a) Without exception the eligible rent will be assessed as an old case if:

- the claim relates to 'exempt accommodation' (para. 7.22); or
- the claimant is an 'exempt claimant'.

Standard cases (paras. 8.5-6)

(b) Where (a) does not apply and:

- (regardless of the landlord type or rent level) the dwelling is let on a protected tenancy (paras. 7.27-30); or
- the dwelling let by a registered housing association on a shared ownership tenancy (para. 2.19);
- the authority accepts that the rent/ accommodation is reasonable and either:
    - the dwelling is former public sector stock; or
    - the landlord is a registered housing association.

Rent referral cases (chapter 9)

Former public sector stock transferred on or after 7th October 2002

(c) Where (a) and (b) do not apply and the letting is a former local authority, new town or NIHE property which was transferred on or after 7th October 2002 it will be a rent referral case only if:

- the new landlord is a registered housing association; and
- there has been a rent increase since the transfer took place; and
- the authority considers that the rent is unreasonably high.

Former public sector stock transferred before 7th October 2002

(d) Where (a), (b) and (c) do not apply and the letting is a former local authority, new town or NIHE property which was transferred before 7th October 2002 it will be a rent referral case only if:

- the new landlord is a registered housing association; and
- there has been a rent increase since the transfer took place; and
- the authority considers that either
    - the rent is unreasonably high; or
    - the accommodation is unreasonably large.

All other registered social landlord non transferred stock

(e) Where (a), (b), (c) and (d) do not apply and the landlord is a registered housing association the claim will be a rent referral case only if:

- the authority considers that either:
  - the rent is unreasonably high; or
  - the accommodation is unreasonably large.

LHA cases (chapter 9)

(f) All other housing association or stock transfer property that does not fall under items (a)-(e) above (for example a stock transfer property where the new landlord is not a registered housing association).

high or (for stock transferred before 7th October 2002) the dwelling is unreasonably large;

- any other type of claim not covered by paragraph 7.22 where the landlord is an English county council, a housing association which is not a registered housing association, almshouse, charity, or other type of not-for-profit body;
- the letting relates to a resettlement place, night shelter or hostel which does not fall within the definition of a hostel for HB purposes (para. 10.21).

Table 8.5 provides a summary of those types of claim which cannot be LHA cases.

Definitions and terms used

'Old cases'

7.15 Especially in the voluntary and charitable sector, the amount of a claimant's eligible rent depends very much on whether the claim is treated as an old case. (Strictly speaking, this method of assessment can apply to any type of standard or rent referral case including council and NIHE (para. 8.4) tenants – but the greatest impact is on the voluntary and charitable sector.) In broad terms, all cases where the claimant occupies 'exempt accommodation' (para. 7.22) and certain cases where the claimant has been on HB since before 2nd January 1996 will be treated as old cases and the rent will be assessed as described in paragraph 8.7.

7.16 The term old case does not appear in any legislation or official guidance but is used in this guide and by many administrators and advisers as convenient shorthand. Other terms may be in use locally such as 'old scheme'. The term old case is used because, regardless of the actual age of the case, the rules for assessing the eligible rent are based on the rules that were in force before January 1996.

7.17 A claim will be an old case:

- if the claimant is an 'exempt claimant'; or
- if the dwelling to which the claim relates is 'exempt accommodation' (para. 7.22).

Otherwise, he or she will be treated as a standard or a rent referral case.

'Exempt claimants'

7.18 An 'exempt claimant' will be treated as an old case and so be exempt from both the LHA and local reference rent rules if he or she:

- was 'entitled to' HB on Monday 1st January 1996 (Monday 1st April 1996 in Northern Ireland); and
- has remained 'entitled to and in receipt of' HB continuously since that date (disregarding breaks in HB entitlement/receipt of up to 104 weeks if they or their partner are a 'welfare to work beneficiary': table 12.2; or in any case disregarding breaks of four weeks or less); and
- has not moved home since that date, or has moved only because a fire, flood, explosion or natural catastrophe made his or her former home uninhabitable.

7.19 A person will also be an 'exempt claimant' if they have had an exemption transferred to them from another exempt claimant (para. 7.20).

7.20 Exemption is transferred in the following three ways from one claimant ('A') to another claimant ('B') (and 'B' therefore falls within the old). 'Partner' and 'member of the household' have their specific HB meanings (paras. 4.3 onwards):

- A dies; and B was (until then) his or her partner or any other member of the household;
- A leaves the dwelling; and B was (until then) his or her partner;
- A is 'detained in custody pending sentence upon conviction or under a sentence imposed by a court' (and is not entitled to HB under the rules about absences from home: chapter 3); and B is (or was until then) his or her partner.

7.21 Additionally, in all three cases:

- at the date of his or her death, departure or detention, A must be in receipt of HB (or a 'welfare to work beneficiary' – table 12.2 – who was in receipt of HB no more than 104 weeks previously);

7.17 HB 12D(1),(2),13C(5); HB60+ 12D(1),(2),13C(5); CPR sch 3 para 4; NIHB 13C(1),(2),14C(5); NIHB60+ 13C(1),(2),14C(5); NICPR sch 3 para 4

7.18 CPR sch 3 para 4(1)(a),(2)-(4),(9),(10); NICPR sch 3 para 4(1)(a),(2),(3),(8),(9)

7.20 CPR sch 3 para 4(5)-(10); NICPR sch 3 para 4(4)-(6),(8),(9)

- B must occupy the dwelling as a home on that date (or be treated as occupying it: para. 3.3 onwards);
- B's claim for HB must be made within four weeks of that date (or awarded to fall within those four weeks: paras. 5.51-54);
- B's claim is then treated as having been made on that date;
- B then continues to be exempt for as long as he or she:
  - remains 'entitled to and in receipt of' HB continuously (disregarding breaks in HB entitlement/receipt of up to 104 weeks in the case of a 'welfare to work beneficiary': table 12.2; or in any case disregarding breaks of four weeks or less), and
  - does not move to occupy a new dwelling as his or her home, or moves only because a fire, flood, explosion or natural catastrophe makes his or her home uninhabitable;
- B's exemption is then transferred to any other claimant in the same way as described above (para. 7.20). There is no limit to the number of transfers of exemption so long as the above conditions are complied with in each case.

Example: Old cases – exempt claimants and transferring exemption

Mrs Sawable is a magician's assistant. Her husband lives with her. She was in receipt of HB on 1st January 1996.

- So she is an exempt claimant from 2nd January 1996.

Mrs Sawable remains continuously entitled to and in receipt of HB.

- So she continues to be an exempt claimant.

Mrs Sawable dies in May 2008. Mr Sawable makes a claim for HB within four weeks of her death.

- So, because of the rules about 'transferred exemption', he is an exempt claimant.

'Exempt accommodation'

7.22 A dwelling will be 'exempt accommodation' and be dealt with as an old case (regardless of when the claim is made) if:

- the accommodation is 'provided by':
  - a housing association, whether registered or unregistered,
  - a registered charity,
  - a non-profit-making voluntary organisation,
  - in England only, a county council, or
  - any other registered social landlord,

7.22 CPR sch 3 para 4(1)(b),(10); NICPR sch 3 para 4(1)(b),(9) where (in each of the cases) 'that body or a person acting on its behalf also provides the claimant with care, support or supervision'; or

- in Great Britain only, it is a resettlement place for which the provider previously received grant funding from the DWP under section 30 of the Jobseekers Act 1995 (sometimes referred to as resettlement grant).

Note that the rule only applies to each individual home which satisfies the conditions above and not to the whole of that landlord's stock.

7.23 In deciding whether somewhere is 'exempt accommodation', the phrase care, support or supervision has its ordinary English meaning – but it must be more than minimal (*R(H) 7/07* – a case where less than ten minutes per week was provided, on average, to each tenant or likewise in *CH/779/2007* where the only evidence of support provided was to accompany the tenant to tenant participation meetings). What matters in deciding this question is the support which is actually available in reality to the claimant *(CH/779/2007).* What it means for accommodation to be 'provided by' the organisation concerned seems to be limited to cases in which the tenant's immediate landlord is one of the relevant bodies *(CH/3900/2005).* Circular A22/2008 provides helpful guidance.

7.24 What it means for care, support or supervision to be 'provided on behalf of' the organisation concerned was decided in *R(H) 2/07.* In this case, the claimant and two others (all with learning difficulties) rented a house from a housing association. Their carer, who lived there too, was provided by an independent firm largely funded by the council's social services department. Since the house was provided by the association, the question was whether the care, etc, was provided on its behalf. The commissioner decided that the care was provided by the firm on behalf of social services, not on behalf of the association, so the accommodation was not 'exempt accommodation'. For the care to be provided on the association's behalf, there would have to be 'some respect in which the [care provider] acts for [the association], either because [the association] would otherwise be legally obliged to provide the care or because [the association] has engaged [the care provider] to provide it for [them]'. The mere fact that the association benefited from the care arrangement, or might have to replace it if it were withdrawn, did not mean the care was provided on the association's behalf.

'Housing association' and 'registered housing association'

7.25 For HB purposes, a 'housing association' means a society, body of trustees, or company:

- whose objects or powers include the power to provide, manage, construct or improve housing; and
- which does not trade for profit or, if it does, is limited by its constitution

7.25 HB 2(1); HB60+ 2(1); NIHB 2(1); NIHB60+ 2(1)

not to pay interest or dividends above a limit (currently 5%) set by the Treasury or, in Northern Ireland, the Department of Finance and Personnel.

A 'housing association' may (or may not) also be a charity, registered with the Charity Commissioners.

7.26 A 'registered housing association' means a housing association which is registered with the Tenant Services Authority (in England), Welsh Ministers (in Wales), Scottish Ministers (in Scotland) or the Department for Social Development (in Northern Ireland).

'Protected tenant' and 'protected tenancy'

7.27 The terms 'protected tenant' and 'protected tenancy' are not terms used in the legislation or guidance. In ordinary usage these terms are used to describe certain tenancies in which the security and rent levels are regulated by the Rent Acts. The Rent Acts governed the law for many types of tenancy prior to 1989 and still apply to certain tenancies which started before then. In this guide the terms are used to mean all pre-January 1989 tenancies in Great Britain, and certain pre-October 1978 tenancies in Northern Ireland, whether or not the tenancy is protected by the Rent Acts or the rent has been registered (i.e. fixed) by the rent officer. Protected tenancies have their eligible rent calculated as a 'standard case'.

7.28 In England and Wales a letting will be a protected tenancy if it is:

- any kind of letting that was entered into before 15th January 1989;
- a housing association secure tenancy;
- any other kind of housing association letting where the rent officer is entitled to register a rent;
- any other type of private sector letting where the rent officer is entitled to register a rent.

7.29 In Scotland a letting will be a protected tenancy if:

- it is any kind of letting that was entered into before 2nd January 1989;
- it is a housing association or any other kind of private sector letting where the rent officer is entitled to register a rent.

7.30 In Northern Ireland a letting will be a protected tenancy if it is a protected or statutory tenancy to which article 3 of the Housing (Northern Ireland) Order 1978 applies, i.e. either the rent is controlled or is fixed by a rent officer. In broad terms this includes certain pre-October 1978 tenancies.

7.27 HB sch 2 paras 4-8; HB60+ sch 2 paras 4-8; NIHB sch 3 para 4; NIHB60+ sch 3 para 4

'LHA case'

7.31 'LHA case' means any type of case in which the eligible rent is determined by reference to the local housing allowance. It is the method of assessing the eligible rent for the majority of private sector tenancies and is described in chapter 9.

'Rent referral case'

7.32 The term 'rent referral case' is not used in any law or guidance. In this guide we use it to refer to all those cases covered in chapter 10 where the rent officer's figures are binding in calculating the eligible rent. It applies to any kind of claim which is not a standard, old, or LHA case. Note that the authority is also required to refer certain other kinds of case to the rent officer (e.g. in an old case where the authority considers the claim to be unreasonable) but in this guide we do not refer to these as rent referral cases because the authority makes the decision about the eligible rent and the rent officer's figures are advisory. Table 10.1 identifies certain types that can never be rent referral cases.

'Standard case'

7.33 The term 'standard case' is not used in any HB law or guidance. In this guide we use it refer to the method of assessing the eligible rent for local authority (including local authority 'ALMO') and NIHE tenants. It also includes the vast majority of registered housing association lettings (i.e. where the authority accepts that the rent/dwelling size is reasonable or the dwelling is let on a shared ownership tenancy) as well as any kind of protected tenancy. It is therefore the method of assessment for the majority of HB cases. Note that in this guide it does not refer to the method of assessing income in non-passport benefit claims which was used in earlier versions of the HB scheme (and is still used by some administrators and advisors).

7.31 HB 12D; HB60+ 12D; NIHB 13C; NIHB60+ 13C

7.32 HB 12C; HB60+ 12C; NIHB 13B; NIHB60+ 13B

7.33 HB 12B; HB60+ 12B; NIHB 13A; NIHB60+ 13A

8 Standard and old cases

8.1 This chapter describes how the eligible rent is worked out for the vast majority of social housing tenants (i.e. council tenants of the benefit authority, NIHE and housing association tenants) which in this guide we call 'standard cases'. It also describes how the eligible rent is worked out for those cases that are assessed under pre-January 1996 rules which in this guide we call 'old cases'. It covers:

- how to calculate the eligible rent for standard cases (council, NIHE and most housing association tenants);
- how to calculate the rent for old cases;
- when the eligible rent is apportioned (e.g. joint tenancies) in standard and old cases;
- which service charges are eligible for HB in standard and old cases;
- how and when the eligible rent in standard and old cases might be further restricted.

For a detailed description of the rules as to which types of tenancy qualify as standard or old cases see chapter 7.

8.2 Note that some of the rules in this chapter – such as the treatment of service charges – also apply to the letting and tenancy types covered in chapter 10. Any common rules are identified as they arise.

Eligible rent in standard and old cases

8.3 The eligible rent for local authority/NIHE tenants (i.e. rent rebate cases) is always dealt with as a standard case, as is any housing action trust letting or any kind of protected tenancy (regardless of the landlord type). Tenants of registered housing associations, (former public sector) stock transfer properties and certain mobile homes sited on local authority land are also treated as standard cases except where the authority considers that the claim is unreasonable (para. 7.7 and table 7.4) when they are treated as rent referral cases. For the treatment of any other type of stock transfer letting see table 7.4 or paragraphs 7.7-14.

8.4 Note that any type of letting which could be a standard case (e.g. a stock transfer property) can also be an old case – and where it is, the old case rules will always take precedence. However, there is no practical difference in the method of assessment (although the sources of law are different) unless the authority considers that the claim is unreasonable and decides to restrict the rent.

Eligible rent in standard cases

8.5 The method of assessment for standard cases is simply:

- the actual rent;
- minus amounts for service charges which are ineligible for HB (paras. 8.17 onwards).

8.6 In all these cases:

- non-weekly rents need to be converted to a weekly figure (para. 6.68);
- adjustments must be made in the case of joint occupiers (para. 8.9) or where the accommodation includes business premises (para. 8.11);
- it is the authority (not the rent officer) which decides how much the eligible rent is and who deals with all matters relating to service charges;
- it is possible, but rare, for the net figure to be reduced further if the authority considers the claim to be unreasonable (paras. 8.45-48). (But note the claim will be a rent referral case and not a standard case if the home is let by a registered social landlord and the authority considers the claim to be unreasonable.)

Example: Eligible rent for a council tenant

A claimant rents a council flat. His actual rent is £65 per week. This figure includes £5 per week for the cleaning and lighting of communal areas and £12 per week for the use of an emergency alarm service.

His eligible rent is calculated as follows. The charge for the communal areas is eligible for HB. However, the charge for the emergency alarm service is not eligible, so this has to be deducted from his actual rent to find his eligible rent. His eligible rent is therefore £53 per week.

Eligible rent in old cases

8.7 In old cases (paras. 7.15-17), the claimant's eligible rent is worked out as a standard case (paras. 8.5-6) except:

- if a claimant's rent has been fixed by a rent officer (i.e. a registered rent) the claimant's eligible rent must not exceed the registered rent;
- if the claimant has any type of assured tenancy where the rent has been set by a rent assessment committee then the rent less any ineligible service

---

8.5 HB 12B(2); HB60+ 12B(2); NIHB 13A(2); NIHB60+ 13A(2)

8.6 HB 12B(3),(4),(6); HB60+ 12B(3),(4),(6); NIHB 13A(3),(4),(7); HB60+ 13A(3),(4),(7)

8.7 CPR sch 3 para 5(1),(2); NICPR sch 3 para 5(1),(2)

charges must not exceed the rent assessment committee's figure for one year from the date it has effect (in practice this rarely ever happens);

- whether or not a rent has been fixed by a rent officer or rent assessment committee, if the authority considers that the rent is unreasonably high or the dwelling unreasonably large then, in certain circumstances, it must restrict the eligible rent to a lower figure (paras. 8.49);
- if the rent is increased during an existing HB award, then in certain circumstances, the authority must apply a restriction to all or part of the increase (para. 8.67).

Where the rent is apportioned

8.8 The rules in this section (paras. 8.8-11) apply to standard, old, and rent referral cases only. They do not apply to LHA cases (see paras. 9.20 and 9.24).

Joint occupiers

8.9 In the case of a claimant who is a joint occupier (para. 4.49), the figures used in calculating eligible rent are apportioned between the joint occupiers (but see paragraph 6.33 regarding the treatment of non-dependants). In doing this, the authority must determine how much of the actual rent on the dwelling is fairly attributable to each of the joint occupiers, taking into account the number of people paying towards the rent, the proportion of rent paid by each, and any other relevant circumstances – such as the size and number of rooms each occupies, and whether there is any written or other agreement between them. The authority must then apportion the figures used in calculating the claimant's eligible rent on the same basis. The rent is apportioned among all the joint occupiers even if one of them (or more than one) is a student *(Naghshbandi v LB Camden and the Secretary of State for Work and Pensions)*. However, HB for rates in Northern Ireland is apportioned in the same way as CTB (para. 11.26).

8.10 In *CH/3376/2002* the commissioner dealt with a case where there were two joint tenants, one of whom was absent. He held that the proportion of rent paid is not necessarily the predominant factor (though in appropriate cases it can be), and apportioned the whole of the rent to the tenant who was present, taking account of a wide range of personal factors including his age, health, sick mother, local connections, attempts to ameliorate the situation and lack of control over the other tenant's (his step-son's) failure to pay the rent and whether it was appropriate to expect the claimant to seek alternative accommodation.

8.9 HB 12B(4),12C(2); HB60+ 12B(4),12C(2); NIHB 13A(4),13B(2); HB60+ 13A(4),13B(2)

Example: Joint occupiers

Tom, Dick and Harry

Three unrelated friends in their thirties, Tom, Dick and Harry, jointly rent a three-bedroom housing association house, where the rent for the whole house is £150 per week (and this does not include any service charges). They have a bedroom each and share the kitchen and all other facilities. They have each contributed one-third of the rent in the past. Harry loses his job and claims HB, saying that his share remains one-third.

Harry's eligible rent is very likely to be regarded as £50 per week. It is possible that a fairer split would be something other than one-third each, but unlikely based on the information given.

Tom moves out

Tom moves out. He is not replaced. Dick and Harry agree between them that they should contribute equally to the rent.

Harry's eligible rent is now very likely to be regarded as £75 per week – unless the authority considers that the new rent is unreasonable and has the power to restrict it (as described in later parts of this chapter).

Business premises

8.11 Rent on any part of a property which is used for business, commercial or other non-residential purposes is not eligible for HB. For example, if a claimant rents both a shop and the flat above it, only the rent relating to the flat is eligible for HB. If the rent on the business premises is not specified separately from the rent on the home, it is necessary for the authority to decide how much relates to each. For self-employed claimants who work from home, see paragraph 15.23.

Service charges

8.12 This section (paras. 8.12-44) deals with service charges (and related charges) which may be included in a claimant's actual rent, or payable as well as the rent. It applies to standard cases, old cases and rent referral cases (chapter 10). With the exception of LHA boarders (para. 9.53) it does not apply to LHA cases (para. 9.23). It explains which charges are eligible for HB in standard, old and rent referral cases and which are not. It covers:

- general information about service charges (including their definition);
- who is responsible for valuing services (the rent officer or the authority);

8.11 HB 12B(3),12C(2); HB60+ 12B(3),12C(2); NIHB 13A(3),13B(2); HB60+ 13A(3),13B(2)

8.12 HB 12(8),12B(2),(5),13(2),(5),(7); HB60+ 12(8),12B(2),(5),13(2),(5),(7); ROO sch 1 paras 7,9; NIHB 12(8),13A(2),(6),14(2),(5),(7), sch 2 paras 7,9; NIHB60+ 12(8),13A(2),(6),14(2),(5),(7), sch 2 paras 7,9

- which service charges are eligible or ineligible for HB;
- how service charges are valued;
- the rules about specific types of service charge.

This section is relevant only in the calculation of HB for rent (not CTB, or HB for rates in Northern Ireland).

The importance of service charges

8.13 Many tenants pay for services either in with their rent (whether or not they are mentioned in their letting agreement) or separately. As illustrated in the examples, there are two main methods of showing service charges in letting agreements:

- a claimant's rent may be shown as so much per week (or month, etc) including certain services; or
- it may be shown as so much per week (or month, etc) with an amount for service charges being due on top of the rent.

Examples: Service charges

1. A council tenant claimant's rent is expressed as being £100 per fortnight including £20 per fortnight for fuel for the claimant's own room and £10 per fortnight for heating, lighting, cleaning and maintaining communal areas. In this case the eligible rent is £80 per fortnight (£40 per week). The ineligible charge for fuel for the claimant's own room is deducted.
2. A housing association claimant's rent is expressed as being £70 per fortnight plus £20 per fortnight for fuel for the claimant's own room and £10 per fortnight for heating, lighting, cleaning and maintaining communal areas. In this case the eligible rent is £80 per fortnight (£40 per week). The eligible charge for the communal areas is added.

Notes

- The facts in the two examples are the same but are expressed differently.
- Information about the service charges illustrated is given later in this chapter.
- The terms 'net rent' and 'gross rent' are sometimes used to distinguish between different methods of expressing a rent figure. But they are used in different ways nationally and are best avoided for HB purposes.

8.14 Whether a service charge is eligible for HB affects the amount of a claimant's eligible rent (para. 7.5), which in turn affects the amount of his or her HB.

- If a charge is 'eligible for HB', this means that it is a charge which can be included in a claimant's eligible rent. With certain exceptions (mentioned below as they arise), it does not need to be valued; and no deduction is made for it at any stage in deciding the amount of a claimant's eligible rent unless the charge for it is excessive (para. 8.23).

- If a charge is 'ineligible for HB', this means that it is a charge which cannot be included in a claimant's eligible rent. With certain exceptions, it needs to be valued and deducted at some point in deciding the amount of a claimant's eligible rent (para. 8.15).

Councils, housing associations and many other landlords provide details of service charges to their tenants (and in many cases, tenants have a right to this information: for good information on this, see the *Housing Rights Guide* by Geoffrey Randall, published by Shelter). It is in their interests as well as their tenants' to bear in mind the detailed rules when deciding what services to provide and how much to charge for them.

Who deals with service charges

8.15 In Great Britain, service charges may be dealt with by the authority or the rent officer (or both of them) in assessing a claimant's eligible rent. In Northern Ireland, service charges are always dealt with by the NIHE. Fuller details are given in the remainder of this chapter, but in general terms:

- in rent referral cases (chapter 10) including LHA boarders (para. 9.53), the rent officer provides the council with figures which are already adjusted to take account of most service charges: in effect, the rent officer values them;
- in standard and old cases, it is the authority which assesses all matters relating to service charges.

Definition of 'services'

8.16 The law defines 'services' as 'services performed or facilities... provided for, or rights made available to, the occupier...' and 'service charge' as any periodical charge for any such service.

Which service charges are eligible?

8.17 Service charges are eligible for HB, so long as they:

- have to be paid as a condition of occupying the dwelling as a home; and
- are not listed in the regulations as ineligible (as described in the following paragraphs); and
- are not excessive in relation to the service provided (para. 8.23).

The rules about specific types of service charge, and whether they are eligible for HB, are in paragraphs 8.24 onwards.

8.16 HB 12(8); HB60+ 12(8); CPR sch 3 para 5; NIHB 13(8); NIHB60+ 13(8); NICPR sch 3 para 5

8.17 HB 12(1),(8),12B(2), 13(2); HB60+ 12(1),(8),12B(2),13(2); CPR sch 3 para 5(1); ROO sch 1 para 7; NIHB 13(1),(8),13A(2),14(2), sch 2 para 7; NIHB60+ 13(1),(8),13A(2),14(2), sch 2 para 7; NICPR sch 3 para 5(1)

8.18 The first of the above conditions need not have applied from the date the letting agreement began. A service charge is eligible for HB (subject to the other conditions) whenever the claimant agreed to pay it, if the only alternative would have been to lose his or her home. (Note also that a different rule applies in the case of charges for garages, land, etc: paras. 8.11 and 8.44.)

8.19 Details of which service charges are eligible for HB (subject to the above points) follow, and are summarised in table 8.1. Helpful advice on services is given by the DWP (GM paras. A4.700-950).

8.20 Sometimes services are provided 'free' to a claimant but this is often because the charge is wholly funded from elsewhere. The DWP points out in relation to hostel residents (though the point is relevant to all claims) that 'HB should be based only on items included in the resident's charge. [Authorities] must confirm which services are included in the hostel charge' (GM para. A4.1950).

Valuing ineligible service charges

8.21 When the authority has the duty of valuing ineligible service charges (para. 8.15), this is done as follows:

- if the amount can be identified from the letting agreement or in some other way, the authority uses the amount so identified as the value;
- but if this identified amount is unrealistically low for the service provided, or if the amount cannot be identified, the authority must decide what amount is fairly attributable to the value;
- however, different rules can apply for water charges, fuel and meals (paras. 8.24-33).

Valuing eligible service charges

8.22 If (unusually) it is necessary to value eligible service charges, the authority values them as follows:

- if the amount can be identified from the letting agreement or in some other way, the authority uses the amount so identified as the value;
- but if this identified amount is excessive, or if the amount cannot be identified, the authority must decide what amount is fairly attributable to the value.

8.21 HB 12B(2),13(1), sch 1 para 3; HB60+ 12B(2),13(1), sch 1 para 3; ROO sch 1 para 7; NIHB 13A(2),14(2) sch 1 para 3, sch 2 para 7; NIHB60+ 13A(2),14(2), sch 1 para 3, sch 2 para 7

8.22 HB 12B(2),13(2), sch 1; HB60+ 12B(2),13(2), sch 1; ROO sch 1 para 7; NIHB 13A(2),14(2), sch 1, sch 2 para 7; NIHB60+ 13A(2),14(2), sch 1, sch 2 para 7

Table 8.1: Service charges summary

As described throughout this chapter, further details apply in many of the following cases.

Type of service charge	Eligible for HB?
Water charges	NO
Provision of a heating system	YES
Fuel for communal areas	YES
Other fuel	NO
Meals	NO
Furniture/household equipment	YES
Communal window cleaning	YES
Other exterior window cleaning which the occupier(s) cannot do	YES
Other window cleaning	NO
Communal cleaning	YES
Other cleaning	NO
Emergency alarm systems	NO
Counselling and support	NO
Medical/nursing/personal care	NO
Day-to-day living expenses	NO
Most communal services relating to the provision of adequate accommodation	YES

Excessive eligible service charges

8.23 In deciding whether an eligible service charge is excessive, the authority must take account of the cost of comparable services. If it is excessive, the authority must decide how much would be reasonable for that service and disallow the excess.

Water charges

8.24 In Great Britain, water charges (including any sewerage or environmental charges) are not eligible for HB (except those payable in respect of communal

T 8.1 HB sch 1 paras 1,5; HB60+ sch 1 paras 1,5; NIHB sch 1 paras 1,5; NIHB60+ sch 1 paras 1,5

8.23 HB 12B(6),12C(2), sch 1 para 4; HB60+ 12B(6),12C(2), sch 1 para 4; NIHB 13A(7),13B(2), sch 1 para 4; NIHB60+ 13A(7),13B(2), sch 1 para 4

areas). So if such charges are included in a claimant's rent, an amount must be deducted for them. (No deduction is made at any stage if the claimant pays water charges direct to the water company, since in such a case the water charges are not included in the claimant's rent.) The same applies in Northern Ireland, though for the time being, until a separate system for water charging is in place, water charges remain eligible for HB in respect of rates (although the rates element is deducted from the rent).

8.25 In rent referral cases (i.e. chapter 10), the rent officer deducts an amount for such charges (paras. 10.26 onwards and 10.44). In all other cases (i.e. this chapter), the authority decides the value as follows:

- if the water charge varies according to consumption, either the actual amount or an estimate;
- otherwise, if the claimant's accommodation is a self-contained unit, the actual amount of the water charge;
- otherwise, a proportion of the water charge for the self-contained unit. The proportion should equal the floor area of the claimant's accommodation divided by the floor area of the self-contained unit (but in practice authorities sometimes use different, simpler methods).

Water charges for communal areas are, however, eligible for HB.

Fuel

8.26 Charges for fuel (such as gas, electricity, etc, and also any standing charges or other supply costs) are not eligible for HB. So if such charges are included in a claimant's rent, an amount must be deducted for them. (No deduction is made at any stage if the claimant pays fuel charges direct to the fuel company, since in such a case the fuel charges are not included in the claimant's rent.)

8.27 There are two exceptions to the above:

- a charge for the provision of a heating system is eligible for HB, but only if it is separate from the fuel charge;
- a fuel charge for communal areas is eligible for HB, but only if it is separate from the fuel charge for the claimant's own accommodation. Communal areas are areas of common access (e.g. halls, stairways, passageways) and, in sheltered accommodation only, they also include common rooms (e.g. a dining room or lounge).

8.28 In rent referral cases (chapter 10) and LHA boarders (para. 9.53), the rent officer (or NIHE) deducts an amount for such charges (para. 10.26 onwards). In standard and old cases, the rules depend on whether the amount of the fuel charge is known to the authority, as described below.

8.24 HB 2(1),12B(2),(5),13(2); HB60+ 2(1),12B(2),(5), 13(2); ROO sch 1 para 7; NIHB 13A(2),(6),14(2), sch 2 para 7; NIHB60+ 13A(2),(6),14(2), sch 2 para 7

8.26 HB 12B(2),13(2), sch 1 paras 5-8; HB60+ 12B(2),13(2), sch 1 paras 5-8; ROO sch 1 para 7; NIHB 13A(2),14(2), sch 1 paras 5-8, sch 2 para 7; NIHB60+ 13A(2),14(2), sch 1 paras 5-8, sch 2 para 7

Table 8.2: Standard weekly fuel deductions

If the claimant and any family occupy more than one room	
Fuel for heating	£21.55
Fuel for hot water	£2.50
Fuel for lighting	£1.75
Fuel for cooking	£2.50
Fuel for any other purpose	NIL
Fuel for all the above	£28.30
If the claimant and any family occupy one room only	
Fuel for heating and any hot water and/or lighting	£12.90
Fuel for cooking	£2.50
Fuel for any other purpose	NIL
Fuel for all the above	£15.40

8.29 If the amount of a fuel charge is identifiable, the authority uses this figure as the value of the fuel charge. However, if this is unrealistically low or includes an element for communal areas which cannot readily be separated out, the fuel charge is treated as unidentifiable.

8.30 If the amount of a fuel charge is not identifiable (or not 'readily identifiable'), the authority decides its value by reference to standard amounts depending on what the fuel is for, as shown in table 8.2. As shown there, the standard amounts are lower for claimants who only occupy one room. If the authority uses these standard amounts, it must invite the claimant to provide evidence on which the 'actual or approximate' amount of the charge may be estimated; and, if reasonable evidence is provided, the authority must estimate the value of the fuel charge.

Meals

8.31 Charges for meals are not eligible for HB. So if such charges are included in a claimant's rent, an amount must be deducted for them.

8.32 For these purposes, 'meals' includes the preparation of meals (e.g. where meals are prepared somewhere else and then delivered) and also the provision of unprepared food (e.g. cereal, bread still in its wrappings).

T 8.2 HB sch 1 para 6; HB60+ sch 1 para 6; NIHB sch 1 para 6; NIHB60+ sch 1 para 6

8.31 HB 12B(2),13(2), sch 1 paras 1(a)(i),2; HB60+ 12B(2),13(2), sch 1 paras 1(a)(i),(2); ROO sch 1 para 7; NIHB 13A(2),14(2), sch 1 paras 1(a)(i),(2), sch 2 para 7;
NIHB60+ 13A(2),14(2), sch 1 paras 1(a)(i),(2), sch 2 para 7

8.33 In rent referral cases (chapter 10) and LHA boarders (para. 9.53) the rent officer (or NIHE) does not deduct an amount for such charges, though there are uncommon exceptions to this (para. 10.26 onwards). So both in these cases and in standard and old cases, the authority decides the value by reference to standard amounts depending on what meals are provided, as shown in table 8.3. Those amounts cannot be varied; the actual amount the landlord charges for meals is never used. As shown in the table, one deduction applies for each person whose meals are paid for in the claimant's rent (whether this is the claimant, a member of the family or some other person such as a non-dependant). No deduction applies for anyone whose meals are not included (for example, a baby). When appropriate, deductions are calculated separately for each person (for example fewer meals may be provided for someone who goes out to work than for someone who does not).

Table 8.3: Standard weekly meals deductions

A separate amount is assessed and deducted for each person whose meals are provided.

If at least three meals are provided every day	
For the claimant, and each other person from the first Monday in September following his or her 16th birthday	£22.95
For each child	£11.60
If breakfast only is provided	
For the claimant, and each other person of any age	£2.80
All other cases	
For the claimant, and each other person from the first Monday in September following his or her 16th birthday	£15.25
For each child	£7.65

Furniture and household equipment

8.34 Charges for the use of these are eligible for HB; unless there is an intention that they will become part of the claimant's personal property, in which case they are ineligible. Ineligible amounts are valued by the rent officer in rent referral cases (chapter 10) and LHA boarders (para. 9.53), otherwise by the authority.

T 8.3 HB sch 1 para 2; HB60+ sch 1 para 2; NIHB sch 1 para 2; NIHB60+ sch 1 para 2

8.34 HB 12B(2),13(2), sch 1 para 1(b); HB60+ 12B(2),13(2) sch 1 para 1(b); ROO sch 1 para 7; NIHB 13A(2),14(2), sch 1 para 1(b), sch 2 para 7; NIHB60+ 13A(2),14(2), sch 1 para 1(b), sch 2 para 7

Cleaning and window cleaning

8.35 Charges for the following are eligible for HB; unless the cost is met by Supporting People (para. 8.40) – in which case they are not eligible for HB:

- cleaning communal areas;
- cleaning communal windows; and
- cleaning the outsides of windows which no-one in the household can do.

Any other cleaning and window cleaning (such as cleaning the claimant's own accommodation) is never eligible for HB (but may be met by Supporting People).

Other communal services, etc

8.36 Charges for the following communal services are eligible for HB:

- children's play areas;
- equipment for receiving free-to-view broadcasts ('Freeview' channels) and its relay into the home through the communal areas, including any charges for the installation, upgrade and maintenance of that equipment (less any element included for subscription channels) (but see also paragraph 8.38);
- communal laundry facilities;
- other services which are related to the provision of adequate accommodation.

8.37 The DWP advises (GM para. A4.730, and see chapter A4 generally) that the last item includes:

- portering and refuse removal;
- lifts, communal telephones and entry phones; and
- the time people such as scheme managers and caretakers spend on eligible services.

Other day-to-day living expenses, etc

8.38 Charges for the following are not eligible for HB. So if charges for them are included in a claimant's rent, an amount must be deducted for them. The amount is valued by the rent officer in rent referral cases (chapter 10) and LHA boarders (para. 9.53), otherwise by the authority:

- laundry (e.g. washing sheets, etc, for the claimant);
- transport;
- sports facilities;

8.36 HB 12B(2),13(2), sch 1 para 1(a); HB60+ 12B(2),13(2), sch 1 para 1(a); ROO sch 1 para 7; NIHB 13A(2),14(2), sch 1 para 1(a), sch 2 para 7; NIHB60+ 13A(2),14(2), sch 1 para 1(a), sch 2 para 7

8.38 HB 12B(2),13(2), sch 1 para 1(a),(g); HB60+ 12B(2),14(2), sch 1 para 1(a),(g); ROO sch 1 para 7; NIHB 13A(2),14(2), sch 1 para 1(a),(g), sch 2 para 7; NIHB60+ 13A(2),14(2), sch 1 para 1(a),(g), sch 2 para 7

- TV (and radio) rental, licence and subscription fees and any other charges for providing equipment to the individual home (e.g. a TV, individual satellite dish, set top box);
- any other leisure items or day-to-day living expenses; or
- any other services which 'are not related to the provision of adequate accommodation'.

Support charges

8.39 Support charges are never eligible for HB. This includes charges for:

- cleaning and window cleaning over and above that mentioned in paragraph 8.35;
- emergency alarm systems;
- counselling and support; and
- medical, nursing and personal care.

8.40 Claimants who need such services may be able to have the cost met by Supporting People, a government programme for funding support services administered by local authorities (in Northern Ireland by the NIHE) and independent of HB/CTB.

8.41 In some situations there remain difficulties in distinguishing what constitutes a support charge as above (which is not eligible for HB) and what is merely part of the rent as any landlord would charge it (and which would therefore be eligible for HB: para. 8.42). Chasing rent arrears would usually be an example of the latter: most landlords would regard it as part and parcel of their day-to-day work. But it might become an example of the former if it formed a substantial part of the work of staff in a hostel for residents with difficulty budgeting.

Overheads including management costs and council tax

8.42 Whether the landlord's normal overheads (such as maintenance, insurance and repair costs) count as 'services' or simply as part of the claimant's rent is an arguable point. But in either case they are eligible for HB even if the letting agreement refers to them as service charges – what matters is the substance of the agreement, not the form of the tenancy *(CH/3528/2006)*. In particular, this includes any part of the rent towards the landlord's liability for council tax (e.g. if the claimant has a resident landlord or lives in a house made up of bedsits). No amount is deducted for these items at any stage, so they do not normally need to be valued.

8.39 HB 12B(2),13(2), sch 1 para 1(c)-(f); HB60+ 12B(2),13(2), sch 1 para 1(c)-(f); ROO sch 1 para 7; NIHB 13A(2),14(2), sch 1 para 1(c)-(f), sch 2 para 7; NIHB 13A(2),14(2), sch 1 para 1(c)-(f), sch 2 para 7

Increases to cover arrears of rent

8.43 If a claimant's rent has been increased in order to recover arrears of rent or other charges, that part of the rent is ineligible for HB. This rule applies only if an individual claimant's rent is increased to cover his or her own arrears on a current or former home. It does not apply when landlords increase rents on all their properties as a result of arrears generally.

Garages, land, etc

8.44 The rent on a garage (or any other buildings, gardens or land included in the claimant's letting agreement) is eligible for HB if:

- they are used for occupying the dwelling as a home; and
- the claimant acquired them at the same time as the dwelling; and
- the claimant has no option but to rent them at the same time.

They are also eligible for HB if the claimant has made or is making reasonable efforts to end liability for them.

Rent restrictions in standard cases

8.45 In standard cases the authority has a general power to reduce claimant's eligible rent to below the usual figure (i.e. para. 8.6) if 'it appears to the authority that in the particular circumstances of the case the eligible rent… is greater than it is reasonable to meet by way of housing benefit.'

8.46 In such a case, the eligible rent is reduced to 'such lesser sum as seems to that authority to be an appropriate rent in that particular case'. In doing this an authority must have regard to factors such as the personal circumstances of the claimant: *R v HBRB of the City of Westminster ex parte Laali.*

8.47 In theory at least, it is possible for the authority to reduce the eligible rent for any kind of letting which is a standard case – including a council or NIHE tenancy. In practice, reducing a council tenant's rent using this rule is virtually unheard of although the Court of Appeal has recognised this as a possibility *(Burton v Camden London Borough Council).* Whatever the tenancy type, a reduction can only be applied if the authority has properly exercised its judgment and discretion (paras. 1.40-42).

8.48 In practice, reductions under this rule for any kind of tenancy – whether a council tenancy or otherwise – are rare. One example of where this power may be used would be where the claimant has a protected tenancy (para. 7.27) with a registered rent since, unlike in old cases (para. 8.7), there is no specific rule that the eligible rent must not exceed the registered rent.

8.43 HB 11(3); HB60+ 11(3); NIHB 11(3); NIHB60+ 11(3)

8.44 HB 2(4)(a); HB60+ 2(4)(a); NIHB 2(4)(a); NIHB60+ 2(4)(a)

Rent restrictions in old cases

8.49 The following rules (paras. 8.50-66) apply in old cases only where the authority considers the rent or dwelling size to be unreasonable. Where this occurs the authority will make a referral to the rent officer. (In Northern Ireland the NIHE will be required to make a rent decision.) However, it is the authority that makes the decision as to whether it is required to restrict the rent and if so by how much. In effect the rent officer's figures are advisory and merely form part of the overall evidence the authority must consider.

8.50 In all old cases, before a restriction can be made the rent is assessed in the usual way (para. 8.7). Therefore any ineligible service charges (such as support charges – para. 8.39) must be deducted first before a restriction is applied.

8.51 Further, the rules about restrictions described below (paras. 8.53-66) do not apply where in certain circumstances:

- the claimant could previously afford the rent (para. 9.57);
- a member of the household has died within the last 12 months (para. 9.59).

8.52 A separate set of rules applies for restricting rent increases where there is an existing HB award (para. 8.67).

Eligible rent restrictions

8.53 The rules about eligible rent restrictions in old cases are summarised in table 8.4. In applying them, authorities:

- must not take a blanket approach (GM para. A4.962): each step must be considered in the individual circumstances of each case and each step is open to appeal;
- must not restrict a claimant's eligible rent just because of the subsidy rules. The requirements of the HB regulations (described below) are the only test that is relevant in deciding whether or not benefit should be restricted.

There has been much case law about these matters, well explained in CPAG's regularly revised *Housing Benefit and Council Tax Benefit Legislation* (Lorna Findlay and others, Child Poverty Action Group). The most important cases are described below.

8.49 CPR sch 3 para 5(1); NICPR sch 3 para 5(1)

Table 8.4: HB restrictions for old cases: a summary

Step one: Is the rent or size unreasonable?

The claimant's HB can be restricted only if, compared with suitable alternative accommodation:

- the rent is unreasonably high; or
- the dwelling is unreasonably large; or
- a rent increase is unreasonable.

Step two: Is the claimant in a protected group?

Protections against HB restrictions can apply for claimants:

- who could afford their accommodation when their letting began; or
- who have had a death in their home; or
- who have one or more children or young persons, or are aged 60 or more, or are sick or disabled.

Step three: Should the eligible rent be restricted?

If the rent is unreasonable (step one) and none of the protections applies (step two), the authority must decide how much the claimant's eligible rent should be reduced.

Deciding what is 'unreasonable' by finding comparables

8.54 The first question is whether:

- the rent is unreasonably high; or
- the accommodation is unreasonably large for all the occupiers; or
- a rent increase is unreasonably high; or
- a rent increase is unreasonably soon after another increase during the previous year.

8.55 As regards size, the question of who counts as an occupier is open to interpretation (since 'occupier' is not further defined for these purposes) and appeal (chapter 19), but it is not limited to the groups listed in paragraph 9.61. Though the *Swale and Marchant* case (para. 10.36) may affect how some authorities interpret 'occupier' for these purposes, there is an argument that that case was about the definition of 'occupier' in a different context and so is not binding here.

8.54 CPR sch 3 para 5(1); NICPR sch 3 para 5(1)

8.56 In all the above cases, authorities:

- must make a comparison (as regards the rent, size or rent increase, as appropriate) with suitable alternative accommodation (paras. 8.57-58);
- may additionally take account of figures provided by the rent officer (if the case was referred to the rent officer: chapter 10) – and the DWP advises that they 'must' do this (GM para. A4.1122), bearing in mind that the rent officer's function is different;
- must not, at this stage, take into account the impact of the subsidy rules on their own finances (para. 8.65).

8.57 Authorities should make the comparison by working through the following questions:

(a) what is the actual rent (including all eligible and ineligible services) for the claimant's dwelling?

(b) what type of alternative accommodation is suitable for the claimant? and, in order to determine this, what services are needed to make the alternative accommodation suitable and what other factors need to be taken into account (para. 8.58)?

(c) what rent (including all eligible and ineligible services) would be payable for such accommodation?

(d) is the rent in (a) unreasonably high by comparison with the rent in (c)?

The above is based on *R v Beverley BC HBRB ex p Hare.* As regards (d) above, 'unreasonably high' means more than just 'higher': *Malcolm v Tweeddale DC HBRB.* Commissioners have confirmed this approach *(CH/4306/2003)* and have confirmed *(CH/2214/2003)* that it applies to unreasonable rent increases (as well as to unreasonably high rents/large accommodation).

8.58 In deciding what alternative accommodation would be suitable for the claimant (para. 8.57(b)), authorities:

- must take account of the nature of the alternative accommodation and the exclusive and shared facilities provided, having regard to the age and state of health of all the occupiers (as defined in para. 9.61). 'For example, a disabled or elderly person might have special needs and require more expensive or larger accommodation' (GM para. A4.1171);
- must only take into account alternative accommodation with security of tenure which is reasonably equivalent to what the claimant currently has (GM para. A4.1170);
- 'must have a sufficiency of information to ensure that like is being compared with like... Unless that can be done, no safe assessment can be made of the reasonableness of the rent in question or the proper level of value' *(Malcolm v Tweeddale DC HBRB)*;

8.58 CPR sch 3 para 5(1); NICPR sch 3 para 5(1)

- may take account of alternative accommodation outside the authority's own area if there is no comparable accommodation within it. But if this is necessary, it is unreasonable to 'make comparisons with other parts of the country where accommodation costs differ widely from those which apply locally' (GM para. A4.1172).

Protected groups

8.59 Three groups of claimants are protected against the effect of the above rules about HB restrictions. The first two groups, and the rules applying to them, are the same as those described in paragraphs 9.57-60; the details of the third group, and the rules applying to it, are described below.

Vulnerable people

8.60 A claimant falls within this protected group if any of the occupiers of his or her home (as defined in paras. 10.55-56) is:

- aged 60 or more; or
- responsible for a child or young person in the household (paras. 4.26-40); or
- incapable of work for social security purposes (para. 12.24) including those with limited capability for work. This is decided by the DWP, not the authority; and is decided by reference to the present-day definition of 'incapable of work' *(CH/4424/2004).*

In such a case, the authority must not reduce the claimant's eligible rent unless there is suitable alternative accommodation available (para. 8.61) and it is reasonable to expect the claimant to move (para. 8.62).

8.61 What counts as suitable alternative accommodation was described earlier (para. 8.58). The point here is that it must be available. For example, accommodation the claimant has recently left, or an offer of accommodation the claimant has refused, may be available – but only while it actually remains available to the claimant, and not after it has been let to someone else. In *R v East Devon DC HBRB ex p Gibson,* the judge emphasised that the authority was not an accommodation agency, and said: 'It is... quite sufficient if an active market rent is shown to exist in houses in an appropriate place at the appropriate level of rent to which the [eligible] rent is restricted. There must, however, be evidence at least of that... otherwise the [claimant], if he had to move, would have nowhere to go. It is, however, sufficient, as I wish to stress, to point to a range of properties, or a bloc of property, which is available without specific identification of particular dwelling houses.' The DWP follows this and emphasises that 'authorities should regard accommodation as not available if, in practice, there is little or no possibility of the claimant being able to obtain it, for example because it could only be obtained on payment of a large deposit which the claimant does not have' (GM para. A4.1222).

8.59 CPR sch 3 para 5(1); NICPR sch 3 para 5(1)

8.60 CPR sch 3 para 5(1); NICPR sch 3 para 5(1)

8.62 In deciding whether it is reasonable to expect the claimant to move, authorities must take into account:

- the claimant's prospects of retaining employment; and
- the effect on the education of a child or young person who would have to change school (this means any child or young person mentioned in para. 9.61).

In *R v Sefton MBC ex p Cunningham,* the judge emphasised the authority's duty to take individual circumstances into account when considering 'suitability', 'availability' and 'reasonableness'. In that case, the authority's decision was overturned because there was no evidence that it had considered the effect of a move on the claimant's eight-year-old child's education.

Restricting the eligible rent

8.63 The final question (if it applies at all, considering the above points) is of how much to restrict the eligible rent. If the authority has decided that the claim is unreasonable and the claimant is not entitled to one of the protections described above then it must make a restriction. However, in deciding what level to apply it must use its judgment and discretion as to how much and, according to the circumstances of the case, it may be as little as a penny a week. In considering the level of the restriction, the authority must work through the following questions:

(a) are there any circumstances which may make a small reduction appropriate?

and if so

(b) what is the appropriate amount for the reduction? and

(c) how was that appropriate amount arrived at?

The above is based on the judgments in *Mehanne v Westminster CC HBRB,* and *R v Beverley BC HBRB ex p Hare.* As regards (b) above, the authority must not reduce the claimant's eligible rent below the cost of comparable alternative accommodation: *R v Brent LBC ex p Connery.*

8.64 As regards all the above questions, authorities must consider what is appropriate in the individual circumstances of each case. There may be cases in which the minimum reduction is appropriate. There are also cases in which the minimum reduction is appropriate for the time being but may be increased later on. In practice, in such cases some authorities still tend to restrict claimants' eligible rents to what the rent officer has recommended (in cases which have been referred to the rent officer: chapter 10). However, the rent officer's figures do not take into account personal circumstances at all, whereas the question of what is 'appropriate' places a duty on authorities to do so.

8.62 CPR sch 3 para 5(1); NICPR sch 3 para 5(1)

8.63 CPR sch 3 para 5(1); NICPR sch 3 para 5(1)

The impact of subsidy

8.65 In *R v Brent LBC ex p Connery* it was held that an authority was entitled, except when acting in those cases where an absolute duty was to be fulfilled, to take into account the implications for its own financial situation (e.g. subsidy) when exercising its discretion. As described earlier, there are three main questions to be considered in applying the rules about HB restrictions:

- whether the rent, size or rent increase is unreasonable;
- whether people fall within the protected groups; and
- whether to reduce the eligible rent or disallow a rent increase and, if so, by how much.

8.66 The first two are questions of fact. Subsidy considerations cannot therefore play a part in answering them. The DWP's opinion is that the authority 'cannot restrict on financial grounds alone' in answering the third question (GM para. A4.1173).

Restrictions on rent increases in old cases

8.67 Where the rent is increased during an existing HB award the authority must restrict all or part of the increase if it considers that either:

- the level of increase is unreasonable in comparison with suitable alternative accommodation; or
- the increase is unreasonable because it is less than a year since the last increase (in deciding this it may take account of the rent officer's figures).

However, the claimant will be protected from restriction if any of the occupiers in his/her home have recently died and they have not moved since the death occurred. This protection lasts for 12 months from the date of the death and is described in detail in paragraph 9.59. In considering the level of the restriction the same considerations as in paragraphs 8.63-64 apply.

8.67 CPR sch 3 para 5(2); NICPR sch 3 para 5(2)

9 Local housing allowances

9.1 This chapter explains how to work out the eligible rent of a claimant who falls within the local housing allowance (LHA) scheme. It covers:

- when LHA figures start to apply, and when they can change;
- which category or size of dwelling applies to each claimant;
- eligible rent in an LHA case and the '£15 cap';
- how 'broad rental market areas' are set;
- how the individual LHA figures are set;
- the different rules for LHA boarders; and
- the protections for certain groups of claimant.

9.2 The LHA scheme was introduced nationally on 7th April 2008. The transitional rules which applied in 18 areas from then to 5th April 2009 are in the 2008-09 edition of this Guide. Chapter 7 describes which kinds of HB case fall within each of the HB schemes.

Who falls within the LHA scheme?

9.3 Private sector HB cases are LHA cases if:

- a claim is made and the date of claim falls on or after 7th April 2008; or
- a claimant moves home on or after 7th April 2008.

There are, however, exceptions, and these are all given in table 9.1.

Overview of the LHA scheme

9.4 The key features of the LHA scheme are:

- a claimant's eligible rent simply equals the LHA figure that applies to them;
- however no claimant can get more than £15 per week more than their actual rent;
- the LHA figures are fixed from time to time by the rent officer;
- the LHA figures depend on the category or size of accommodation applicable to the claimant, and on the area they live in;
- the LHA figures are publicly available;
- people who fall within the LHA scheme are also encouraged to have their HB paid to them rather than their landlord (para. 16.28).

9.5 Apart from the last point, none of the above applies to people who get meals in their rent: for them the LHA scheme works differently (para. 9.48).

9.3 HB 2(1), 13C(1),(2)(a)-(c); HB60+ 2(1), 13C(1),(2)(a)-(c)

Table 9.1 Tenancy types which are never LHA cases

The following are never LHA cases (regardless of when HB is claimed):

- council and NIHE lettings (i.e. all lettings where HB is awarded as a rebate: para. 16.14)
- registered housing association lettings (paras. 7.25-26)
- mobile homes, caravans and houseboats (para. 10.8)
- hostel lettings (para. 10.21)
- shared ownership cases (para. 7.8)
- any letting which is exempt accommodation (social accommodation where care, support or supervision is provided: para. 7.22)
- registered rent cases (also known as protected tenancies: paras. 7.27-30)

Terminology

9.6 In day-to-day work and in this guide, the term 'local housing allowance' is used to describe the claimant's eligible rent in an LHA case. In the law, this phrase is indeed used. So too is the phrase 'maximum rent (LHA)', but this is not used in day-to-day work or in this guide.

When LHA figures start and change

When LHAs start to apply to a case

9.7 A claimant falls within the national LHA scheme from:

- their date of claim for HB, if this falls on or after 7th April 2008; or
- the date they move home, if they do so on or after 7th April 2009.

The figures then last until they have to be reviewed as described in paragraph 9.11.

Awards for past periods

9.8 If HB is backdated (for up to six months: para. 5.53) or awarded retrospectively (for up to three months: para. 5.51), the LHA figure which applies is the one relating to the beginning of that past period (and the 12 months, till the LHA is reconsidered, is counted from that earlier date: para. 9.11).

T 9.1 HB 13C(5)-(6); HB60+ 13C(5)-(6)

9.7 HB 2(1),12D(1),(2),13C(1),(2)(a)-(c),13D(12); HB60+ 2(1),12D(1),(2),13C(1),(2)(a)-(c),13D(12); NIHB 2(1),13(1),(2),14C(1),(2)(a)-(c),14D(10); NIHB60+ 2(1),13C(1),(2),14C(1),(2)(a)-(c),14D(10)

9.8 HB 13C(2)(a); HB60+ 13C(2)(a); NIHB 14C(2)(a),114A(10); NIHB60+ 14C(2)(a),95A(10)

Examples: When LHAs start

1. A new claim

A claimant has lived in her home since 2006. She decides to claim HB.

Her date of claim falls on Thursday 2nd July 2009.

So she falls within the LHA scheme from Thursday 2nd July 2009.

(Her HB will probably start the following Monday: para. 5.48.)

2. A move

A claimant has lived in her home since 2005, and has been on HB since 2007.

She moves home on Monday 20th April 2009.

So she falls within the LHA scheme from Monday 20th April 2009.

Gaps in entitlement

9.9 In many areas of the country (but not all) figures available under the LHA scheme have been higher than those under other HB schemes. The DWP eventually advised authorities that if a claimant (not yet falling within LHAs) comes off HB for a week and then reclaims it, then in the new claim they fall within LHAs (DWP circular HB/CTB G10/2008). Other theories abound. In particular there does not seem to be anything to stop someone 'making a claim for HB' while they are already on HB. But this theory needs to be tested.

Extended payments

9.10 The award of an extended payment of HB no longer triggers a fresh claim (para. 17.59), so it can no longer move someone onto the LHA scheme.

When is the LHA reviewed?

9.11 Once a person falls within the LHA scheme, the LHA figure which applies to them remains the same until one of the following events occurs:

- the category or size of dwelling applying to them changes (typically because someone has moved in or out: table 9.2); or
- a member of the family or a relative (para. 9.62) with no separate right of occupation dies (referred to in the law as a 'linked person') even if this would not change the category or size of dwelling applying to the claimant; or
- the claimant moves (whether within the area of the authority or outside it); or

9.9 HB 13C(2)(a); HB60+ 13C(2)(a); NIHB 14C(2)(a); NIHB60+ 14C(2)(a)

9.10 HB 13C(2)(a); HB60+ 13C(2)(a); NIHB 14C(2)(a); NIHB60+ 14C(2)(a)

9.11 HB 2(1),12D(1),(2),13C(2)(d),(3),(4),(6); HB60+ 2(1),12D(1),(2),13C(2)(d),(3),(4),(6); NIHB 2(1),13C(1),(2),14C(2)(d),(3),(4),(6); NIHB60+ 2(1),13C(1),(2),14C(2)(d),(3),(4),(6)

- 12 months have passed. This applies only if the person has been continuously on HB. If they have come off and reclaimed, see paragraphs 9.7 and 9.9.

9.12 Only the first event always means that the claimant's HB will change. In the second event the claimant's HB is unlikely to change (because of the protection for bereavement: para 9.59). In the third and fourth events, the claimant's HB changes only if a different LHA figure now applies to them.

When does the new LHA apply from?

9.13 When the LHA figure applying to a claimant changes, this is done from:

- the day of the event (para. 9.11) if that day is a Monday (but see below);
- the Monday following the event if the event falls on any other day of the week.

9.14 As regards the first point above, there is a degree of doubt about whether this is what the law really means. Some have interpreted the law (taking account of the rules about two or more changes: para. 17.35) as meaning that such changes are done from the Monday afterwards (and this would be much more logical as the other effects of the change will take effect from the following Monday).

Examples: When LHAs are reviewed

1. A new claim

A claimant has lived in her home since 2006. She decides to claim HB.

Her date of claim falls on Wednesday 2nd July 2008.

So she falls within the LHA scheme from Wednesday 2nd July 2008.

(Her HB will probably start the following Monday: para. 5.48.)

If her circumstances do not change in any relevant way (para. 9.11):

- Her LHA is reviewed 12 months later, on Thursday 2nd July 2009.
- And if the LHA is then different, it applies from Monday 6th July 2009.

2. A move

A claimant has lived in his home since 2005, and has been on HB since 2007. He moves home in 2008.

The date he moves home is Monday 21st April 2008.

So he falls within the LHA scheme from Monday 21st April 2008.

If his circumstances do not change in any relevant way (para. 9.11):

- His LHA is reviewed 12 months later, on Tuesday 21st April 2009.
- And if the LHA is then different, it applies from Monday 27th April 2009.

9.13 DAR 7A,8(15); NIDAR 7A

3. A change of circumstances

A claimant has lived in her home since 2005, and has been on HB since 2007. She moves home in 2008.

The date she moves home is Monday 21st April 2008.

So she falls within the LHA scheme from Monday 21st April 2008.

A non-dependant then moves in – so she requires an extra bedroom.

The non-dependant moves in on Wednesday 16th July 2008.

And the new LHA applies from Monday 21st July 2008.

If her circumstances then do not change in any relevant way (para. 9.11):

- Her LHA is reviewed 12 months later, on Thursday 16th July 2009.
- And if the LHA is then different, it applies from Monday 20th July 2009.

Which date's LHA figure is used?

9.15 When the authority has to apply a new LHA figure, it always does this by reference to a particular date (even though it may not apply to the claimant's HB case until the following Monday). In the case of a claim for HB, this means the date of claim. In the case of a move, this means the date of the move. In the case of a change of circumstances (para. 9.11), this means the day the change actually happens. In the case of an annual review (the fourth event in para. 9.11), this means the anniversary of the date by reference to which the last LHA was fixed.

Categories and sizes of dwelling

9.16 This section is about which category or size of dwelling applies to a claimant in LHA cases. This is important because a claimant's eligible rent is then the LHA figure for that category of dwelling for their area. The categories are like those used in rent officer referral cases, but not always identical. Table 9.2 shows which category applies to which groups of claimant.

Which occupiers are included?

9.17 In deciding the size of accommodation the claimant qualifies for (table 9.2), the following occupiers are taken into account:

- the claimant and any family member (partner, children, young persons: para. 4.11)

9.15 HB 2(1),13(1),(2); HB60+ 2(1),13(1),(2); NIHB 2(1),14(1),(2); NIHB60+ 2(1),14(1),(2); DAR 7A,8(15); NIDAR 7A

9.16 HB 13D(2),(3); HB60+ 13D(2),(3); NIHB 14D(2),(3); NIHB60+ 14D(2),(3)

- non-dependants (para. 4.41);
- sub-tenants and boarders in the claimant's home (paras. 4.48 and 50-51);
- other people (apart from joint tenants: para. 9.20) who 'occupy as their home the dwelling to which the claim or award [of HB] relates'.

9.18 The above quotation means that live-in carers are included. Although it seems to suggest that foster children are included, this is not the DWP's intention.

Table 9.2: Categories of accommodation

Details of the occupiers	LHA category
'Young individuals' (Most single claimants under 25: para. 9.19)	One-bedroom shared accommodation
Other single claimants and couples without children who have in their accommodation: • exclusive use of at least two rooms (counting only bedrooms and living rooms, but regardless of whether they share other facilities); or • exclusive use of one room and of a bathroom, a toilet and a kitchen or cooking facilities	One-bedroom self-contained accommodation
Other single people and couples without children	One-bedroom shared accommodation
All lone parents and couples with children plus all cases where the occupiers include non-family members (para: 9.17)	Accommodation with the number of bedrooms indicated below

Counting up bedrooms

A bedroom is allocated for each of the following – but in England, Scotland and Wales only up to a maximum of five bedrooms* (paras. 9.38-40):

- each lone parent or couple;
- each other person aged 16+;
- two children under 16 of the same sex;
- two children under 10 of the same or opposite sex;
- any other child.

* For properties of six or more rooms in Northern Ireland see para. 10.49.

9.17 HB 13D(12); HB60+ 13D(12); NIHB 14D(10); NIHB60+ 14D(10)

Examples: What size dwelling?

1. A single claimant

A single claimant aged 27 is renting a bedsit in a house in multiple occupation.

So she qualifies for the LHA for one-bedroom shared accommodation.

2. The claimant moves

The same claimant as above moves to a one-bedroom self-contained flat.

So she qualifies for the LHA for one-bedroom self-contained accommodation.

3. A younger single claimant

A single claimant aged 23 is renting a bedsit in a house in multiple occupation.

He qualifies for the LHA for one-bedroom shared accommodation.

4. The claimant moves

The same claimant as above moves to a one-bedroom self-contained flat.

Because he is under 25, he still qualifies for the LHA for one-bedroom shared accommodation.

5. A couple with two children

A couple have two children, a boy aged 7 and a girl aged 9.

The children are under 10, so are expected to share a bedroom, so the couple qualify for the LHA for two-bedroom accommodation.

6. The older child reaches 10

The same couple as above, but the daughter reaches 10.

Now one of the children is aged 10 or more, and they are of opposite sexes, so they are no longer expected to share a bedroom, so the couple qualify for the LHA for three-bedroom accommodation.

7. A couple with a lodger

A couple without children have a lodger in their home.

They qualify for two-bedroom accommodation.

Definition of 'young individual'

9.19 For the purposes of the LHA scheme, every claimant who is a 'single claimant' (para. 4.10) and is under the age of 25 is a 'young individual' unless he or she:

- is under the age of 22 and was formerly in social services care under a court order (under section 31(1)(a) of the Children Act 1989 in England and Wales, or equivalent provisions in Scotland and Northern Ireland) which applied (or continued to apply) after his or her 16th birthday;

9.19 HB 2(1); HB60+ 2(1); NIHB 2(1); NIHB60+ 2(1)

- is under the age of 22 and was formerly provided with accommodation by social services (under section 20 of the Children Act 1989 in England and Wales, or equivalent provisions in Scotland and Northern Ireland) but is no longer in that accommodation or remains in it but the accommodation is no longer provided by social services;
- has one or more non-dependant(s);
- qualifies for a severe disability premium in the assessment of his or her HB (para. 12.32), income support or JSA(IB).

(There are further exceptions in the law (paras. 10.7 and 10.41), but these apply only to rent referral cases, not LHAs.)

Joint tenants

9.20 In a joint tenancy, each joint tenant is allocated the category applying to himself or herself. This is likely to be one-bedroom shared accommodation in the majority of cases, because in a joint tenancy it is unlikely that a joint tenant will meet the conditions required to qualify for one-bedroom self-contained accommodation (table 9.2).

Joint tenants with non-dependants

9.21 If amongst joint tenants, one has a non-dependant (for example three friends live together and the mother of one of them lives with them), that joint tenant qualifies for two-bedroom accommodation (and any non-dependant deduction applies to that joint tenant alone).

9.22 If joint tenants 'share' a non-dependant (for example, two sisters live together and their mother lives with them), each of them qualifies for two-bedroom accommodation (but any non-dependant deduction is split between them). What may appear at first sight to be generosity in this method, is tempered by the £15 cap, since the cap applies to each claim, and in the case of a joint tenant is measured against their share of the actual rent.

Examples: Joint occupiers

1. Three friends

Three friends jointly rent a house.

They each (if each claims HB) qualify for the LHA for one-bedroom shared accommodation.

9.20 HB 13D(12); HB60+ 13D(12); NIHB 14D(10); NIHB60+ 14D(10)

9.22 HB 13D(12),74(5); HB60+ 13D(12),55(5); NIHB 14D(10),72(5); NIHB60+ 14D(10),53(5)

9.23 HB 12B(1),13D(1); HB60+ 12B(1),13D(1); NIHB 13A(1),14D(1); NIHB60+ 13A(1),14D(1)

2. Two sisters and their mother

Two sisters jointly rent a house and their mother lives with them.

Their mother is the non-dependant of each of them.

So each sister (if each claims HB) qualifies for the LHA for two-bedroom accommodation – and in each of their cases there is half a non-dependant deduction.

Eligible rent and the £15 cap

Eligible rent in an LHA case

9.23 The eligible rent of a clamant whose case falls within LHAs (apart from a boarder: para. 9.48) is simply the LHA figure for the category or size of dwelling they require and the broad rental market area they live in. No adjustments are made for ineligible service charges (since this is all done by the rent officer in setting the LHA figures). It is, however, possible for the claimant to be awarded a discretionary housing payment (para. 22.2), if their eligible rent under LHAs does not cover their whole rent. It is also possible for the claimant to qualify for more if they fall within the 'protected groups' (para. 9.56).

The £15 cap

9.24 If a claimant's LHA is more than his or her actual rent, the claimant's eligible rent is limited to the actual rent plus £15, and a joint tenant's eligible rent is limited to their share of the actual rent plus £15. Although the number of cases is expected to reduce as time goes by, this does mean that a claimant can receive more HB than they need to pay their rent – but never more than £15 per week more.

Impact on assessment of service charges

9.25 The above is true even if the claimant's actual rent includes service charges which would normally be ineligible for HB. Indeed, to assess the eligible rent of a claimant who falls within the LHA scheme, the authority does not need to know what service charges are included in someone's rent. It merely needs to know what the actual rent is, in order to apply the £15 cap.

Impact on payments to landlords

9.26 If a claimant's eligible rent is more than their actual rent, and it has been decided to pay the HB to their landlord (paras. 16.34 and 41), the most that can be paid to the landlord is:

9.24 HB 13D(4)-(6),(12); HB60+ 13D(4)-(6),(12); NIHB 14D(4)-(6),(10); NIHB60+ 14D(4)-(6),(10)

9.25 HB 13D(12); HB60+ 13D(12); NIHB 14D(10); NIHB60+ 14D(10)

9.26 HB 92(2A); HB60+ 73(2A); NIHB 95(2A); NIHB60+ 76(2A)

- if the claimant is not in arrears to the landlord, the actual rent;
- if the claimant is in arrears to the landlord, the whole of the claimant's HB until the arrears are cleared, and then just the actual rent.

In such cases any amount which cannot be paid to the landlord is paid to the claimant.

Examples: The £15 cap

1. Sole tenant

A claimant is a sole tenant of her home. Her actual rent is £92 a week. The LHA which applies to her is £125 per week.

So the claimant's eligible rent is her actual rent of £92 plus £15, which is £107 per week.

This is true even if the claimant's actual rent includes amounts for ineligible service charges.

2. Joint tenants

Three friends jointly rent a house for £180 per week. They have identical rooms. The LHA which applies to each of them is the amount for one-bedroom shared accommodation, which in their area is £80 per week each.

So the eligible rent of each of them is their share of the actual rent of £60 plus £15, which is £75 per week.

Can the eligible rent be even lower?

9.27 The general rule in LHA cases is that a claimant's eligible weekly rent can never be lower than the lower of:

- the claimant's actual weekly rent plus £15; or
- the weekly LHA figure which applies to them.

For example, if the claimant's actual rent is £80, and the LHA is £120, then the claimant's eligible rent is £95. But if the claimant's actual rent is £110, and the LHA is £120, then the claimant's eligible rent is £120.

9.28 However, it appears that the 'over-riding power to reduce eligible rent' (described in paras. 8.45-48) applies to LHA cases – enabling the authority to restrict the eligible rent to below the LHA figure. (This is because of the definition of the term 'cap rent' in the regulations.)

9.28 HB 12B(1),(6),13D(4)(b),(12); HB60+ 12B(1),(6),13D(4)(b),(12)

The amount of the LHA

9.29 It is the rent officer (para. 10.5) who determines:

- the 'broad rental market areas' for LHAs; and
- the LHA figures for each of those areas.

These are described in turn in the next two sections.

Publicity

9.30 The broad rental market areas, and the LHAs applying in them, are public information, and the authority must 'take such steps as appear to it appropriate' to bring them to the attention of people who may be entitled to HB. Most authorities have published them on their websites and elsewhere. They are also available for the whole country at *https://lha-direct.therentservice.gov.uk/Secure/Default.aspx*

If the rent officer amends the areas or figures

9.31 If the rent officer amends any broad rental market area or any LHA figure, the amendment is taken into account in HB as follows:

- if a claimant's LHA goes down as a result, this is implemented as a change of circumstances from the Monday following the date the rent officer makes their amendment (so this should not result in the claimant being overpaid);
- if a claimant's LHA goes up as a result, this is implemented back to the date the LHA in question applied from (so the claimant gets his or her arrears).

9.32 Note that the above rule applies when rent officers are correcting their areas or figures because there has been a mistake: different rules apply when they are setting new ones because of a change in the rental market (para. 9.46).

Appeals about the areas or figures

9.33 Unlike the law on rent officer referrals, there is no right of appeal to another rent officer about a broad rental market area or about the amount of an LHA figure. Nor is there a right of appeal to a tribunal (though an appeal to a tribunal can be about the number of occupiers and therefore which particular LHA figure is to be applied). This means that any challenge would have to be by judicial review in the High Court (Sheriff Court in Scotland).

9.34 Some judicial reviews were begun (e.g. in relation to the London broad rental market areas) before LHAs came in, but at the time of writing all had been settled by negotiation. Those judicial reviews were begun by authorities, but it would seem that an individual claimant might also be able to do this.

9.30 HB 13E; HB60+ 13E; NIHB 14E; NIHB60+ 14E

9.31 HB 18A; HB60+ 18A; ROO 7A(4); NIHB 14F; NIHB60+ 14F

Determining broad rental market areas

9.35 The way the rent officer determines each broad rental market area changed from 5th January 2009. It is now the same for both LHA cases and rent referral cases (para. 10.29) (except that in Northern Ireland it applies to LHA cases only), and is defined in the law as follows:

- The area must be one where a person 'could reasonably be expected to live having regard to facilities and services for the purposes of health, education, recreation, personal banking and shopping, taking account of the distance of travel, by public and private transport, to and from those facilities and services'.
- It must contain 'residential premises of a variety of types' held on a 'variety of tenancies'.
- It must contain 'sufficient privately rented premises' to ensure that the rent officer's figures 'are representative of the rents that a landlord might reasonably be expected to obtain in that area'.

The areas are then normally defined by reference to post codes.

9.36 In practice, some council areas contain more than one broad rental market area, some are made up of just one, and some broad rental market areas are made up of more than one council area. The DWP takes the view that the areas can be fairly large, and that *R (Heffernan) v the Rent Service* (in which the House of Lords criticised this in relation to rent referral cases) no longer applies.

When the rent officer determines the areas

9.37 The first national set of broad rental market areas was set and notified to authorities by 20th March 2008. Since then, rent officers can amend the broad rental market areas and notify authorities of this – for example, because they consider they were wrong from the outset (para. 9.31) or because things have changed in the real world which affects how they set the areas (para. 9.46).

Determining the LHA figures

9.38 The rent officer determines LHA figures for the following categories of dwelling:

- one-bedroom shared accommodation;
- one-bedroom self-contained accommodation;
- two-bedroom dwellings;
- three-bedroom dwellings;

9.35 ROO sch 3B paras 4,5; NIED sch paras 4,5

9.37 ROO 4B(1A); NIED 3(1)

9.38 ROO 4B(6), sch 3B para 1; NIED 3(6), sch para 1

- four-bedroom dwellings; and
- five-bedroom dwellings.

In each case the rent officer must give a weekly figure and an approximate monthly equivalent: it is the weekly figure which is used in assessing HB.

More than five bedrooms?

9.39 In England, Scotland and Wales, since 6th April 2009 the maximum size of accommodation available in an LHA case is a five-bedroom dwelling – regardless of the number of people included in the HB claim. For differences in the LHA and rent referrals in Northern Ireland, see paragraphs 10.48-49.

Transitional protection for large households

9.40 Before 6th April 2009 larger categories of accommodation were available under the LHA scheme. Transitional protection in those cases works as follows:

- The eligible rent of anyone already on HB before 6th April 2009 continues as it was before that date, until the next occasion their case is reconsidered (under the normal LHA rules: para. 9.11).
- Then, for 26 weeks, their eligible rent is the greater of what it has been to date, or what it would be as a result of the reconsideration.
- But if their case then comes up for reconsideration again within those 26 weeks (under the normal LHA rules: para. 9.11), their transitional protection comes to an early end, and their eligible rent is simply what it is as a result of the reconsideration.

Data, assumptions and medians

9.41 The rent officer sets the LHA figures by taking account of the range of rents which a landlord 'might reasonably have been expected to obtain' on dwellings which:

- are let on assured tenancies;
- have the relevant number of rooms for the category in question;
- are in the relevant broad rental market area; and
- are in a reasonable state of repair.

9.42 In doing this, the rent officer must:

- 'assume that no-one who would have been entitled to [HB] had sought or is seeking the tenancy': in practice they do this simply by ignoring any rent payable by a person on HB; and
- exclude the value of all ineligible service charges.

9.39 HB 13D(2)(c); HB60+ 13D(2)(c)

9.40 HB12L; HB60+ 12L

9.41 ROO sch 3B para 2(1),(5); NIED sch para 2(1),(5)

9.42 ROO sch 3B para 2(7); NIED sch para 2(7)

9.43 Having collected the data as described above, the LHA is then the median of all the data. A median is found by putting all the rental figures in a row (having converted them where necessary to a weekly figure), and then selecting the middle one. (Unlike an average it is relatively unaffected by extremes in the data, and so extremes are not excluded).

9.44 If the result of the above calculations resulted (most unusually) in the LHA figure for a larger category of dwelling being lower than the LHA figure for a smaller category, the figure for the larger is increased to equal that for the smaller.

When the rent officer determines the LHA figures

9.45 The first national set of LHA figures was set and notified to authorities with the broad rental market areas on 20th March 2008.

9.46 The rent officer then issues further figures, between ten and eight working days before the end of each calendar month, to apply from the first day of the next calendar month.

Statistics provided to the rent officer

9.47 In order to assist the rent officer in excluding the effect of HB on market rents (para. 9.42), each authority sends the rent officer statistics. This is done between the first and fifth working day of every month, and contains the following details for everyone who was receiving HB in the private sector at any time in the previous month:

- the address of the dwelling including postcode and any room number;
- in the case of a houseboat, mobile home or caravan, the mooring or plot;
- the date the letting began;
- the rent payable and the period of the letting;
- if the claimant has the use of two or more bedrooms, the number of bedrooms and living rooms (excluding bedrooms shared with a joint tenant, non-dependant, boarder or sub-tenant);
- whether the claimant and any partner has exclusive use of only one bedroom, and if so whether they have exclusive or shared use of a kitchen, bathroom, toilet and living room;
- the date their HB began, and if appropriate the date it stopped.

9.43 ROO sch 3B para 2(2)-(4),(6),(9)-(11); NIED sch para 2(2)-(4),(6),(9)-(11)

9.44 ROO sch 3B regs 3; NIED sch para 3

9.45 ROO 2,4B(2A),(3A); NIHB sch 2 para 15; NIHB60+ sch 2 para 15; NIED 3(2),(3)

9.47 HB 114A(1),(2); HB60+ 95A(1),(2)

LHA boarders

9.48 The following rules apply in Great Britain to a claimant who is an 'LHA boarder'. This means anyone where 'rent under the tenancy is attributable to board and attendance' – and only if their date of claim for HB, or date of their move, falls on or after 7th April 2008 (para. 9.7). The reference to 'board' means that at least some food is provided and the reference to 'attendance' means that some other service must be provided as well.

9.49 In effect the eligible rent for an LHA boarder is assessed in exactly the same way as that of a rent referral boarder case (para. 10.13) – and in Northern Ireland there are no LHA boarders, only rent referral boarder cases. The differences between LHA boarders (in Great Britain) and rent referral boarder cases are to do with the referral procedure (para. 9.50 onwards) and who is paid the HB (para. 16.28).

Rent referrals for LHA boarders

9.50 When the authority receives a claim from an LHA boarder, it refers the individual details of that case to the rent officer in the following two stages.

9.51 First the authority applies to the rent officer for a 'board and attendance determination', and supplies only the following information:

(a) the address of the dwelling including the postcode and any room number;

(b) the length of the tenancy and when it began;

(c) whether the rent includes charges for any ineligible fuel, meals or water;

(d) whether the rent includes charges for any ineligible cleaning, window cleaning, emergency alarm systems, medical, nursing or personal care, or general counselling and support; and

(e) the total rent payable, after deducting (only) the authority's valuation of the charges mentioned in (d).

9.52 It is then the rent officer who determines whether a 'substantial' amount of the rent under the tenancy is attributable to board and attendance (and thus whether the case is an LHA boarder case), and informs the authority of the outcome. Anecdotal evidence consistently suggests that rent officers do not consider breakfast alone to be 'substantial'.

9.48 HB 13C(5)(e); HB60+ 13C(5)(e); NIHB 14C(5)(e); NIHB60+ 14C(5)(e)

9.50 HB 13D(10),(11); HB60+ 13D(10),(11)

9.51 HB 114A(3),(4); HB60+ 95A(3),(4)

9.51 HB 12D(3),(5),13ZA; HB60+ 12D(3),(5),13ZA; CPR sch 3 para 5; NIHB 13C(3),(5),14A; NIHB60+ 13D,14A; NICPR sch 3 para 5

9.52 ROO 4C(1)

9.53 If the rent officer notifies the authority that it is an LHA boarder case, the authority provides all the information (apart from the information it has already provided) it normally provides in a rent officer referral (table 10.3) and this counts as the date of the referral. The rent officer then makes a determination on the same basis as any other rent officer referral (paras. 10.32-44), and all the rules about rent officer referrals apply, including the rules about redeterminations (appeals to the rent officer).

9.54 If the rent officer notifies the authority that the case is not an LHA boarder case, the authority simply treats the case as a (non-boarder) LHA case and all the rules earlier in this chapter apply.

Eligible rent for LHA boarders

9.55 The eligible rent for an LHA boarder is calculated in the same way as in any other rent referral case including the rules about making deductions for meals (para. 10.13).

The protected groups

9.56 This section explains the two protections which apply in LHA cases. They also apply in rent referral cases (chapter 10) and old scheme cases (chapter 8). But if a claimant's eligible rent would be greater (which would be rare) using the LHA figure, the LHA figure is used and the protections are not needed (and do not apply).

People who could formerly afford their accommodation

9.57 A claimant falls within this protected group if:

- they or any combination of the occupiers of their home (para. 9.61) could afford the financial commitments there when the liability to pay rent was entered into (no matter how long ago that was); and
- neither the claimant nor any partner has received HB for any period in the 52 weeks prior to their current claim. Receipt of CTB during those weeks is ignored.

9.58 The protection in such cases lasts for the first 13 weeks of the award of HB. During those weeks, the claimant's eligible rent is worked out in the same way as in a standard case (para. 8.3 onwards) – and this cannot be restricted in any way. The protection gives the claimant time to move without the additional pressure of having insufficient HB.

9.53 HB 14(4A), 114A(5); HB60+ 14(4A), 95A(5); ROO 4C(2); NIHB 16(3A); NIHB60+ 16(3A)

9.55 ROO sch 1 para 7(1); NIHB sch 2 para 7; NIHB60+ sch 2 para 7

People who have had a bereavement

9.59 A claimant falls within this protected group if:

- any of the occupiers of their home (para. 9.61) has died within the last 12 months (including occupiers who were temporarily absent); and
- the claimant has not moved home since the date of that death.

9.60 The protection in such cases lasts until 12 months after that death. During that period it works as follows. If the claimant was on HB at the date of the death, their eligible rent must not be reduced to below whatever was their eligible rent immediately before that date (it is, however, increased if any rule requires this). If the claimant was not on HB at the date of the death, their eligible rent is worked out in the same way as in a standard case (para. 8.3 onwards) – and this cannot be restricted in any way.

Examples: The protected groups

Bereavement

A claimant makes a claim for HB after the death of her husband. She has not moved since her husband's death. Her actual rent is high.

Because of the protection for people who have had a bereavement, her eligible rent must not be restricted in any way until the first anniversary of her husband's death. Until then, her eligible rent is her actual rent minus amounts for any ineligible services.

Redundancy

A claimant makes a claim for HB after he is made redundant. His actual rent is high. He moved to this address when he was in a well-paid job and could easily afford the rent and outgoings. He has not been on HB in the last 52 weeks.

Because of the protection for people who could formerly afford their accommodation, his eligible rent must not be restricted in any way for the first 13 weeks of his award of HB. During those weeks, his eligible rent is his actual rent minus amounts for any ineligible services.

9.59 HB 12D(3),(5),13ZA; HB60+ 12D(3),(5),13ZA; CPR sch 3 para 5; NIHB 13C(3),(5),14A; NIHB60+ 13D,14A; NICPR sch 3 para 5

Who is an 'occupier'?

9.61 For the purposes of the above protected groups, the only 'occupiers' taken into account are:

- the claimant and any family (partner, children, young persons: para. 4.11); and
- any 'relative' of the claimant or partner (including non-dependants, boarders, sub-tenants and joint occupiers) who has no separate right to occupy the dwelling.

In the law, the term 'linked persons' is also used to refer to the above occupiers.

Who is a 'relative'?

9.62 A 'relative' is defined as:

- a parent, daughter, son, sister or brother;
- a parent-in-law, daughter-in-law, son-in-law, step-daughter or step-son, including equivalent relations arising through civil partnership;
- a partner of any of the above (i.e. by marriage or civil partnership, or by living together as husband and wife or civil partners); or
- a grandparent, grandchild, aunt, uncle, niece or nephew.

9.61 HB 2(1),12D,13ZA; HB60+ 2(1),12D,13ZA; CPR sch 3 para 5; NIHB 2(1),13C,14A; NIHB60+ 2(1),13C,14A; NICPR sch 3 para 5

9.62 HB 2(1); HB60+2(1); NIHB 2(1); NIHB60+2(1)

10 Rent referral cases

10.1 This chapter explains how to work out the eligible rent of a claimant who falls within the rent referral scheme (or 'rent officer referral cases'). It covers:

- which cases are rent referral cases;
- how the eligible rent is worked out;
- when referrals are made;
- how the rent officer or Northern Ireland Housing Executive make their determinations;
- how appeals and errors are dealt with; and
- the protections for certain groups of claimant.

10.2 The rent referral scheme ceased to apply for most new cases on 7th April 2008 (when local housing allowances came in: chapter 9). As described in this chapter, it continues for many claims made before that date and for certain types of accommodation. Chapter 7 describes which kinds of HB case fall within each of the HB schemes.

Who falls within the rent referral scheme?

10.3 The rent referral scheme described in this chapter applies only to people renting from a private landlord (as opposed to a housing association or council, though in uncommon cases it can apply to someone renting from a housing association). It applies to:

- all HB claims, whenever made, relating to caravans, houseboats, mobile homes, hostels, and dwellings with board and attendance (para. 7.10); and
- any other private sector case where the claimant has been on HB at that address since before 7th April 2008 (para. 7.13).

There are, however, exceptions, and these are all given in table 10.1.

10.4 The key features of the rent referral scheme are:

- individual HB cases are referred to the rent officer (or in Northern Ireland the Executive makes a rent decision) at various times;
- the rent officer (or the Executive) sets one or more figures which are binding in assessing eligible rent (subject to appeal: paras. 19.102 onwards);
- people who fall within the rent referral scheme can choose whether their HB is paid to them or to their landlord (para. 16.47).

10.3 HB 12C,14, sch 2; HB60+ 12C,14, sch 2; NIHB 12C,15 sch 3; NIHB60+ 12C,15, sch 3

Table 10.1 Tenancy types which are never rent referral cases

The following are never referred to the rent officer:

- council and NIHE lettings (i.e. all lettings where HB is awarded as a rebate: para. 16.14)
- shared ownership cases (para. 7.8)
- registered rent cases (also known as protected tenancies: paras. 7.27-30)

The following are never referred to the rent officer unless the authority considers that the accommodation is unreasonably large or the rent is unreasonably expensive (para. 7.9 and table 7.4):

- registered housing association lettings (paras. 7.25-26) *
- caravans, mobile homes and houseboats on land belonging to the authority itself (para. 16.14)
- gypsies' and travellers' caravans and mobile homes where the payments are to the county council (para. 2.26)

* But in the case of transferred stock (i.e. former council and new towns lettings transferred to a housing association or other owner) this applies only if there has been a rent increase since the date of the transfer.

The rent officer

10.5 Rent officers are independent of the authority. In England, they are employed by the Rent Service, which comes under the Valuation Office Agency; in Wales by the Rent Officer Service, which comes under the Welsh Assembly; and in Scotland by the Rent Registration Service, which comes under the Scottish Government.

The Northern Ireland Housing Executive

10.6 The NIHE in Northern Ireland, as well as administering the HB scheme (chapter 11), has the same functions as the Rent Officer does in the UK.

Definition of 'young individual'

10.7 Some of the rules in this chapter relate only to 'young individuals' (e.g. the 'single room rent': para. 10.41). Broadly speaking this means most single claimants under the age of 25. The full definition and the exceptions are the

T 10.1 HB 14(1),(2)(b), sch 2; HB60+ 14(1),(2)(b), sch 2; NIHB 15(1),(3)(b), sch 3; NIHB60+ 15(1),(3)(b), sch 3

10.7 HB 2(1),13(5),(6); HB60+2(1),13(5),(6); ROO 6(2); NIHB 2(1),14(6),(7); NIHB60+ 2(1),14(6),(7)

same as in LHA cases (para. 9.19). Additionally, in rent referral cases only, people do not count as a 'young individual' if they rent from a hostel (paras. 10.20-21) or a registered social landlord.

Which cases are rent referral cases

10.8 The following are all rent referral cases:

(a) a caravan, houseboat or mobile home;

(b) a hostel (paras. 10.20-21);

(c) a boarder (paras. 10.13-14); and

(d) any other letting from a private landlord where the date of claim for HB was before 7th April 2008, and the claimant has been continuously on HB at their current address since before that date (para. 9.3).

10.9 In addition to those mentioned above, some older claims for HB and some registered social landlord cases are also referred to the rent officer (paras. 7.12-13). In those cases, the rules in this chapter about when and how the referral is made apply, but in old cases only the rent officer's figures are advisory rather than binding (para. 8.49).

Eligible rent

The general rule

10.10 In a rent referral case the rent officer may provide the authority with one or two or all of the following determinations (or in Northern Ireland the Executive may make one or two or all of them):

- a claim-related rent determination (in all cases);
- a local reference rent determination (in some cases);
- a single room rent determination (only in the case of a 'young individual': para. 10.7).

The claimant's eligible rent is then the lowest of the above (or if there is only one, that one). This often means that the claimant's eligible rent is lower than their actual rent.

10.11 In the law the term 'maximum rent' is used as an alternative for 'eligible rent' in rent referral cases. The term is not used in this guide or in day-to-day work. The next section explains how the various rent determinations are made.

10.8 HB 12C,14, sch 2; HB60+ 12C,14 sch 2; NIHB 13B,15, sch 3; NIHB60+ 13B,15, sch 3

10.10 HB 2(1),12C,13(1)-(3),(5); HB60+ 2(1),12C,13(1)-(3),(5); NIHB 2(1),13C,14(1)-(3),(5); NIHB60+ 2(1),13C,14(1)-(3),(5)

Joint tenants

10.12 The eligible rent of a claimant who is a joint tenant is the same as above (paras. 10.10-11) except that before deciding which of the figures is the lowest, the claim-related rent determination and any local reference rent determination have to be apportioned between the joint tenants (but this does not apply to the single room rent determination). The apportionment is done as described in paragraphs 8.9-10.

Boarders

10.13 The eligible rent of a claimant whose rent includes at least some meals is the same as above (paras. 10.10-11) except that before deciding which of the figures is the lowest, the standard amount for meals (table 8.2) is always deducted from any local reference rent determination, and is also deducted from the claim-related rent determination if the rent officer has said that it includes meals (but is never deducted from the single room rent determination).

10.14 The above calculation also applies to 'LHA boarders' (paras. 9.48-55).

The 50% top-up

10.15 A few claimants get a '50% top-up'. This just means their eligible rent is half-way between the local reference rent determination and the claim-related rent determination. The only claimants who get this are people who have been on HB continuously since before 6th October 1997, have not moved home since then, and have been getting a 50% top-up continuously since then.

Can the eligible rent be even lower?

10.16 If, during an award of HB, a claimant's actual rent reduces to below the eligible rent calculated as above (which would be rare), the eligible rent is reduced to match the actual rent minus any ineligible service charges included in it. For these purposes ineligible service charges are assessed as in paras. 8.12 onwards.

10.17 Also, the 'over-riding power to reduce eligible rent' (described in paras. 8.45-48) applies to rent referral cases – enabling the authority to restrict the eligible rent to below the rent officer's figure.

10.12 HB 12C(2); HB60+ 12C(2); NIHB 13B(2); NIHB60+ 13B(2)

10.13 HB 13(4)-(7); HB60+ 13(4)-(7); NIHB 14(4)-(7); NIHB60+ 14(4)-(7)

10.15 HB 13(4); HB60+ 13(4); NIHB 14(4); NIHB60+ 14(4); CPR sch 3 para 8; NICPR sch 3 para 8

10.16 HB 13ZB; HB60+ 13ZB; NIHB 14B; NIHB60+ 14B

10.17 HB 12B(1)(6),12C(2),(3); HB60+ 12B(1)(6),12C(2),(3)

Examples: Eligible rent in rent referral cases

1. Sole tenant

A claimant under the age of 25 is a sole tenant of her home. Her actual rent is £80 per week The rent officer has provided the following figures:

- a claim-related rent determination of £70 per week;
- a local reference rent determination of £65 per week;
- a single room rent determination of £60 per week

So her eligible rent is simply the lowest of the above figures, which is £60 per week.

2. Joint tenants

Three claimants in their 30s jointly rent a house for £180 per week. They have identical rooms. The rent officer has provided the following figures:

- a claim-related rent determination of £150 per week;
- a local reference rent determination of £135 per week;
- no single room rent determination (because none of them are under 25).

The two figures given have are divided between the three joint tenants, giving £50 per week and £45 per week.

So the eligible rent of each of them is the lower of those two figures, which is £45 per week.

When referrals are made

10.18 In rent referral cases, in order to obtain the figures needed to calculate eligible rent, the authority must refer the details of the case to the rent officer, and the Executive in Northern Ireland must make a rent decision, within three working days of each of the following events:

- whenever it receives a new HB claim (but this can apply only in cases (a) to (c) in para. 10.8);
- whenever it receives notice of a 'relevant change of circumstances' (see below);
- when it receives a request for a 'pre-tenancy determination' (para. 10.22);
- whenever 52 weeks have passed since it last made a referral for the dwelling.

10.19 For the above purposes:

- table 10.2 defines what counts as a 'relevant change of circumstances';

10.18 HB 14(1)-(3),(6)-(8) sch 2 para 2; HB60+14(1)-(3),(6),(7),(9) sch 2 para 2; NIHB 15,16,sch 3 para 2; NIHB60+15,16,sch 3 para 2

- table 10.3 lists the information the authority must give to the rent officer; and
- table 10.4 shows the date rent officer's figures (in Northern Ireland the Executive's figures) take effect in the assessment of HB.

Table 10.2: 'Relevant changes of circumstances'

- Except in hostel cases (para. 10.21), there has been a change in the number of occupiers.
- Any child or young person in the household has reached the age of 10 or 16 – but only if, at the last referral, the rent officer gave a size-related rent determination (para. 10.34).
- There has been a change in the composition of the household – but only if, at the last referral, the rent officer gave a size-related rent determination (para. 10.34). (One example is when two people have ceased to be a couple.)
- There has been a substantial change or improvement in the condition of the dwelling – regardless of whether there has been an associated change in the rent. (For example, central heating has been installed.)
- The claimant has moved to a new dwelling.
- There has been a substantial change in the terms of the letting agreement (excluding a change in a term relating to rent alone) – regardless of whether there has been an associated change in the rent. (For example, the landlord has taken over the responsibility for internal decorations from the tenant or vice versa.)
- There has been a rent increase and:
  - the rent increase was made under a term of the letting agreement (which need not be in writing but must be a term of the letting in question, not merely a provision of law: *CH/3590/2007*) and that term is the same (or substantially the same) as at the previous referral to the rent officer; and
  - at the previous referral, the rent officer did not make any of the following determinations: a 'significantly high rent determination', a 'size-related rent determination' or an 'exceptionally high rent determination' (paras. 10.33-37).
- At the previous referral to the rent officer, the claimant was not a 'young individual' (para. 10.7), but the claimant in the current case is a 'young individual'.

T 10.2 HB 14(1), sch 2 para 2; HB60+14(1), sch 2 para 2; NIHB 15(1), sch 3 para 2; NIHB60+15(1), sch 3 para 2

Table 10.3: Summary of information given to the rent officer

- The address of the dwelling.
- A description (drawn from a fixed list, such as 'bedsit or rooms or studio flat', 'detached house').
- How many living rooms, bed-sitting rooms, bedrooms, bathrooms/toilets there are in the dwelling and the tenancy altogether, how many for the exclusive use of claimant and household, and how many for their shared use.
- Whether the dwelling and the tenancy have central heating, a garden, a garage, a parking space, and whether and to what extent the tenancy is furnished.
- What the rental period is (e.g. weekly, calendar monthly).
- The length of the tenancy, when it began, and if applicable when it ended.
- The landlord's or agent's name and business address, and whether they are a housing association or registered social landlord.
- The relationships between the claimant and other occupiers of the dwelling.
- The age and gender of under-18-year-old occupiers.
- Whether the claimant is a young individual (para. 10.7).
- If the referral relates to a period before 7th April 2008, that fact.
- Any other information reasonably needed to make determinations or to visit.

Representative referrals for hostel cases

10.20 In the case of a hostel (para. 10.21), once one rent referral has been done, the figures in that case apply to any other case in that hostel if:

- it is similar (e.g has the same number of bed spaces);
- there has been no 'relevant change of circumstances' (table 10.2); and
- no more than 12 months have passed.

T 10.3 HB 114A(6)-(10),(12); HB60+ Reg 95A(6)-(10),(12)

10.20 HB 14; HB60+ 14; NIHB 15; NIHB60+ 15

Table 10.4: When rent referral figures are implemented

Reason triggering the referral	Date rent officer figure is implemented from
A claim	The start of the award of HB
A 'relevant change of circumstances'	The date the change itself takes effect (typically the following Monday: chapter 17)
52 weeks have passed	If the rent officer's new determination means that the claimant qualifies for: *more HB or the same amount, and the claimant's rent is payable weekly or in multiples of weeks:* the day the referral was due, unless that is not a Monday, in which case from the Monday immediately before that day *more HB or the same amount, and the claimant's rent is payable otherwise than above:* the day the referral was due (which could be any day of the week) *less HB (regardless of when rent is payable):* the Monday following the date the rent officer determination 'was received' by the authority.

Examples: Rent referrals and implementation dates

The claimant's first ever claim for HB was received by the authority on Tuesday 8th May 2007 and the authority referred the details to the rent officer that very day. The authority awarded HB from Monday 14th May 2007.

- The rent officer's figures therefore applied from Monday 14th May 2007.

There are no changes in the claimant's circumstances, so the next rent referral is made 52 weeks after the last one, which is Tuesday 6th May 2008. The rent officer's reply is received by the authority on Thursday 15th May 2008.

T 10.4 DAR 7A(3),8(6A),(6B); NIDAR 7A(3),8(6A),(6B)

- If the rent officer's new figures mean the claimant is entitled to more HB (or the same amount) and the claimant's rent is due weekly or in multiples of weeks, then they apply to her case from Monday 5th May 2008.
- If the rent officer's new figures mean the claimant is entitled to more HB (or the same amount) and the claimant's rent is due calendar monthly or daily, then they apply to her case from Tuesday 6th May 2008 (on a daily basis).
- If the rent officer's new figures mean the claimant is entitled to less HB, then they apply to her case from Monday 19th May 2008 (the Monday after the authority received them).

The claimant 's non-dependant (who has been there all along so far) moves out on Saturday 8th June 2008. Because this is a relevant change of circumstances, a further referral is required on Saturday 8th June 2008 and can be made up to three days after that date. It is in fact made on Monday 10th June 2008.

- The resulting new figures (whether higher, lower or the same) apply to the claimant's case from the Monday after the change of circumstances, namely Monday 10th June 2008.

What is a 'hostel'?

10.21 A 'hostel' is defined for HB purposes as any building (other than a care home or independent hospital: paras. 2.15-16) to which both the following apply:

- it provides domestic accommodation which is not self-contained together with meals or adequate facilities for preparing food; and
- it is:
  - managed or run by a registered housing association or registered social landlord, or
  - run on a non-commercial basis, and wholly or partly funded by a government department or agency or local authority, or
  - managed by a registered charity or non-profit-making voluntary organisation which provides care, support or supervision with a view to assisting the rehabilitation of the residents or their resettlement into the community.

10.21 HB 2(1); HB60+2(1); NIHB 2(1); NIHB60+2(1)

Pre-tenancy determinations (PTDs)

10.22 In rent referral cases, the authority can make a referral to the rent officer (in Northern Ireland the Executive can make a rent decision) before a claimant moves in to their dwelling (or before they enter a new letting agreement there, so long as it is at least 11 months since their last agreement began). This is called a pre-tenancy determination (PTD). It is done if the claimant completes and signs an application requesting this and the landlord of the dwelling signs to show their consent.

10.23 In Great Britain, the timetable for forwarding the PTD to the rent service is two working days – unless the application is invalid (in which case the authority notifies the claimant of why it is invalid) or there is already a rent officer determination which is relevant to the case (in which case the authority notifies the claimant of this within four working days).

10.24 The rent officer makes the same determinations as in any other rent referral case, and should reply within five working days (or in Northern Ireland the Executive makes a rent decision within seven working days). In practice the response is usually quicker.

10.25 When the authority receives an HB claim on a dwelling to which a PTD applies, the authority uses the PTD in assessing the claimant's eligible rent (instead of making a further rent referral) – unless it is by now more than 12 months old or there has been a relevant change of circumstances (table 10.2).

The rent determinations

10.26 The rent officer (in Northern Ireland the Housing Executive) may provide one or more of the following determinations. More information on each is given in the next few paragraphs:

- a claim-related rent determination;
- a local reference rent determination;
- a single room rent determination;
- certain determinations relating to service charges.

The rent officer does not make any determinations if the referral is withdrawn by the authority. The rent officer is not required to visit the dwelling but does so in some cases.

General rules and assumptions about determinations

10.27 In making the determinations described below (paras. 10.32-44), the rent officer (in Northern Ireland the Housing Executive):

10.22 HB 14; HB60+14; ROO 3(1); NIHB 16; NIHB60+16

10.26 ROO sch 1 paras 1-7; NIHB sch 2 paras 1-7; NIHB60+ sch 2 paras 1-7

- must base these on the facts as they stood on the date on which the authority made the referral, unless the claimant had left the accommodation by that date, in which case they are based on the facts as they stood at the end of the claimant's letting;
- provides these for the same period (e.g. weekly, calendar monthly) as that for which the authority supplied the information to the rent officer (table 10.3);
- must 'assume that no one who would have been entitled to housing benefit had sought or is seeking the tenancy';
- must ignore all rents payable to housing associations, other registered social landlords and registered charities;
- must include the value of any meals provided to the claimant (except that, in the case of an exceptionally high rent determination in a case arising from before 7th April 2008, the rent officer may choose whether to include meals or not);
- must exclude the value of all other service charges which are ineligible for HB (para. 8.12 onwards).

Areas

10.28 In Great Britain, the rent officer makes his or her determinations by reference to the 'broad rental market area', the 'neighbourhood' or the 'vicinity'. In Northern Ireland, all determinations are made by reference to the 'locality' (para. 10.48). The meanings of these various terms are given below.

10.29 'Broad rental market area' (used in determining local reference rents: para. 10.38; and single room rents: para. 10.41) is defined for rent referral cases in the same way as it is in LHA cases (see paras. 9.35-36). 'Broad rental market areas (local reference rent)' – to give them their full name – replaced 'localities' for rent referral cases from 5th January 2009.

10.30 'Neighbourhood' (used in determining exceptionally high rents: para. 10.37) means:

- in the case of dwelling in a town or city, 'that part of that town or city where the dwelling is located which is a distinct area of residential accommodation';
- in the case of a dwelling not in a town or city, 'the area surrounding the dwelling which is a distinct area of residential accommodation' and where there are dwellings satisfying the size criteria (table 10.5).

10.27 ROO sch 1 paras 1-5,7,8; NIHB sch 2 paras 1-5,7,8; NIHB60+ sch 2 paras 1-5,7,8

10.28 ROO sch 1 paras 1-4; NIHB sch 2 paras 1-5

10.29 ROO sch 1 para 4(6),(7)

10.30 ROO sch 1 para 3(5)

10.31 'Vicinity' (used in determining significantly high rents: para. 10.33; and size-related rents: para. 10.34) means:

- 'the area immediately surrounding the dwelling';
- however, for size-related rents only (not significantly high rents), if 'the area immediately surrounding the dwelling' contains no dwellings matching the size criteria (table 10.5), 'vicinity' instead means 'the area nearest to the [claimant's] dwelling where there is such a dwelling'.

Claim-related rent determinations

10.32 In all cases, the rent officer must make a 'claim-related rent determination.' This is the only, lower or lowest of the following (the latter three are described in the following paragraphs):

- the referred rent, adjusted (as regards service charges) in accordance with the general rules and assumptions (para. 10.27);
- the significantly high rent;
- the size-related rent;
- the exceptionally high rent.

Significantly high rent determinations

10.33 The rent officer determines whether the referred rent for the dwelling is 'significantly higher than the rent which the landlord might reasonably have been expected to obtain'. If it is, he or she makes a significantly high rent determination: this is the amount 'the landlord might reasonably have been expected to obtain' for the dwelling, having regard to 'the level of rent under similar tenancies [or licences] of similar dwellings in the vicinity (or as similar as regards tenancy [or licence], dwelling and vicinity as reasonably practicable'. 'Vicinity' is defined in para. 10.31. Also, the general rules and assumptions apply (para. 10.27). In Northern Ireland 'broad rental market area' is used instead of 'vicinity'.

Size-related rent determinations

10.34 Except in the case of site rents for caravans or mobile homes and mooring charges for houseboats, the rent officer also determines whether the dwelling exceeds the size criteria given in paragraph 10.35 and table 10.5. If it does, he or she makes a size-related rent determination: this is the amount 'the landlord might reasonably have been expected to obtain' on a dwelling which:

- is in 'the same vicinity' (in Northern Ireland 'locality'); and
- is let under a similar tenancy under the same terms as the tenancy of the dwelling in question; and

---

10.31 ROO sch 1 para 1(4)

10.32 ROO sch 1 para 6; NIHB sch 2 para 6; NIHB60+ sch 2 para 6

10.33 ROO sch 1 para 1; NIHB sch 2 para 1; NIHB60+ sch 2 para 1

- matches those size criteria; and
- is in a reasonable state of repair; and
- in other respects, matches the claimant's dwelling 'as closely as reasonably practicable'.

'Vicinity' is defined in para. 10.31. Also, the general rules and assumptions apply (para. 10.27).

Table 10.5: The size criteria for rent referral cases

These are relevant for size-related rent determinations (para. 10.34), exceptionally high rent determinations (para. 10.37) and local reference rent determinations (para. 10.38). For who counts as an occupier for these purposes, see paragraphs 10.35-36.

- One room is allowed as a bedroom for each of the following occupiers, each occupier coming only within the first category which applies to him or her:
  - a couple (para. 4.13);
  - a single person aged 16 or more;
  - two children of the same sex under the age of 16;
  - two children (of the same or opposite sexes) under the age of 10;
  - a child under the age of 16.
- One, two or three living rooms are allowed as follows:
  - one if there are one to three occupiers;
  - two if there are four to six occupiers;
  - three if there are seven or more occupiers.
- The size criteria relate to the total number of bedrooms or living rooms allowed (under either of the above headings). It is irrelevant whether the claimant actually uses those as bedrooms or living rooms. The rent officer is not permitted to take account of personal circumstances such as disability.

10.35 The size criteria (table 10.5) allow for every 'occupier'. Who counts as an occupier is decided by the authority. It includes:

- the claimant and any family (partner, children, young persons: para. 4.11);
- non-dependants (para. 4.41);

10.34 ROO sch 1 para 2; NIHB sch 2 para 2; NIHB60+ sch 2 para 2

T 10.5 ROO sch 2; NIHB sch 2 para 10; NIHB60+ sch 2 para 10

- sub-tenants and boarders in the claimant's home (para. 4.48 and 4.50);
- joint occupiers; and
- other people who 'occupy the dwelling as their home'.

10.36 The Court of Appeal in *R v Swale BC HBRB ex p Marchant* held in 1999 that a child who spends time in the homes of each of his or her parents (who live apart) counts as an 'occupier' only in the home of the parent who is 'responsible' for him or her (para. 4.33) – typically the one who receives child benefit. However, the more recent *Hockenjos* case (para. 4.35) may over-ride this in appropriate circumstances. *Marchant* does not apply in other difficult situations. One example is that of a grown-up child who lives away from home for part(s) of the year (perhaps as a student) but returns home from time to time (perhaps in the holidays). It is clear that he or she counts as an 'occupier' in weeks in which he or she is treated as a non-dependant. In other weeks (if any), it can be argued that he or she counts as an 'occupier' (since the definition of 'occupier' appears flexible and is unaffected in this situation by the *Marchant* case), but it is unlikely that all local authorities will agree with this. Matters such as this are open to appeal.

Exceptionally high rent determinations

10.37 Except in the case of hostels (para. 10.21) or care homes and independent hospitals (para. 2.15-16), the rent officer also determines whether either of the figures described above (paras. 10.33-36), or (if he or she has not made a determination in either of those cases) the referred rent for the dwelling, is 'exceptionally high'. If it is, he or she makes an exceptionally high rent determination: this is 'the highest rent, which is not an exceptionally high rent and which a landlord might reasonably have been expected to obtain' on a dwelling which:

- is in 'the same neighbourhood'(in Northern Ireland 'locality'); and
- matches the size criteria (table 10.5); and
- is let on an assured tenancy (in Northern Ireland an uncontrolled letting);
- is in a reasonable state of repair.

'Neighbourhood' is defined in para. 10.30. Also the general rules and assumptions apply (para. 10.27).

Local reference rent determinations

10.38 Except in the case of hostels (para. 10.21) or care homes and independent hospitals (para. 2.15-16), the rent officer also determines whether any of the figures described above (paras. 10.33-37), or (if he or she has not made a determination in any of those cases) the referred rent for the dwelling, is

10.37 ROO 6(2) sch 1 para 3; NIHB sch 2 para 3; NIHB60+ sch 2 para 3

10.38 ROO 6(2) sch 1 para 4; NIHB sch 2 para 4; NIHB60+ sch 2 para 4

greater than the 'local reference rent' described below. If it is, he or she makes a local reference rent determination (in other words, notifies the authority of the local reference rent). If it is not, he or she notifies the authority that it is not.

10.39 In determining the 'local reference rent', the rent officer takes account of the range of rents 'which a landlord might reasonably have been expected to obtain' on dwellings which:

- are in 'the same broad rental market area' (in Northern Ireland 'locality': para. 10.48); and
- match the size criteria (table 9.5) or have the same number of rooms as the claimant's dwelling, if less; and
- in the case of one-room dwellings, are in the same category as the claimant's dwelling (see below); and
- are let on an assured tenancy (in Northern Ireland an uncontrolled letting) or a similar tenancy or licence, including a student letting when appropriate; and
- are in a reasonable state of repair.

'Broad rental market area' is defined in para. 10.29 (for Northern Ireland see para. 10.48). Also the general rules and assumptions apply (para. 10.27).

The categories (mentioned above) of one-room dwellings are:

- one-room dwellings where a 'substantial' part of the rent is 'fairly attributable' to 'board and attendance' included within the rent;
- other one-room dwellings where the tenant shares a kitchen, toilet, bathroom and living room ('room suitable for living in') with someone who is not a member of his or her household (paras. 4.3-9 and 10.35); and
- other one-room dwellings.

For the purposes of deciding whether it is a one-room dwelling in the first place, the definition of a 'room' is the same as in the third bullet in table 10.5.

10.40 The 'local reference rent' is then the figure which is half-way between:

- the lowest such rent which is not an 'exceptionally low rent'; and
- the highest such rent which is not an 'exceptionally high rent'.

Single room rent determinations

10.41 Except in the case of hostels (para. 10.21) or care homes and independent hospitals (paras. 2.15-16), and only if the authority states in the referral that the claimant is a 'young individual' (para. 10.7 and see also para. 9.19), the rent officer also determines whether the claimant's rent is greater than the 'single room rent' described below. If it is, he or she makes a single room rent determination (in other words, notifies the authority of the single room rent). If it is not, he or she notifies the authority that it is not.

10.41 ROO 6(2) sch 1 para 5; NIHB 15(3)(a), sch 2 para 5; NIHB60+ 15(3)(a), sch 2 para 5

10.42 In determining the 'single room rent', the rent officer takes account of the range of rents 'which a landlord might reasonably have been expected to obtain' on dwellings which:

- provide exclusive use of one bedroom;
- provide no other bedroom;
- provide shared use of a living room ('room suitable for living in');
- provide shared use of a toilet and bathroom;
- provide shared use of a kitchen (and no exclusive use of facilities for cooking food);
- do not provide board and attendance;
- are in 'the same broad rental market area';
- are let on an assured tenancy (in Northern Ireland an uncontrolled letting) or a similar tenancy or licence, including a student letting when appropriate;
- are in a reasonable state of repair.

'Broad rental market area' is defined in para. 10.29 (see para. 10.48 for Northern Ireland). Also the general rules and assumptions apply (para. 10.27).

10.43 The 'single room rent' is then the figure which is half-way between:

- the lowest such rent which is not an 'exceptionally low rent'; and
- the highest such rent which is not an 'exceptionally high rent'.

Service charges determinations

10.44 Except in the case of a hostel (para. 10.21), the rent officer must determine the value of the ineligible service charges (apart from meals) he or she excluded in making the claim-related rent determination (unless the amount is negligible).

Joint occupiers

10.45 In the case of accommodation occupied by joint occupiers, the rent officer's determinations (apart from the single room rent determination) relate to the dwelling as a whole. It is for the authority to make any necessary apportionment (para. 8.9).

Notification and time limits

10.46 In Great Britain only, the rent officer has a duty to notify the authority of the following:

- the claim-related rent (all cases);
- the local reference rent (if any);

10.44 ROO sch 1 paras 6(3),7; NIHB sch 2 paras 6(3),7; NIHB60+ sch 2 paras 6(3),7

10.45 HB 12C(2),(3),13(5); HB60+ 12C(2),(3),13(5); ROO 2(1)(a); NIHB 2(1)(a),13B(2),(3),14(5); NIHB60+ 2(1)(a),13B(2),(3),14(5)

10.46 ROO sch 1 para 9

- the single room rent (if any);
- except in the case of a hostel (para. 10.21), the value of the ineligible service charges (apart from meals and support charges) he or she has excluded in making his or her claim-related rent determination;
- whether the claim-related rent includes an amount for ineligible meals (as can be the case if it is an exceptionally high rent determination).

10.47 The rent officer should notify the authority of the above determinations within five working days or, if the rent officer intends to visit the dwelling, within 25 working days (or, in either case, as soon as reasonably practicable after that). The period begins on the day the rent officer receives the referral from the authority or (if he or she has requested this) on the day he or she receives further information needed from the authority.

Differences in rent determinations and the LHA in Northern Ireland

10.48 In Northern Ireland all of the rent determinations in rent referral cases are set by reference to the 'locality'. Locality is not defined but it probably has a different meaning for each type of determination which is similar, but not identical to, 'vicinity' (para.10.31), for a significantly high rent and size-related rent determination, and 'neighbourhood' (para. 10.30) for an exceptionally high rent determination. In the case of a local reference rent and single room rent 'locality' probably means a fairly wide area but not as wide as a 'broad rental market area'. (The Heffernan case (para. 9.36) may be relevant.)

10.49 Unlike in Great Britain (table 9.2 and para. 9.39) there is no limit on the number of bedrooms when setting the size of accommodation for the LHA. If a property of more than five bedrooms is needed then the NIHE will set a rate once a claim is made (and not before). This rate will then apply to all subsequent claims. A prospective tenant who is likely to be entitled to accommodation with more than five bedrooms may obtain the figures in advance of making their claim if they complete a form and have their landlord's signed consent: in effect this is the same as a pre-tenancy determination (para. 10.22).

The protected groups

10.50 In rent referral cases the same protections apply as in LHA cases:

- the 13-week protection applies for people who could afford the accommodation when they first took it on (para. 9.57): and
- the 12-month protection applies for people who have had a bereavement in the household (para. 9.59).

10.47 ROO 2(1)(a),3(1)(a)

10.48 NIHB sch 2 paras. 1-5; NIHB60+ sch 2 paras. 1-5

10.49 NIHB 14D(7)-(9); NIHB60+ 14D(7)-(9)

10.50 HB 13ZA; HB60+ 13ZA; CPR sch 3 para 5; NIHB 14ZA; NIHB60+ 14ZA; NICPR sch 3 para 5

11 Eligible council tax and rates

11.1 This chapter describes how help with certain local taxes (in Great Britain, the council tax; in Northern Ireland domestic rates) is calculated. In England, Scotland and Wales, CTB is worked out by reference to the claimant's 'eligible council tax'. In Northern Ireland HB for rates is worked out by reference the claimant's 'eligible rates'. This chapter explains these two terms and how to work out the eligible council tax/rates in all cases. It covers

- in Great Britain, an overview of the council tax itself, and who has to pay it;
- the exemptions, disability reductions, discounts and discretionary powers, which can reduce or eliminate council tax liability;
- how to calculate the eligible council tax for CTB and second adult rebate purposes;
- in Northern Ireland, an overview of domestic rates, and who has to pay them;
- the exemptions, disability reductions, and transitional relief, which can reduce the amount of rates payable;
- how to calculate the eligible rates for HB purposes;
- how to calculate any rate relief and lone pensioner allowance which may be payable in addition to, or without any HB for rates.

Paragraphs 11.2-31 apply to England, Scotland and Wales only and paragraphs 11.32 onwards to Northern Ireland.

Council tax overview

11.2 The council tax is the means by which local people help meet the cost of local public services in Great Britain. It is a tax on residential properties known as dwellings. In England, Scotland and Wales the same authorities that are responsible for administering HB/CTB (para. 1.18) are also responsible for the billing and collection of the tax. Table 11.1 lists the key considerations that arise when considering council tax liability, etc. Fuller details of the council tax are in CPAG's regularly revised *Council Tax Handbook* (Alan Murdie and Martin Ward, Child Poverty Action Group), which covers many matters not included in this guide (such as billing, payment, penalties, appeals, and so on).

Dwellings and valuation bands

11.3 One council tax bill is issued per dwelling, unless the dwelling is exempt (para. 11.11). A dwelling means a house, a flat, etc, whether lived in or not, and also houseboats and mobile homes that are used for domestic purposes.

Table 11.1: Council tax: key considerations

- Which dwelling is being considered?
- What valuation band does it fall into?
- How much is the council tax for that band?
- Who is liable to pay the council tax there?
- Is the dwelling exempt from council tax altogether?
- Do they qualify for a disability reduction?
- Do they qualify for a discount?
- Do they qualify for main CTB or second adult rebate?
- Should the council use its power to reduce liability?

11.4 The amount of tax depends first on which valuation band a dwelling has been allocated to, and this is shown on the bill. The lower the valuation band, the lower the tax. An amount for each band is fixed each year by the billing or local authority, and often includes amounts for other bodies (such as a county council, a parish council, the police, etc).

11.5 In England and Scotland, dwellings are valued as at 1st April 1991 (taking effect from 1st April 1993) and there are eight valuation bands – band A to band H. In Wales, dwellings are valued as at 1st April 2003 (taking effect from 1st April 2005); and there are nine valuation bands – band A to band I.

11.6 The valuation list holds current details of which band dwellings are in. In England and Wales it can be seen at either the local valuation office or the authority's main office or viewed on-line at the Valuation Office Agency's site, *www.voa.gov.uk.* In Scotland it may be seen at the authority's main office.

Who is liable to pay council tax?

11.7 Council tax is normally payable by someone resident in the dwelling (but there are also exceptions described in the next paragraph). A 'resident' is someone aged 18 or over, solely or mainly resident in the dwelling. Where there is more than one resident the liable person is the one with the greatest legal interest in the dwelling. So if a resident home-owner has a lodger, the home-owner is liable, not the lodger. If a resident council, housing association or private tenant has a lodger, the tenant is liable, not the lodger.

11.8 The most common exceptions to the above rule are that the owner (or other landlord) is liable for council tax on:

- a 'house in multiple occupation'. This means a dwelling occupied by separate households with separate lettings but some shared facilities;
- many hostels and care homes; and

- unoccupied dwellings (unless they are exempt).

In other words, the residents (in the first two cases) are not liable, but many owners pass on the cost of paying the council tax (along with any other overheads) when fixing the rent.

Joint liability

11.9 There are two ways in which joint liability (or 'joint and several liability') arises:

- if there is more than one resident with the greatest (or only) legal interest in the dwelling they are jointly liable for the council tax. For example two sisters who jointly own their home, or three friends who jointly rent their home, are jointly liable;
- if the liable person has a partner living with him or her, then the partner is jointly liable (even if he or she has no legal interest in the property). This applies to couples and polygamous arrangements.

For exceptions see the next paragraph. For how jointly liable residents are dealt with in CTB, see paragraphs 11.26-30. There are further rules (not in this guide) about joint liability for unoccupied properties.

Students and people with severe mental impairment

11.10 The exceptions to the above rules on joint liability relate to students and people who are severely mentally impaired. A person counts as 'severely mentally impaired' as described in category 13 in appendix 6; and as a student (for these purposes) as described in category 6 of that appendix. Such a person is not jointly liable if there is another resident with the same legal interest in the dwelling who is neither severely mentally impaired nor a student. See the next paragraph if they are all severely mentally impaired, or all students.

Exemptions

11.11 Only dwellings, rather than people, can be exempt from the council tax. The following occupied dwellings are exempt from council tax:

- dwellings where all the residents are students;
- in England and Wales only, dwellings where all the occupants (though their normal residence is elsewhere) are students;
- halls of residence mainly occupied by students;
- where all the occupiers are severely mentally impaired, including cases where the only other occupiers are students (but this does not apply to dwellings where the owner rather than the occupier is liable (para. 11.8);
- dwellings occupied only by people under 18;
- armed forces accommodation;

- in England and Wales only, annexes or similar self-contained parts of a property which are occupied by an elderly or disabled relative of the residents living in the rest of it; and
- in Scotland only, certain dwellings used as trial flats by registered housing associations for pensioners and disabled people.

11.12 Various unoccupied dwellings are also exempt. For example, an unoccupied dwelling which is substantially unfurnished is exempt for six months – and there are many other categories.

Examples: Council tax liability, exemptions and discounts

Unless stated below, none of the following are students, severely mentally impaired, or under 18.

A couple with a lodger

A couple live in a house which the man owns in his name only. They have children in their 20s living at home, and a lodger who rents a room and shares facilities.

The couple are jointly liable for the council tax, because the man is the resident with the greatest legal interest in the dwelling and the woman is jointly liable with him by being his partner. There is no reason to suppose they qualify for exemption, or a disability reduction or a discount.

A lone parent

A lone parent owns her home and lives there with her three children, all under 18.

The lone parent is solely liable for the council tax, because she is the resident with the greatest legal interest in the dwelling. She is the only (adult) resident so she qualifies for a 25% discount.

Three sharers

Three friends jointly rent a house (in other words all their names are on the tenancy agreement). No-one else lives with them.

They are all jointly liable for the council tax, because they are all residents with the greatest legal interest in the dwelling. There is no reason to suppose they qualify for exemption, or a disability reduction or a discount.

The sharers' circumstances change

One of the sharers leaves and is not replaced. One of the others becomes a full-time university student.

The remaining non-student resident is now the only liable person (para. 11.11), and qualifies for a 25% discount because the student is disregarded when counting the residents (para. 11.17).

Disability reductions

11.13 The council tax bill is reduced if a dwelling has at least one disabled resident and provides:

- an additional bathroom or kitchen for the use of the disabled person;
- an additional room, other than a bathroom, kitchen or toilet, used predominantly to meet the disabled person's special needs – such as a downstairs room in a two storey house which has to be used as a bedroom by the disabled person because of the nature of the disability; or
- sufficient floor space to enable the use of a wheelchair required by the disabled person within the dwelling.

11.14 In each case the authority must be satisfied that the facility in question is either essential, or of major importance, for the disabled person (who may be an adult or a child) in view of the nature and extent of the disability. Disability reductions are not limited to specially adapted properties.

11.15 The effect of the reduction is that the person is liable for the amount that would be due if his or her dwelling was in the next lowest valuation band (or in the case of a band A dwelling, one-sixth less than normal).

Discounts

11.16 The council tax bill is reduced if:

- there is only one resident in the dwelling. In this case the discount is always 25 per cent; or
- there are no residents in the dwelling (unless the dwelling is exempt). In this case, the discount can be 50% or (depending on the individual authority) any lower amount or even nil (in other words in some cases there is no discount).

11.17 When considering the number of people in the dwelling, certain people including students, apprentices, carers, severely mentally impaired people and under-18-year-olds are disregarded. Appendix 6 describes the categories of person who are disregarded. A person can be disregarded for the purpose of awarding a discount but still liable to pay the tax.

Obtaining an exemption, disability reduction or discount

11.18 An authority is expected to take reasonable steps to ascertain whether exemptions, disability reductions and discounts apply to the dwellings in its area. These can be awarded on the basis of information available to it, or someone can write requesting this. There is no time limit on obtaining exemptions, disability reductions or discounts, though the authority is entitled to seek appropriate evidence.

Other reasons why liability may be lower

11.19 In addition to the disability reductions and discounts mentioned above, authorities can offer a discount for prompt payment of the tax or the adoption of certain payment methods. In some areas council tax may be 'capped' by the government to a lower figure, and in a few areas there may be a 'transitional reduction' in liability because of recent re-organisation of authority boundaries.

Power to reduce council tax liability

11.20 In England only, an authority may reduce any liability for council tax. This is a wide power, which permits the authority to reduce liability 'to such extent as it thinks fit' and 'includes power to reduce an amount to nil'. This can be done 'in relation to particular cases or by determining a class of case in which liability is to be reduced to an extent provided by the determination.'

11.21 This power exists under section 13A of the Local Government Finance Act 1992, as inserted by section 76 of the Local Government Act 2003 (itself brought into force by section 128(2) of the 2003 Act). No further rules are given about how to get such a reduction, so a person could write in and ask, or (in theory) an authority could design its own rules without any such request. Similarly, no mention is made of any kind of appeals mechanism, though presumably these matters could be judicially reviewed.

Impact on discretionary housing payments

11.22 The above power to reduce council tax liability is separate from the power to make discretionary housing payments (para. 22.2). The government contributes to awards of DHPs, which can be granted only to people on HB/CTB. Neither of those points apply to the above power.

Eligible council tax

11.23 Only a person who is liable for council tax is eligible to claim for CTB or second adult rebate. A claimant's 'eligible council tax' is the figure used in calculating his or her entitlement to CTB and/or second adult rebate. The eligible council tax figure used in calculating CTB can differ from that used in calculating second adult rebate, as mentioned in the appropriate places below. An example is at the end of the chapter.

11.24 A claimant's weekly eligible council tax is calculated by working through the following steps:

1. Start with the council tax due on his or her home.
2. If the claimant is entitled to a disability reduction, use the council tax figure after that reduction has been made.

11.24 CTB 57(1),(2),62(1); CTB60+ 40(1),(2), 46(1)

3. If the claimant is entitled to a discount, use the council tax figure after that discount has been made.
4. Apportion the result if the claimant is a joint occupier (see below).
5. Convert it to a weekly figure (as described in para. 6.68).

11.25 All the above steps apply when calculating eligible council tax for CTB purposes and the 'student only' type of second adult rebate (para. 6.38). But steps 3 and 4 are omitted when calculating eligible council tax for the general type of second adult rebate (para. 6.40 – and see para. 11.30). See also paragraph 11.31 about other items which can affect a council tax bill.

Apportionment for joint occupiers

11.26 A joint occupier is one of two or more people who are jointly liable to pay the council tax on a dwelling, other than just a couple or polygamous arrangement. In such cases, the figures used in calculating eligible council tax are apportioned between the joint occupiers for CTB purposes (but not second adult rebate: para. 11.30).

11.27 This apportionment is found by dividing the total council tax liability by the number of people who are jointly liable.

11.28 If amongst several jointly liable people some are a couple or polygamous marriage, the law is unclear. The DWP advises (GM para. A2.91: example) that if there are three jointly liable people, two of whom are a couple, then the couple are eligible for CTB on two-thirds of the council tax liability and the other person on one-third.

11.29 In most cases, students and people who are severely mentally impaired are not jointly liable for council tax (para. 11.10) so the apportionment ignores them.

Variations when calculating general second adult rebate

11.30 As mentioned in paragraph 11.25, there are two differences in the rules for calculating eligible council tax for general second adult rebate purposes:

- Step 3 in paragraph 11.24 does not apply. In other words, a claimant's eligible council tax is calculated as though he or she did not qualify for any council tax discount. This is for mathematical reasons. As illustrated in the following example, a claimant who qualifies for a discount does not lose it.
- Step 4 in paragraph 11.24 does not apply. In other words, there is no apportionment between joint occupiers. Instead, the apportionment will be done after the calculation of second adult rebate is otherwise complete (as described in para. 6.55).

11.26 CTB 57(3),(4); CTB60+ 40(3),(4)

Example: Eligible council tax

The claimant and his household

A claimant's dwelling falls in band D, which in his area is £900 per year. With him lives only his niece (as his non-dependant). The claimant is a full-time student with income from several sources, including a grant towards his disablement needs. His niece is on income support. The claimant qualifies for:

- a disability reduction, because he has a large enough house to use his wheelchair indoors (para. 11.13). This is worth £100 per year; and
- a 25% council tax discount, because he is a full-time student, so there is only one countable resident in his home, his niece (para. 11.17). This is worth £200 per year.

Eligible council tax for CTB

In calculating CTB his eligible council tax is the figure obtained by deducting both the disability reduction and the discount from the amount for the dwelling. This is (£900 – £100 – £200 =) £600, the weekly equivalent of which is (to the nearest penny) £11.51 (para. 11.24).

It turns out, though, when the authority assesses his entitlement to CTB, that he does not qualify because he has too much capital.

Eligible council tax for second adult rebate

In calculating second adult rebate his eligible council tax is the figure obtained by deducting the disability reduction from the amount for the dwelling but not the discount (para. 11.30). This is (£900 – £100 =) £800, the weekly equivalent of which is (to the nearest penny) £15.34.

Because his niece is on income support, he qualifies for second adult rebate equal to 25% of the last figure (table 6.6). This is (to the nearest penny) £3.84. On an annual basis this is £200.

His resulting liability for council tax

The following are the annual figures:

The council tax for the dwelling is	£900
He is granted his disability reduction of	– £100
He is granted his discount of	– £200
He is granted second adult rebate of	– £200
So his resulting liability is	= £400

Other items affecting eligible council tax

11.31 The following additional rules apply to main CTB and also to both types of second adult rebate:

- in the case of an authority which offers discounts against its council taxes for people who pay in a lump sum or by a method other than cash (e.g. direct debit), CTB is calculated on liability before those discounts are subtracted;
- if lower council taxes are set as a result of council tax 'capping' procedures, these apply from the beginning of the financial year, and CTB is calculated (throughout the financial year) on the lower amount;
- if a council tax bill is increased to recover an earlier overpayment of CTB or of community charge benefit, CTB is calculated before those amounts are added;
- if a penalty is added to a council tax bill, CTB is calculated as if that penalty was not included; and
- if council tax liability is reduced (para. 11.20), CTB is calculated on the reduced amount.

Rates overview

11.32 Domestic rates are the means by which local people help meet the cost of local public services in Northern Ireland. Rates are a tax on residential properties known as dwellings. They are made up of local rates which help fund district councils, and regional rates which help fund centrally delivered services. Land and Property Services are responsible for the billing and collection of the tax.

Table 11.2: Domestic rates: key considerations

- Which dwelling is being considered?
- What is the capital value (or social sector value) for that dwelling?
- What is the aggregate rate poundage in that district?
- Who is liable for the rates?
- Is the dwelling exempt from rates altogether?
- Do they qualify for a disability reduction?
- Do they qualify for full or partial HB on their rates?
- Do they qualify for rate relief on any remaining rates?
- Do they qualify lone pensioner allowance on any remaining rates?

Dwellings and annual rates

11.33 The domestic rate is an annual bill. One rates bill is issued per dwelling; unless the dwelling is exempt (para. 11.38). A 'dwelling' means any house, flat, etc, whether lived in or not, and also a houseboat or mobile home that is used for domestic purposes.

11.34 The amount of rates depends first on the capital value which the dwelling has been allocated, and this is shown on the bill. The lower the capital value the lower the annual rates bill. An annual rate in the pound ('rate poundage') is fixed each year by the district council and levied together with the regional rate poundage. The amount of annual rates charged is calculated by multiplying the capital value by the aggregate rate poundage, however, the amount may be lower than this due to capping or transitional relief (para. 11.35).

11.35 The capital value of the dwelling is set as the assessed sale value of dwelling as at 1st January 2005, capped to a maximum value of £500,000. However, for NIHE and registered housing association tenants the capital value is substituted by a 'social sector value' which is calculated by the DSD based on the rent paid for the property. The system for assessing rates started on the 1st April 2007 where a household experienced an increase as a result of the change transitional relief will apply and phase the increase in over a three year period.

11.36 Capital values (including substitute social sector values) and the rate poundage can be viewed on-line at Land and Property Services website, *www.lpsni.gov.uk*.

Liability for rates

11.37 One rates bill goes to the owner or occupier of each dwelling. For example:

- the rates bill for NIHE and housing association tenants goes to the NIHE or housing association – and so increases the overall amount payable by the tenant;
- the rates bill for some private sector tenants goes to the landlord – who may include this amount in setting the amount of rent due;
- the rates bill for some private sector tenants goes to the tenant;
- the rates bill for an owner-occupied dwelling goes to the owner-occupier.

Exemptions

11.38 Occupied dwellings are exempt from rates if:

- all the householders are under 18; or
- all the householders were in care before they attained age 16 and are currently all aged under 22; or

- all the householders/occupiers are students; or
- the landlord is a registered charity.

Exemptions are not automatic: an application must be made to the Land and Property Services.

Disability reductions

11.39 The rates bill is reduced by 25% for dwellings which have been adapted or extended because of the occupant's disability. Reductions are not automatic: an application must be made to Land and Property Services.

Rate rebates, rate relief and lone pensioner allowance

11.40 Anyone who is liable to pay rates on their normal home (including tenants whose rent includes an amount towards their landlord's rates) can get any or all of rate rebate, rate relief or lone pensioner allowance. There are two exceptions for rate rebate and rate relief but not lone pensioner allowance. These are:

- certain people who are migrants or recent arrivals in the UK (chapter 20);
- most full-time students (table 21.1).

11.41 A person is eligible for all three of these schemes whether they pay rates direct to Land and Property Services, or via the rent they pay their landlord. Unless a tenant receives a rate bill in their own name, it is always assumed that the rent they pay their landlord includes an element for rates.

11.42 However, in the case of a tenanted dwelling, a rate rebate, rate relief or lone pensioner allowance cannot be awarded until a rates bill is issued. Once it is issued, a rate rebate and rate relief are awarded retrospectively if the claimant notifies the NIHE within one month of receiving it, a time limit which can be extended in special circumstances. Otherwise they are awarded from the Monday after the claimant notifies the NIHE. In the case of lone pensioner allowance, the award will start from the date rates liability commenced, or the date the person qualifies if later.

Rate rebates and eligible rates

What are rate rebates?

11.43 A rate rebate (HB for rates) reduces a claimant's rates. It is worked out in a similar way to HB for rent. It is funded by subsidy payable to Land and Property Services or NIHE. For where to apply for a rate rebate, see paragraphs 1.18 and table 1.5.

11.40 NICBA 129(1)(a); NIHB 8(1)(a),9(1); 10(1),53(1); NIHB60+ 8(1)(a); 9(1),10(1)

11.41 NIHB 12(2), 13(3)(b),(6); NIHB60+ 12(2), 13(3)(b),(6)

Eligible rates

11.44 A claimant's eligible rates is the figure used in calculating his or her entitlement to rate rebate (HB for rates). It is calculated by working through the following steps:

1. Start with the annual rates due on his or her home (paras. 11.34-35) after any capping or transitional relief that may apply;
2. If the claimant is entitled to a disability reduction, use the rates figure after that has been made.
3. Apportion the result if the claimant is a joint occupier (para. 11.46).
4. Convert it to a weekly figure (as described in para. 6.68).

Note that unlike HB for rent, there is no power to restrict the eligible rates if the dwelling is too expensive or too large.

Impact of rates changes on eligible rent

11.45 When a tenant's rent includes an amount for rates (para. 11.41), a change in the rates (such as the new amount applying from each April, or following the award of a disability reduction) means the person's eligible rent changes too. Since there is no duty on the tenant or landlord to advise of changes to rates, the NIHE alters the tenant's HB for rent and HB for rates automatically when advised by Land and Property Services.

Apportionment of eligible rates

11.46 The eligible rates figure is apportioned if:

- someone occupies only part of a rateable unit – for example a lodger or someone living in a multi-occupied property. In this case only the proportion of the rates payable for their accommodation is eligible for a rate rebate;
- two or more people are jointly liability to pay rates – for example in a joint tenancy (see para. 8.9);
- part of the rateable unit is in business use – such as a shop with a flat above. This is done in the same way as for eligible rent (para. 8.11).

Calculating rate rebate

11.47 The method of calculating rate rebates (HB for rates) is given in paragraphs 6.4-15 and 6.68. As with HB for rent, non-dependant charges may apply: see paragraphs 6.17-35 for details. Examples of the calculation are at the end of this chapter.

11.44 NIHB 11(1)(a), 12(3), 78(3); NIHB60+ 11(1)(a), 12(3), 59(3)

11.45 NIHB 12(1),(2); 84(2)(a),(b); NIHB60+; 12(1),(2),65(2)(a),(b)

11.46 NIHB 12(2),(4)-(6); NIHB60+; 12(2),(4)-(6)

Example: Calculation of eligible rates

A dwelling has a capital value of £135,000 in an area where the rate poundage is £0.0057777 per £1 of capital value. Capping and transitional relief do not apply so the annual rates payable are:

£135,000 x 0.0057777 = £780.00

The weekly eligible rates (to the nearest 1p) are therefore:

£780.00 ÷ 365 x 7 =	£14.96 if paid separately from rent or
£780.00 ÷ 52 =	£15.00 if paid along with rent

Awarding rate rebate as a credit or as a payment

11.48 A rate rebate is awarded as a credit to the rates account for the dwelling in question, but there is one exception. The NIHE may choose (at its discretion) to pay HB for rates as an allowance (along with any HB for rent) if:

- the claimant's rent includes an amount for rates (para. 11.41); and
- the claimant qualifies for HB for rent (or would do but for any non-dependant deduction or the application of the taper percentage).

11.49 When HB is paid as an allowance, it is paid to either the claimant or landlord, following the same rules as HB for rent (paras. 16.12-48). In addition to those rules, if the total HB (for rent and rates) is £2 per week or less it can be paid four-weekly; and if it is less than £1 per week it can be paid every six months.

Rate relief

What is rate relief?

11.50 The rate relief scheme was introduced on 1st April 2007 following changes in the assessment of domestic rates from being a theoretical rental value to the open market capital value. Because of the way rate rebates are calculated, people receiving a rate rebate get no financial benefit from a change in their rates. The rate relief scheme gives them an extra reduction to compensate for this.

11.51 Rate relief is not part of the HB scheme, and is funded from the rates themselves rather than from government subsidy. Some people may not be eligible for HB but will qualify for rate relief and as the same information is required from the claimant a full HB assessment is always carried out.

11.48 NIHB 87(2),88,89(5); NIHB60+ 68(2),69,70(5)

Who gets rate relief?

11.52 There is no need to claim rate relief. It is considered automatically for everyone who:

- qualifies for a rate rebate; but
- still has rates to pay – other than any non-dependant deduction or repayment of an overpayment.

So people who get a full rate rebate cannot get rate relief. Nor can people whose only rates due are because of a non-dependant deduction or the repayment of an overpayment. Everyone else who claims a rate rebate can get rate relief. A person who does not qualify for HB can claim rate relief separately if he/she has rates to pay.

Calculating rate relief

11.53 Rate relief is calculated in the same way as a rate rebate – except that:

- rate relief is worked out on the amount of rates remaining after rate rebate has been granted – ignoring any non-dependant deduction;
- if the claimant or partner is aged 60+, the personal allowance in the applicable amount is higher (para. 11.54);
- there is a higher capital limit of £50,000 if the claimant or partner is aged 60 or over (tariff income applies as in HB);
- the taper percentage used in the calculation is 12% of excess income.

Examples of the calculation are given at the end of this chapter.

11.54 The personal allowances for rate relief are:

- for under 60s: the same as in rate rebates;
- for people aged 60+ or whose partner is: £149.50 for a single claimant or lone parent, £218.30 for a couple;
- for people aged 65+ or whose partner is: £172.96 for a single claimant or lone parent, £248.05 for a couple.

Awarding rate relief

11.55 Rate relief is used to reduce the amount of rates payable on the dwelling. For owner-occupiers and private tenants, it is credited to the rates account by Land and Property Services. For NIHE and housing association tenants, it is awarded to the landlord and so reduces the overall rent and rates payable by the claimant.

11.52 NISR 2007/203; NISR 2007/244

11.54 NISR 2007/244

11.55 NISR 2007/203; NISR 2007/204

Reconsiderations and appeals

11.56 The rules about getting a written statement of reasons, requesting a reconsideration, and requesting an appeal, are the same as those relating to HB for rent (chapter 19). Although rate relief is not a social security benefit, an appeal tribunal nonetheless deals with appeals and, whenever practicable, deals with the rate relief appeal at the same time as any HB appeal.

Overpayments of rate relief

11.57 The conditions for recovering overpaid rate relief are the same as those for recovering overpaid HB for rent (paras. 18.10-14).

11.58 Recoverable overpayments of rate relief can be recovered by any lawful method, but the main methods used are:

- charging them back to the rates account;
- deducting them from the claimant's future rate relief.

11.59 A recoverable overpayment of rate relief can be charged back to the rates account. But this method is not normally used in the case of NIHE or housing association tenants, unless the person has died or left and there remains sufficient credit on their account to make recovery from it.

11.60 A recoverable overpayment of rate relief may be deducted from the claimant's future award of rate relief. The deduction is limited to £9.75 per week, increased to £12.80 in a case where fraud has been proved. But this limit does not apply to deductions from lump sum arrears of rate relief. Deductions to recover rate relief overpayments are additional to those to recover HB overpayments.

Lone pensioner allowance

What is lone pensioner allowance?

11.61 Lone pensioner allowance was introduced on 1st April 2008 following a review of domestic rating policy by the Northern Ireland Executive, which concluded that single people over 70 required further assistance to help with rates charges. In some respects it is similar to the single person discount within council tax but applies only to people aged 70 or above. People who do not qualify for either HB or rate relief may qualify for lone pensioner allowance.

11.62 Lone pensioner allowance is not part of either the HB or rate relief schemes and is funded by the Northern Ireland Executive.

11.56 NISR 2007/203; NISR 2007/204

11.57 NISR 2007/203; NISR 2007/204

Who gets lone pensioner allowance?

11.63 Anyone aged 70 or over who lives alone (but see para. 11.64 for details of limited exceptions) and has to pay rates on their normal or only home will receive lone pensioner allowance. The allowance is not means tested; however, it is not awarded automatically, but must be claimed either along with a claim for HB and/or rate relief or separately. If a person qualifies for full HB and/or rate relief they cannot also get lone pensioner allowance as this is based on the rates still left to pay.

Living alone

11.64 In limited circumstances a person can still be classed as living alone and thus qualify for lone pensioner allowance even though someone else lives in their household. This applies in the following circumstances:

- if the person living with the claimant is a resident carer (conditions apply);
- if the person living with the claimant is aged less than 18;
- if the claimant is receiving child benefit for the person;
- if the person living with the claimant is severely mentally impaired (conditions apply).

Calculating lone pensioner allowance

11.65 As lone pensioner allowance is not means tested anyone who qualifies will receive a 20% reduction on the rates charge they have to pay. Where the person also receives any or all of HB, rate relief or a disability reduction the allowance is applied to the amount of rates left to pay. If the person does not receive HB, rate relief or a disability reduction the allowance will be applied to the full rates charge. Examples of lone pensioner allowance calculations are at the end of this chapter.

Awarding lone pensioner allowance

11.66 Like rate relief, lone pensioner allowance is used to reduce the amount of rates payable on the dwelling. For owner-occupiers and private tenants, it is credited to the rate account by Land and Property Services. For NIHE and housing association tenants, it is awarded to the landlord and so reduces the overall rent and rates payable by the claimant.

Overpayments of lone pensioner allowance

11.67 Overpayments of lone pensioner allowance are only likely to occur when the claimant ceases to live alone or no longer has rates to pay. Overpayments of lone pensioner allowance cannot be recovered from either HB or rate relief unless the claimant agrees to this but can be recovered by any other lawful method. In the case of owner-occupiers or private tenants this will most likely be by charging

---

11.63 NISR 2008/124

them back to the rates account. In the case of NIHE or housing association tenants, if the tenant has died or left there may be sufficient credit on their account or assets in an estate to make recovery. In the unlikely event that a person again qualifies for lone pensioner allowance recovery may be effected by deduction from lump sum arrears of the new award.

Appeals

11.68 Appeals relating to lone pensioner allowance will be considered by the Valuation Tribunal and must be made within 28 days of being notified of the decision. This differs from the usual time limit of one month within both the HB and rate relief schemes.

Examples: Rate rebate, rate relief and lone pensioner allowance

A claimant without a non-dependant

A couple in their 40s have no non-dependants. They are not on JSA(IB) or income support. Their income exceeds their applicable amount by £20 per week. Their eligible rates are £15 per week.

	£
Rate rebate (HB for rates)	
Eligible rates	15.00
minus 20% of excess income (20% of £20.00)	– 4.00
equals weekly rate rebate	11.00
Rate relief	
Rates due after rate rebate	4.00
minus 12% of excess income (12% of £20.00)	– 2.40
equals weekly rate relief	1.60

A claimant with a non-dependant

A single claimant in her 50s has a non-dependant son living with her. The claimant is not on JSA(IB) or income support. Her income exceeds her applicable amount by £10 per week. Her eligible rates are £18.00 per week. Her son works full-time with gross income of £400 per week.

Rate rebate (HB for rates)	**£**
Eligible rates	18.00
minus non-dependant deduction	– 6.95
minus 20% of excess income (20% of £10.00)	– 2.00
equals weekly rate rebate	9.05
Rate relief	
Rates due after rate rebate – ignoring non-dependant deduction	2.00
minus 12% of excess income (12% of £10.00)	– 1.20
equals weekly rate relief	0.80

Lone pensioner allowance

A person aged 72 lives alone and has a weekly rates charge of £18. She does not receive either HB or rate relief

	£
Weekly rates to pay	18.00
Minus lone pensioner allowance (20% of £18)	3.60
Net amount to pay	14.40

If the same person receives £10 per week HB and £2 per week rate relief.

	£
Weekly rates to pay	18.00
Minus HB	10.00
Minus rate relief	2.00
Rates left to pay	6.00
Minus lone pensioner allowance (20% of £6)	1.20
Net amount to pay	4.80

12 Applicable amounts

12.1 An applicable amount is the figure used in calculating HB and main CTB to reflect the basic living needs of the claimant and family. This chapter covers:

- personal allowances;
- general rules about additional amounts;
- the detailed rules for each of these in turn; and
- further rules and special cases.

12.2 A claimant's applicable amount is the same for both HB and CTB. It is the total of any personal allowances and additional amounts which apply in their case. 'Applicable amounts' are also known as 'appropriate amounts' (in the case of 60+s). The 'additional amounts' are also known as 'premiums' or 'components'.

All claimants have an applicable amount but for those in receipt of JSA(IB), ESA(IR), IS or guarantee credit it is not required to calculate their HB/CTB as they are entitled to maximum HB/CTB (paras. 6.5 and 13.4). Consequently, this chapter does not apply to these claimants.

12.3 As described in the relevant places in this chapter, there are some differences in the law depending on whether:

- the claimant or any partner is aged 60 or over; and
- the claimant and any partner are both under the age of 60.

Personal allowances

Single people, couples, lone parents and children

12.4 Personal allowances are awarded for the claimant and any other family members (para. 4.11). There are different amounts for single claimants, couples and lone parents. Additions are made for children and young persons (sometimes known as dependants' allowances). The amounts, which vary with age, are given in table 12.1.

Polygamous marriages

12.5 The applicable amount for a claimant in a polygamous marriage (para. 4.23) is the sum of the following. If the following could combine to produce

---

12.2 CBA 135; NICBA 131; HB 22; HB60+ 22; NIHB 20; NIHB60+ 20; CTB 12; CTB60+ 12

12.3 HB 5; HB60+ 5; NIHB 5; NIHB60+ 5; CTB 5; CTB60+ 5

12.4 HB 22(a),(b), sch 3 paras 1,2; HB60+ 22(a),(b), sch 3 paras 1,2; NIHB 20(a),(b), sch 4 paras 1,2; NIHB60+ 20(a),(b), sch 4 paras 1,2; CTB 12(a),(b), sch 1 paras 1,2; CTB60+ 12(a),(b), sch 1 paras 1,2

12.5 HB 23; HB60+ sch 3 para 1; NIHB 21; NIHB60+ sch 4 para 1; CTB 13; CTB60+ sch 1 para 1

more than one result, the result which is most favourable to the claimant applies:

- where none of the partners in a polygamous marriage is aged 60 or over:
  - the personal allowance of £100.95, unless (in HB only) all the members of the polygamous marriage are under 18, in which case £76.90; and
  - £36.65 for each spouse in excess of two;
- where at least one of the partners in a polygamous marriage is aged 60 or over but none of the members of the marriage are over 65:
  - the personal allowance of £198.45; and
  - £68.45 for each spouse in excess of two;
- where at least one of the members of a polygamous marriage is aged 65 or over:
  - the personal allowance of £225.50; and
  - £75.10 for each spouse in excess of two;
- additions to the personal allowance for any child or young person as in any other case including, if appropriate, any premiums in respect of them.
- family premium if there is at least one child or young person;

Any special rules with respect to additional amounts for partners in polygamous marriages are dealt with as they arise in this chapter.

Additional amounts

12.6 Many claimants – but not all – qualify for one or more additional amounts – also known as 'premiums' or 'components'. Table 12.1 lists these and gives their amounts. An additional amount is awarded if its conditions of entitlement are satisfied. Entitlement to many of them is triggered by certain qualifying social security benefits. General points and special rules such as when a person is treated as being 'in receipt' of a qualifying benefit are given in paragraphs 12.41-49. Paragraphs 12.14-40 set out the specific conditions for each additional amount.

How many premiums at once?

12.7 Except as described in the remainder of this chapter, there are no limitations on how many additions can be awarded at a time. However, as mentioned throughout, some can be awarded only if the claimant and any partner are both under the age of 60, whereas others can be awarded regardless of the claimant's or partner's age.

ESA and its impact on HB/CTB

12.8 The biggest change to HB/CTB additional amounts – which took effect on 27th October 2008 – was due to the introduction of employment and support allowance (ESA). ESA is for people with a 'limited capacity for work'. For claims made on or after that date, income-related ESA (ESA(IR)) replaces income support; and contributory ESA (ESA(C)) replaces incapacity benefit.

Table 12.1: Weekly applicable amounts

Personal allowances

Single claimant	aged under 25 – on main phase ESA	£64.30
	aged under 25 – other	£50.95
	aged 25+ but under 60	£64.30
	aged 60+ but under 65	£130.00
	aged 65+	£150.40
Lone parent	aged under 18 – on main phase ESA	£64.30
	aged under 18 – other	£50.95
	aged 18+ but under 60	£64.30
	aged 60+ but under 65	£130.00
	aged 65+	£150.40
Couple	both under 18 – claimant on main phase ESA	£100.95
	both under 18 – other	£76.90
	at least one aged 18+ but both under 60	£100.95
	at least one aged 60+ but both under 65	£198.45
	at least one aged 65+	£225.50
Plus for each dependent child		£56.11

Additional amounts

Family premium	baby rate	£27.80	
	normal rate	£17.30	
Disability premium	single claimant/lone parent	£27.50	*
	couple (one/both qualifying)	£39.15	*
Disabled child premium	each dependent child	£51.24	
Enhanced disability premium	single claimant/lone parent	£13.40	*
	couple (one/both qualifying)	£19.30	*
	each dependent child	£20.65	
Work related activity component	single claimant/lone parent/couple	£25.50	*
Support component	single claimant/lone parent/couple	£30.85	*
Carer premium	claimant or partner or each	£29.50	
Severe disability premium	single rate	£52.85	
	double rate	£105.70	

* *Only awarded when the claimant and any partner are under 60.*

Examples: applicable amounts

Except for the lone parent in the fourth example, none of the following qualifies for any of the premiums for disability or for carers.

Single claimant aged 23

Personal allowance:	
Single claimant aged under 25	£50.95
No additional amounts apply	
Applicable amount	£50.95

Couple with two children aged 13 and 17

The older child is still at school so still counts as a dependant of the couple.

Personal allowances:	
Couple at least one over 18 (and both under 60)	£100.95
Child aged 13	£56.11
Child aged 17	£56.11
Additional amount: family premium (normal rate)	£17.30
Applicable amount	£230.47

Couple aged 38 and 65

Personal allowance:	
Couple at least one aged 65	£225.50
Applicable amount	£225.50

Disabled lone parent with baby

The lone parent is in receipt of the highest rate of the care component of disability living allowance and so qualifies for a disability premium and enhanced disability premium. Her baby is aged under one year.

Personal allowances:	
Lone parent aged over 18 (and under 60)	£64.30
Child	£56.11
Additional amounts:	
Family premium ('baby' rate)	£27.80
Disability premium (single rate)	£27.50
Enhanced disability premium (single rate)	£13.40
Applicable amount	£189.11

12.9 After a 13 week 'assessment period', a claimant's ESA(IR) or ESA(C) goes up by one of the following two amounts:

- claimants get a 'work-related component' added to their ESA if they are capable of 'work-related activity' (preparing for work);
- claimants get a 'support component' added to their ESA if they are not capable of work-related activity.

12.10 This later period is known as the 'main phase' of ESA. In the early months of ESA, many people's ESA assessment was delayed and they did not get their component on time – but in all cases the relevant component must be awarded retrospectively to the start of the claimant's 14th week on ESA (and this is then also done for HB/CTB: para. 12.20; and see also para. 12.41 for people getting national insurance credits but no actual ESA).

12.11 The two 'components' were introduced (for balancing reasons) into HB and CTB at the same time (paras. 12.18-19 below). They are irrelevant to HB/CTB if the clamant or partner is on ESA(IR) (because for them the authority does not assess an applicable amount), but do affect HB/CTB if the claimant or partner is on ESA(C).

'Better off' problems

12.12 Unfortunately, the new HB/CTB components complicated the rules about disability premium and enhanced disability premium (paras. 12.21, 12.29). Then, even worse, several 'better off' problems accidentally resulted – in the sense that a couple can be better or worse off (sometimes by over £30 per week: see the 'better off' example given later) depending on which of them is the claimant for HB/CTB purposes and which the partner. They are all described below.

12.13 The result of these 'better off' problems is that authorities have been advised to alert couples when they would be better off if they swapped the claimant role (DWP circular A11/2008). It would, however, be straightforward to amend the law to avoid the problems and the DWP may do this.

Family premium

12.14 The condition for this premium is that there is at least one child or young person in the claimant's family – whether the claimant is in a couple or is a lone parent. The terms 'child', 'young person', 'family', 'couple' and 'lone parent' are defined in paragraphs 4.10-40.

12.15 There are two main rates of this premium (and see also para. 12.16):

- the 'baby' rate is awarded to couples and lone parents with at least one child aged under one year;
- the normal rate is awarded to other couples and lone parents (with at least one child or young person).

12.14 HB sch 3 para 3; HB60+ sch 3 para 3; NIHB sch 4 para 3; NIHB60+ sch 4 para 3; CTB sch 1 para 3; CTB 60+ sch 1 para 3

12.16 Higher 'protected rates' of family premium apply to certain lone parents aged under 60. They are £32.70 ('baby' protected rate) and £22.20 (normal protected rate). The conditions are in the next paragraph.

12.17 A lone parent qualifies for the protected rate if they are aged under 60 and on 5th April 1998 they were entitled to HB or CTB and satisfied the conditions for the (then existing) lone parent rate of the family premium. The protected rate ceases permanently to apply as soon as any of the following apply after 5th April 1998:

- there is a break in their entitlement to HB or CTB (ignoring breaks due only to rent-free periods);
- they ceased to be a lone parent at any time since that date;
- they became entitled to JSA(IB) or IS, or ceased to be entitled to both those benefits, at any time since that date; and
- they reached the age of 60 or became entitled to a disability premium or either of the following components at any time since that date.

Work-related activity component and support component

12.18 For a single claimant or lone parent, the conditions for these two components are:

- the claimant must be under 60;
- the claimant is awarded the work-related activity component in their HB/CTB applicable amount whenever (and only when) they are awarded it in their ESA(C);
- the claimant is awarded the support component in their HB/CTB applicable amount whenever (and only when) they are awarded it in their ESA(C).

12.19 For a couple (or polygamous marriage) the rules are as follows:

- both of them must be under 60;
- if only one partner in a couple gets a component in their ESA(C), they get (one lot of) that component in their HB/CTB applicable amount;
- if both partners in a couple qualify for the same component in their ESA(C), they get (one lot of) that component in their HB/CTB applicable amount;
- if in a couple one partner qualifies for one component in their ESA(C) and the other partner qualifies for the other component in their ESA(C), they get (one lot of) the claimant's component in their HB/CTB applicable amount.

The last point leads to a 'better off' problem – because it makes a difference which one in the couple is the claimant for HB/CTB purposes (paras. 12.12-13).

12.16 HB sch 3 para 3(3)-(5); NIHB sch 4 para 3(3)-(5); CTB sch 1 para 3(3)-(5)

12.18 HB sch 3 paras 21-24; NIHB sch 4 paras 21-24; CTB sch 1 paras 21-24

12.19 HB sch 3 paras 21-24; NIHB sch 4 paras 21-24; CTB sch 1 paras 21-24

12.20 If a person's ESA assessment is delayed with the effect that their ESA component is awarded retrospectively (para. 12.10), their HB/CTB component is also awarded retrospectively to the start of the claimant's 14th week on ESA. This does not normally lead to an over- or under-payment of HB/CTB.

Disability premium

12.21 The conditions for a disability premium are as follows – and in the case of a couple, the couple rate is awarded even if only one partner fulfils the conditions:

- the claimant and any partner must be under 60;
- the claimant (or in the case of a couple, either partner) must count as 'disabled or long-term sick' in one of the ways described in paragraphs 12.22-24 – but note that it must be the claimant, not the partner, in the cases described in para. 12.24; and
- the claimant must not be on ESA(C), nor during a period of disqualification from ESA(C) – but note that it does not matter if the partner is on ESA(C).

The last point leads to a 'better off' problem (as illustrated in the example) because it makes a difference which one in the couple is the claimant for HB/CTB purposes (paras. 12.12-13).

Example: A 'better off' problem for couples

Information

A couple (both under 60) meet the condition for a disability premium which relates to being disabled or long-term sick (e.g. one of them is on DLA or is registered blind), but one partner in the couple is on ESA(C).

Entitlement to additions in the HB/CTB applicable amount

This depends on which partner is the HB/CTB claimant.

(a) If the HB/CTB claimant is on ESA(C):

their HB/CTB applicable amount does not include a disability premium (at any point), but it does include a work-related activity or support component from the claimant's 14th week on ESA(C).

(b) If the HB/CTB partner is on ESA(C):

their HB/CTB applicable amount includes a couple-rate disability premium (from the beginning), but it never includes a work-related activity or support component.

Conclusion

So they are better off if (b) applies to them – by over £25 per week in HB and over £5 per week in CTB, during the first 13 weeks on ESA(C) (and by a lower amount after that).

12.21 HB sch 3 para 12; NIHB sch 4 para 12; CTB sch 1 para 12

'Disabled or long-term sick'

12.22 The following are the ways of counting as 'disabled or long-term sick' in order to qualify for a disability premium (para. 12.21). They are that the claimant or any partner:

(a) is blind or has recently regained their sight (paras. 12.45-47); or

(b) receives disability living allowance; or

(c) receives a benefit which is treated as attendance allowance (para. 12.44); or

(d) receives war pensioner's mobility supplement;

(e) receives the disability element or severe disability element of working tax credit; or

(f) has an invalid vehicle supplied by the NHS or gets DWP payments for car running costs; or

(g) is incapable of work and satisfies the further conditions in either of the next two paragraphs.

In the case of items (b) and (c) special rules apply where the qualifying benefit is lost after a period in hospital – see paragraph 12.49 and table 12.3 for details.

12.23 The claimant or any partner counts as 'disabled or long-term sick' if they are 'in receipt' of (para. 12.41) severe disablement allowance or incapacity benefit payable at the long-term rate (which starts after 52 weeks of incapacity for work), or are terminally ill and receive it at the short-term higher rate (which starts after 28 weeks of incapacity for work). See also paragraph 12.48 where the qualifying person starts on a government training scheme.

12.24 As an alternative to paragraphs 12.22-23, the claimant (but not the claimant's partner) counts as disabled or long-term sick and qualifies for the disability premium if they:

- are incapable of work; and
- have been incapable of work for a 'qualifying period' (calculated as described below) of:
  - 28 weeks (196 days) if they are terminally ill, or
  - 52 weeks (364 days) in any other case.

After the qualifying period is completed, there are further 'linking rules' (described below). See paragraph 12.48 where the qualifying person starts on a government training scheme.

12.25 This way of qualifying for a disability premium helps (para. 12.24) people who are incapable of work but who do not get incapacity benefit. For couples, it

12.22 HB sch 3 para 13(1)(a),(b),(2); NIHB sch 4 para 13(1)(a),(b),(2); CTB sch 1 para 13(1)(a),(b),(2)

12.23 HB sch 3 para 13(1)(a)(i),(7); NIHB sch 4 para 13(1)(a)(i),(7); CTB sch 1 para 13(1)(a)(i),(7)

12.24 HB sch 3 para 13(1)(b); NIHB sch 4 para 13(1)(b); CTB sch 1 para 13(1)(b)

must be the claimant – not their partner – who qualifies. It is therefore important which partner makes the claim (para. 5.4).

12.26 'Incapable of work' means the same here as it does for incapacity benefit. Broadly, during the first 28 weeks the person must demonstrate that they are incapable of following their normal job and thereafter (or from the outset if they have no normal occupation) any work. Broadly, a person is 'terminally ill' if their death can be expected within six months. The decision about whether a person is incapable of work is always made by a Decision Maker at the Jobcentre Plus office (*R(H) 3/06* and see GM para. BW3.148).

The 'qualifying period' and the 'linking rules'

12.27 The qualifying period (para. 12.24) need not be continuous. Any number of periods can be added together so long as the gap between each is eight weeks or less (104 weeks or less, in the case of a 'welfare to work beneficiary': table 12.2). A 'gap' means a period during which the person either is capable of work or is disqualified from incapacity benefit. Once a person has completed the qualifying period, there are linking rules as follows:

- the claimant does not qualify for a disability premium during a gap;
- after a gap of eight weeks or less (104 weeks or less, in the case of a 'welfare to work' beneficiary: table 12.2), the person qualifies for a disability premium straight away;
- after a gap of more than eight weeks (104 weeks in the case of a 'welfare to work' beneficiary), the person does not qualify for a disability premium until they have completed a fresh qualifying period.

Breaks in entitlement to HB or CTB during the qualifying period or after it have no effect on this rule.

Disabled child premium

12.28 The condition for this premium to be applied is that a child or young person in the family:

- is blind or has recently regained their sight (paras. 12.45-47); or
- receives disability living allowance (either component payable at any rate).

A disabled child premium is awarded for each child or young person who qualifies. If the child/young person dies the premium continues for eight weeks following the death. Special rules apply if the child is in hospital – see paragraph 12.49 and table 12.3 for details.

12.27 HB sch 3 paras 11(5), 13(3),(4),(6),(8); NIHB sch 4 paras 11(5), 13(3),(4),(6),(8); CTB sch 1 paras 11(5), 13(3),(4),(6),(8)

12.28 HB sch 3 para 16; HB60+ sch 3 para 8; NIHB sch 4 para 16; NIHB60+ sch 4 para 8; CTB sch 1 para 16; CTB60+ sch 1 para 8

Table 12.2: Definition of 'welfare to work beneficiary'

For all HB/CTB purposes, this means a person who:

- has been incapable of work for at least 28 weeks (196 days); and
- has stopped receiving one of the benefits or advantages which is described in paragraphs 7.18 and 12.27 and is dependent on that person being incapable of work; and
- has – within seven days of ceasing to be incapable of work – started:
  - remunerative work (paras. 6.27-29 onwards), or
  - Work Based Training for Adults (in England and Wales), or
  - Training for Work (in Scotland); and
- has notified the DWP of the fact that he or she has started work, and has done so within one month of the date on which he or she ceased to claim that he or she is incapable of work (or, in certain cases, has won a social security appeal relating to this).

Such a person counts as a welfare to work beneficiary for 104 weeks only. The DWP is responsible for informing the claimant that protection applies (GM para. BW3.159).

Enhanced disability premium

12.29 This premium can be awarded in respect of a child or young person in the family and/or in respect of the claimant or partner if they are both aged under 60. Two or more of these premiums are awarded if appropriate – for example, if a claimant or partner qualifies and also one or more children or young persons. Special rules apply where disability living allowance is lost following a period in hospital (para. 12.49 and table 12.3).

12.30 The conditions for an enhanced disability premium in the case of the claimant or partner are as follows – and in the case of a couple who meet the conditions, it is always the couple rate which is awarded (never the single rate):

- the claimant and any partner must be under age 60; and either
- the claimant (or in the case of a couple, either partner) receives the highest rate of the care component of disability living allowance; or
- the claimant qualifies for an ESA support component (paras 12.9, 12.19).

The last point leads to a 'better off' problem because it makes a difference which one in the couple is the claimant for HB/CTB purposes (paras. 12.12-13).

T 12.2 HB sch 3 para 13(8)

12.29 HB sch 3 para 15; HB60+ sch 3 para 7; NIHB sch 4 para 15; NIHB60+ sch 4 para 7; CTB sch 1 para 15; CTB60+ sch 1 para 7

12.31 The condition for an enhanced disability premium in the case of a child or young person is that they receive the highest rate of the care component of disability living allowance.

Severe disability premium

12.32 There are three conditions for this premium:

- the claimant must be receiving one of the following qualifying benefits:
  - the middle or highest rate of the care component of disability living allowance, or
  - attendance allowance at either rate, or
  - a benefit which is treated as attendance allowance (para. 12.44); and
- they must have no non-dependants (but see paragraph 12.34 below for exceptions); and
- no-one must be receiving carer's allowance in respect of them (but see paragraphs 12.35 and 12.41 for circumstances where the carer will be treated as either in receipt or not in receipt of carer's allowance).

In the case of a couple, except where one member is blind (para. 12.45), both members must be in receipt of a qualifying benefit. Special rules apply where a qualifying benefit is lost following a period in hospital (paras. 12.33, 12.35, 12.49 and table 12.3).

12.33 A single claimant or lone parent who satisfies all three conditions gets the single rate of severe disability premium. In the case of a couple or a polygamous marriage, a severe disability premium is awarded as follows:

- if both members of a couple satisfy all three conditions, they get the double rate;
- if both members of a couple satisfy the first two conditions but only one satisfies the third condition, they get the single rate;
- if, in a couple, the claimant only satisfies all three conditions, and their partner is blind or recently regained their sight (paras. 12.45-47), they get the single rate. In this case, if the 'wrong' partner makes the claim, they should be advised to 'swap the claimant role';
- if a couple have been getting the double rate, but one partner then ceases to satisfy the first condition because of having been in hospital for four weeks, they get the single rate from that point;
- in the case of a polygamous marriage, the double rate of severe disability premium if all members of the marriage satisfy all three conditions in paragraph 12.32; the single rate if all members of the marriage satisfy the

12.32 HB sch 3 para 14(2); HB60+ sch 3 para 6(2); NIHB sch 4 para 14(2); NIHB60+ sch 4 para 6(2); CTB sch 1 para 14(2); CTB60+ sch 1 para 6(2)

first two of those conditions but someone receives a carer's allowance in respect of caring for one of them; and the single rate if the claimant satisfies all three conditions and all the other members of the marriage are blind or recently regained their sight (paras. 12.45-47).

12.34 For the purposes of determining the second condition, the following persons do not prevent the award of a severe disability premium:

- any person aged under 18 or who is excluded from the definition of a non-dependant (paras, 4.42-43);
- non-dependants who are blind or recently regained their sight (paras. 12.45-47);
- non-dependants receiving:
  - the middle or highest rate of the care component of disability living allowance, or
  - attendance allowance, or
  - a benefit which is treated as attendance allowance (para. 12.44).

12.35 For the purpose of determining whether the severely disabled person has a carer receiving carer's allowance in respect of them (para. 12.32) the following considerations apply:

- the carer will not be in receipt of carer's allowance if it is overlapped by other benefits (paras 12.41 and 12.43);
- a backdated award of carer's allowance is ignored as regards any period before the first payment is made: in other words the backdated part does not cause an overpayment;
- in the case of couples or polygamous marriages the carer will be treated as in receipt of a carer's allowance if they have lost it because the claimant or the partner they are caring for has been in hospital for four weeks or more. This will ensure that a couple in receipt of the single rate will continue to receive it at the same rate when one member goes into hospital (paras 12.32-34);
- the carer will be treated as if they are in receipt of carer's allowance if it is not awarded because of the loss of benefit rules following certain benefit fraud convictions.

12.33 HB sch 3 para 14(3); HB60+ sch 3 para 6(3); NIHB sch 4 para 14(3); NIHB60+ sch 4 para 6(3); CTB sch 1 para 14(3); CTB60+ sch 1 para 6(3)

12.34 HB sch 3 para 14(4); HB60+ sch 3 para 6(6); NIHB sch 4 para 14(4); NIHB60+ sch 4 para 6(6); CTB sch 1 para 14(4); CTB60+ sch 1 para 6(6)

12.35 HB sch 3 paras 14(5)-(7),19; HB60+ sch 3 paras 6(7)-(8),11; NIHB sch 4 paras 14(5)-(7),19; NIHB60+ sch 4 paras 6(7)-(8),11; CTB sch 1 paras 14(5)-(7),19; CTB60+ sch 1 paras 6(7)-(8),11

Example: Severe disability premium, etc

A husband and wife are both under 60 and both receive the middle rate of the care component of disability living allowance. Neither of them is or has recently been registered or certified blind. Their daughter of 17 is in full-time employment and lives with them. Their son lives elsewhere and receives carer's allowance for caring for the husband. No-one receives carer's allowance for the wife.

Disability premium: Because of receiving disability living allowance, they are awarded the couple rate of disability premium.

Enhanced disability premium: Because they get the middle (not the highest) rate of the care component of disability living allowance, this cannot be awarded.

Severe disability premium:

- Both receive the appropriate type of disability living allowance.
- Although their daughter is a non-dependant, she is under 18.
- Someone receives carer's allowance for caring for only one of them.

So they are awarded the single rate of severe disability premium (for the second reason in para. 12.33).

Carer premium

12.36 The condition to qualify for this premium is that the claimant (or, in the case of a couple, either partner) is entitled to (paras. 12.38, 12.41) carer's allowance or was entitled to carer's allowance within the past eight weeks.

12.37 A single claimant who satisfies the condition gets one carer premium. A couple will get one or two carer premiums, one if one of them fulfils the condition, two if both do. In the case of a polygamous marriage a carer premium will be awarded for each partner that satisfies the conditions.

12.38 A claimant only has to be 'entitled' and not 'in receipt' so where carer's allowance is overlapped by another benefit (see examples) that would be sufficient. Further, once a person has claimed carer's allowance and their entitlement has been established (whether or not they receive it) it continues indefinitely until they no longer satisfy the conditions for it (e.g. the person being cared for dies or the carer starts work). Note that it does not matter whether their original claim for carer's allowance was made before their claim for HB/CTB: they will continue to be 'entitled' to carer's allowance and qualify for the premium without the need to make a further claim for carer's allowance *(CIS/367/2003)*.

12.36 HB sch 3 paras 7(2),17; HB60+ sch 3 paras 5(2),9; NIHB sch 4 paras 7(2),17; NIHB60+ sch 4 paras 5(2),9; CTB sch 1 paras 7(2),17; CTB60+ sch 1 paras 5(2),9

12.39 A person will be treated as in receipt of carer's allowance if they lose it as a result of taking part in a government training scheme (para. 12.48).

Interaction of carer and severe disability premium

12.40 Although entitlement to carer's allowance results in the award of a carer premium for the carer, the person cared for may lose a severe disability premium (though not retrospectively: para. 12.35). However this happens only if the carer's allowance (or part of it) is actually being paid to the carer (para. 12.41) – and not in the situation illustrated in the second example. It is therefore possible for a couple who care for each other to qualify for a severe disability premium (at the single or double rate) and two carer premiums.

Example: Carer premium and overlapping benefits

Claimant over age 65

A claimant and her partner are both aged over 80 and in receipt of retirement pension. She looks after her partner who has been in receipt of attendance allowance since 7th February 2009. On 12th February 2009 she made a claim for carer's allowance and was notified by the DWP that she was entitled to carer's allowance but it could not be paid because it was overlapped by her retirement pension (in other words, payment of the latter prevents payment of the former).

On 7th April 2009 she makes a claim for HB/CTB for the first time and is awarded HB/CTB from 12th April 2009 (para. 5.51). The award includes the carer premium. If her partner subsequently dies, she would no longer be entitled to carer's allowance, but the premium would continue for a further eight weeks.

Claimant under 65

A claimant aged 33 is in receipt of incapacity benefit. He cares for his severely disabled sister who receives the high care rate of disability living allowance. She lives alone in her own flat. He claims carer's allowance and is entitled to it but it cannot be paid because it is overlapped by his incapacity benefit. Once having claimed carer's allowance he remains 'entitled' to it indefinitely until such time as he no longer meets the conditions for it (e.g. he starts work, becomes a student or his sister dies or no longer qualifies for disability living allowance). While he remains entitled to carer's allowance he should be awarded the carer premium on his HB/CTB without the need for a further claim for carer's allowance even if there are breaks in his HB/CTB award. Note that his sister would also be entitled to the severe disability premium because although he is 'entitled' to carer's allowance he is not 'in receipt' of it (para 12.41).

12.40 HB sch 3 para 19; HB60+ sch 3 para 11; NIHB sch 4 para 19; NIHB60+ sch 4 para 11; CTB sch 1 para 19; CTB60+ sch 1 para 11

General rules and special cases

Being 'in receipt' of a benefit including 'main phase ESA'

12.41 Receipt of a state benefit forms part of the condition for many of the rules in this chapter. For these purposes, a person is 'in receipt' of a benefit only if it is paid in respect of himself or herself, and only during the period for which it is awarded. Except as described in paragraph 12.43 below, a person will not be in receipt where they are entitled to that benefit but it cannot be paid due to the overlapping benefit rules.

A further rule applies for 'main phase ESA' (para. 12.10). For the purposes of qualifying for the personal allowances (table 12.1), a claimant counts as being 'on main phase ESA', in the 14th and subsequent weeks of ESA, even if they are being awarded only national insurance credits (but no payments of ESA itself) as a result of their ESA claim.

DWP concessionary payments

12.42 For the purpose of entitlement to any premium, a DWP concessionary payment compensating for non-payment of any qualifying benefit is treated as if it were that benefit.

Overlapping social security benefits

12.43 Where a claimant is entitled to a qualifying benefit but does not receive it because of the rules about overlapping social security benefits (for example if widow's pension is payable instead of incapacity benefit) then the claimant will not normally be treated as being in receipt of the qualifying benefit except in the following circumstances:

- if they qualify for the carer's premium (para. 12.36);
- if they qualified for that premium before the relevant qualifying benefit was overlapped. In such cases they will continue to be treated as in receipt of the qualifying benefit during any period in which they would be in receipt of that benefit but for the overlapping benefit rules. This rule protects claimants from a reduction in their benefit merely because they became entitled to an overlapping benefit at some later date;
- if the qualifying benefit is only partially overlapped (i.e. the overlapping benefit is paid at a rate which is less than the qualifying benefit).

12.41 HB sch 3 para 19; HB60+ sch 3 para 11; NIHB sch 4 para 19; NIHB60+ sch 4 para 11; CTB sch 1 para 19; CTB60+ sch 1 para 11

12.42 HB sch 3 para 18; HB60+ sch 3 para 10; NIHB sch 4 para 18; NIHB60+ sch 4 para 10; CTB sch 1 para 18; CTB60+ sch 1 para 10

12.43 HB sch 3 paras 7,19; HB60+ sch 3 paras 5,11; NIHB sch 4 paras 7,19; NIHB60+ sch 4 paras 5,11; CTB sch 1 paras 7,19; CTB60+ sch 1 paras 5,11

Benefits treated as attendance allowance

12.44 A person will be treated as in receipt of attendance allowance (paras. 6.19, 12.22, 12.32, 12.34, 13.52 and 13.62) if they receive any type of increase for attendance paid with an industrial injuries benefit or war disablement pension. Qualifying payments include constant attendance allowance, 'old cases' attendance payments, severe disablement occupational allowance and exceptionally severe disablement allowance (GM BW2 annex B para. 7).

Meaning of blind or recently regained sight

12.45 For the purpose of determining whether a non-dependant deduction applies (para. 6.19) or entitlement to certain premiums in this chapter (paras. 12.22, 12.28, 12.32-33) a person is 'blind' if they satisfy the appropriate condition in paragraph 12.46 or will be treated as blind if they have recently regained their sight (para. 12.47).

12.46 A person is blind if:

- in England or Wales, they are blind and are registered as such with the local authority social services department; or
- in Scotland, they are certified blind and are registered as such with the local authority social services department; or
- in Northern Ireland, they are blind and are registered as such with the Health and Social Services Board.

12.47 A person who has ceased to be registered as blind (para. 12.46) as a result of having recently regained their sight will continue to be treated as blind for a further 28 weeks following the date on which they were removed from the register.

People on training courses or in receipt of a training allowance

12.48 Once a person qualifies for the disability premium by virtue of being incapable of work (paras. 12.23 and 12.24) or the carer premium by virtue of being in receipt of carer's allowance (para. 12.36), if they go on a government-run or approved training course (para. 13.123) or receive a training allowance, they are treated as if they continue to satisfy the relevant condition. This rule avoids creating a disincentive to training.

People in hospital

12.49 Certain premiums (e.g. severe disability and carer) may be lost as a result of losing a qualifying benefit after a period in hospital – see table 12.3 for details. In

---

12.44 HB 2(1); HB60+ 2(1); NIHB 2(1); NIHB60+ 2(1); CTB 2(1); CTB60+ 2(1)

12.45 HB sch 3 para 13; HB60+ sch 3 para 13; NIHB sch 4 para 13; NIHB60+ sch 4 para 13; CTB sch 1 para 13; CTB 60+ sch 1 para 13

12.48 HB sch 3 para 7(1)(b), 13(5); HB60+ sch 3 para 5(1)(b); NIHB sch 4 para 7(1)(b), 13(5); NIHB60+ sch 4 para 5(1)(b); CTB sch 1 para 7(1)(b), 13(5); CTB60+ sch 1 para 5(1)(b)

addition, after a continuous period in hospital of 52 weeks the claimant's right to benefit will be lost altogether (paras. 3.3, 3.32), or in the case of any dependants (adults or children) they are likely to cease to be treated as a member of the family (paras. 4.24, 4.31). In both cases this will override any special rules in table 12.3.

Table 12.3: Loss of certain premiums after a period in hospital

Disability, disabled child and enhanced disability premium (paras. 12.24 and 12.28-31)

- Where the claimant/partner/child loses their disability living allowance (including in the case of the disability premium one of the benefits in paragraph 12.44) solely because they have been in hospital for four weeks* (12 weeks in the case of a child) or more the relevant premium will continue or, in the case of a new claim, is still awarded.

Severe disability premium (para. 12.32)

- In the case of a single claimant or a lone parent where payment of a qualifying benefit is lost because they have been in hospital for four weeks* then the premium will be lost.
- In the case of couples or polygamous marriages where one or more members would be in receipt of a qualifying benefit but for the fact they have been in hospital for four weeks* they will continue to be treated as in receipt of that benefit and the premium will continue to be awarded – see also paragraph 12.35.

Carer premium (para. 12.36)

- Where a carer goes into hospital, entitlement to carer's allowance is not normally lost until after 12 weeks, after which the carer premium will continue for a further eight weeks (making 20 in total).
- Where a disabled person has been in hospital for four weeks* (12 in the case of a child) they will lose their disability living allowance/attendance allowance or equivalent benefit with the result that their carer will lose entitlement to carer's allowance. The carer premium will continue for a further eight weeks (para. 12.36).

* The four/twelve week period may not be continuous but may be made up of two or more distinct periods which are less than 29 days apart.

T 12.3 HB sch 3 paras 13(1)(a)(iii), 14(5)(a), 15(1),16(a),17(2); HB60+ sch 3 paras 6(7)(a),7,8(a),9(2); NIHB sch 4; paras 13(1)(a)(iii),14(5)(a),15(1),16(a),17(2); NIHB60+ sch 4 paras 6(7)(a),7,8(a),9(2); CTB sch 1 paras 13(1)(a)(iii),14(5)(a),15(1),16(a),17(2); CTB60+ sch1 paras 6(7)(a),7,8(a),9(2)

13 Income and capital

13.1 This and the following two chapters describe how income and capital are dealt with in the assessment of HB and main CTB. Chapters 14 and 15 give additional information relating to employed earners and the self-employed. This chapter covers:

- how different rules apply for different groups of claimants;
- general matters;
- benefits, pensions, and other state help;
- the home, property and possessions;
- savings and investments;
- trust funds and awards for personal injury;
- other items of income and capital;
- notional income and capital; and
- the separate rules used for claimants on savings credit.

13.2 The claimant is treated as having the income and capital of any partner and all references in this chapter to the income or capital of a claimant should be read as also referring to the income or capital of a partner (para. 13.6). The income and capital of a child or young person is always disregarded.

The different rules for different groups of claimants

Second adults and non-dependants

13.3 Income and capital are assessed differently for all purposes relevant to second adult rebate (para. 6.59) and to non-dependant deductions (paras. 6.23-25); this chapter does not apply in such cases.

Claimants on JSA(IB), ESA(IR), IS or guarantee credit

13.4 If a claimant is on JSA(IB), ESA(IR), IS or guarantee credit (or his or her partner is), the whole of his or her (and any partner's) income and capital is fully disregarded. There are no exceptions whatsoever. The remainder of this chapter therefore does not apply in such cases. (Para. 6.4 shows how their entitlement to HB/CTB is assessed.) If the claimant or partner receives arrears of these benefits

---

13.4 HB sch 4 para 12, sch 5 paras 4,5, sch 6 paras 5,6; HB60+ 26;
NIHB sch 5 para 12, sch 6 paras 4,5, sch 7 paras 5,6; NIHB60+ 24;
CTB sch 3 para 12, sch 4 paras 5,6, sch 5 paras 5,6; CTB60+ 16

all their income and capital are disregarded for the period that they cover and thereafter are treated as capital (para. 13.11) which is usually disregarded for one year (para. 13.38).

Claimants on savings credit

13.5 If a claimant is on savings credit (or his or her partner is), there are special rules for assessing income and capital. The rules for people on savings credit are in paragraphs 13.157-164.

Other cases: whose income and capital counts

13.6 In all cases other than the above (paras. 13.3-5), for the purposes of assessing HB and CTB, a claimant is treated as possessing any income and capital belonging to:

- the claimant themself; and
- any partner.

13.7 If it appears that a claimant (not on JSA(IB), ESA(IR), IS or guarantee credit) and non-dependant have entered into arrangements to take advantage of the HB or CTB scheme, the authority may treat the claimant as possessing the non-dependant's income and capital (instead of, not as well as, their own). This is very rare.

Differences in assessment depending on age

13.8 The rules for people aged 60+ (or whose partner is) are different from those for people aged under 60 (and whose partner is). While the two sets of regulations frequently produce the same effect, there are some differences (e.g. the amount of disregard for income from (sub-)tenants: table 13.2). The rules and differences are given at the relevant places in the remainder of this and the next two chapters.

13.9 In particular the approach to which types of income do and do not count in the assessment of HB/CTB is different for the two age groups:

- if the claimant or any partner is aged 60+, nothing counts as income unless the law says it does (an approach which suits computers);
- if the claimant and any partner are under 60, everything counts as income unless the law says it does not (an approach which makes it pointless to create imaginative new kinds of income).

13.6 HB 25,45; HB60+ 25; NIHB 22,42; NIHB60+ 23; CTB 15,35; CTB60+ 15

13.7 HB 26; HB60+ 24; NIHB 23; NIHB60+ 22; CTB 16; CTB 60+ 14

13.8 HB 27, 44; HB60+ 28; NIHB 24, 41; NIHB60+ 26; CTB 17, 34; CTB60+ 18

13.9 HB 31(1); HB60+ 29(1); NIHB 28(1); NIHB60+ 27(1); CTB 21(1); CTB60+ 19(1)

Definitions and general matters

Distinguishing capital from income

13.10 The distinction between income and capital is usually straightforward. Typical examples are in table 13.1. If a difficulty arises, the DWP advises (GM paras. BW1.70-71): 'As a general rule, capital includes all categories of holdings which have a clear monetary value... A payment of capital can normally be distinguished from income because it is (i) made without being tied to a period, and (ii) made without being tied to any past payment, and (iii) not intended to form part of a series of payments.'

13.11 A commissioner has confirmed that the HB/CTB regulations do not (except in the case of income for 60+s: para. 13.9) provide a definition of income or capital; instead they 'operate at the stage after the money has been classified' *(CH/1561/2005)*. In considering how income can turn into capital, the commissioner (agreeing with R*(SB) 2/83* and *R(IS) 3/93*) held: 'A payment of income is treated as income when received. It remains income for the period in which it is paid. Any surplus remaining at the end of that period metamorphoses [changes] into capital.' (The case was about social security benefits but applies to other regular payments of income: para. 13.94.)

Which types of income and capital count

13.12 As described in the later parts of this chapter, some types of income and capital are wholly disregarded; some are partly disregarded; and some are counted in full (table 13.1). Also, in some cases a claimant can be treated as having income or capital he or she does not in fact possess: this is known as 'notional' income or capital (para. 13.142).

Why capital is assessed

13.13 A claimant's capital is first assessed under the rules in this chapter, then taken into account as follows:

- if it amounts to more than £16,000, the claimant is not entitled to HB or main CTB at all; otherwise
- the first £6,000 is completely ignored in the assessment of HB and main CTB;
- the remainder up to £16,000 is treated as generating 'tariff income' (para. 13.14).

The £6,000 and £16,000 figures are called the 'lower capital limit' and 'upper capital limit'. The lower capital limit is expected to increase to £10,000 for 60+s from November 2009 (Budget report, April 2009).

13.13 HB 43,52; HB60+ 29(2),43; NIHB 40,49; NIHB60+ 27(2),41; CTB 33,42; CTB60+ 19(2),33

Table 13.1: Examples of capital and income

Capital which is (wholly or partly) taken into account

- Savings in a bank, etc
- National Savings Certificates, stocks and shares
- Property (unless it falls within one of the numerous disregards)
- Redundancy pay (with some exceptions)
- Tax refunds

Capital which is disregarded

- The home a claimant owns and lives in
- A self-employed claimant's business assets
- Arrears of certain state benefits
- Certain compensation payments
- A life insurance policy which has not been cashed in

Income which is (wholly or partly) taken into account

- Earnings from a job or from self-employment
- Pensions
- Certain state benefits (e.g. contribution-based jobseeker's allowance, retirement pension)
- Rent received from a sub-tenant or boarder in the claimant's home
- Tariff income from capital

Income which is disregarded

- Reimbursement of expenses wholly incurred in the course of a job
- Certain state benefits (e.g. disability living allowance, attendance allowance)
- Charitable or voluntary payments
- Maintenance received for a child
- Fostering payments

These are just some examples, and are simplified. The detailed rules are given later in this chapter.

Tariff income

13.14 'Tariff income' is assessed as follows (and illustrated in the examples):

- deduct £6,000 from the total amount of assessed capital;
- then divide the remainder by 250 if the claimant and any partner are aged under 60, but 500 if the claimant or any partner is aged 60+;
- then, if the result is not an exact multiple of £1, round the result up to the next whole £1. This is the claimant's weekly tariff income.

Examples: Calculating tariff income

Claimant under 60

A single claimant aged 59 has capital, assessed under the rules in this chapter, of £8,085.93.

This first £6,000 is disregarded, leaving a remainder of £2,085.93. Divide the remainder by 250 and round the answer up to the next whole £1. The claimant has tariff income of £9.

Claimant aged 60+

A single claimant aged 6 has capital, assessed under the rules in this chapter, of £8,085.93.

This first £6,000 is disregarded, leaving a remainder of £2,085.93. Divide the remainder by 500 and round the answer up to the next whole £1. The claimant has tariff income of £5.

How capital is assessed

13.15 The whole of a claimant's capital (including that of any partner) is taken into account from the date it is received (but see para. 13.17), unless it is disregarded as described in this chapter.

Valuing capital in general

13.16 The following rule applies whenever a property, shares, or anything else has to be valued for HB/CTB purposes. Other parts of this chapter mention considerations that also have to be taken into account for specific items. The rule has three steps:

- take the current market or surrender value of the capital item;
- then disregard 10% if selling it would involve costs;
- then disregard any debt or charge secured against it.

Other than secured debts, a claimant's debts (e.g. rent arrears) cannot be set off against their capital *(CH/3729/2007)*.

13.15 HB 44; HB60+ 44; NIHB 41; NIHB60+ 42; CTB 34; CTB60+ 34

13.16 HB 47; HB60+ 45; NIHB 44; NIHB60+ 43; CTB 37; CTB60+ 35

13.17 In practice, a claimant's capital is usually valued at his or her date of claim and revalued only if there is a reasonably large change. But it should be revalued whenever there is a change which affects entitlement to HB/CTB.

13.18 Authorities may seek the assistance of the Valuation Office Agency in London in valuing capital items such as dwellings or other property. Forms authorities may use for this purpose appear in the Guidance Manual (BW1 annex E).

Valuing jointly held capital

13.19 The following rule applies when a capital item (e.g. a property) is held jointly by two or more people. An example is given below:

- first assume that all the joint owners own an equal share in the capital item;
- then value the person's resulting assumed share (as in para. 13.16) and count that as his or her capital.

13.20 The above rule does not apply when an item is held in distinct, known shares (e.g. one person holds a one-third share and the other a two-thirds share) and in such cases the actual share should be valued (as in para. 13.16) and counted as the person's capital *(Secretary of State for Work and Pensions v Hourigan,* reported as *R(IS) 4/03).* That actual share may itself have minimal value *(CH/1953/2003).*

Examples: Valuing capital

Shares wholly owned by a claimant

A claimant owns 1,000 shares in a company. The sell price is currently £0.50 each.

For HB/main CTB purposes, from the current market value (1,000 x £0.50 = £500) deduct 10% (£50) giving £450. Assuming no loan or other encumbrance is secured on the shares, the value for HB/main CTB purposes is therefore £450.

A jointly owned property

A claimant and her sister inherit some land from their father. In his will, he stipulated that it was a joint inheritance. The land has recently been valued by the Valuation Office Agency, and the authority accepts their valuations, which are as follows:

- if the whole of the land was sold, it would fetch £10,000;
- if a half-share in the land was sold, the half-share would fetch only £4,000.

The claimant has recently taken out a loan for £2,000 using the land as security (and none of the loan has yet been repaid).

13.19 HB 51; HB60+ 49; NIHB 48; NIHB60+ 47; CTB 41; CTB60+ 39

For HB/CTB purposes, the claimant's share of the capital in the land is valued as follows:

- first the claimant is treated as owning half of the land;
- then this half share is valued. Using the Valuation Office Agency's figure, the authority values the half share at £4,000;
- then 10% is deducted towards sales costs: £4,000 minus £400 leaves £3,600;
- then the claimant's loan is deducted: £3,600 minus £2,000 leaves £1,600.

So for HB/CTB purposes, the claimant has capital of £1,600 (plus any other capital she may have).

Why income is assessed

13.21 A claimant's earned and unearned income, assessed under the rules described in this chapter and chapters 14 and 15, is compared with his or her applicable amount in calculating how much HB or CTB he or she is entitled to (paras. 6.8-11).

How income is assessed

13.22 The whole of a claimant's income (including that of any partner) is taken into account, unless it is disregarded as described in this chapter (though for people aged 60+ what counts as income in the first place is limited: paras. 13.8-9).

13.23 The HB and CTB rules distinguish earned income (i.e. earnings received by employed earners or by the self-employed) from unearned income (e.g. pensions, benefits, rent received by the claimant, and so on). Chapter 14 deals with earnings from a job, chapter 15 with self-employed earnings. The rules about unearned income are in this chapter.

Deciding which weeks income belongs to

13.24 The general objective for HB/CTB purposes is '[calculating or] estimating the amount which is likely to be [the claimant's or partner's] average weekly income'. However, there are many specific rules and these are given in this and the next two chapters as they arise. Where there is no specific rule, it is usually straightforward to decide according to the facts of the case which week or weeks a claimant's income belongs to for HB/CTB purposes – though in the case of tax credits this can 'amount, in reality, to a task of nightmare proportions' (TH/1/2009 [GP]).

13.22 HB 27,31,40; HB60+ 30; NIHB 24,28,37; NIHB60+ 28; CTB 17,21,30; CTB60+ 20

13.24 HB 27(1); HB60+ 30(1); NIHB 24(1); NIHB60+ 28(1); CTB 17(1); CTB60+ 20(1)

Arrears of income

13.25 In broad terms, it is usually the case that if a claimant receives arrears of income, then those arrears are treated as being income belonging to the week or weeks to which they relate (except to the extent that they are income which is disregarded). It is because of this that certain arrears of income are disregarded as capital (*CH/1561/2005,* and see para. 13.11). Exceptions to this and further specific rules are given in this and the next chapter as they arise.

Income tax

13.26 The income tax payable on any kind of income, even income not listed elsewhere in this guide, is disregarded in the assessment of that income.

Converting income to a weekly figure

13.27 For HB/CTB purposes, income must be converted (if necessary) to a weekly figure. The details are given in paragraph 6.68.

Social security benefits, tax credits and war pensions

13.28 This section gives the rules about the assessment for HB/CTB purposes of social security benefits and pensions, tax credits, and war pensions. Paragraphs 13.29-36 give general rules, paragraphs 13.37 onwards give rules for individual benefits.

State benefits and tax credits: general rule for current payments

13.29 Except where otherwise indicated (paras. 13.37-63), social security benefits and pensions are counted in full as unearned income. All the following social security benefits and tax credits are counted in full:

- bereavement allowance;
- carer's allowance;
- child benefit (except for 60+s: para. 13.49);
- child tax credit (but see also paras. 13.35 and 13.46-48);
- employment and support allowance (contribution-linked);
- incapacity benefit and severe disablement allowance;
- industrial injury disablement benefit (except certain increases, para. 13.52);
- jobseeker's allowance (contribution-based);
- maternity allowance;
- retirement pensions;
- working tax credit (but see also paras. 13.35 and 13.46-48).

13.25 HB 31(2),79(6),(7); NIHB 28(2),77(8),(9); CTB 21(2),67(8),(9)

13.26 HB sch 5 para 1; HB60+ 33(12); NIHB sch 6 para 1; NIHB60+ 31(11); CTB sch 4 para 1; CTB60+ 23(12)

13.29 HB 31(1); HB60+ 29(1); NIHB 28(1); NIHB60+ 27(1); CTB 21(1); CTB60+ 19(1)

13.30 Except in the case of working tax credit and child tax credit (para. 13.46), the period over which these are taken into account is 'the period in which that benefit is payable'.

Social security benefits: general rule for arrears

13.31 Except when indicated in the following paragraphs (see in particular para. 13.32), arrears of social security benefits and pensions are counted as unearned income for the period they cover.

Example: Arrears of incapacity benefit

A claimant, who has been receiving HB and CTB for many years, has been receiving incapacity benefit since January 2008. It has been taken into account as her income for HB/CTB purposes from that date. In June 2009, following a successful appeal, she is paid arrears of incapacity benefit for the period from September 2007 to January 2008.

The arrears are her income for the period from September 2007 to January 2008. The authority may therefore reassess her entitlement to HB/CTB for that period, which may result in an overpayment (chapter 18).

Social security benefits: large arrears due to official error

13.32 In the case of several benefits (e.g. DLA: para 13.53), arrears are disregarded as capital for 52 weeks from the date of payment. In those cases (and they are identified throughout this section as they arise), there is a lengthened disregard if:

- the underpayment was due to official error; and
- the amount of the arrears is £5,000 or more.

In such cases, the arrears are then disregarded (if this would be longer than the 52 weeks) for as long as the claimant or any partner remain continuously entitled to HB/CTB (including periods for which the partner remains continuously entitled after the claimant's death).

Reduced state benefits

13.33 If the amount of a social security benefit is reduced (for example, in order to recover a previous overpayment), the gross amount (i.e. before the reduction) is counted as unearned income. (But there are exceptions: paras. 13.34-35.)

13.30 HB 31(2); HB60+ 33(6); NIHB 28(2); NIHB60+ 31(6); CTB 21(2); CTB60+ 23(6)

13.31 HB 79(7); HB60+ 33(6); NIHB 77(9); NIHB60+ 31(6); CTB 67(9); CTB60+ 23(6)

13.32 HB sch 6 para 9; HB60+ sch 6 paras 18,21,22; NIHB sch 7 para 9; NIHB60+ sch 7 paras 18,21,22; CTB sch 5 para 9; CTB60+ sch 4 paras 18,21,22

13.34 However, if the amount of a state benefit is reduced due to the overlapping social security benefit rules, or (for 60+s) due to hospitalisation, the net amount (i.e. after the reduction) is counted as unearned income.

Reduced tax credits

13.35 If the amount of working tax credit (WTC) or child tax credit (CTC) (para. 13.46) has been reduced to recover an overpayment which arose in a previous tax year, the net amount of WTC or CTC (i.e. after the deduction) is counted as unearned income.

Increases in social security benefits for dependants

13.36 With some social security benefits, an increase can be added for a dependent partner, or other dependent adult(s) or child(ren). For under-60s, an increase for any member of the family (para. 4.11) counts as unearned income if the benefit it is paid with counts as unearned income. The same applies for 60+s, but only to increases for a partner.

JSA(IB), ESA(IR), IS or pension credit

13.37 Current payments of:

- savings credit count in full as unearned income – but there are special rules for assessing HB/CTB for anyone on savings credit (paras. 13.157-164);
- guarantee credit, JSA(IB), ESA(IR) and IS are disregarded in full as income (together with any other income or capital the claimant or their partner possesses: para. 13.4).

13.38 Arrears of all of the above benefits, including payments compensating for non-payment of them, are disregarded as income; and are disregarded as capital for 52 weeks from the date of payment, or longer for some large underpayments (para. 13.32).

13.39 It is worth noting that the further rules about the date an award, change or end of entitlement to pension credit takes effect can also operate in a way that effectively causes payments of pension credit to be disregarded as income (para. 17.25 and table 17.5).

13.33 HB 40(5); HB60+ 29(3),(4); NIHB 37(3); NIHB60+ 27(3),(4); CTB 30(5); CTB60+ 19(3),(4)

13.35 HB 2(1),40(6); NIHB 2(1),37(4); CTB 2(1),30(6)

13.36 HB sch 5 para 52; HB60+ 29(1)(j); NIHB sch 6 para 54; NIHB60+ 27(1)(h); CTB sch 4 para 52; CTB60+ 19(1)(j)

13.37 HB sch 5 paras 4, 5, 7, sch 6 para 9; HB60+ 26, 27,44(3), sch 6 paras 21,22; NIHB sch 6 paras 4, 5,8, sch 7 para 9; NIHB60+ 24, 25,42(3), sch 7 paras 21, 22; CTB sch 4 paras 4,5,8, sch 5 para 9; CTB60+ 16,17,34(3), sch 4 paras 21,22

Certain former JSA(IB) or income support claimants

13.40 The whole of a claimant's unearned income is disregarded if he or she lost entitlement to JSA(IB) or IS on 1st April 2003, and the only reason for this was that the assessment of his or her JSA(IB) or IS no longer included support charges because they became payable by Supporting People (para. 8.40). This applies only if the claimant and any partner are under 60, only to CTB and HB for rates in Northern Ireland (but not to HB for rent anywhere in the UK). It mainly affects long leaseholders and is rare.

HB, CTB and discretionary housing payments

13.41 Current payments of HB/CTB are disregarded as income.

13.42 Arrears of HB/CTB, including payments compensating for non-payment of them, are disregarded as income; and are disregarded as capital for 52 weeks from the date of payment, or longer for some large underpayments (para. 13.32).

13.43 Discretionary housing payments (para. 22.2) are disregarded in full as income; and are disregarded as capital for 52 weeks from the date of payment, or longer for some large underpayments (para. 13.32).

13.44 Note that in the case of the 60+s, discretionary housing payments are disregarded as income because they are not counted as income (para. 15.9).

Social fund payments and loans

13.45 Disregard payments and loans from the social fund in full (both as income and capital) – including winter fuel payments.

Working tax credit and child tax credit

13.46 Working tax credit (WTC) and child tax credit (CTC) are assessed as follows for HB/CTB purposes. If the claimant or any partner is aged 60+, CTC is disregarded, but WTC is counted, as unearned income. For under 60s, both are counted as unearned income. In each case, the period over which they are taken into account is the period they cover, as follows:

(a) in the case of a daily instalment, the one day in respect of which it is paid;

(b) in the case of a weekly instalment, the period of seven days ending on the day on which it is due to be paid;

13.40 CTB sch 4 para 6; NIHB sch 6 para 6

13.41 HB sch 5 paras 51,62, sch 6 para 9; HB60+ 29(1)(j), sch 6 paras 21,22; NIHB sch 6 paras 53,62, sch 7 para 9; NIHB60+ 27(1)(h), sch 7 paras 21,22; CTB sch 4 paras 37,55A,62, sch 5 para 9; CTB60+ 19(1)(j), sch 4 paras 21,22

13.44 SI 2008 No. 698; NISR 2008 No. 112

13.45 HB sch 5 para 31 sch 6 para 20; HB60+ 29(1); NIHB sch 6 para 32 sch 7 para 21; NIHB60+ 27(1); CTB sch 4 para 33, sch 5 para 20; CTB60+ 19(1)

(c) in the case of a two-weekly instalment, the period of 14 days commencing six days before the day on which the instalment is due to be paid (because two-weekly instalments of WTC/CTC are due at the end of the first week of the two weeks they cover);

(d) in the case of a four-weekly instalment, the period of 28 days ending on the day on which it is due to be paid (though there may be exceptions due to the way the Inland Revenue pays these).

13.47 There are two further rules for special circumstances:

- Certain recipients of WTC qualify for a disregard from their earnings of £16.85 per week (para. 14.24). If (uncommonly) their earnings are insufficient for this £16.85 disregard to be made in full from them (as described in para. 14.26), £16.85 is instead disregarded from their WTC.
- Certain claimants with child care costs qualify for a disregard from their earnings (para. 14.15). If (uncommonly) their earnings are insufficient for this disregard to be made in full from them, any balance of the disregard is made from their WTC.

13.48 Arrears of WTC and CTC are never counted as income; and are disregarded as capital for 52 weeks (one year for 60+s) from the date of payment, or longer for some large underpayments (para. 13.32). (The effect of this rule is that the arrears themselves cannot create an overpayment of HB/CTB.) The same rule applies to payments compensating for non-payment of WTC/CTC.

Child benefit and guardian's allowance

13.49 If the claimant or any partner is aged 60+ (or from October 2009 any age) both are disregarded. In all other cases child benefit counts in full as income but guardian's allowance is disregarded.

Statutory maternity, paternity and adoption pay

13.50 Statutory maternity, paternity and adoption pay count as earnings (as described in para. 14.46).

13.46 HB 32; HB60+ 29(1)(b),32; NIHB 29; NIHB 27(1)(b),30; CTB 22; CTB60+ 19(1)(b),22

13.47 HB 27(1),(2),34(e), sch 4 para 17; sch 5 para 56; HB60+ sch 4 para 9, sch 5 para 21; NIHB 24(1),(2),31(e), sch 5 para 17, sch 6 para 58; NIHB60+ sch 5 para 9, sch 6 para 22; CTB 17(1),(2),24(e), sch 3 para 56, sch 4 para 9; CTB60+ sch 2 para 9, sch 3 para 21

13.48 HB 46(9), sch 6 para 9; HB60+ 44(3), sch 6 paras 18,21; NIHB 43(8), sch 7 para 9; NIHB60+ 42(3), sch 7 para 18,21; CTB 36(9), sch 5 para 9; CTB60+ 34(3), sch 4 para 18,21

13.49 HB sch 5 para 50; HB60+ 29(1)(j); NIHB sch 6 par 52; NIHB60+ 27(1)(h); CTB sch 4 para 51; CTB60+ 19(1)(j)

13.50 HB 35(1)(i); HB60+ 29(1)(j); NIHB 32(1)(i); NIHB60+ 27(1)(h); CTB 25(1)(i); CTB60+ 19(1)(j)

Benefits for sickness, incapacity and disability

13.51 Most benefits for sickness and/or disability are treated under the general rule (13.29-30) and so count in full as income, including carer's allowance, ESA(C), incapacity benefit (but see para. 13.33), severe disablement allowance and industrial injuries disablement benefit (except certain increases). The only exceptions are:

- ESA(IR) (paras. 13.4 and 13.37);
- war disablement pensions (paras. 13.58-62);
- disability living allowance and attendance allowance (para. 13.52-53);
- those benefits treated as attendance allowance (para. 12.44) which are paid as increases to industrial and war disablement pensions (paras. 13.52-53);
- statutory sick pay (which counts as earnings as described in para. 14.46).

Benefits for attendance and mobility

13.52 Current payments of the following are disregarded in full as income:

- disability living allowance;
- attendance allowance;
- any benefit treated as attendance allowance (para. 12.44);
- war pensioners mobility supplement; and
- payments compensating for non-receipt of the above.

13.53 Arrears of the above are disregarded in full as income. They are also disregarded as capital for 52 weeks from the date of payment, or longer for some large awards of arrears (para. 13.32).

State retirement pension: payments and deferral

13.54 State retirement pension counts in full as unearned income. A person who chooses to defer their state retirement pension can choose between a lump sum now, or increased payments later, and can change their mind about this (subject to conditions). The amount of a lump sum is disregarded as capital (until and unless the person opts to have increased payments rather than a lump sum). Increased payments count in full as income. For treatment of occupational and personal pensions see paras. 13.93-94. For winter fuel payments see para. 13.45.

13.52 HB sch 5 paras 6-9; HB60+ 29(1)(j), sch 6 para 21; NIHB sch 6 paras 7-10; NIHB60+ 27(1)(h); CTB sch 4 paras 7-10; CTB60+ 19(1)(j), sch 4 para 21

13.53 HB sch 6 para 9; NIHB sch 7 para 9; CTB sch 5 para 9

13.54 HB 60+ sch 6 para 26A; SI 2005/2677 Reg 11,12, CPR 2; NIHB60+ sch 7 para 28; CTB 60+ sch 4 26A

Christmas bonus

13.55 The 'Christmas bonus' of £10, which is awarded each year to certain claimants on long-term benefits (e.g. retirement pension and disability living allowance) is disregarded as income.

Widowed parent's allowance

13.56 Disregard £15 per week from current payments (subject to the overriding £20 disregard: para. 13.156). Arrears from current payments are counted as unearned income for the period they cover apart from the £15 per week disregard.

Bereavement payment

13.57 Bereavement payment is a lump-sum, one-off payment and so counts as capital (not income).

War pensions for bereavement and disablement

13.58 The following rules apply to:

- war widow's, war widower's and war disablement pensions, war pensions for surviving civil partners, and also guaranteed income payments under the Armed Forces and Reserve Forces Compensation Scheme;
- payments to compensate for non-payment of any of the above;
- analogous payments of any of the above from governments outside the UK.

See also the rules for gallantry awards (para. 13.130) and Second World War payments etc (paras. 13.111-113).

13.59 In England, Wales and Scotland £10 per week is disregarded as income from the above payments for the period they cover (subject to the over-riding £20 disregard, para. 13.156), plus any additional amount from a 'local scheme'. Most councils operate a 'local scheme' whereby a larger amount (usually 100%) of any current payments or arrears of the first item are disregarded as income (para. 22.12).

13.60 In Northern Ireland all of the above payments (including any amounts for attendance or mobility: para. 13.52) are disregarded in full as income for the period they cover.

13.55 HB sch 5 para 32; HB60+ 29(1)(j); NIHB sch 6 para 33; NIHB60+ 27(1)(h); CTB sch 4 para 33; CTB60+ 19(1)(j)

13.56 HB sch 5 para 16; HB60+ sch 5 paras 7,8; NIHB sch 6 para 17; NIHB60+ sch 6 paras 8,9; CTB sch 4 para 17; CTB60+ sch 3 paras 7,8

13.57 HB60+ 29(1)(j); NIHB60+ 27(1)(h); CTB60+ 19(1)(j)

13.58 HB sch 5 paras 7-9,15,52-54; HB60+ 29(1), sch 5 paras 1-6, sch 6 paras 21,22; NIHB sch 6 paras 8-10,15,16,54-56; NIHB60+ 27(1), sch 6 paras 1-7, sch 7 paras 21,22; CTB sch 4 paras 8-10,16,52-54; CTB60+ 19(1), sch 3 paras 1-6, sch 4 paras 21,22

13.61 In England, Wales, Scotland and Northern Ireland there is no disregard of the capital value of arrears of any of these payments apart from any amounts for attendance or mobility (para. 13.52).

13.62 Arrears of amounts granted for attendance (para. 12.44) or mobility (para. 13.52) are disregarded as capital for 52 weeks from the date of payment, or longer for some large underpayments (para. 13.32). The same applies to payments compensating for non-receipt of such amounts.

'Pre-1973' war widows and widowers special payment

13.63 Special payments paid to 'pre-1973' war widows, widowers and surviving civil partners (from April 2009 paid at £77.32 per week) are disregarded as income. If the claimant and partner are aged under 60 any arrears are also disregarded as capital for up to 52 weeks.

Social services payments for care and support

13.64 This section gives the rules about the treatment of certain payments for childcare, community care and other support services. In Great Britain these payments are usually made by the local authority social services department or by a voluntary body on their behalf. In Northern Ireland these payments are made by various public sector bodies including the Health and Social Services Board; a Health and Social Services Trust; a Juvenile Justice Centre or by a voluntary body on their behalf.

Fostering, boarding out and respite care payments

13.65 If the claimant or any partner is aged 60+ disregard all such payments in full (as income): there are no further conditions. If the claimant and any partner are under 60, disregard these payments in full as income if they are received from a local authority or voluntary organisation or (in the case of respite care payments) a primary care trust; and also disregard (in the case of respite care payments), contributions required from the person cared for. Any sum accumulated from allowances paid counts as capital and cannot be disregarded as an implied trust *(CIS/3101/2007)*.

13.63 HB sch 5 paras 43, 53-55, sch 6 para 39; HB60+; sch 5 para 23;
NIHB sch 6 paras 45, 55-57, sch 7 para 40; NIHB60+ sch 6 para 24;
CTB sch 4 paras 44,53-55, sch 5 para 39; CTB60+ sch 3 para 22

13.65 HB sch 5 paras 26,27; HB60+ 29(1); NIHB sch 6 paras 27,28; NIHB60+ 27(1);
CTB sch 4 paras 27,28; CTB60+ 19(1)

Adoption allowances and special guardianship payments

13.66 If the claimant or partner is aged 60+ disregard all such payments in full (as income): there are no further conditions. If the claimant and partner are under 60:

- count these payments as unearned income up to the dependant's allowance and any disabled child premium for the child or young person concerned; and
- disregard the remainder.

(Special guardianship payments are payments for support services.)

Community care and other social services payments

13.67 If the claimant or partner is aged 60+ disregard all such payments in full (as income): there are no further conditions. If the claimant and partner are under 60, disregard in full (both as income and capital):

- any social services payment made for the purposes of avoiding taking children into care or to children and young persons who are leaving or have left care;
- any payment made by social services to a young person formerly in their care which is passed on to the claimant. To qualify the young person must be aged 18 or over and continue to live with the claimant;
- any social services community care payment.

Supporting people payments

13.68 Supporting people payments (usually administered by social services to assist people with certain support costs in their home) are disregarded in full as income.

The home, property and possessions

13.69 This section is about how things the claimant owns affect his or her entitlement to HB and main CTB, including the home, a former or future home, other property and rent received by the claimant.

13.66 HB 2(1), sch 5 para 25; HB60+ 29(1); NIHB 2(1), sch 6 para 26; NIHB60+ 27(1); CTB sch 4 para 26; CTB60+ 19(1)

13.67 HB sch 5 paras 26,28,28A,57, sch 6 paras 19,19A,58-60; HB60+ 29(1); NIHB sch 6 paras 27,29,29A,59, sch 7 paras 20,20A,55-57; NIHB60+ 27(1); CTB sch 4 paras 27,29,29A,57, sch 5 paras 19,60-62; CTB60+ 19(1)

13.68 HB sch 5 para 63, sch 6 para 57; HB60+ 29(1); NIHB sch 6 para 63, sch 7 para 54; NIHB60+ 27(1); CTB sch 4 para 63, sch 5 para 59; CTB60+ 19(1)

Homes and other property

13.70 The claimant's current, former or future home can be disregarded and so can a home or other property (including non-domestic property) which the claimant has never occupied, if the conditions in the following paragraphs apply. The disregards described below can apply one after another, so long as the relevant conditions are met (as illustrated in the example).

The claimant's home

13.71 Disregard the capital value of the dwelling normally occupied as the claimant's home, and any land or buildings (including in Scotland croft land) which are part of it or are impracticable to sell separately. There is no time limit. This disregard is limited to one home per claim but see the other headings below.

A relative's home

13.72 Disregard the capital value of the home of a partner or relative of anyone in the claimant's family, if that partner or relative is aged 60+ or incapacitated. There is no time limit. The property may be occupied by others as well as the partner or relative. Any number of properties may be disregarded under this rule. 'Relative' is defined in paragraph 9.62. 'Incapacitated' is not defined for this purpose; in particular, it is not linked to premiums or state benefits.

An intended home

13.73 Disregard the capital value of a property which the claimant intends to occupy as a home as follows:

- in all cases, for 26 weeks from the date of acquisition or such longer period as is reasonable; and/or
- if the claimant is taking steps to obtain possession (e.g. if there are squatters or tenants), for 26 weeks from the date the claimant first seeks legal advice or begins legal proceedings, or such longer period as is reasonable; and/or
- if the property requires essential repairs or alterations, for 26 weeks from the date the claimant first takes steps to render it fit for occupation or reoccupation as his or her home, or such longer period as is reasonable. This could apply for example to the normal home of a claimant in temporary accommodation.

13.71 HB sch 6 para 1; HB60+ 2(1), sch 6 para 26; NIHB sch 7 para 1; NIHB60+ 2(1), sch 7 para 26; CTB sch 5 para 1; CTB60+ sch 4 para 26

13.72 HB sch 6 para 4(a); HB60+ sch 6 para 4(a); NIHB sch 7 para 4(a); NIHB60+ sch 7 para 4(a); CTB sch 5 para 4(a); CTB60+ sch 4 para 4(a)

13.73 HB sch 6 paras 2,27,28; HB60+ sch 6 paras 1-3; NIHB sch 7 paras 2,28,29; NIHB60+ sch 7 paras 1-3; CTB sch 5 paras 2,27,28; CTB60+ sch 4; paras 1-3

A former home

13.74 There is no disregard of the capital value of a claimant's former home as such. However, a former home may well fall within one of the following headings (which also apply to other property): if it does not, then it is taken into account as capital.

Property for sale

13.75 Disregard the capital value of any property the claimant intends to dispose of (e.g. sale or transfer), for 26 weeks from the date when the claimant first takes steps to dispose of it, or for such longer period as is reasonable. This can apply to a former or second home or any other property. It can apply to more than one property.

Couples and divorce, dissolution and estrangement

13.76 If a claimant has divorced their partner or dissolved their civil partnership with them or become estranged from them, disregard the whole capital value of the claimant's former home (and any land or buildings which are part of it or are impracticable to sell separately) as follows:

- for any period when it is occupied by the former partner if he or she is now a lone parent. This could begin straight after the divorce/estrangement, or later on, and there is no time limit in this case;
- in any other case, for 26 weeks from the date of divorce, dissolution or estrangement (e.g. if the former partner is not a lone parent at the time, or the property is empty). The time limit in this case cannot be extended, but the property may fall within one of the other disregards afterwards.

Note that (unlike in the next paragraph) the claimant must have formerly lived there as his or her home for this disregard to apply. 'Divorce' (in the case of married couples) and 'dissolution' (in the case of civil partners) have their ordinary meaning. 'Estrangement' (in all cases) means more than just physical separation, namely that the couple in question consider their relationship to be over *(CH/117/2005)*; it need not be an acrimonious split and the fact that one party might want them to get back together is irrelevant *(CH/3777/2007)*.

Couples and polygamous marriages: separation

13.77 If a claimant has not divorced their partner, dissolved their civil partnership with them, or become estranged from them, but the HB/CTB rules treat him or her as no longer being in a couple or polygamous marriage (e.g.

13.75 HB sch 6 para 26; HB60+ sch 6 para 7; NIHB sch 7 para 27; NIHB60+ sch 7 para 7; CTB sch 5 para 26; CTB60+ sch 4 para 7

13.76 HB sch 6 para 25; HB60+ sch 6 para 6; NIHB sch 7 para 26; NIHB60+ sch 7 para 6; CTB sch 5 para 25; CTB60+ sch 4 para 6

13.77 HB sch 6 para 4(b); HB60+ sch 6 para 4(b); NIHB sch 7 para 4(b); NIHB60+ sch 7 para 4(b); CTB sch 5 para 4(b); CTB60+ sch 4 para 4(b)

because of the rules about absence of a partner: para. 4.24), disregard the whole capital value of any property currently occupied as a home by the former partner. There is no time limit. Note that (unlike in the previous paragraph) it is irrelevant who used to live there. This rule does not apply if the reason the two people do not live in the same household as a couple is that the relationship has broken down even if the two remain on civil terms *(CH/3777/2007)*.

Example: The capital value of a property following relationship breakdown

- A married couple in their forties jointly own the house they live in. They do not own any other property. They have one child at school. They claim CTB. The man is the claimant.

  The value of the house is disregarded as capital: it is their normal home (para. 13.71). However, they turn out not to qualify for CTB because they have too much income.
- The couple separate (but are not estranged).The man leaves and rents a room in a shared house. He does not intend to return (and so they no longer count as a couple: para. 4.24). He claims HB and CTB for the flat.

  In the man's claim, his share of the house is disregarded: it is the home of his former partner from whom he is separated (para. 13.77).
- They divorce. The terms of the divorce are that the man retains a one-third share in the house; but that the house cannot be sold until their child is 18.

  In his claim, his share of the house is disregarded: it is his former home and is occupied by his former partner from whom he is divorced and who is a lone parent (para. 13.76).
- More than 26 weeks after their divorce, their child leaves school. The house is not put up for sale and the man does not seek his share of its value.

  In his claim, his one-third share in the house must now be taken into account (paras. 13.76 and 13.19).
- The house is put up for sale.

  In the man's claim, his share in the house is now disregarded as capital for 26 weeks (or longer if reasonable: para. 13.75).
- The house is sold, and the man puts his share into a bank account and starts trying to raise a mortgage using the money. It seems likely that he will be able to buy somewhere within the next two or three months.

  In his claim, this money is disregarded: it is the proceeds of the sale of his former home and he plans to use it to buy another property within 26 weeks (para. 13.80).

Disputed assets when a relationship ends

13.78 When a relationship ends, ownership of a property may be in dispute. This can sometimes mean the current market value of the property (paras. 13.16-20) is nil until ownership of the property is settled.

Housing association deposits

13.79 If the claimant and any partner are under 60, disregard in full as capital any amount deposited with a housing association (para. 7.25) in order to secure accommodation. There is no such disregard if the claimant or any partner is aged 60+.

Money from selling a home

13.80 If the claimant and any partner are under 60, disregard in full as capital:

- money from the sale of the claimant's former home – this could include, for example, any compensation paid resulting from compulsory purchase (specific provision is made in the Northern Ireland regulations) or money held by a solicitor following a sale; and
- money refunded by a housing association with which it was deposited (para. 13.79),

but only if it is intended for purchasing another home within 26 weeks, or such longer period as is reasonable. (However, interest accrued on the money is counted as capital in the normal way: para. 13.97.) If the money is available but is subject to a dispute as to the claimant's share, then the claimant cannot benefit from the extended disregard by taking a hard line in negotiations even if it compromises their position. Neither can they benefit from the disregard if they have not yet decided what they will do with the money when they receive it (both points: *CH/2255/2006*). If the claimant or any partner is aged 60+, a different rule applies (para. 13.81).

Money for buying a home

13.81 If the claimant or any partner is aged 60+, payments (or amounts deposited in the claimant's name) for the sole purpose of buying a home are disregarded for one year from the date of receipt. Apart from lasting longer, this is wider than the rule for under 60s (para. 13.80). It includes home sale proceeds and money refunded by a housing association, but also (for example) money given or loaned by a relative for that purpose.

13.79 HB sch 6 para 11(a); NIHB sch 7 para 11(a); CTB sch 5 para 11(a)

13.80 HB sch 6 paras 3,11(b); NIHB sch 7 paras 3,11(b); CTB sch 5 paras 3,11(a)

13.81 HB60+ sch 6 paras 18,20(a); NIHB60+ sch 7 paras 18,20(a); CTB60+ sch 4 paras 18,20(a)

Valuing property generally

13.82 The general rules about valuing capital apply to a property which has to be taken into account as capital for HB/CTB purposes (paras. 13.16-20). In such cases, an authority can get a free valuation of property from the Valuation Office Agency (and a form which can be used for this purpose is in GM chapter BW1 annex D).

Valuing property which is rented out

13.83 Unless it forms part of the capital assets of a business (or in certain circumstances a former business: para. 15.7), property a claimant owns and has rented out is valued as described earlier (paras. 13.16-20). However, the fact that it is rented out will affect its market value; for example, the presence of a sitting tenant can reduce it: *CH/1953/2003*. For information about rental income see the following.

Table 13.2: Rent received from people in the claimant's home

Rent, keep, etc, from household members

- Disregard the whole of any rent, 'keep', etc, received from a child or young person in the family (paras. 4.26-40) or from a non-dependant (para. 4.44).

Rent from boarders (as defined in para. 4.48)

- Disregard the first £20.00 of that rent.
- Count only half the rest as unearned income.
- A separate £20.00 is disregarded for each individual boarder who is charged for – even a child – regardless of whether they have separate agreements.

Rent from (sub-)tenants (as defined in paras. 4.50-51)

- Disregard the first £20.00 of that rent (including any other payments within the gross charge – such as heating – which is not board).
- Count all the rest as unearned income.
- A separate £20.00 is disregarded for each (sub-) tenancy.

13.83 HB sch 6 para 7; HB60+ sch 6 para 5; NIHB sch 7 para 7; NIHB60+ sch 7 para 5; CTB sch 5 para 7; CTB60+ sch 4 para 5

T 13.2 HB sch 5 paras 21,22,41; HB60+ 29(1), sch 5 paras 9,10; NIHB sch 6 paras 23,44; NIHB60+ 27(1), sch 6 paras 10,11; CTB sch 4 paras 21,23; CTB60+ 19(1), sch 3 paras 9,10

Table 13.3: Rent received on property other than the claimant's home

If the claimant or any partner is aged 60+

Rent received on property (other than the claimant's home) is disregarded in full as income in all circumstances.

If the claimant and any partner are under 60 and the property's value is disregarded as capital

This applies to rent received on one of the types of property (other than the claimant's home) whose capital value is disregarded (as described in paras. 13.71-77 and 15.7):

- Take the amount of the rental income for an appropriate period (e.g. six months, a year).
- Disregard any payment towards mortgage repayments (both interest and capital repayments) or any council tax (in Northern Ireland domestic rates) or water charges the claimant is liable to pay during that period on the property (note that other outgoings cannot be disregarded).
- Count the balance (converted to a weekly figure) as the claimant's unearned income.

If the claimant and any partner are under 60 and the property's value counts as capital

This applies to rent received on one of the types of property whose value is taken into account as his or her capital (even if for some reason the capital value is nil for HB/main CTB purposes):

- Take the amount of the rental income for an appropriate period (e.g. six months, a year).
- Deduct any outgoings incurred in respect of the letting (e.g. agents' fees, tax due on the income, repairs, cleaning, council tax, water charges, repayments of mortgages/loans, etc).
- The balance (if any) is capital (not income) for HB/main CTB purposes.

T 13.3 HB 46(4), sch 5 para 17(1),(2); HB60+ 29(1), sch 5 para 22; NIHB 43(4), sch 6 para 18(1),(2); NIHB60+ 27(1), sch 6 para 23; CTB 36(4), sch 4 para 18(1),(2); CTB60+ 19(1), sch 3 para 24

Receiving rent

13.84 Table 13.2 shows how rent received by the claimant from people living in his or her home is taken into account. See also the example. Table 13.3 shows how rent received from property other than the claimant's home is taken into account.

13.85 The value of the right to receive rent is disregarded as capital.

Example: Letting out a room

A couple in their 20s are on HB and CTB. They have a spare room and they let it out to a man for £80.00 per week inclusive of fuel for heating etc, and water charges (but not meals). He is their sub-tenant.

For the purposes of their HB/CTB, their income from this sub-tenant is £80.00 minus £20.00, which is £60.00 per week.

Later, the same couple agree with the man that if he increases what he pays to £100.00 per week, they will feed him. He is now their boarder.

For the purposes of their HB/CTB, their income from this boarder is £100.00 minus £20.00, which is £80.00, the result being divided in two, which is £40.00 per week.

Note that the rules therefore mean that a claimant is usually better off renting out a room to a boarder than to a (sub-)tenant.

Payments for work on the home

13.86 The following disregard applies to such payments:

- If the claimant and any partner are under 60, payments (from anyone) solely for essential repairs or improvements to the home, and grants from a local authority to purchase, alter or repair an intended home, are disregarded as capital for 26 weeks from the date of payment, or such longer period as is reasonable.
- If the claimant or any partner is aged 60+, payments, or amounts deposited in the claimant's name, (from anyone) solely for essential repairs or improvements to the home or an intended home are disregarded for one year from the date of receipt.

13.84 HB sch 6 para 33; HB60+ sch 6 para 28; NIHB sch 7 para 34; NIHB60+ sch 7 para 30; CTB sch 5 para 33; CTB60+ sch 4 para 28

13.86 HB sch 6 paras 10,38; HB60+ sch 6 paras 18,20(b); NIHB sch 7 paras 10,39; NIHB60+ sch 7 paras 18,20(b); CTB sch 5 paras 11,38; CTB60+ sch 4 paras 18,20(b)

Tax refunds for mortgage interest

13.87 If the claimant and any partner are under 60, tax refunds for interest on a mortgage taken out for purchasing a home, or for carrying out home repairs or improvements, are disregarded in full as capital. There is no such disregard for 60+s.

Mortgage and loan protection policies

13.88 The following applies if a claimant has taken out insurance against being unable (perhaps because of sickness) to pay his or her mortgage or any other loan (for example a car loan), and is now receiving payments under that insurance policy. In such cases, if the claimant or any partner is aged 60+, all payments received under that insurance policy are disregarded (as unearned income). If the claimant and any partner are under 60 they are disregarded only insofar as they cover the cost of:

- the repayments on the mortgage or other loan; and
- any premiums due on the policy in question; and
- (only in the case of a mortgage protection policy) any premiums on another insurance policy which was taken out to insure against loss or damage to the home and which was required as a condition of the mortgage.

Compensation and insurance payments for the home or possessions

13.89 Such payments are disregarded (as capital) if they are for repair or replacement following loss of, or damage to, the claimant's home or personal possessions. If the claimant and any partner are under 60, they are disregarded for 26 weeks from the date of payment, or such longer period as is reasonable. If the claimant or any partner is aged 60+, they are disregarded for one year from the date of receipt.

Compensation for compulsory purchase

13.90 The treatment of compensation for compulsory purchase of the claimant's home depends on the type of payment being made. The rules are:

- compensation for the market value of the home (but not other property) is disregarded for 26 weeks or longer (one year for 60+s) (paras. 13.80-81);
- elements of disturbance payments for the replacement of fixtures and fittings are disregarded for 26 weeks or longer (one year for 60+s) (para. 13.89);
- there is no specific rule to deal with other elements of the disturbance payments (such as the cost of a removal van) – this is probably unintended.

13.87 HB sch 6 para 21; HB60+ 29(1); NIHB sch 7 para 22; NIHB60+ 27(1); CTB sch 5 para 21; CTB60+ 19(1)

13.88 HB sch 5 para 29; HB60+ 29(1); NIHB sch 6 para 30; NIHB60+ 27(1); CTB sch 4 para 30; CTB60+ 19(1)

13.89 HB sch 6 para 10; HB60+ sch 6 paras 18,19; NIHB sch 7 para 10; NIHB60+ sch 7 paras 18,19; CTB sch 5 para 10; CTB60+ sch 4 paras 18,19

However, where the service provider is paid directly or the service is provided free then it can be disregarded (paras. 13.126 and 13.151).

- Home loss payments count in full as capital except where they are intended to be used to buy a new home (13.81).

Personal possessions

13.91 Disregard in full (as capital) the value of the claimant's personal possessions. A personal possession is any physical asset other than land and assets used for business purposes *(R(H)7/08)*. If the claimant and any partner are under 60, the law specifically mentions that if they were purchased for the purpose of obtaining or increasing entitlement to HB/CTB, their capital value should be taken into account. If the claimant or any partner is aged 60+, the same applies, but under the deprivation of capital rule (para. 13.143).

Savings, investments and private income

13.92 This section is about savings, investments, insurance policies, etc. When these are taken into account, they are valued as described in paragraphs 13.16-20. (But for national savings certificates, see para. 13.98.) The following terms are used below:

- the 'surrender value' (of an insurance policy, for instance) means what the claimant would be paid if he or she cashed it in now rather than waiting for it to mature;
- the 'value of the right to receive income' (from an annuity, for instance) means what the claimant would be paid in return for transferring the right to receive the income to someone else.

Occupational and personal pensions

13.93 These count in full as unearned income, after deducting tax and disregarding any amount required to be paid by a court pension-splitting order *(CH/1672/2007)*. However, disregard as capital any amount held in a pension scheme and the value of the right to receive money from it (para. 13.92).

13.94 Payments under the Pension Protection Fund are counted as unearned income (and for 60+s this is because of the definition of 'retirement pension income'). These are government payments to people who have lost out on their occupational pension scheme because it was under-funded when it began to be wound up and because the employer is now insolvent or has ceased to exist (and so cannot make up the shortfall).

13.91 HB sch 6 para 12; HB60+ sch 6 para 8; NIHB sch 7 para 12; NIHB60+ sch 7 para 8; CTB sch 5 para 12; CTB60+ sch 4 para 8

13.94 HB 35(2),40(10), sch 5 para 1, sch 6 para 31; HB60+ 29(1)(x),33(12), sch 6 para 24; NIHB 32(2),37(8), sch 6 para 1, sch 7 para 32; NIHB60+ 27(1)(v),31(11), sch 7 para 24; CTB 25(2),30(11), sch 4 para 1, sch 5 para 31; CTB60+ 19(1)(x),23(12), sch 5 para 24

Savings and cash

13.95 These count in full as capital. For example, money in a bank account (or under the mattress) is counted as capital (but see the next paragraph).

Income paid regularly into an account

13.96 Regular payments of income (e.g. earnings, benefits, pensions) into a claimant's bank or similar account should not be counted as capital for the period they cover (para. 13.11). For example, if earnings are paid in monthly, only what is left at the end of the month is capital. In practice, authorities often do not do this unless claimants ask them to.

Interest

13.97 Except where other rules in this chapter state otherwise, interest or other income derived from capital (on a bank account, etc) is counted not as income but as capital. If the claimant and any partner are under 60, the law spells out that this is done from the date it is due to be credited to the claimant, and it seems logical that this would also apply to 60+s.

National Savings and Ulster savings certificates

13.98 These count as capital, and since 1st October 2007 are valued as in paragraph 13.16 (i.e. their market value). The DWP advises authorities (GM BW1.440) to use the valuation calculator on *www.nsandi.com*. For further guidance on valuing, see GM BW1.441-451.

Shares and other investments

13.99 These count as capital. They are valued as described in the general rules (paras. 13.16-20), with the effect that:

- shares are valued at their 'sell' price. Then disregard 10% towards the cost of their sale;
- unit trusts are valued at their 'sell' price. Normally this already allows for notional sales costs. If it does not, disregard 10% for this;
- income bonds count in full.

Life insurance policies

13.100 Disregard (as capital) the surrender value of a life insurance policy (para. 13.91). (This includes instruments, such as bonds, which have a life insurance

---

13.95 HB 44(1); HB60+ 44(1); NIHB 41(1); NIHB60+ 42(1); CTB 34(1); CTB60+ 34(1)

13.97 HB 46(4); HB60+ 29(1), sch 5 paras 22,24; NIHB 43(4); NIHB60+ 27(1), sch 6 paras 23,25; CTB 36(4); CTB60+ sch 3 paras 23,24

13.100 HB sch 6 para 17; HB60+ sch 6 para 11; NIHB sch 7 para 18; NIHB60+ sch 7 para 11; CTB sch 5 para 17; CTB60+ sch 4 para 11

element: R(IS)7/98.) But count as capital any money actually received from it (e.g. if the claimant actually cashes in all or part of it).

Funeral plan contracts

13.101 If the claimant or any partner is aged 60+, disregard the value of a funeral plan contract. To qualify, the contract provider (which would normally be a firm or company but need not be so) must contract to provide or secure the provision of a funeral for the claimant or partner in the UK, and that must be the sole purpose of the contract. There is no such disregard if the claimant and any partner are under 60.

Annuities

13.102 If the claimant has an annuity, it means he or she has invested an initial lump sum with an insurance company which, in return, pays the claimant a regular income. Count this in full as unearned income. Disregard (as capital) the surrender value of the annuity, and also the value of the right to receive income from it (para. 13.92). Unless the claimant is legally required to do so (para. 13.93) money paid over from an annuity to a former spouse cannot be disregarded as an implied trust and in any case an annuity paid by a former employer cannot normally be assigned *(CH/1076/2008)*.

Home income plans

13.103 If the claimant has a home income plan, it means he or she raised a loan using his or her home as security, has invested the loan as an annuity and, in return, gets a regular income. Part of this income is used to repay the loan, part may be used to repay the claimant's mortgage, and part may be left over for the claimant to use. Count the income received by the claimant as unearned income, but only after deducting (if they have not been deducted at source):

- any tax payable on that income;
- any repayments on the loan which was raised to obtain the annuity; and
- any mortgage repayments made using the income (using the figures for the repayments which apply after tax has been deducted from them).

Disregard (as capital) the surrender value of the annuity, and the value of the right to receive income from it (para. 13.92).

13.101 HB60+ sch 6 para 12; NIHB60+ sch 7 para 12; CTB60+ sch 4 para 12

13.102 HB sch 6 para 13; HB60+ 29(1), sch 6 para 25; NIHB sch 7 para 13; NIHB60+ 27(1), sch 7 para 25; CTB sch 5 para 13; CTB60+ 19(1), sch 4 para 25

13.103 HB 41(2), sch 5 para 18, sch 6 para 13; HB60+ 29(1), sch 5 para 11, sch 6 para 29; NIHB 38(2), sch 6 para 19, sch 7 para 13; NIHB60+ 27(1), sch 6 para 12, sch 7 para 31; CTB 31(2), sch 4 para 64, sch 5 para 13; CTB60+ 19(1), sch 3 para 11, sch 4 para 29

Equity release schemes

13.104 If the claimant is in an equity release scheme, it means that he or she receives (loaned) payments which are advanced by a lender at regular intervals and are secured on his or her home. If the claimant or any partner is aged 60+, such payments count in full as income (even though they are a loan). If the claimant and any partner are under 60, there is no specific rule in the law (but see para. 13.136).

Life interest and liferent

13.105 If a claimant has a life interest or (in Scotland) liferent, it means he or she has the right to use a property or other asset during his or her or someone else's lifetime, after which it will pass to someone else. The actual value to the claimant (if any) of the life interest or liferent is counted as capital; and any actual income the claimant receives from it is counted as earned or unearned income as appropriate. Disregard as capital the value of the right to receive income from it (para. 13.92).

Reversionary interest

13.106 If a claimant has a reversionary interest, it means he or she will not possess a property or other asset until some future event (for example, the death of a relative). Disregard in full the capital value of a reversionary interest. (Different rules apply to a property the claimant has rented out: table 13.3).

Trust funds and compensation payments

13.107 This section is about personal injury payments and trusts including special trusts and compensation schemes which are treated favourably (i.e. disregarded). Apart from these special schemes the rules about the treatment of all other personal injury payments and trusts changed on 2nd October 2006.

- For the rules about special trusts and compensation schemes which are treated favourably see paragraphs 13.108-113.
- For the rules about all other payments for personal injury and other trusts see paragraphs 13.114-120.

Macfarlane, Independent Living and similar trusts

13.108 Payments from any of the following trusts are usually disregarded in full as described in para. 13.109):

- The Independent Living Fund ((2006) (to help severely disabled people to live independently);

13.104 HB60+ 29(1)(w),(8); NIHB60+ 27(1)(u),(8); CTB60+ 19(1)(w),(8)

13.105 HB sch 6 para 15; HB60+ sch 6 para 27; NIHB sch 7 para 16; NIHB60+ sch 7 para 29; CTB sch 5 para 15; CTB60+ sch 4 para 27

13.106 HB sch 6 para 7; HB60+ sch 6 para 5; NIHB sch 7 para 7; NIHB60+ sch 7 para 5; CTB sch 5 para 7; CTB60+ sch 4 para 5

- The Macfarlane Trust, the Macfarlane (Special Payments) Trust, the Macfarlane (Special Payments) (No. 2) Trust, (for people with haemophilia infected with HIV through blood products);
- 'The Fund', and the Eileen Trust (for people who contracted HIV through NHS products);
- The Skipton Fund (for people infected with hepatitis C through blood products);
- The Variant Creutzfeldt-Jacob Disease Trust (for people who have contracted variant CJD and their families).

13.109 Any payments made from the first three trusts are disregarded in full as income and capital. Also disregarded are payments from the Skipton Fund (which are made as lump sum capital payments). Payments from the second and third of these trusts can still be disregarded if they are passed on to certain relatives as a gift or an inheritance (and are always disregarded if the person who receives it or their partner is aged 60+). For further details see GM para. BW2.620. Payments from the fifth trust are made as a lump sum capital payment (as an interim and final award). They are disregarded indefinitely if they are made to the person who has contracted vCJD, or to their partner or surviving partner. They are disregarded for two years if made to parent or guardian of a child who has vCJD.

The London Bombing Charitable Relief Fund and compensation for the families of the disappeared

13.110 Payments from the London Bombing Charitable Relief Fund (set up to assist victims of the bombings on 7th July 2005) are disregarded, without time limit, as both income and capital. In Northern Ireland only, compensation payments by the Secretary of State to the families of the disappeared are disregarded (as capital) for 52 weeks from the date of receipt.

Second World War payments

13.111 Disregard in full (as capital), without time limit, the *ex gratia* payments of £10,000 made by the Secretary of State to people who were imprisoned or interned by the Japanese during the Second World War. Authorities need not attempt to identify the particular £10,000: £10,000 should simply be disregarded from the capital the claimant has.

13.108 HB 2(1), sch 5 para 35, sch 6 paras 24,34,55; HB60+ 29(1), sch 6 para 14;
NIHB 2(1), sch 6 para 37, sch 7 paras 25,35,52; NIHB60+ 27(1), sch 7 para 14;
CTB sch 4 para 36, sch 5 paras 24,34,57; CTB60+ 19(1), sch 4 para 14

13.110 HB 2(1), sch 5 para 35, sch 6 para 25; HB60+ 29(1), sch 6 para 16;
NIHB 2(1), sch 6 para 37, sch 7 paras 25,58; NIHB60+ 27(1), sch 7 paras 16,27;
CTB 2(1), sch 4 para 36, sch 5 para 24; CTB60+ 19(1), sch 4 para 16

13.111 HB sch 5 para 15(g), sch 6 paras 54,56; HB60+ 29(1), sch 6 paras 13,15;
NIHB sch 6 para 15(f), sch 7 paras 51,53; NIHB60+ 27(1), sch 7 paras 13,15;
CTB sch 4 para 16(g), sch 5 paras 56,58; CTB60+ 19(1), sch 4 paras 13,15

13.112 Also disregard in full as capital, without time limit, any payment (apart from a war pension) made to compensate for the fact that, during the Second World War, the claimant or partner or either's deceased spouse or civil partner:

- was a slave labourer or a forced labourer; or
- had suffered property loss or personal injury; or
- was a parent of a child who had died.

13.113 Subject to the over-riding £20 disregard (para. 13.156), £10.00 per week is disregarded as income from any pension paid by the German or Austrian Government to the victims of Nazi persecution for the period it covers. There is no disregard of the capital value of arrears.

Personal injury payments of income

13.114 Payments of income for a personal injury (of the claimant or any partner), including payments from a trust, are disregarded in full as income.

Personal injury payments of capital

13.115 Payments of capital for a personal injury (of the claimant or any partner), including payments from a trust, are disregarded in full. There is no time or other limit if the claimant or any partner is aged 60+ and in their case the disregard equals the amount of the personal injury payment: the particular money need not be kept track of. If the claimant or any partner is under 60, there are two limits:

- the disregard lasts only for 52 weeks from the payment date (sometimes referred to as a 'grace period' since within this period the money is likely to be spent or, if not, it should be possible to form a trust to hold the money); and
- there is only one 52-week disregard per personal injury. If someone gets two or more payments for the same personal injury, the 52 weeks runs only from the first such payment.

Personal injury payments held in a trust

13.116 Any payments for personal injury (of the claimant or any partner) which are held in a trust are disregarded in full (as capital) without time limit (and if the claimant and any partner are under 60, so is the value of the right to receive income from them: para. 13.92). If the claimant or any partner is aged 60+ the

13.114 HB sch 5 para 14; HB60+ sch 5 para 12; NIHB sch 6 para 14; NIHB60+ sch 6 para 13; CTB sch 4 para 15; CTB60+ sch 3 para 12

13.115 HB sch 5 para 14A; HB60+ sch 6 para 17; NIHB sch 7 para 14A; NIHB60+ sch 7 para 17; CTB sch 5 para 14A; CTB60+ sch 4 para 17

13.116 HB sch 6 para 14; HB60+ sch 6 para 17; NIHB sch 7 para 14; NIHB60+ sch 7 para 17; CTB sch 5 para 14; CTB60+ sch 4 para 17

disregard equals the amount of the personal injury payment: the particular money need not be kept track of. If the trust pays the money out to the claimant it is then also disregarded for the reasons in the previous two paragraphs.

Personal injury payments administered by a court

13.117 Compensation for personal injury (of claimant or partner), if paid into a court and administered by the court on the compensated person's behalf, is disregarded in full (as capital) without time limit. The same applies to money which is held by someone other than a court but is administered subject to the order or direction of a court. If the compensated person is under 18, the same points apply to compensation for the death of a parent.

Personal injury payments under a court order or out-of-court settlement

13.118 If the claimant and any partner is under 60, periodic payments under a court order for personal injury (of claimant or partner) are counted as unearned income. If the claimant or any partner is aged 60+, the following periodic payments are disregarded (as income):

- payments under a court order for accident, injury or disease of the claimant, partner or child;
- payments in an out-of-court settlement for injury of the claimant or partner.

Property held in a trust

13.119 If the claimant or any partner is aged 60+, the value of any property held in a trust for the claimant's or partner's benefit is disregarded – so long as the trust makes payments or has a discretion to make payments to the claimant or partner. There is no such disregard if the claimant and any partner are under 60.

Payments received from a discretionary trust

13.120 If a discretionary trust (one which the claimant has no absolute right to take money from) makes a payment of capital to a claimant, that capital (insofar as it remains unspent) becomes part of their capital for HB/CTB purposes. If such a trust makes a payment of income to a claimant, it is counted in full as income if the claimant and any partner are under 60; but if the claimant or any partner is aged 60+:

- £20 is disregarded if the payments are for food, ordinary clothing or footwear or household fuel; rent, council tax or water charges for which

---

13.117 HB sch 6 paras 45,46; HB60+ sch 6 para 17; NIHB sch 7 para 45; NIHB60+ sch 7 para 17; CTB sch 5 paras 47,48; CTB60+ sch 4 para 17

13.118 HB 41(5); HB60+ sch 5 paras 14,15; NIHB 38(4); NIHB60+ sch 6 paras 15,16; CTB 31(5); CTB60+ sch 3 paras 14,15

13.119 HB60+ sch 6 para 30; NIHB60+ sch 7 para 32; CTB60+ sch 4 para 30

13.120 HB60+ sch 5 para 12; NIHB60+ sch 6 para 13; CTB60+ sch 3 para 12

the claimant or partner is liable; or housing costs (such as mortgage interest payments) that could be met by guarantee credit (but this is subject to the over-riding £20 disregard: para. 13.156);

- the whole amount is disregarded if the payments are for anything else.

Other items of income and capital

Maintenance for a child

13.121 Disregard £15 of maintenance received by the claimant or partner, but only if there is at least one child or young person in the family, and only if the maintenance is paid by one of the following:

- if the claimant or any partner is aged 60+, by a current or former married partner or civil partner of either of them; but
- if the claimant and any partner are under 60, by:
  - a former partner of either of them, or
  - a parent of any child or young person in the claimant's family (so long as that parent is not in the claimant's family), or
  - the Secretary of State (under child support provisions) in lieu of maintenance.

The definitions of 'partner', 'child', 'young person', 'family' are in chapter 4. The £15 disregard applies whether the maintenance is payable to the claimant or to a child or young person. If two or more maintenance payments are received in any week, the maximum disregard is £15 per week. (The rules before 27th October 2008 were different.)

Maintenance for an adult

13.122 If maintenance is received by a claimant or partner in respect of themself:

- if the claimant or any partner is aged 60+, disregard the whole amount;
- if the claimant and any partner are under 60 and have at least one dependent child in the family (and the claimant is thus entitled to the family premium), disregard £15 per week;
- if the claimant and any partner are under 60 and do not have a dependent child in the family, count the whole amount as unearned income.

(The rules before 27th October 2008 were different.)

13.121 HB sch 5 para 47; HB60+ 29(1), sch 5 para 20; NIHB sch 6 para 49; NIHB60+ 27(1), sch 6 para 21; CTB sch 4 para 48; CTB60+ sch 3 para 20

13.122 HB sch 5 para 47; HB60+ 29(1), sch 5 para 20; NIHB sch 6 para 49; NIHB 60+ 27(1), sch 6 para 21; CTB sch 4 para 48; CTB60+ 19(1), sch 3 para 20

The New Deal and other government training schemes

13.123 People on New Deal or other government training schemes are normally also on JSA(IB), ESA(IR) or IS (paras. 13.4 and 13.37-38). The rules for people on a training scheme but who are not on JSA(IB), ESA(IR) or IS are so rarely needed that they are not given in full here but there are two possibilities:

- If the claimant or any partner is aged 60+, all such payments are disregarded as income: there are no further conditions (para. 13.9); but if they form part of the claimant's capital (which is improbable) they count as capital: there are no special disregards.
- If the claimant and any partner are aged under 60, treatment of the payment as income or capital depends on the particular type of training scheme (e.g. Access to Work, Lone Parent Work Search, Better Off In Work Credit). For details see GM paras. 597-611.

Sports awards

13.124 If the claimant or any partner is aged 60+, these are disregarded if paid as income but counted if paid as capital. If the claimant and any partner are under 60, they are dealt with as follows:

- Any amounts awarded in respect of the claimant's or a member of the family's food (excluding vitamins, minerals or other special performance-enhancing dietary supplements), ordinary clothing or footwear (excluding school uniform and sportswear), household fuel, rent, council tax, or water charges, are counted in full as income or capital as appropriate.
- Any other amounts are disregarded as unearned income, and as capital for 26 weeks from the date of payment.

Charitable and/or voluntary payments

13.125 Payments which are charitable and/or voluntary (such as payments from family, friends or charities) are assessed as follows:

- payments of income are disregarded in all circumstances;
- lump sum payments in kind (i.e. payments of goods rather than money) are disregarded (as capital);
- other payments of capital are disregarded if the claimant or any partner is aged 60+, but count as capital if the claimant and any partner are under 60.

13.123 HB 2(1),46(7), sch 5 paras 13,49,58,60,61; sch 6 paras 8,35, 43,44,49; NIHB 2(1),43(7), sch 6 paras 12,51,60, sch 7 paras 8,36,44; CTB 2(1),36(7), sch 4 paras 14,50,58,60,61, sch 5 paras 8,35,43,45,51

13.124 HB 2(1), sch 5 para 59, sch 6 para 50; HB60+ 29(1); NIHB 2(1), sch 6 para 61, sch 7 para 49; NIHB60+ 27(1); CTB 2(1), sch 4 para 59, sch 5 para 52; CTB60+ 19(1)

13.125 HB 46(6), sch 5 para 14, sch 6 para 34; HB60+29(1); NIHB 43(6), sch 6 para 14, sch 7 para 35; NIHB60+ 27(1); CTB 36(6), sch 4 para 15, sch 5 para 34; CTB60+ 19(1)

These rules are of particular importance when a claimant has no income other than the above (e.g. during a period when he or she fails to 'sign on') and thus qualifies for maximum HB/CTB (para. 6.9).

Payments in kind

13.126 A 'payment in kind' is a payment made in goods (e.g. fuel, food) rather than in money (e.g. cheques, cash). Regular payments in kind are dealt with as follows. If the payments are voluntary or charitable, see paragraph 13.125. If the payments are earned income they are usually disregarded (para. 14.33). If the payments are made in the course of business to a self-employed claimant, their value counts in full as self-employed income (because there is no specific disregard in such a case). If the payments are unearned (i.e. in any other case), their value is disregarded.

Concessionary coal and cash in lieu

13.127 Concessionary coal is disregarded as income, being a payment in kind. Cash in lieu of concessionary coal counts as income if the claimant and any partner are aged under 60 *(R v Doncaster Metropolitan Borough Council and Another ex p Boulton),* but is disregarded as income if the claimant or any partner is aged 60+.

Health benefits and prison visits payments

13.128 If the claimant or any partner is aged 60+, all the following payments are disregarded in full (as income). If the claimant and any partner are under 60, all the following are disregarded in full as unearned income and also disregarded as capital for 52 weeks from the date of payment:

- payments for travel for hospital visits;
- health service supplies or payments in lieu of free milk and vitamins;
- health in pregnancy grant;
- healthy start vouchers;
- Home Office payments for travel for prison visits.

Jurors' allowances

13.129 If the claimant or any partner is aged 60+ these are disregarded. If the claimant and any partner are under 60, they are disregarded except insofar as they compensate for loss of earnings or loss of a social security benefit.

13.126 HB 40(1), sch 5 para 23; HB60+ 29(1); NIHB 37(1), sch 6 para 24; NIHB60+ 27(1); CTB 30(1), sch 4 para 24; CTB60+ 19(1)

13.127 HB 40(1), sch 5 para 23; HB60+ 29(1); NIHB 37(1), sch 6 para 24; NIHB60+ 27(1); CTB 30(1), sch 4 para 24; CTB60+ 19(1)

13.128 HB sch 5 paras 44-46, sch 6 paras 40-42; HB60+ 29(1); NIHB sch 6 paras 46-48, sch 7 paras 41-43; NIHB60+ 27(1); CTB sch 4 paras 45-47, sch 5 paras 40-42; CTB60+ 19(1)

13.129 HB sch 5 para 39; HB60+ 29(1); NIHB sch 6 para 41; NIHB60+ 27(1); CTB sch 4 para 41; CTB60+ 19(1)

Gallantry awards

13.130 If the claimant and any partner are under 60, the following are disregarded (as both income and capital without time limit). If the claimant or any partner is aged 60+ they count in full as capital (apart from any amounts paid as income, which are disregarded):

- Victoria Cross and George Cross payments;
- the lump sum payments of up to £6,000 for those who have agreed not to receive any further payments of income from those; and
- analogous awards for gallantry from this country or another country.

Parental contributions to students

13.131 The following rules apply to contributions made by claimants to a student son or daughter ('student' is defined in paras. 21.4-15):

- If a claimant has been assessed as being able to make a contribution to the student's grant (other than a discretionary grant) or student loan, the whole amount of the assessed contribution is disregarded in the assessment of the claimant's income.
- If a claimant contributes towards the maintenance of a student under the age of 25, who has a discretionary grant or no grant, the amount of the contribution is disregarded in the assessment of the claimant's income – but only up to a maximum weekly figure. The maximum weekly figure is £50.95 minus the weekly amount of any discretionary grant.

So far as possible the above are disregarded from unearned income, then any balance is disregarded from earned income.

Education Maintenance Allowances

13.132 Disregard Education Maintenance Allowances or Awards, including Assisted Places Allowances (as unearned income). These include payments under the national scheme for 16 to 18-year-olds in non-advanced education and also payments towards a child's travel to school.

13.133 If the claimant and any partner are under 60, disregard Education Maintenance Allowance bonuses as capital for 52 weeks from the date of payment. There is no such disregard for 60+s.

13.130 HB sch 5 para 10, sch 6 para 47; HB60+ 29(1); NIHB sch 6 para 11, sch 7 para 46; NIHB60+ 27(1); CTB sch 4 para 11, sch 5 para 49; CTB60+ 19(1)

13.131 HB sch 4 para 11, sch 5 paras 19,20; HB60+ sch 4 para 6, sch 5 paras 18,19; NIHB sch 5 para 11, sch 6 paras 20,21; NIHB60+ sch 5 para 6, sch 6 paras 19,20; CTB sch 3 para 11, sch 4 paras 19,20; CTB60+ sch 2 para 6, sch 3 paras 18,19

13.132 HB sch 5 para 11; HB60+ 29(1); NIHB sch 6 para 12; NIHB60+ 27(1); CTB sch 4 para 12; CTB60+ 19(1)

13.133 HB sch 6 para 51; NIHB sch 7 para 49; CTB sch 5 para 53

Career development loans

13.134 In Great Britain only, career development loans are paid under arrangements between the Learning and Skills Council and certain national banks. If the claimant or any partner is aged 60+, they are disregarded as income. If the claimant and any partner are under 60, only the element of the loan which relates to living expenses is taken into account, and even this is disregarded if the course which the loan supports has been completed. Note that this exemption does not apply to other types of loan for living expenses for people who are undertaking education or training.

Assistance with repaying student loans

13.135 Disregard (as unearned income) any payment made to a former student to help with repaying his or her student loan. This applies whether the payer pays it direct or via the ex-student. It includes Government payments under the Teacher Repayment Loan Scheme, but also includes any other case.

Loans

13.136 A genuine loan increases a person's capital (until and to the extent that he or she spends it, perhaps on the thing it was lent for). However, it is at least possible for a loan to be income (*Morrell v Secretary of State for Work and Pensions* reported as *R(IS) 6/03,* and see para. 13.11) depending on the circumstances of the case, but the burden of proof that it should be lies with the authority *(CH/2675/2007).* However, the law expressly requires this in the case of student loans (paras. 21.30-35), career development loans for the under-60s (para. 13.134) and equity release schemes for 60+s (para. 13.104) (although in the case of the first two certain elements can be disregarded).

Outstanding instalments of capital

13.137 If the claimant or partner is aged 60+, outstanding instalments of capital count as capital when received (para. 13.15).

13.138 If the claimant and any partner are under 60 and if, at the claimant's date of claim for HB/CTB (or at the date of any subsequent reconsideration of the claim), he or she is entitled to outstanding instalments of capital (i.e. instalments due after that date), the authority must consider whether the sum of the outstanding instalments and the claimant's other capital exceeds £16,000:

- If it does, the outstanding instalments are disregarded as capital but are counted as income. The law does not set out a way of doing this.
- If it does not, the outstanding instalments are counted as capital from the date of claim (or reconsideration).

13.134 HB 41(4), sch 5 para 13; HB60+ 29(1); CTB 31(4), sch 4 para 14; CTB60+ 19(1)

13.135 HB sch 5 para 12; HB60+ 29(1); CTB sch 4 para 13; CTB60+ 19(1)

13.138 HB 41(1), sch 6 para 18; NIHB 38(1), sch 7 para 19; CTB 31(1), sch 5 para 18

Capital outside the UK

13.139 The following rules apply if a claimant possesses capital in a country outside the UK.

- If there is no prohibition in that country against bringing the money to the UK, value it at its market or surrender value in that country; then disregard 10% if selling it would incur costs; then disregard any mortgage or other 'encumbrance' (e.g. a loan) secured on it; then disregard any charge which would be incurred in converting it into sterling; and count the remainder as capital.
- If there is such a prohibition, value it at what a willing buyer in the UK would give for it; then disregard 10% if selling it would incur costs; then disregard any mortgage or other 'encumbrance' (e.g. a loan) secured on it; and count the remainder as capital.

Income outside the UK

13.140 The following rules apply if a claimant is entitled to income payable in a country outside the UK.

- If there is no prohibition in that country against bringing the money to the UK, treat it as income in the normal way, allowing any disregard which may apply (including any earnings disregard in the case of earned income); also disregard any charge for converting it into sterling.
- If there is such a prohibition, disregard it; also (but only if the claimant and any partner are under 60) disregard as capital the value of the right to receive income from it (para. 13.92).

Expenses for unpaid work

13.141 Expenses for unpaid work (whether for a charity, voluntary organisation, friend or neighbour) are disregarded. (For expenses for paid work, see para. 14.39.)

13.139 HB 48, sch 6 para 23; HB60+ 46, sch 6 para 23; NIHB 45, sch 7 para 24; NIHB60+ 44, sch 7 para 23; CTB 38, sch 5 para 23; CTB60+ 36, sch 4 para 23

13.140 HB sch 5 paras 24,33, sch 6 para 16; HB60+ sch 5 paras 16,17; NIHB sch 6 paras 25,34, sch 7 para 17; NIHB60+ sch 6 paras 17,18; CTB sch 4 paras 25,34, sch 5 para 16; CTB60+ sch 3 paras 16,17

13.141 HB sch 5 para 2; HB60+ 29(1); NIHB sch 6 para 2; NIHB60+ 27(1); CTB sch 4 para 2; CTB60+ 19(1)

Notional income and capital

13.142 In the situations described below a claimant is treated, for HB/main CTB purposes, as possessing income and/or capital he or she does not in fact possess – known as 'notional' income and/or capital. The notional income or capital is assessed as if it was actual income or capital and any relevant disregards must be applied.

Deprivation

13.143 If a claimant deliberately deprives himself or herself of capital or income in order to qualify for HB (or for more HB), he or she is treated as still having it for HB purposes. The same applies independently for CTB. It is the claimant's intention which must be taken into account (not the item he or she spent the money on).

13.144 Authorities sometimes (wrongly) confuse what the money was spent on with what the claimant's intentions were. A recent commissioner's decision illustrates this *(R(H) 1/06)*. The claimant was a schizophrenic man without an appointee who lived in 'an intolerable level of chaos'. He had a very big windfall and telephoned the authority to arrange for his HB to be stopped. When he re-claimed four months later, he had almost none of this capital left. It was agreed by the parties that the money had gone on 'alcohol and high living'. The authority said he had deprived himself of this money. The commissioner was satisfied that it had not been shown that the claimant appreciated what he was doing, or the consequences of it, and held that the test whether someone spent capital 'for the purpose of' getting (more) HB is subjective. The commissioner remitted the case to a differently constituted tribunal with various directions including that the tribunal take proper account of the claimant's mental state and capabilities.

13.145 If the claimant or any partner is aged 60+, one special rule applies. It is that repaying or reducing a debt, or purchasing goods or services reasonable in the claimant's circumstances is never deprivation. The rule is automatic, and applies regardless of the claimant's intention. For any other question of deprivation in the case of this age group, and for all questions of deprivation in the case of under 60s, the claimant's intention is the only determining factor.

13.142 HB 42(11),(12),49(7); HB60+ 47(5); NIHB 39(11),(12),46(7); NIHB60+ 45(5); CTB 32(11),(12),39(7); CTB60+ 37(5)

13.143 HB 42(1),49(1); HB60+ 41(8),47(1); NIHB 39(1),46(1); NIHB60+ 39(8),45(1); CTB 32(1),39(1); CTB60+ 31(8),37(1)

13.145 HB60+ 47(2); NIHB60+ 45(2); CTB60+ 37(2)

Diminishing notional capital

13.146 If a claimant is treated as having notional capital for the above reason (paras. 13.143-145), the amount of notional capital taken into account is reduced each week, broadly speaking, by the amount of any HB, CTB, JSA(IB), ESA(IR) or IS (but not WTC or CTC), lost as a result of the claimant being treated as having notional capital. For further details, see GM paras. BW1.760-807.

Money available on application

13.147 The claimant can be treated as having money which he or she has not applied for but could. The details follow.

13.148 If the claimant or any partner is aged 60+, the rule is limited to the following two items, and does not apply to any other kind of income, or any kind of capital at all:

- state retirement pension (but not the increased amount a person does not get if they choose a lump sum instead: para. 13.54); and
- private or occupational pensions.

13.149 If the claimant and any partner are under 60, any income or capital which the claimant could have on application (in other words, simply by applying for it) is treated as possessed by him or her from the date it could be obtained. For example, this rule is sometimes used in the case of unclaimed child benefit.

13.150 The rule does not apply to:

- working tax credit or child tax credit;
- income which could be obtained in the form of a DWP rehabilitation allowance;
- payments under the flexible New Deal;
- payments (of income or capital) made to a provider of a New Deal arrangement;
- income or capital which could be obtained from a discretionary trust or a trust for personal injury (paras. 13.114-120);
- capital which could be obtained from the London Bombing Charitable Relief Fund (para. 13.110); or
- any kind of disregarded capital.

Also the DWP advises that this rule should not be applied in the case of income from any other social security benefit unless the authority is sure about the amount the person could receive (GM para. BW2.682).

13.146 HB 50; HB60+ 48; NIHB 47; NIHB60+ 46; CTB 40; CTB60+ 38

13.148 HB60+ 2(1),41; NIHB60+ 2(1),39; CTB60+ 2(1),31

13.149 HB 42; NIHB 39; CTB 32

Payments given to one person but used by another

13.151 If income (including payments in kind: para. 13.126) is paid in A's name but used by B for food, household fuel, clothing or footwear (other than school uniform and sportswear), eligible rent (apart from any non-dependant deduction), council tax, water charges or in Northern Ireland eligible rates, it is treated as belonging to B. If the claimant and any partner are under 60, the rule applies also to capital (but not for 60+s).

13.152 This rule must not be used in relation to occupational or personal pensions (including payments from the Pension Protection Fund: para. 13.94) if the intended beneficiary is bankrupt or sequestered, and payment is made to a trustee (or similar) for him or her, and any family have no other income.

Up-ratings

13.153 If the April up-rating date for social security benefits or tax credits is different from that for HB/CTB, they are generally treated as up-rated on the same date as HB/CTB (paras. 17.34-35). The same applies if the 'Assessed Income Figure' (used when the claimant or partner is on savings credit: para. 13.160) changes at that time.

Work paid at less than the going rate

13.154 This rule applies only if the claimant and any partner are under 60. If the claimant is paid less than the going rate for a job, he or she is treated as having whatever additional pay is reasonable in the circumstances. The means of the employer must be taken into account; and this rule does not apply to voluntary work or to claimants on a government training programme or DWP-approved work placement. When this rule is used, disregard notional tax and national insurance contributions and apply the earnings disregards (paras. 14.14-26).

Relationship to a company

13.155 This rule applies only if the claimant and any partner are under 60. It applies to a claimant who is not the sole owner of, or a partner in, a company, but whose relationship to that company is analogous to someone who is. In such cases, the claimant's share of the capital of that company is assessed as though he or she was the sole owner or partner and any actual share of the company he or she possesses is disregarded.

13.151 HB 42(6)(a),(13),49(3),(8); HB60+ 42; NIHB 39(6)(a),(14),46(3),(8); NIHB60+ 40; CTB 32(a),(13),39(4),(8); CTB60+ 32

13.153 HB 42(8); HB60+ 41(9),(10); NIHB 39(8); NIHB60+ 39(11),(12); CTB 32(8); CTB60+ 31(9),(10)

13.154 HB 42(9),(10); NIHB 39(9),(10); CTB 32(9),(10)

13.155 HB 49(5),(6); NIHB 46(5),(6); CTB 39(5),(6)

The over-riding £20 disregard from certain income

13.156 In any particular claim for HB/main CTB, the maximum weekly disregard per claim is £20 from any or all of the following:

- in the case of authorities in Great Britain which do not operate a local scheme (para. 22.12), certain war pensions for bereavement or disablement (para. 13.59);
- widowed parent's allowance (para. 13.56);
- if the claimant and any partner are under 60, student loan and access fund income (chapter 21);
- if the claimant or any partner is aged 60+, certain payments made by trusts (para. 13.120).

This rule is so rare that in practice it is never needed, and the DWP is considering whether it should be abolished (circular HB/CTB U1/2009, forthcoming).

Assessing people on savings credit

13.157 This section explains how income and capital are assessed for HB/CTB if the claimant or any partner is on savings credit (so long as they are not also on guarantee credit). It over-rides the rules described earlier in this chapter.

Income and capital is assessed by the DWP

13.158 A claimant on savings credit has had their income and capital assessed by the DWP (i.e. the pension, disability and carers service). With the exceptions mentioned below, the authority must use the DWP's assessment of income and capital in assessing the claimant's HB/CTB. Table 17.5 gives more information about the date these figures take effect.

The DWP must notify the authority

13.159 The DWP must notify the authority of its assessment of income and capital within two working days of the following (or in either case as soon as reasonably practicable thereafter):

- the date the DWP did the assessment, if the person has already claimed or is already on HB/CTB by that time; or
- the date the authority informs the DWP that the claimant or partner has claimed HB/CTB, in all other cases.

13.156 HB sch 5 para 34; HB60+ sch 5 para 12(3); NIHB sch 6 para 35; NIHB60+ sch 6 para 13(3); CTB sch 4 para 35; CTB60+ sch 3 para 12(3)

13.158 HB60+ 27(1); NIHB60+ 25(1); CTB60+ 17(1)

13.159 HB60+ 27(2),(3); NIHB60+ 25(2),(3); CTB60+ 17(2),(3)

13.160 In particular, the DWP must include in the decision notice its 'assessed income figure' ('AIF'). This is the DWP's assessment of the person's net weekly income (including tariff income).

13.161 If the DWP notifies the authority of new figures at any time, this is implemented as a change of circumstances (supersession) in the HB/CTB claim (table 17.1 and para. 17.5).

When the authority adjusts the DWP's assessed income figure

13.162 Once the DWP has notified the authority of the claimant's assessed income figure, it is adjusted by the authority – but only if one (or more) of the things in table 13.4 applies. This is simply to reflect differences in assessing income for pension credit purposes as opposed to HB/CTB purposes.

When the authority adjusts the DWP's capital figure

13.163 The capital figure notified by the DWP is never (apart from the one exception below) adjusted. In particular, if the DWP notifies a figure above £16,000, the claimant is not entitled to HB/CTB at that time.

13.164 The one exception works as follows. If the DWP notified the authority that the claimant's capital was £16,000 or lower and then the claimant's capital rises above £16,000 during the course of the DWP's 'assessed income period' (the period during which the DWP does not reconsider the amount of a claimant's income or capital) then entitlement to HB/CTB ends.

13.162 HB60+ 27(4),(5); NIHB60+ 25(4),(5); CTB60+ 17(4),(5)

13.163 HB60+ 27(6),(7); NIHB60+ 25(6),(7); CTB60+ 17(6),(7)

13.164 HB60+ 27(8); NIHB60+ 25(8); CTB60+ 17(8)

Table 13.4: Claimants on savings credit: adjustments to the DWP's assessed income figure (AIF)

All the amounts mentioned in this table are weekly.

(a) Start with the DWP's assessed income figure

(b) Add the amount of savings credit payable

(c) If the claimant receives the following, deduct the amount shown*:

• earned income if the claimant is a lone parent	£5 (table 14.1)
• earned income if the claimant meets the conditions for the additional earnings disregard	£16.85 (para. 14.24)
• earned income if the claimant meets the necessary conditions for the child care disregard	the whole amount, up to the appropriate limit (para. 14.15)
• maintenance received from a current or former married partner or civil partner	the full HB/CTB disregard ** (paras. 13.121-122)
• pensions for war bereavement or disablement	any amount disregarded under a local scheme (i.e. any amount over £10: para. 22.12)

(d) Make the following (very rare) adjustments if appropriate:

- add the income of any partner who was ignored in assessing pension credit but has to be taken into account in HB/CTB
- if the authority determines that the income and capital of a non-dependant should be used instead of the income and capital of the claimant and partner (para 13.7), use this income instead of the DWP's assessment

* In each case the deduction equals the difference between what is disregarded in the assessment of pension credit and what is disregarded in HB/CTB.

** This may change during the course of 2009-10.

Example: A war widow on savings credit

Information

A war widow aged 81 gets savings credit of £12.00 per week. She also gets a war widow's pension of £57.00 per week and retirement pension and an occupational pension, and has some capital.

The DWP notifies the authority of its assessed income figure (AIF) of £202.00 and notifies her capital as being £7,000. The authority dealing with her claim has a local scheme whereby it disregards the whole of a war widow's pension.

Assessment

The authority (table 13.4) starts with the DWP's assessed income figure (£202.00) and adds her savings credit (£12.00), giving a total of £214.00. It then disregards all but £10.00 of the war widow's pension of £57.00 (in other words, it disregards £47.00). This gives her net income for HB/CTB purposes as being £167.00 per week. It must use this figure in calculating her entitlement to HB/CTB.

The authority must accept that her capital is £7,000 at the outset (and must not calculate tariff income because the DWP has already included this in the AIF). If evidence later arises of an increase in her capital, perhaps taking it above £16,000, it then becomes the authority's duty to re-assess her capital; but no action is taken upon this re-assessment unless the amount is greater than £16,000.

14 Employed earners

14.1 This chapter explains how employed earners' income is assessed. It covers:

- deciding who is an employed earner;
- assessing gross earnings over an appropriate period (the assessment period);
- making the right deductions and conversions to arrive at a net weekly earned income figure after disregards that is used in the benefit calculation;
- the earned income disregards;
- the disregard for child care costs;
- the additional disregard for people working at least 16/30 hours per week;
- particular kinds of earnings and expenses; and
- starting work, absences from work and ending work.

14.2 This chapter applies only if the claimant and any partner are not on JSA(IB), ESA(IR), income support or pension credit. It applies to the assessment of a claimant's earnings and to those of any partner. In some cases the rules are different depending on whether the claimant or any partner are under 60 or aged 60+. For more information on these points, and other general considerations, see paragraphs 13.2-9.

14.3 This chapter does not apply to the earnings of a non-dependant or second adult. The law does not lay down any particular way of assessing earnings in such cases, although it must be gross (not net) of tax and national insurance. In practice, most authorities assess a non-dependant or second adult's income under the rules in this chapter, but using the total (gross) earnings figure rather than the net earnings figure.

Who is an 'employed earner'?

14.4 A person is an 'employed earner' if they are gainfully employed in Great Britain (or in the Republic of Ireland or Northern Ireland) either under a contract of service, or in an office (including elective office), with general earnings. Employed earners who are gainfully employed under a contract of service include employees who work for a wage or salary. The employed earners who work 'in an office' include directors of limited companies (para. 14.38), local authority councillors (para. 14.34) and clergy.

14.4 CBA 2(1)(a); HB 2(1); CTB 2(1); NIHB 2(1); NIHB60+ 2(1); CTB 2(1); CTB60+ 2(1)

The assessment of earnings

14.5 The authority needs to work out a net weekly earnings figure after appropriate disregards to use in the benefit calculation. To do this it must:

- identify that there are earnings derived or likely to be derived from employment as an employed earner;
- establish the gross earnings over an appropriate assessment period;
- deduct amounts attributable to income tax and Class 1 national insurance contributions;
- deduct half of any approved pension contribution;
- convert the net amount if necessary to a weekly figure;
- deduct a fixed earned income disregard and, if appropriate, amounts for child care costs and for certain people working 16/30 hours or more per week.

In certain circumstances notional (rather than actual) earnings are used but this does not apply where the claimant or any partner is aged 60 or over (para. 13.154).

Gross earnings

14.6 Gross earnings means the total amount of earnings after the deduction of expenses wholly and exclusively incurred in the performance of the employment (*R(IS) 16/93* and see para. 14.40) but before any authorised deductions by the employer for tax, etc.

The assessment period

14.7 The authority must identify an appropriate assessment period that can be used as the basis for calculating or estimating an average weekly earnings figure. Its aim should be to identify the period that provides the most accurate basis on which to do this. The law gives the following guidelines for this:

(a) if the earnings relate to a period of one week or less, then weekly gross earnings equal the amount for that period;

(b) if the earnings are regular and do not fluctuate, then weekly gross earnings are found by taking an average over the period running up to the date of claim or any supersession (see para. 14.8);

(c) if the claimant has not been employed long enough for (b) to apply, then weekly gross earnings are based on what the claimant has been paid, so long as this is representative;

(d) if the claimant's hours vary over a recognisable cycle, then weekly gross earnings are averaged over the period of the complete cycle (including any periods where the claimant does no work, but excluding other absences).

14.7 HB 2(1),29; HB 60+ 2(1),33; NIHB 2(1),26; NIHB60+ 2(1) 31; CTB 2(1),19; CTB60+ 2(1),23

This is specified in the law only for 60+s but would equally be reasonable for under 60s;

(e) if it would be fairer to do so, or there is as yet no evidence of earnings, then weekly gross earnings should be assessed from a certificate of (actual or estimated) earnings. Authorities usually include these with their application forms for claimants to give to their employers to complete;

(f) if some other method would produce a fairer estimate of weekly gross earnings, then that method is used.

When earnings begin or change during an award, the above points apply again.

14.8 When applying method (b) above, there are small differences for under 60s as opposed to 60+s:

- if the claimant and any partner are under 60, they are averaged over:
  - the previous five weeks if the claimant is paid weekly, or
  - the previous two months if the claimant is paid monthly, or
  - any period which would produce a fairer result;
- if the claimant or any partner is aged 60+, they are averaged over:
  - the previous four payments if the last two are less than one month apart, or
  - the previous two payments if those are one month or more apart, or
  - any period which would produce a fairer result.

Calculating net earnings

14.9 Net earnings are the gross earnings over the assessment period less:

- income tax;
- Class 1 national insurance contributions;
- half of any sum paid by the employee towards an occupational or personal pension scheme.

Deducting income tax and national insurance contributions

14.10 If the claimant's actual gross earnings are used as described above, any income tax or Class 1 national insurance contributions deducted (or paid from them) must be deducted from those earnings. If the claimant's gross earnings are estimated, notional amounts for the income tax payable (using the basic rate of tax applicable to the assessment period and less only the personal allowance for a person aged under 65, whatever the claimant's actual circumstances) and Class 1 national insurance contributions must be deducted from those estimated earnings

---

14.8 HB 29; HB60+ 33; NIHB 26; NIHB60+ 31; CTB 19; CTB60+ 23

14.9 HB 36; HB60+ 36; NIHB 33; NIHB60+ 34; CTB 26; CTB60+ 26

14.10 HB 36; HB60+ 36; NIHB 33; NIHB60+ 34; CTB 26; CTB60+ 26

on a pro-rata basis. Note that from 6 April 2008 the 10% starting rate for earned income was removed and the previous 22% basic rate of tax was reduced to 20%.

14.11 If a claimant in Northern Ireland works in the Republic, the amounts deducted are those which the NIHE estimates would have been deducted if they worked in Northern Ireland.

Deducting half of pension contributions

14.12 Whether the claimant's actual or estimated gross earnings are used, half of any contributions they make (or which would be payable on the estimated earnings) to an occupational or personal pension scheme, must be deducted from the gross earnings figure.

Conversion to a weekly figure

14.13 If a claimant's earnings are paid other than weekly, they must be converted to a weekly figure as described in paragraph 6.70.

Earned income disregards

14.14 An earned income disregard must be deducted from the claimant's earnings. The amount depends on the type of case (table 14.1). Only one of the amounts shown in table 14.1 is deducted from the joint earnings of a couple or polygamous marriage. (In certain cases, there are further disregards: paras. 13.131, 14.15 and 14.24.)

Table 14.1: Weekly earned income disregards

£25 – lone parents

The weekly disregard is for anyone who counts as a lone parent for HB/CTB purposes.

£20 – certain people who are disabled or long-term sick

This weekly disregard (per single claimant or per couple) applies in all the following cases:

- where the claimant and any partner are under 60 and the claimant's applicable amount includes a disability premium (para. 12.21) or severe

---

14.11 NIHB 33; NIHB60+ 34

14.12 HB 36; HB60+ 36; NIHB 33; NIHB60+ 34; CTB 26; CTB60+ 26

14.14 HB 36(2), sch 4; HB60+ 36(1), sch 4; NIHB 33(2), sch 5; NIHB60+ 34(1), sch 5; CTB 26(2), sch 3; CTB60+ 26(1), sch 2

disability premium (para. 12.32); work related activity component or a support component (para. 12.9).

- where the claimant or any partner are 60+ and in receipt of:
  - disability living allowance
  - attendance allowance
  - a mobility supplement
  - long-term incapacity benefit
  - severe disablement allowance
  - the disability or severe disability element of working tax credit;
  - main phase employment and support allowance;

  or are
  - registered blind
  - treated as incapable of work (para. 12.24) for a continuous period of 196 days if terminally ill; or 364 days in any other case
  - treated as having limited capability for work or limited capability for work related activity (i.e. ESA credit only cases).

Note: If the claimant or any partner to whom a £20 disregard applies becomes 60 and either had an award of HB/CTB within eight weeks of becoming 60 then they re-qualify for the £20 disregard provided that:

- they qualified for the £20 disregard under the previous award; and
- continued in employment after that award ended, and
- there is no break of more than eight weeks in HB/CTB entitlement or employment.

£20 – certain carers and certain people in special occupations

Except where the preceding disregards of £25 or £20 apply, this weekly disregard (per single claimant or per couple) applies in the following cases:

- single claimants and couples who are awarded a carer premium
- single claimants and couples employed in the special occupations listed in paragraph 14.31.

Other single claimants and couples

In any case not mentioned above, the weekly disregard is:

- £10 per couple
- £5 per single claimant

Note

Other earned income disregards are described in paragraphs 14.15 and 14.24.

The child care disregard

14.15 In addition to the disregards in table 14.1, up to £175 (for one child) or £300 (for two or more children) per week per HB/main CTB claim is disregarded for child care costs in the circumstances described below.

Who can qualify?

14.16 The following groups can get the child care disregard in the circumstances described:

- lone parents in remunerative work (para. 14.17);
- couples if both are in remunerative work (para. 14.17);
- couples if one of them (claimant or partner) is in remunerative work and the other one incapacitated (para. 14.18), or in hospital, or in prison (whether serving a sentence or on remand).

Remunerative work

14.17 In general terms, 'remunerative work' means at least 16 hours per week (see paras. 6.27-29 for the full definition). For the purposes of the child care disregard certain people are treated as in remunerative work even when they are not. A person on maternity, paternity or adoption leave is treated as in remunerative work if they:

- were in remunerative work in the week before the leave started;
- are incurring relevant child care charges (para. 14.19); and
- are entitled to statutory maternity, paternity or adoption pay, maternity allowance or income support because of paternity leave.

The maximum periods for which statutory maternity and adoption pay and maternity allowance can be paid has been extended from 26 to 39 weeks for babies that were expected on or after 1st April 2007 or children that were expected to be placed for adoption on or after that date (DWP A7/2007 paras.1-5). People should be treated as in remunerative work from the day on which the leave starts to the earliest of:

- the day the leave ends;
- the date entitlement to the statutory pay or allowance ends – if no child care element of working tax credit is in payment on that date; or
- the date that entitlement to the child care element of working tax credit ends.

A person on (or on any combination of): statutory sick pay, short-term incapacity benefit at the lower rate, employment and support allowance, or income support because of incapacity for work, or credited with earnings because of incapacity for work, or limited capacity for work, should be treated as in remunerative work

---

14.15 HB 28; HB60+ 31; NIHB 25; NIHB60+ 29; CTB 18; CTB60+ 21

14.17 HB 28(2)-(4),(14)-(15); HB60+ 31(2)-(4), (14)-(15); NIHB 25(2)-(4), (14)-(15); NIHB60+ 29(2)-(4), (14)-(15); CTB 18(2)-(4), (14)-(16); CTB60+ 21(2)-(4), (14)-(15)

if they were in remunerative work immediately before the first day of the sick pay, etc. They are treated as in remunerative work for a maximum period of 28 weeks. For those paid income support on the grounds of incapacity for work, or credited with earnings because of incapacity for work or limited capability for work, the first day of the 28 weeks begins on the day the person is first paid income support or the first day of the period in which the earnings are credited.

Incapacitated

14.18 The other member of the couple is 'incapacitated' where:

- they are aged 80 or over;
- the claimant's applicable amount includes a disability premium because of the partner's incapacity;
- the claimant's applicable amount includes the support component or the work related activity component because the partner has limited capability for work;
- they are aged less than 80 and except for the age criteria would satisfy the conditions for the disability premium (para. 12.21) or would satisfy one of those conditions but have not been treated as incapable of work because the DWP has decided that their incapacity has arisen from their own misconduct or failure to take up medical treatment;
- the claimant's applicable amount would include a disability premium (para. 12.21) because of the other member's disability but they have been disqualified by the DWP;
- the claimant's applicable amount would include the support component or the work-related activity component on account of their partner's limited capability for work but the partner is being treated as not having limited capability under a determination made in accordance with the Employment and Support Allowance Regulations;
- the claimant has been treated as incapable of work (para. 12.24) for a continuous period of at least 196 days (breaks in continuity of 56 days should be ignored in calculating the 196 days);
- the claimant has been treated as having limited capability for work and has been treated as having limited capability for work for a continuous period of at least 196 days (breaks of 84 days or less should be ignored in calculating the 196 days);
- they receive (in GB) the NI equivalent of the following, or (in NI) the GB equivalent:
  - disability living allowance (DLA),
  - attendance allowance (AA),
  - short-term higher rate or long-term incapacity benefit,

14.18 HB 28(11); HB60+ 31(11); NIHB 25(11); NIHB60+ 29(11); CTB 18(11); CTB60+ 21(11)

- severe disablement allowance (SDA),
- industrial injuries constant attendance allowance, or
- an increase of a war pension or disablement pension similar to DLA, AA or an increase in disablement pension
- main phase employment and support allowance;

- any of the above pensions or allowances, except short-term higher rate or long-term incapacity benefit, have stopped because of hospitalisation; or
- the claimant has an invalid carriage or other vehicle provided under the prescribed legislation.

Relevant child care costs

14.19 The above groups qualify for the disregard if the claimant or partner pays one or more of the following to care for at least one child in their family (so long as that child satisfies the age condition – see below):

- a registered child-minder, nursery or play scheme; or
- a child-minding scheme for which registration is not required (e.g. run by a school, local authority or, in Northern Ireland, Crown property); or
- child care approved for working tax credit purposes; or
- any other out-of-school-hours scheme provided by a school on school premises or by a local authority (in Northern Ireland an education and library board or HSS trust) – but, in this case only, the child must be aged 8 or more.

The disregard does not, however, apply to payments in respect of compulsory education, nor to payments made by a claimant to his or her partner (or *vice versa*) if the child is the responsibility of at least one of them (para. 4.33), nor to payments for care given by a relative (para. 9.62) for care wholly or mainly in the child's home.

The age condition

14.20 A child satisfies the age condition until:

- the first Monday in September after their 15th birthday; or
- if the child meets the conditions for a disabled child premium (para. 12.28), or would do so except for having regained sight, the first Monday in September after their 16th birthday.

The amount of the child care disregard from earnings

14.21 The amount of the disregard equals what the claimant or partner pays, up to a maximum of:

14.19 HB 28(7),(8); HB60+ 31(7),(8); NIHB 25(7),(8); NIHB60+ 29(7),(8); CTB 18(7),(8); CTB60+ 21(7),(8)

14.20 HB 28(6),(13); HB60+ 31(6),(13); NIHB 25(6),(13); NIHB60+ 29(6),(13); CTB 18(6),(13); CTB60+ 21(6),(13)

- £175.00 per week per HB/main CTB claim for claimants with one child who meets the above criteria (paras. 14.19-20); or
- £300.00 per week per HB/main CTB claim for claimants with two or more children who meet those criteria.

14.22 The disregard is made as far as possible from the earnings (from employment or self-employment) of a claimant and/or partner who satisfies the conditions in paragraph 14.16. Any balance, if the earnings are not enough, is disregarded from any working tax credit or child tax credit the claimant or partner receives (para. 13.47). Apart from that, it cannot be disregarded from unearned income.

14.23 The amount the claimant or partner pays is averaged over whichever period, up to a year, gives the most accurate estimate of the charges, taking account of information given by the person providing the care.

The additional earnings disregard

14.24 In addition to the earned income disregards mentioned above, a disregard of £16.85 per week is made if at least one of the following conditions is met (but see para. 14.26 for the exception to this rule):

- the claimant, or any partner receives the working tax credit 30 hours element; or
- the claimant or any partner is aged at least 25 and that person is engaged in remunerative work for on average at least 30 hours per week; or
- the claimant is in a couple who have at least one dependent child or young person and at least one member of the couple is engaged in remunerative work for on average at least 16 hours per week; or
- the claimant is a lone parent who is engaged in remunerative work for on average at least 16 hours per week; or
- the claimant's applicable amount includes a disability premium because of their disability or the work related activity component or the support component and the claimant is engaged in remunerative work for on average at least 16 hours per week;
- the claimant's applicable amount includes a disability premium because of their partner's disability or the work related activity component or the support component and one member of the couple is engaged in remunerative work for on average at least 16 hours per week;

14.21 HB 27(1)(c),(2),(3); HB60+ 30(1)(c),(2),(3); NIHB 24(1)(c),(2),(3); NIHB60+ 28(1)(c),(2),(3); CTB 17(1)(c),(2),(3); CTB60+ 20(1)(c),(2),(3)

14.22 HB 27(1)(c); HB60+ 30(1)(c); NIHB 24(1)(c); NIHB60+ 28(1)(c); CTB 17(1)(c); CTB60+ 20(1)(c)

14.23 HB 28(10); HB60+ 31(10); NIHB 25(10); NIHB60+ 29(10); CTB 18(10); CTB60+ 21(10)

14.24 HB sch 4 para 17; HB60+ sch 4 para 9; NIHB sch 5 para 17; NIHB60+ sch 5 para 9; CTB sch 3 para 16; CTB60+ sch 2 para 9

- the claimant or any partner receives the 50-plus element of working tax credit;
- the claimant or any partner would qualify for the 50-plus element of working tax credit if they were to make an application (regulation 18 of the Working Tax Credit (Entitlement and Maximum Rate) Regulations 2002 (SI 2002/2005 as amended by SI 2003/2815) sets out the entitlement conditions for the 50-plus element and GM BW2 annex E paras. 6-12 provides the procedures to help identify this group);
- the claimant is aged at least 60, meets the conditions for the disabled/ long-term sick earned income disregard (table 14.1) and does paid work averaging at least 16 hours per week;
- The claimant or partner is aged at least 60, one of them does paid work averaging at least 16 hours per week and that person's circumstances meet the condition for the disabled/long-term sick earned income disregard (table 14.1).

14.25 For the above purposes, the question of whether anyone works 16 hours or more per week on average is decided as in paragraphs 6.27 onwards; and the question of whether anyone works 30 hours or more per week on average is decided in the same way (apart from the different number of hours).

14.26 The above £16.85 earned income disregard is not made if it (along with the other earned income disregard(s) which apply in any particular case) would result in a negative earned income figure. In such a case, a £16.85 disregard is instead made from working tax credit (para. 13.47).

Particular kinds of earnings and expenses

Bonuses, tips and commission

14.27 All forms of bonuses, tips and commission derived from the employment are included in the assessment of gross earnings.

Arrears of earnings

14.28 Any arrears of pay count as earnings for the period they relate to.

Tax refunds

14.29 If the claimant and any partner are under 60, tax refunds on earnings count as capital (not earnings), including in Northern Ireland any similar payments from the Irish Republic.

14.26 HB sch 5 para. 56; HB60+ sch 5 para. 21; CTB sch 4, para. 56; CTB60+ sch 3, para. 21

14.27 HB 35(1); HB60+ 35(1); NIHB 32(1); NIHB60+ 33(1); CTB 25(1); CTB60+ 25(1)

14.28 HB 79(7); HB60+ 59(7); NIHB 77(9); NIHB60+ 57(9); CTB 67(9); CTB60+ 50(9)

14.29 HB 46(2); NIHB 43(2); CTB 36(2)

Earnings paid in a lump sum

14.30 If the claimant and any partner are under 60 and have earnings that are paid in a lump sum (or in any other form which could in broad terms be characterised as capital), they are however counted as earnings. They are averaged over the period they cover.

Special occupations annual bounty

14.31 If the claimant and any partner are under 60 and receive a bounty paid by the special occupations this counts as capital (not earnings) if it is paid annually or at longer intervals. For these purposes the 'special occupations' means part-time fire-fighters, auxiliary coast guards, part-time life-boat workers, and members of the Territorial Army or similar reserve forces.

Non-cash vouchers

14.32 If an employee receives non-cash vouchers that are taken into account for the purposes of calculating national insurance contributions, their value is counted as employed earnings. The value of such vouchers should appear on pay slips (circular HB/CTB A17/99). Non-cash vouchers that are not taken into account for the purposes of calculating national insurance contributions are disregarded as a payment in kind (para. 14.33).

Payments in kind

14.33 With the exception of certain non-cash vouchers (para. 14.32), payments in kind (i.e. payments of goods rather than money) do not count as earnings and are completely disregarded (para. 13.126). The DWP advises (GM paras. BW2.99-101) that credits received by way of Local Exchange Trading Schemes ('LETS') do not count as payments in kind, but should be given a cash value as earnings.

Councillors' allowances

14.34 Councillors' allowances, except for expenses payments, count as employed earnings *(R(IS) 6/92).* (For further advice on these, see GM paras. BW2.83-95.)

Royalties, etc

14.35 The following two paragraphs apply to:

- royalties or other payments received for use of, or the right to use any copyright, design, patent or trademark; or
- any Public Lending Right Scheme payment for authors including any

---

14.30 HB 41(3); NIHB 38(3); CTB 31(3)

14.31 HB 46(1); NIHB 43(1); CTB 36(1)

14.32 HB 35(1)(k); HB60+ 35(1)(g); NIHB 32(1)(l); NIHB60+ 33(1)(g); CTB 25(1)(k); CTB60+ 25(1)(g)

14.35 HB 37(3), HB60+ 29(1)(q)-(r), NIHB 34(3), NIHB60+ 27(1)(o)(p), CTB 27(3), CTB60+ 19(1)(q)(r)

analagous payments received under any similar international public lending right scheme.

For the paragraphs to apply the claimant must be the first owner of the copyright, design, patent or trademark (i.e. not producing the work as an employee in the course of their employment) or an original contributor to the book, etc.

14.36 If the claimant or any partner is aged 60+

- these payments count as income;
- these payments. together with other occasional payments (presumably of the same type), should be treated as if made in respect of a year;
- the items in para 14.35 are added to any other earnings when it comes to applying the appropriate earned income disregards.

14.37 If the claimant and any partner are under 60 the payments identified in para 14.35 should be taken into account for the number of weeks (including part weeks) calculated by dividing the amount of the payment by:

- the amount of HB (for HB purposes) or CTB (for CTB purposes) that would have been paid had the payments identified in para 14.35 not been received; plus
- the appropriate earned income disregards in the claimant's case.

Company directors

14.38 Company directors (registered with Companies House) are 'office holders' (para. 14.4) and are therefore employed earners:

- the income paid by the company to the director is assessed as earned income under the usual rules;
- their interest (or share of it) in the company is assessed as capital.

Work expenses

14.39 The treatment of work expenses met by an employer is as follows:

- if they are for travel to work, or for the cost of caring for a child or other dependant, these must be added in as part of the employee's earnings;
- if they are for other items wholly, exclusively and necessarily incurred in the performance of the job, these are disregarded in full.

14.36 HB60+ 33(4),(5),(8); NIHB60+ 31(4),(5),(8); CTB60+ 23(4),(5),(8)

14.37 HB 37(4); NIHB 34(4); CTB 27(4)

14.39 HB 35(1)(f),(2)(b), sch 5 para 3; HB60+ 29(1)(f),(2)(b); NIHB 32(1)(f),(2)(b), sch 6 para 3; NIHB60+ 33(1)(f),(2)(b); CTB 25(1)(f),(2)(b), sch 4 para 3; CTB60+ 19(1)(f),(2)(b)

14.40 Work expenses met by an employee and not paid back by the employer may not be disregarded against the employee's earnings (but see paragraph 14.16 as regards child care expenses); but where they are wholly and exclusively (see para. 15.22) and necessarily incurred in the performance of the employment (e.g. travel costs between work places as opposed to travel to the claimant's place of employment) they should be deducted from the earnings figure to arrive at the gross earnings figure that is used as the starting point for the calculation of net earnings (*R(IS) 16/93* followed in *CIS 507/94*). Also note that some employed earners may not have a 'place of employment'. In *CH/1330/2008* the Commissioner held that the claimant – a care worker who could be asked to work anywhere in a particular authority' area – had no actual place of employment. Consequently all of the travel expenses paid by the employer should be disregarded in these circumstances.

Expenses in unpaid work

14.41 Expenses received by a person doing unpaid work are disregarded in full if they are paid by a charitable organisation or non-profit-making voluntary organisation, or if the person does any kind of work voluntarily.

Starting work

14.42 When a claimant starts work, earnings should be taken into account from the beginning of the job – not (if different) the first pay day (but note the rules on 'extended payments' – paras. 17.54-59 – and also the general rules about when changes of circumstances are taken into account – chapter 17).

Advances or loans from an employer

14.43 Any advance of earnings or any loan from an employer count as capital, not earnings.

Absences from work and ending work

14.44 The general rules are described below. More details are in tables 14.2 and 14.3 (and see also the general rules about when changes of circumstances are taken into account: chapter 17).

14.41 HB sch 5 para 2; HB60+ 29(1); NIHB sch 6 para 2; NIHB60+ 27(1); CTB sch 4 para 2; CTB60+ 19(1)

14.43 HB 46(5); NIHB 43(5); CTB 36(5)

14.44 HB 35; HB60+ 35; NIHB 32; NIHB60+ 33; CTB 25; CTB60+ 25

Holiday pay

14.45 Holiday pay counts as earnings (but see tables 14.2 and 14.3). Any holiday pay from employment which ended before the first day of HB/CTB entitlement is disregarded. Before 1st October 2007 such holiday pay would have been taken into account where the claimant and any partner were under 60. Also note that the disregard does not apply to holiday pay taken into account during an award of benefit. Where the claimant and any partner are aged under 60, any holiday pay payable more than four weeks after the following event counts as capital:

- the beginning of an absence or break from work (table 14.2), or
- ending work (table 14.3).

Sick pay, maternity pay, paternity pay and adoption pay

14.46 Statutory sick, maternity, paternity and adoption pay and employer's sick, maternity, paternity and adoption pay, and corresponding Northern Ireland payments (or in Northern Ireland, corresponding GB payments or payments from the Republic), count as earnings (but see table 14.2).

Retainers

14.47 Retainers are payments made for a period when no actual work is done, for example to employees of school meals services during the school holidays. These count as earnings (but see tables 14.2 and 14.3).

Strike pay

14.48 Strike pay does not count as earned income (since it is not paid by an employer). If the claimant and any partner are under 60, it counts as unearned income (but see tables 14.2 and 14.3). If the claimant or any partner are aged 60+ it is disregarded.

Redundancy payments

14.49 Redundancy payments (including those paid periodically rather than in a lump sum) do not count as earnings. They count as capital (but see table 14.3 for the treatment of other payments which may be made on redundancy – such as payments in lieu of notice (i.e. instead of notice) and compensation payments).

14.45 HB 35(1)(d),46(3); HB60+ 35(1)(d), sch 4 para 8; NIHB 32(1)(d),43(3); NIHB60+ 33(1)(d), sch 5 para 8; CTB 25(1)(d),36(3); CTB60+ 25(1)(d), sch 2 para 8

14.46 HB 2(1), 35(1)(i),36(3); HB60+ 35(1)(h)-(j); NIHB 2(1), 32(1)(i)(j),33(3); NIHB60+ 33(1)(h)-(j),(l); CTB 2(1)25(1)(i),26(3); CTB60+ 25(1)(h)-(j)

14.47 HB 35(1)(e); HB60+ 35(1)(e); NIHB 32(1)(e); NIHB60+ 33(1)(e); CTB 25(1)(e); CTB60+ 25(1)(e)

14.48 HB60+ 29(1); NIHB60+ 27(1); CTB60+ 19(1)

14.49 HB 35(1)(b),(g); HB60+ 35(1)(b); NIHB 32(1)(b),(g); NIHB60+ 33(1)(b); CTB 25(1)(b),(g); CTB60+ 25(1)(b)

Table 14.2: Absences from work

Periods while someone receives a retainer

- Reassess earnings if they change (for example, if the person is paid less during the summer holidays). (See also para. 14.7(d).)

Holidays, absences without good cause, and strikes

- Reassess earnings if they change (for example, if the person is paid less during holidays, or nothing during a strike). (See also the general rule about holiday pay: para. 14.45.)

Sick leave, maternity leave, paternity leave, adoption leave, lay off, suspension and other absences with good cause

The following rules apply so long as the employment has not terminated.

- If the absence for any of these reasons began before the first day of entitlement to HB/CTB count only the following as earnings (and only if they are received during the absence):
  - retainers;
  - statutory or employer's sick, maternity, paternity or adoption pay;
- If the absence for any of these reasons begins on or after the person's first day of entitlement to HB/CTB reassess earnings if they change (for example if the person gets a lower rate of pay for any of these reasons). (See also the general rule about holiday pay: para. 14.45.)

Table 14.3: Ending work

60+ – ending work

If the claimant or any partner is aged 60+ disregard any earnings (except royalties etc, para. 14.36) from employment which ended before the first day of entitlement to HB/CTB.

Under 60 – ending remunerative work

(16 or more hours per week: para 6.27)

Where the claimant and any partner are under 60 and remunerative work ends before the first day of entitlement to HB/CTB for any reason other than retirement disregard all earnings except:

T 14.2 HB sch 4 paras 1(c), 2; CTB sch 3 paras 1(c), 2

- a retainer;
- any award of compensation made for unfair dismissal (i.e. under section 112(4) or 117(3)(a) of the Employment Rights Act 1996);
- any sum payable in respect of arrears of pay following an order for reinstatement or re-engagement under the Employment Rights Act 1996;
- a sum payable by way of pay following an order under the Employment Rights Act 1996 or the Trade Union and Labour Relations (Consolidation) Act 1992 for the continuation of a contract of employment;
- any remuneration following a protective award under the Trade Union and Labour Relations (Consolidation) Act 1992;
- an employment tribunal award of the amount of a guarantee payment (under section 34 of the Employment Rights Act 1996);
- an employment tribunal award of remuneration or compensation (under section 70 of the Employment Rights Act 1996) including any payment made following the settlement of a complaint to an employment tribunal or of court proceedings.

NB: Before 1st October 2007 payments in lieu of remuneration, payments in lieu of notice (para. 14.49) and holiday pay (para. 14.45) would also have been taken into account as income.

Under 60 – ending part-time work

(Under 16 hours per week: para 6.27)

If employment ends before the first day of entitlement to HB/CTB disregard all earnings except for retainers.

Other circumstances

In all cases (remunerative/non-remunerative work and 60+/under 60) if employment ends on or after the first day of entitlement the authority should reassess to take changes and ending of earnings into account under the general rules about changes of circumstance (chapter 17).

T 14.3 HB sch 4 paras 1(b), 2; HB 60+ sch 2 para 8; CTB sch 3 paras 1(b), 2; CTB 60+ sch 2 para 8

15 The self-employed

15.1 This chapter gives the rules for assessing self-employed income (and capital). It covers:

- deciding who is self-employed;
- deciding what assessment period to use;
- assessing the total income during that period;
- assessing allowable expenses during that period;
- calculating pre-tax profit (chargeable income) for that period;
- allowing for tax and national insurance;
- allowing for half of any pension contributions;
- calculating net profit.

15.2 This chapter applies only if the claimant and any partner are not on JSA(IB), ESA(IR), income support or pension credit. Apart from that, it applies to the self-employed capital and income of a claimant and any partner. In some cases the rules are different depending on whether the claimant or any partner are under 60 or aged 60+. For more information on these points, and other general considerations, see paragraphs 13.2-9.

15.3 This chapter does not apply to the self-employed income of a non-dependant or second adult: the law does not lay down any particular way of assessing income from self-employment in such cases, although it must be gross (not net) of tax and national insurance; and in practice most authorities assess their income under the rules in this chapter, but using the pre-tax profit figure rather than the net income figure.

Who is 'self-employed'?

15.4 A person is self-employed if they are gainfully employed in Great Britain (or in Northern Ireland gainfully employed in NI or the Republic) in employment that does not count as 'employed earner' employment (para. 14.4). Sometimes a person may also be employed as an employed earner – in which case there is income from both self-employment and 'employed earner' employment to be assessed.

15.5 A person may be a sole trader or in a business partnership, and therefore be a self-employed earner. But someone who is a director of a limited company is an office holder in the company and should be treated as an employed earner (para. 14.38).

15.4 CBA 2(1)(b); HB 2(1); HB60+ 2(1); NIHB 2(1); NIHB 60+ 2(1); CTB 2(1); CTB60+ 2(1)

15.6 The following do not count as self-employed income:

- fostering and respite care payments (para. 13.65);
- Sports Council awards (para. 13.124);
- rent received by the claimant on their home (table 13.2);
- rent received by the claimant on property other than their home (table 13.3) *(R(FC) 2/92),* unless the renting of property constitutes gainful self-employment (perhaps because of the number of properties rented out).

Capital, etc

15.7 Assets of a business wholly or partly owned by a claimant are disregarded as capital when he or she:

- is self-employed in that business – so long as the assets are held in the course of self-employment *(CH/4258/2004);*
- has ceased to be self-employed – for as long as is reasonably needed for disposal. In these circumstances, income from (the former) self-employment is also disregarded (apart from royalties and similar payments).
- is not self-employed because of sickness or disability, but intends to be as soon as able to. In this case, the assets are disregarded for 26 weeks from the date of any claim for HB/CTB, and then for whatever period is reasonable to enable the return to self-employment.

15.8 It is sometimes necessary to decide whether capital is personal or part of the business. In general, the test depends on whether the capital is 'part of the fund employed and risked in the business' (*R(SB) 4/85* para 11). For example, an amount in a self-employed claimant's personal bank account is not disregarded as a business asset if it is neither employed nor risked in the business.

Income: the assessment period

15.9 The income and expenses of a self-employed person are estimated by reference to an 'assessment period'. This should be whatever period is appropriate to enable the most accurate estimation of average weekly earnings *(CH/329/2003).* If the claimant and any partner are under 60 the period must not be longer than one year. If the claimant or any partner is aged 60+ it must be a year (so long as the claimant has been self-employed for at least a year). The year

15.6 HB 37(2); HB60+ 38(2); NIHB 34(2); NIH60+ 36(2); CTB 27(2); CTB60+ 28(2)

15.7 HB sch 6 para 8; HB60+ sch 6 paras 9,10; NIHB sch 7 para 8; NIHB60+ sch 7 paras 9,10; CTB sch 5 para 8; CTB60+ sch 4 paras 9,10
Also HB sch 4 para 2A, HB60+ sch 4 para 8, CTB sch 3 para 2A

15.9 HB 2(1), 30; HB60+ 2(1), 37; NIHB 2(1), 27; NIHB60+ 2(1), 35; CTB 2(1), 20; CTB60+ 2(1), 27

does not need to be the year immediately before the claim or the date the claim is looked at. In all cases, the general principle is that income and expenses in the assessment period are used to calculate HB and CTB.

People who have been self-employed for at least a year

15.10 For people who have been self-employed for some time, the DWP advises that the assessment period should normally be that of the last year's trading accounts, but that a shorter or different period may be used if that period is more representative of the current trading position (GM para. BW2.330).

15.11 A person who claims HB/CTB during the course of self-employment should usually have evidence of his or her recent actual income and expenses from that self-employment. It would usually be reasonable in such cases for the authority to ask for the claimant's most recent accounts showing income and expenses (regardless of whether these are prepared by the claimant, an accountant or someone else) but the supplied figures may need adjustment because the way certain items are treated for accounting purposes is different from the way they are treated for HB/CTB purposes (table 15.2).

People who have been self-employed for less than a year

15.12 If someone has been self-employed for less than a year, the assessment period is whatever period (during which they have been self-employed) that will give the most accurate assessment.

People setting up in business

15.13 A person who claims HB/CTB when he or she is just setting up in self-employment cannot possibly have evidence of his or her actual income and expenses from that self-employment. In such cases, the DWP recommends that the claimant's income and expenses should be estimated (GM para. BW2.333). Many authorities have forms claimants can fill in giving their estimates. These estimates (unless they are unreasonable) are typically used to assess the claimant's HB/CTB for a short period, say 13 weeks. The claimant should then be advised to keep proper records of income and expenses during that period, so that he or she can send them in to be used as evidence for the following period.

If the nature of a business changes

15.14 If the nature of a claimant's business changes in such a way as to affect the normal pattern of business, e.g. the loss of a major customer or changing from full-time to part-time self-employment, the authority should again identify an assessment period that allows it to calculate the earnings with the greatest accuracy, e.g. starting with the date the change occurred and ending on the date for which the most recent figures regarding earnings and expenditure are available *(CH/329/2003).*

Can the figures be altered later?

15.15 Once the various figures have been assessed as described above, they can be altered later only if they were based on a mistake of fact or law or there was an official error, or if there has subsequently been a relevant change of circumstances (e.g. as in para. 15.14).

Accounting methods

15.16 Self-employed people usually account for their income and expenditure using one of the following methods:

- a 'cash' basis – counting income as being received on the day they receive the money and counting expenses as being incurred on the day they pay the money out; or
- an 'on paper' basis – counting income as being received on the day they issue their bill or invoice for it and counting expenses as being incurred on the day they receive a bill or invoice for them; or
- the basis required (roughly speaking) for income tax purposes – counting income as being received on the day they issue their bill or invoice or the day they receive the money, whichever happens first and counting expenses as being incurred on the day they receive a bill or invoice or the day they pay the money out, whichever happens first.

15.17 For HB/CTB purposes, it doesn't matter which of the above methods the claimant uses, so long as it is reasonable and representative of their income and expenses, and consistent during their period of trading.

Assessing total earnings

15.18 Having selected an assessment period, the next step is to find the claimant's total earnings. This means all the income/receipts of the business during the assessment period. For this purpose:

- only payments of income are taken into account. A payment of capital into a business (e.g. an investment in the business by a relative or bank) is disregarded (para. 15.7); and
- only income 'derived from' the self-employment is taken into account. Income from some other source falls under whatever rules apply to that kind of income (para. 15.19 and chapter 13).

15.18 HB 37(1), 38(1),(3); HB60+38(1); NIHB 34(1), 35(1),(3); NIHB60+ 36(1); CTB 27(1), 28(1),(3); CTB60+ 28(1)

Grants, loans and the access to work scheme

15.19 These are assessed as follows:

- grants are not usually 'derived from' self-employment. Usually they are a separate source of income or capital – typically voluntary or charitable (para. 13.125);
- genuine loans are not income (para. 13.136). Money from a loan forms part of the claimant's capital. If it is a loan to the business it is therefore disregarded (para. 15.7);
- disabled people setting up in self-employment can get payments under the government's Access to Work scheme: these are disregarded as income (para. 13.123).

Regeneration and renewal schemes

15.20 There have been various government-related schemes for regeneration and renewal (such as the former Business Start Up Allowances and Single Regeneration Budget). Payments under such schemes to self-employed claimants are the income or capital (as appropriate) of the business, not a separate source of income or capital.

Assessing allowable expenses

15.21 Having worked out the total income in the assessment period, the next step is to allow for the expenses incurred in running the business during the assessment period. The two general principles are:

- expenses are allowed for if they are 'wholly and exclusively incurred' for the purpose of the business; but
- the authority cannot allow an expense if it is not satisfied, given the nature and the amount, that it has been 'reasonably incurred'.

Examples of expenses which are usually allowable (subject to the above points) are in table 15.1. The law also contains rules about particular kinds of expenditure and these are summarised in table 15.2.

'Wholly and exclusively incurred' and 'reasonably incurred'

15.22 With many small businesses, particularly when someone is working from home, or only has the use of one car, certain items of expenditure (such as the cost of gas and electricity for heating and lighting including any standing charges, petrol, road fund licence, insurance premiums, etc) may relate to both business and private use. Where such expenses can be apportioned on for example a time

---

15.20 HB 37(1); HB60+38(1); NIHB 34(1); NIHB60+ 36(1); CTB 27(1); CTB60+ 28(1)

15.21 HB 38(3)(a),(7); HB60+ 39(2)(a),(6); NIHB 35(3)(a),(7); NIHB60+ 37(2)(a),(6); CTB 28(3)(a),(7); CTB60+ 34(3),(7)

basis this can be used to identify the amount wholly and exclusively used for business purposes. This process of apportionment should be used not just for items like heating, lighting and petrol but also for items such as the standing charge, road fund licence and insurance where it might have been argued that no proportion could be said to relate exclusively to business use (*R(FC) 1/91* followed in *R(H) 5/07*). Such apportionment is also appropriate in relation to the loan interest and capital repayments for a replacement car used partly for non-business purposes even though the car would have been replaced if the person were not in business *(R(H) 5/07).* In this case the apportionment of both the loan interest and capital repayments should be in accordance with the amount of business mileage as a percentage of total mileage in the assessment period. As in tax law and practice, however, there is no need for this to be the result of a detailed calculation, so long as any estimate is obtained reasonably.

To decide whether expenditure is 'reasonably incurred' the authority must consider the circumstances of the individual case *(R(P)2/54)* including the person's earnings from the business *(R(G) 1/56).* Where an item of expenditure is appropriate and necessary it should always be considered reasonably incurred unless excessive *(R(G) 7/62).* If it is excessive, only that part considered reasonable should be allowed as a deduction.

Table 15.1: Typically allowable types of expenditure

The items in this table do not appear in the law, but are typically allowable in the assessment of self-employed income for HB/CTB purposes (subject to the tests in para 15.21 and the points in paras 15.22-25 and table 15.2). The table does not list every possible allowable expense.

transport	vehicle costs
protective clothing	advertising
postage, carriage and delivery	telephone
legal and accountancy fees	staff costs
subscriptions to professional/trade bodies	fuel costs
rent, rates and other premises costs	cleaning
buying in stocks and supplies	bank charges
hire and leasing charges	stationery
insurance costs	repair costs

Rent – working from home

15.23 An appropriate proportion of the rent paid by someone working from home should also be deducted as a business expense. Relevant factors in arriving at a figure to use would include the size of the working area in relation to the rest of the home and the proportion of time that area is utilised for business as opposed to domestic purposes. A tribunal was found not to have erred where it decided that an appropriate amount to allow for the rent payable in respect of a second bedroom used for business purposes was the difference between the actual rent for the two-bedroomed property and the rent officer's valuation for a one bedroom flat (*R(H) 5/07* para. 12). Where part of someone's rent is identified as a deductible business expense it should also be deducted from the claimant's eligible rent (paras. 7.4 and 8.11).

Table 15.2: Particular types of expenditure

		Allowable?
(a)	Interest payments on any business loan	Yes
(b)	Sums (except interest payments) employed or intended to be employed in setting up or expanding the business	No
(c)	Income spent on repairing an existing business asset (except to the extent that any sum is payable under an insurance policy for this)	Yes
(d)	Capital repayments on loans for repairing an existing business asset (except to the extent that any sum is payable under an insurance policy for this)	Yes
(e)	Capital repayments on loans for replacing business equipment or machinery (the term includes a car: para. 15.22 *(R(H) 5/07)*)	Yes
(f)	Capital repayments on any other business loans	No
(g)	Any other capital expenditure	No
(h)	Depreciation of any capital asset (also called a capital allowance)	No
(i)	Losses incurred before the beginning of the assessment period	No
(j)	Excess of VAT paid over VAT received in the assessment period	Yes
(k)	Proven bad debts	Yes*
(l)	Other debts	No*
(m)	Expenses incurred in the recovery of any debt	Yes
(n)	Business entertainment	No
(o)	Any sum for a domestic or private purpose	No
*	*The regulations state this for under 60s, but it is equally reasonable in the case of 60+s.*	

T 15.2 HB 38(3)(a),(7); HB60+ 39(2)(a),(6); NIHB 35(3)(a),(7); NIHB60+ 37(2)(a),(6); CTB 28(3)(a),(7); CTB60+ 34(3),(7)

Drawings taken by the claimant from the business

15.24 Claimants may take 'drawings' from their business as a kind of wages or salary for themselves. These must not be allowed as a business expense (GM. paras. BW2.390-396)

Couples where one employs the other

15.25 If the claimant pays their partner to work for the business, this is allowable as a business expense. It counts as the partner's earnings. The rules are different if the couple are in a business partnership (para. 15.28).

Self-employed child minders

15.26 For claimants who are self-employed child minders, instead of working out what their actual expenses are, two-thirds of their total earnings are disregarded in lieu of expenses. No actual expenses can be allowed for. An example is given later.

Pre-tax profit (chargeable income)

15.27 The next step is to work out the claimant's 'pre-tax profit' (referred to in the law as 'chargeable income'):

- Total earnings over the assessment period (paras. 15.18-20)
- minus allowable expenses over the assessment period (paras. 15.21-26)
- equals pre-tax profit.

Business partnerships

15.28 If the claimant is self-employed in a partnership, the pre-tax profit (as defined above) should be assessed for the partnership and then split between the business partners. This split should reflect how the business partners actually share their income. This split is required even if the business partners are a couple because it will ensure the correct calculation of notional tax and national insurance (para. 15.34). The rules are different if one partner in a couple employs the other (para. 15.25).

15.29 The rules regarding the business partner's share of the net profit also apply to 'share fishermen'.

15.26 HB 38(9); HB60+ 39(8); NIHB 35(9); NIHB60+ 37(8); CTB 28(9); CTB60+ 29(8)

15.27 HB 38(1)(a),(3); HB60+ 39(1)(a),(3); NIHB 35(1)(a),(3); NIHB60+ 37(1)(a),(3); CTB 28(1)(a),(3); CTB60+ 29(1)(a),(3)

15.28 HB 38(1)(b),(4); HB60+ 39(1)(b); NIHB 35(1)(b),(4); NIHB60+ 37(1)(b); CTB 28(1)(b),(4); CTB60+ 29(1)(b)

Example: A self-employed window cleaner

Dennie Wroclaw, a self-employed window cleaner, provides accounts for his most recent year's trading, showing annual income (with tips) of £10,268 and the following expenses:

- petrol and other costs for van (attributable to business use) £2,356
- telephone costs (attributable to business use) £270
- advertising £507
- meals (while working) £613
- postage and stationery £63
- equipment and overalls £187
- sundry £21
- total £4,017

In assessing his HB/CTB claim, the following points apply:

- the figures all appear reasonable and believable;
- 'sundry' (miscellaneous) is an allowable expense if it is reasonable;
- meals in this instance are not an allowable expense, so his expenses are reduced from £4,017 by £613 (for the meals) to an allowable figure of £3,404.
- his pre-tax profit for the year is £10,268 (total earnings) minus £3,404 (allowable expenses), which is £6,864;
- deductions are then made for notional tax and national insurance (tables 15.3, 15.4) to give his annual net profit (he does not contribute to a pension scheme);
- his annual net profit is converted to a weekly figure (para. 6.70) and the relevant earned income disregards are then made (para. 14.14).

Example: A self-employed childminder

Hendl Drimic, a self-employed childminder, provides evidence that her total earnings are £180 per week.

In assessing her HB/CTB claim, the following points apply :

- it is reasonable to assess her total earnings as £180 per week;
- of this, two-thirds (£120) is disregarded, leaving £60 per week as her pre-tax profit;
- the annual equivalent of her pre-tax profit is too low for deductions to be made for notional tax and national insurance (tables 15.3, 15.4) and she does not contribute to a pension scheme, so her weekly net profit is simply £60;
- the relevant earned income disregards are then made (para. 14.14).

Nil income from self-employment

15.30 If the claimant's allowable expenses exceed his or her total income, then pre-tax profit is nil *(CH/1099/2007)*. So his or her income from the self-employment is nil.

More than one employment

15.31 If a self-employed claimant is engaged in any other employment or self-employment, the losses from one cannot be set against the income from the other nor can any loss by one member of a family be set against the earnings of another *(RH 5/08)*.

If the pre-tax profit appears unrepresentative

15.32 If the pre-tax profit appears unlikely to represent the claimant's income, the authority should consider whether selecting a different assessment period would produce a more accurate estimate (para. 15.9).

Notional income tax and notional NICs

15.33 Allowances are made for income tax and national insurance contributions ('NICs'). However, the authority must work these out itself, based on the claimant's pre-tax profit. The figures calculated by the authority are known as 'notional income tax' and 'notional NICs'. They usually differ from the actual income tax and NICs paid by the claimant. In Northern Ireland, if the claimant is employed in the Republic the authority deducts what it considers would have been deducted had they worked in Northern Ireland.

Table 15.3: Calculating notional income tax (2009-10 tax year)

(a) Start with the annual pre-tax profit figure.

(b) Subtract £6,475*.

(c) If there is a remainder multiply it by 20%**

(d) The result is the amount of notional tax.

Notes

* £6,475 is the personal allowance.

** The 40% tax rate is not used in assessing notional income tax, nor are any allowances taken into account other than as above.

15.31 HB 38(10); HB60+ 39(9); NIHB 35(10); NIHB60+ 37(9); CTB 28(10); CTB60+ 29(9)

15.33 HB 39; HB60+ 40; NIHB 35(12),36; NIHB60+ 37(11),38; CTB 29; CTB60+ 30

Table 15.4: Calculating notional national insurance contributions (2009-10 tax year)

Class 2 NICs

If the annual pre-tax profit figure is £5,075* or more, then the amount of notional class 2 NICs is £124.80.**

Class 4 NICs

(a) Start with the annual pre-tax profit figure (unless this is greater than £43,875***, in which case start with £43,875).

(b) Subtract £5,715.***

(c) If there is a remainder, multiply it by 8%. The result is the amount of notional class 4 NICs.

Notes

The person may have class 2 notional NICs alone, or may have both class 2 and class 4 notional NICs.

* £5,075 is the lower threshold for class 2 NICs. If the person's pre-tax profit is lower, then the notional class 2 NICs figure is nil (regardless of whether the claimant has in fact applied to HM Revenue and Customs for exemption).

** £124.80 is 52 times £2.40 (the weekly rate of class 2 NICs), there being 52 Sundays in the 2009-10 tax year (6th April one year to 5th April the following year).

*** £5,715 is the lower threshold, and £43,875 the upper threshold, for class 4 NICs. The 1% class 4 NIC rate for income above £43,875 is not used in assessing notional NICs. (The regulations have not been amended to keep them up-to-date with NIC rules, but this appears to be their intention.)

The calculations

15.34 The calculations are given in tables 15.3 and 15.4. An example is given near the end of this chapter. The tables apply to annual amounts of pre-tax profit. If a claimant's assessment period was a different length (e.g. 13 weeks), convert pre-tax profit into an annual figure before doing the calculations (para. 6.70). In the case of a couple, work through the calculations separately for each one who has self-employed income.

15.34 HB 39; HB60+ 40; NIHB 36; NIHB60+ 38; CTB 29; CTB60+ 30

15.35 Tables 15.3 and 15.4 give the figures for the tax year from 6th April 2009 to 5th April 2010. The law says authorities should use the tax and national insurance figures 'applicable to the assessment period'. Interpreting this phrase is difficult when accounts span two tax years (as is common). Some authorities split the pre-tax profit and work out two part-year amounts of notional tax/NI. Others take the full annual pre-tax profit, and either use the tax/NI figures which apply at the end date of the assessment period, or use the tax/NI figures which apply at the date of claim for (or supersession of) HB/CTB.

Pension contributions

15.36 An allowance is made for half of any pension contributions payable by self-employed claimants. This applies to periodical (e.g. monthly – but not lump sum) contributions to personal pension schemes (so long as they are tax-deductible), and to (nowadays uncommon) annuities for a retirement pension for the claimant or a dependant.

15.37 If a claimant starts or stops making such payments, or changes their amount, this is a change of circumstances and HB/CTB are reassessed.

15.38 To find the annual equivalent of a pension contribution, multiply a calendar monthly contribution by 12 – or in any other case, divide the contribution by the number of days it covers and multiply by 365.

Net profit

15.39 The final step is to work out the claimant's 'net profit'. It is always advisable to work this out at first on an annual basis:

- pre-tax profit (paras. 15.27-32)
- minus notional income tax and NI contributions, and half of pension contributions (paras. 15.33-38)
- equals net profit.

The law does not say how to convert the result to a weekly figure, but the best way is to divide the annual figure by 365 (366 in a leap-tax-year) and multiply the result by 7.

15.35 HB 39; HB60+ 40; NIHB 36; NIHB60+ 38; CTB 29; CTB60+ 30

15.36 HB 38(11),(12); HB60+ 36(11),(12); NIHB 35(11),(13); NIHB60+ 37(10),(12); CTB 28(11),(12); CTB60+ 29(11),(12)

15.39 HB 38(1)-(3); HB60+ 39(1)-(3); NIHB 35(1)-(3); NIHB60+ 37(1)-(3); CTB 28(1)-(3); CTB60+ 29(1)-(3)

Example: Notional tax and NI contributions and net profit: 2009-10

A claimant's annual pre-tax profit is £8,000. She contributes £360 per year to a personal pension scheme.

Notional income tax (table 15.3)

(a)	Start with the annual pre-tax profit figure. This is	£8,000
(b)	Subtract the personal allowance of £6,475. This leaves	£1,525
(c)	Multiply £1,525 by 20%. This gives	£305
(d)	So her notional tax is:	£305

Notional class 2 NICS (table 15.4)

The annual pre-tax profit figure (£8,000) is greater than £5,075, so the amount of her notional class 2 NICs is £124.80.

Notional class 4 NICS (table 15.4)

(a) Start with the annual pre-tax profit figure (which is not greater than £43,875). This is £8,000.

(b) Subtract £5,715.

(c) Multiply the remainder (which is £2,285) by 8%.

This is £182.80 – which is the amount of her notional class 4 NICs.

Net profit

Annual pre-tax profit	£8,000.00
minus notional income tax	£305
minus notional class 2 NICs	£124.80
minus notional class 4 NICs	£182.80
minus half of annual contributions to pension scheme	£180.00
Equals annual net profit:	£7,207.40
On a weekly basis this is (£7,207.40 ÷ 365 x 7 =)	£138.22

Don't forget to apply the earned income disregards (paras. 14.14, 14.15 and 14.24).

16 Decisions, notices and payment

16.1 This chapter describes the process of decision-making, notices and payment. It covers the following:

- how quickly a claim should be dealt with and benefit paid;
- who must be notified of the authority's decisions;
- the information that must be given to the claimant and others;
- how and when HB/CTB should be paid;
- the requirement to make a payment of HB in 14 days (a payment on account) for rent allowance claimants;
- how often a rent allowance should be paid;
- when HB can be paid direct to a landlord or letting agent;
- who else may receive payment of a rent allowance/CTB.

Dealing with claims and changes

How quickly should the claim be dealt with and benefit paid?

16.2 Once the authority has received a claim and all the information and evidence it reasonably requires from the claimant it must:

- reach a decision on the claim within 14 days or as soon as reasonably practicable after that;
- notify persons affected (para. 16.8) as soon as the claim is decided or as soon as reasonably practicable after that; and
- in the case of HB, make payment within 14 days of the receipt of the claim or as soon as reasonably practicable after that.

In all rent allowance cases if the authority cannot meet the 14 day decision-making timetable it should consider making a payment on account (para. 16.16).

Exceptions to the requirement to decide

16.3 The authority does not have to meet the above time limits however where a claim:

- is not made in the proper time and manner (para. 5.25); or

16.2 HB 89(2),90(1)(a),91(3); HB60+ 70(2),71(1)(a),72(3); NIHB 85(2),86(1)(a),87(3); NIHB60+ 66(2),67(1)(a),68(3); CTB 75(2),76(1)(a); CTB60+ 60(2),61(1)(a)

16.3 HB 89(2); HB60+ 70(2); NIHB 85(2); NIHB60+ 66(2); CTB 75(2); CTB60+ 60(2)

- is not supported by reasonably required information or evidence from the claimant (para. 5.17); or
- has been withdrawn (para. 5.16).

Time period in which other decisions should be made

16.4 From time to time authorities have to make other decisions on a claim, e.g. to supersede an original decision following a change of circumstance. Notice of a decision must be given within 14 days of the decision having been made or as soon as possible after that, except in the case of CTB where a change in entitlement relates solely to a delayed award of a disability reduction or discount or as a result of tax capping (paras. 11.18-19).

Performance

16.5 Authorities have a duty to allocate sufficient resources according to their caseload such that the vast majority of claims can be processed within the 14 day time limit. The fact that many authorities fail to meet this standard is not an excuse but makes the need for judicial intervention 'all the greater' *(R v Liverpool CC ex parte Johnson No. 1).* Authorities in England, Scotland and Wales are expected to report to the DWP on their average processing times for new claims and change events (the 'right time performance indicator') (para. 1.22). The DWP also collects other processing data from authorities. Information on each authority's performance is available on the DWP's Housing Benefits Operational Database (HoBod) *(www.dwp.gov.uk/asd/hobod/).*

Remedies for delays

16.6 Authorities are expected to meet the time limits in most cases. Delays are normally only justifiable, for example, in periods of peak pressure such as the annual up-rating. Where authorities fail to meet the time limits, remedies to ensure that they meet their obligations in the future include:

- complaints to the appropriate ombudsman;
- action in the High Court or Court of Session in Scotland for judicial review to require authorities to make a decision; and
- action in the County Court or Sheriff Court to require authorities to make a payment if they have agreed that the claimant is entitled *(Waveney DC v Jones).*

16.4 HB 90(1)(b); HB60+ 71(1)(b); NIHB 86(1)(b); NIHB60+ 67(1)(b); CTB 76(1)(b); CTB60+ 61(1)(b)

16.7 In England and Wales local authorities and registered social landlords are expected to comply with the Civil Procedure Rules pre-action protocol prior to seeking possession for rent arrears (see *www.justice.gov.uk/civil/procrules_fin/contents/protocols/prot_rent.htm*). Its terms require that possession proceedings should not start against a tenant who has provided the authority with all the evidence required to process their claim, provided that there is a reasonable expectation of entitlement and they have paid any other sums to the landlord not covered by HB. Under the Civil Procedure Rules, the court has the power to summon the authority to explain any delays or problems with a claim, and costs may be sought from the authority where it can be shown that HB problems have caused the litigation.

Who should be notified and how?

Persons affected

16.8 The authority must notify all 'persons affected' by a decision. This means any of the following where their rights, duties or obligations are affected by a decision:

- the claimant;
- where a claimant is unable for the time being to act on his or her own behalf:
  - a deputy (or before October 2007 a receiver) appointed by the Court of Protection with power to claim or receive benefit;
  - in Scotland, a tutor, curator, judicial factor or other guardian acting or appointed in terms of law administering the claimant's estate;
  - an attorney with a general power or a power to receive benefit appointed under the Powers of Attorney Act 1971, the Enduring Powers of Attorney Act 1985 or the Mental Capacity Act 2005 or otherwise;
  - a person appointed by the authority to act for the claimant;
  - a person appointed by the Secretary of State (in practice a manager at the DWP office) to act on the claimant's behalf and treated as an appointee by the authority;
- the landlord or agent – but only in relation to a decision (not) to make direct payments; or
- anyone – including the landlord – from whom the authority has decided that an overpayment is recoverable (paras. 18.28-29).

16.8 HB 2(1),90; HB60+ 2(1),71; NIHB 2(1),86; NIHB60+ 2(1),67; CTB 2(1),76; CTB60+ 2(1),61; DAR 3; NIDAR 3

The term 'person affected' includes corporate bodies such as housing associations and letting companies. The list above puts the status of certain categories of person beyond argument but is not exhaustive and others may also be 'persons affected' *(CH/3817/2004)*. More than one person may be affected by a decision, for example, where the authority decides to recover an overpayment from the landlord, both the landlord and the claimant should be notified.

Information to be provided in a notice

16.9 The authority must send a written notice to each person affected by a decision. Every notice must contain the following information (whatever the decision and regardless of whether the claimant is entitled) explaining the right of that person to:

- request a written statement of the reasons for the decision and the time and manner in which to do this (17.45); and
- request a reconsideration of that decision (para. 19.6) and, where appropriate, to appeal (para. 19.30).

Table 16.1 sets out the additional information that a notice must contain following a decision on a claim for HB/CTB.

16.10 In practice, some notices do not meet these minimum requirements and/or are difficult to understand. Further, some authorities do not keep copies of their notices, thereby placing their staff in the difficult position of being unable to explain to claimants what they have said to them.

16.11 A decision notice is also required where an extended payment is made (para. 17.54); a rent allowance is (not) to be paid direct to the landlord (paras. 16.30-48 and 55-56); the income of a non-dependant is treated as the claimant's (para. 13.7); or there is a recoverable overpayment (paras. 18.11-12 and 18.58-61).

16.9 HB 90 sch 9 paras 1-8; HB60+ 71 sch 8 paras 1-8; NIHB 86 sch 10 paras 1-8; NIHB60+ 67 sch 9 paras 1-8; CTB 76 sch 8 paras 1-8; CTB60+ 61 sch 7 paras 1-8

16.11 HB 90 sch 9 paras 11-13,15; HB60+ 71 sch 8 paras 11-13,15; NIHB 86 sch 10 paras 11-13,15; NIHB60+ 67 sch 9 paras 11-13,15; CTB 76 sch 8 paras 11,16; CTB60+ 61 sch 7 paras 11,16

Table 16.1: Information to be notified following decisions on a claim

(Separate notices are required for HB and CTB decisions)

Where the claimant is entitled to HB and/or CTB

Items to be included in all decision notices where the claimant is entitled

(a) The matters to be notified in every case (para. 16.9).

(b) The claimant's duty to notify the authority of changes of circumstance and examples of the kinds of change that should be reported.

(c) The weekly eligible rent/council tax/rates (and for CTB the details of any rounding of figures).

(d) The normal weekly amount of benefit (and for CTB the details of any rounding of figures).

(e) The first day of entitlement.

Additional items where the claimant is entitled to HB/CTB

(f) The amount and category of any non-dependant deductions.

(g) Except where the claimant is on IS/JSA(IB)/ESA(IR)/guarantee credit the applicable amount and how it is worked out.

(h) Except where the claimant is on IS/JSA(IB)/ESA(IR)/state pension credit the weekly earnings and unearned income.

(i) Where the claimant is entitled to the savings credit only

- the amount of income and capital notified to the authority by the DWP (para. 13.158) or where appropriate the capital figure calculated by the authority (13.164); and
- any adjustment of the DWP's income and capital figures; and
- the amount of savings credit.

(j) HB only, the amount of any deductions for fuel where the amounts in table 8.2 have been applied and the fact that they may be varied if they supply evidence.

(k) HB only, where payment is by rent allowance, the date of payment and period for which payment is being made.

T 16.1 HB sch 9 paras 1-10,14; HB60+ sch 8 paras 1-10,14; NIHB sch 10 paras 1-10,14; NIHB60+ sch 9 paras 1-10,14; CTB sch 8 paras 1-10,13-15; CTB60+ sch 7 paras 1-10,13-15

Additional item where the claimant is entitled to both types of CTB

(l) Where the claimant is entitled to both types of CTB, the fact that they are better off on the type of CTB awarded and the amount of alternative CTB that would otherwise have been payable.

Additional items where the claimant is entitled to second adult rebate

(m) Rates of second adult rebate and related gross income levels.

(n) Gross income of any second adult or the fact that the second adult is on IS/JSA(IB)/ESA(IR)/state pension credit.

Where the claimant is not entitled to HB or CTB

(o) Items (a) and (c)* in all cases.

(p) Where HB/CTB is not payable because of income or, in the case of HB only, the minimum payment rule (para. 6.12):

- items (f) and (j); and
- where the claimant is not on IS/JSA(IB)/ESA(IR)/guarantee credit, items (g) and (h); and
- where appropriate, the fact that HB is not payable because the minimum payment rule applies, the weekly HB that would otherwise be payable.

(q) Where HB/CTB is not payable for any reason other than in (p) above, the reason why it is not payable.

(r) Where second adult rebate is not payable because the income of the second adults is too high or some other reason:

- in the case where the income of the second adults is too high: items (m) and (n); or
- in any other case the reason why it is not payable.

* Details of CTB rounding figures are not required if the claimant is not entitled.

Time and manner of payment

Payment of HB

16.12 Authorities may decide on the time and manner in which to make payments of HB on the basis of the circumstances of the individual case. They are expected to have regard to the reasonable needs and convenience of the person

16.12 HB 91(1); HB60+ 72(1); NIHB 87(1); NIHB60+ 68(1); DAR sch para 1; NIDAR sch para 1

they are paying, as well as the time and frequency with which the liability to make payments arises. Decisions on payment method and frequency are not appealable but a person affected can request a reconsideration at any time (para. 19.6).

16.13 The requirement to consider the needs and convenience of the claimant means that authorities should not make unreasonable demands, such as collection from a place not easily accessible, or insist on payment by crossed cheques or credit transfer arrangements when the payee does not have a bank account *(R(Spiropoulos) v Brighton and Hove CC)* (GM para. A6.120, GLHA para. 5.87). To resolve difficulties the claimant may wish to nominate a third party such as a relative to receive the payments (para. 16.62).

Payment of HB to a housing authority or the NIHE

16.14 Where the landlord is a housing authority or the NIHE (para. 1.18) payment should normally be in the form of a rebate applied to the rent account. There are two exceptions to this rule. From April 2009 where the occupier of a caravan, mobile home or houseboat is liable to make payments in respect of the site or mooring to the housing authority but payments for the caravan, etc, to someone other than the housing authority, e.g. a private landlord, the payments to the housing authority take the form of a rent allowance. The other exception is where the claimant's dwelling is the subject of:

- in England and Wales, an interim management order, a final management order, an interim empty dwelling order or a final empty dwelling order made by that authority under section 102, 113, 133 or 136 of the Housing Act 2004;
- in Scotland, a management control order made by that authority under section 74 of the Antisocial Behaviour etc (Scotland) Act 2004.

Where such orders are made the authority takes over responsibility for managing the property and the rent becomes payable to the authority instead of the landlord. The HB payments, however, continue to take the form of a rent allowance (para. 16.15). They are therefore still dealt with under the rules relating to rent allowances although the benefit is payable to the authority: see circulars A10/2006 and A11/2006 for further information.

Payment of rent allowance for all other cases

16.15 In all other cases, including tenants of private landlords, housing associations (para. 7.25), stock transfer landlords (table 7.4) and other types of landlord (para. 7.14), the claimant is paid by rent allowance. Payment is normally made direct to the claimant, though in certain circumstances a rent allowance must or may be paid to the landlord (paras. 16.34-44) or certain other people (paras. 16.61-63).

16.14 AA 134(1A); NIAA 126(1)(b); HB 91A; HB60+ 72A

16.15 AA 134(1B); NIAA 126(1)(c); HB 91(1),94(1); HB60+ 87(1),75(1); NIHB 87(1),91(1); NIHB60+ 68(1),72(1)

Payments on account (interim payments)

16.16 A payment on account must be paid within 14 days if the following circumstances are met:

- the claimant is to be paid by rent allowance (para. 16.15); and
- the authority is unable to decide on the amount of benefit payable within 14 days of receipt of the claim; and
- that inability has not arisen out of the claimant's failure, without good cause, to provide necessary information or evidence (which the authority has requested from the claimant in writing).

Payments on account are sometimes known as 'interim payments' but the Audit Commission has advised authorities not to use this term because it is not found in the legislation and can cause confusion (DWP HB/CTB G24/2008 para. 22). When a payment on account must be made the authority should pay an amount it considers reasonable on the basis of whatever information is available to it about the individual claimant's circumstances, such as sources of income, and any relevant determination made by a rent officer. Note there is no equivalent rule for claimants who are to be paid a rent rebate (para. 16.14).

16.17 Payments on account are not discretionary and provided that the claimant has done all that is required of them a payment must be made within 14 days. This position was confirmed in the case *R v Haringey LBC ex parte Ayub,* where it was also held that no separate claim or request for a payment on account is required. The fact that no request is necessary is reinforced in DWP guidance (GM A6.158).

16.18 Many authorities fail to make payments on account or only make such payments when the claimant's tenancy is at risk. These practices are unlawful and may expose the authority to judicial review or a complaint to the appropriate ombudsman. Where an authority fails to make a payment the ombudsman is likely to find maladministration and recommend that compensation be paid (*www.lgo.org.uk* (England), *www.ombudsman-wales.org.uk* (Wales), *www.spso.org.uk* (Scotland), *www.ni-ombudsman.org.uk* (Northern Ireland)).

16.19 Good cause for the claimant failing to provide necessary information and evidence would include, for example, a landlord's unwillingness to provide evidence of rent payments. DWP guidance (GM A6.161) advises that a claimant cannot be held responsible for delays in receiving confirmation of IS, JSA(IB), ESA(IR) or pension credit entitlement from the DWP, confirmation of conditions of entry or stay from the Home Office or decisions from the Rent Officer. A claimant cannot be held responsible for a failure to supply information which they have not been asked specifically to provide and must also be given a reasonable time to provide any information which has been requested. The authority is obliged to make an initial payment on account on the 14th day following receipt of the claim based on the information originally available to it.

16.16 HB 93(1); HB60+ 74(1); NIHB 90(1); NIHB60+ 71(1)

16.20 Following a decision to make a payment on account the notice must inform the claimant that if the payment turns out to be more than their actual entitlement it will be recoverable from the person to whom it was paid. If when the claim is finally decided this turns out to be the case future rent allowance payments are adjusted to allow for any under or overpayment made. Decisions about payment on account, except those relating to adjustments, are not appealable (table 19.2).

Frequency of rent allowance payments

16.21 Following any 'payment on account', or first payment, the authority may choose to pay a rent allowance at intervals of two or four weeks or one calendar month or, with the consent of the person entitled to payment, at intervals greater than one month. Except for certain pre-October 1996 transitionally protected claims (para. 16.23), the authority must make payments to claimants at the end of the period to which they relate as follows:

- where payment is being made direct to the landlord every four weeks (or, at the authority's discretion, monthly where there is a monthly rent liability); or
- in any other case every two weeks or other period in accordance with paragraph 16.24.

16.22 Where the authority is paying benefit direct to a landlord for more than one claimant the first payment for a new claimant may be made at a shorter interval than four weeks if it is 'in the interest of efficient administration'. In practice this allows the authority to align any new claimants of a landlord whom they already pay direct into the same payment cycle as their other claimants.

Exceptions for certain pre-October 1996 cases

16.23 The rules in paragraphs 16.21-22 do not apply to claimants who:

- were in receipt of HB on 6th October 1996; and
- have been on HB continuously since without any breaks; and
- have not moved home since that date.

Except where the claimant dies and their surviving partner makes a claim within four weeks, any break in the claim no matter how short results in the payment cycle reverting to the ordinary (post-October 1996) rules (para. 16.21). In all other cases where the pre-October 1996 rules apply authorities have a duty, as far as possible, to make payments two weeks before the end of the period covered in accordance with the same rules about frequency of payment as

---

16.20 HB 93(2),(3); HB60+ 74(2),(3); NIHB 90(2),(3); NIHB60+ 71(2),(3); DAR sch para 1(b); NIDAR sch para 1(b)

16.21 HB 92(1)-(4); HB60+ 73(1)-(4); NIHB 89(1)-(4); NIHB60+ 70(1)-(4)

16.22 HB 92(4)(b); HB60+ 73(4)(b); NIHB 89(4)(b); NIHB60+ 70 (4)(b)

16.23 CPR sch 3 para 7; NICPR sch 3 para 7

described in paragraph 16.21. So a fortnightly rent liability should be paid in advance, while four-weekly or monthly liabilities should be met midway through the period. However, where the tenancy allows for rent to be paid in arrears the authority has the discretion to make payments at the end of the period.

Claimant's right to fortnightly payments

16.24 Where payment is being made to the claimant they can require the authority to make payments every two weeks if their weekly HB is greater than £2. Where the amount of weekly benefit is £2 or less, the authority may pay HB according to the following rules:

- if they are a student once a term;
- where the amount of weekly HB is less than £1 per week, every six months;
- in any other case the authority may choose to pay either at intervals of two weeks, four weeks, one month or, where the claimant has given their consent, any other interval greater than a month.

In all these cases the authority retains discretion to pay the claimant weekly where the circumstances in paragraph 16.25 apply.

Authority's discretion to pay weekly

16.25 Except where HB is paid direct to a landlord, authorities have discretion to pay HB weekly if they consider that:

- paying HB over a longer period would lead to an overpayment; or
- the claimant is liable to pay rent weekly and it is in his or her interest (or that of the family) to receive weekly payments.

The first instance covers cases where there is only a short period of entitlement to HB, or where a change of circumstance is expected in the near future. The second instance may be helpful in cases where claimants have difficulty in budgeting over a longer period. DWP guidance suggests that 'authorities are not expected to make special enquiries as to whether this applies' but if, for example, the social services advise that the claimant has difficulties then weekly payment can be made (GM A6.143).

Payment of CTB and HB for rates in Northern Ireland

16.26 In Northern Ireland payment of HB for rates is normally by rebate; further details can be found in para. 11.48. In Great Britain payment of CTB is normally by means of a rebate (credit) to the individual's council tax account, so reducing their overall liability for the tax. Where the rebate is greater than the tax liability the authority may reduce the liability for the tax in subsequent years. However,

---

16.24 HB 91(2),92(5),(7); HB60+ 72(2),73(5),(7); NIHB 87(2),89(5),(7); NIHB60+ 69(2),71(5),(7)

16.25 HB 92(6); HB60+ 73(6); NIHB 89(6); NIHB60+ 71(6)

16.26 NIHB 88; NIHB60+ 69; CTB 77; CTB60+ 62

any outstanding CTB must be paid direct to the claimant where:

- the tax has been paid for the year, and the claimant requests it;
- the account has been paid and closed (e.g. because the claimant has moved out of the area);
- in any other case, where the claimant is liable for the tax and the authority considers it appropriate.

Where the claimant is to be paid direct, payment should normally be made within 14 days or as soon as reasonably practicable after that.

Who should HB/CTB be paid to?

Overview

16.27 The main rules about who HB and CTB are paid to, are as follows:

- CTB is normally paid by way of a rebate to the claimant's council tax account (para. 16.26);
- HB for council and NIHE tenants, and HB for rates in Northern Ireland, are normally paid by way of a rebate to the claimant's rent or rates account (para. 16.26);
- HB for anyone else, including all private and housing association tenants, can be paid to the claimant or a landlord/agent, depending on the type of case (paras. 16.30-47);
- HB and CTB can be paid to someone else – such as an appointee or executor (paras. 16.61-63).

Changes to the HB payment rules from April 2008

16.28 Before April 2008, it was generally the case that private and housing association tenants could choose whether HB (excluding HB for rates) was paid to them or to their landlord/agent, though there were some specific rules. This is still true for housing association tenants. But since 7th April 2008, in England, Scotland and Wales, for private tenants who fall within the local housing allowance (LHA) scheme, HB is normally paid to the claimant. Table 16.2 summarises when HB is paid to a landlord/agent, and further details are in paragraphs 16.30-47.

'Landlord' and 'agent'

16.29 When HB is payable to a landlord/agent under any of the rules in this chapter, this means it is payable to the landlord if the landlord collects the rent, but to the agent if the agent collects the rent.

16.27 AA 134(1A),(1B),138(1); NIAA 126(1); HB 94; HB60+ 75; NIHB 91; NIHB60+ 72; CTB 78; CTB60+ 63

Table 16.2: When HB is paid to a landlord/agent rather than the claimant

Mandatory rules: all cases

In LHA and non-LHA cases, the authority must pay HB to a landlord/agent if any of the following apply:

- there are arrears of rent of eight weeks or more – unless it is in the overriding interests of the claimant not to pay the landlord/agent;
- part of the claimant's JSA, income support, employment support allowance or pension credit is being paid direct to the landlord/agent; or
- the claimant has died and before the death the authority decided to pay the landlord/agent.

Discretionary rules: LHA cases in Great Britain

In LHA cases, in addition to the above, the authority may pay HB to a landlord/agent if any of the following apply:

- the claimant is likely to have difficulty managing their affairs;
- it is improbable that the claimant will pay their rent;
- for a period not greater than eight weeks while the authority is considering whether either of the above applies;
- the claimant has left the accommodation with arrears owing to the landlord/agent; or
- the authority had to pay the landlord/agent at the claimant's previous address.

Discretionary rules: Northern Ireland and non-LHA cases

In non-LHA cases in Great Britain (or any kind of case in Northern Ireland), in addition to the above, the authority may pay HB to a landlord/agent if any of the following apply:

- the claimant asks for this or agrees to it;
- it is in the best interests of the claimant or family to do so; or
- the claimant has left the accommodation with arrears owing to the landlord/agent.

T 16.2 HB 95-96; HB60+ 76-77; NIHB 92-93 ; NIHB60+ 73-74

Mandatory rules for paying HB to a landlord/agent

When deductions are being made from a passport benefit

16.30 In all rent allowance cases (including all housing association and private cases) the authority must pay the HB to the landlord/agent if part of the claimant's (or partner's) income support, employment support allowance (income-related or contribution based), pension credit (guarantee or savings credit) or JSA (income-based or contribution-based) is being paid to the landlord/agent to meet arrears (or to meet the cost of ineligible services of a hostel resident) as described in appendix 7. This should continue until the DWP stops making the relevant deductions. DWP local offices should inform authorities of appropriate cases (GM A6.187).

When there are eight weeks' rent arrears

16.31 In all rent allowance cases (including all housing association and private cases) the authority must pay the HB to the landlord/agent if the claimant has rent arrears equal to eight weeks or more, except where the authority considers it to be in the overriding interest of the claimant not to pay the landlord/agent. This should continue until there are no longer at least eight weeks' rent arrears.

16.32 For the above purposes, the term 'rent' includes ineligible service charge payments, e.g. for fuel, that must be paid if the claimant is to occupy the home. The authority should estimate the length of time it will take to clear the arrears and review the case when this should have happened (GLHA 5.86).

16.33 This duty to pay a landlord/agent only arises if the landlord/agent (or someone else) informs the authority that there are eight weeks' or more arrears. It is not up to the authority to find this out for itself: *R v Haringey LBC ex parte Ayub.* The question of whether there are eight weeks' rent arrears is a question of fact (paras. 1.31-35). It is for the claimant to show that it is in their overriding interest for payment not to be made direct *(CH/3244/2007 para. 9-10).* This requires something more specific than an unparticularised assertion of a dispute with the landlord. For example in a dispute over the need for essential repairs to be carried out the Commissioner indicated her expectation that the claimant's evidence would include a solicitor's letter setting out the alleged essential repairs and a schedule of disrepair provided by a builder or surveyor *(CH/3244/2007 para. 9).*

16.30 HB 95(1)(a); HB60+ 76(1)(a); NIHB 92(1)(a); NIHB60+73(1)(a)

16.31 HB 95(1)(b); HB60+ 76(1)(b); NIHB 92(1)(b); NIHB60+73(1)(b)

16.32 HB 2(1); HB60+ 2(1); NIHB 2(1); NIHB60+2(1) def: 'rent'

Following a death

16.34 In all rent allowance cases (including all housing association and private cases) the authority must pay the HB to the landlord/agent if the claimant has died, and before the death the authority had already decided to pay the landlord/agent – but only up to the amount of any rent remaining unpaid at the date of the death. This sounds obvious, but it means that an executor cannot argue that the money should instead be paid to them (but see also para. 16.63).

Discretionary payment rules in LHA cases

16.35 The following rules, in paragraphs 16.35-40, apply in England, Scotland and Wales only. In rent allowance cases which fall within the LHA rules (many private tenants but never housing association tenants), the authority pays HB to the claimant or the landlord/agent as follows. If one of the mandatory rules applies (paras. 16.30-34), HB must be paid to the landlord/agent. Otherwise it may be paid to the landlord/agent if:

- the authority considers that the claimant is likely to have difficulty managing their financial affairs; or
- the authority considers that it is improbable that the claimant will pay the rent; or
- for eight weeks while the authority is considering whether either of the above applies; or
- HB remains due to a claimant who has left a dwelling with rent arrears (in which case payment to the landlord/agent is limited to the amount of rent owing; or
- a mandatory payment has already been made by the authority to the landlord/agent in respect of the current HB award (paras. 16.30-34).

In all other cases, the HB is paid to the claimant (or appointee etc: paras. 16.61-63). The next few paragraphs look at this in more detail and give some further rules.

The claimant likely to have difficulty managing financial affairs

16.36 An authority could consider that a claimant is likely to have difficulty managing their financial affairs, for example if the claimant has a learning disorder that makes managing a budget difficult. Other possible indicators are a medical condition, illiteracy, an inability to speak English, fleeing domestic violence, leaving care or leaving prison, debt problems, undischarged bankruptcy, an inability to obtain a bank account, receipt of supporting people or charitable help (GLHA 5.61-5.71).

16.34 HB 97(5); HB60+ 78(5); NIHB 94(5); NIHB60+75(5)

16.35 HB 95(1), 96(1)(c),(3A)-(3B); HB60+ 76(1), 77(1)(c),(3A)-(3B)

Improbable that the claimant will pay the rent

16.37 An authority could consider that it is improbable that the claimant will pay the rent if he or she has consistently failed to pay the rent on past occasions without good reason (GLHA 4.10). The terms of the tests are however predictive – what is likely to happen, not what has happened *(CH/2986/2005).*

Paying a landlord/agent while considering who to pay

16.38 If the authority suspects that either of the above may apply (paras. 16.36-37) it may pay HB to the landlord/agent for up to eight weeks while it is considering who to pay. On the other hand the DWP suggests that the authority may wish to make payments to the claimant to see how he or she handles them (GLHA 5.71). Alternatively the authority might suspend payments (para. 16.54).

DWP guidance

16.39 The DWP has given extensive guidance to authorities on the procedures to be adopted in considering the above discretionary powers (GLHA 4.00-6.102). Authorities should however be aware that in so far as the regulations give a discretion they must exercise it according to the law. Any attempt to impose rules upon themselves or to accept guidance without question may fetter that discretion and render the decision wrong in law *(CH/2986/2005).* The guidance has at various times referred to 'vulnerability' or 'safeguarding', terms which do not appear in the law.

16.40 A claimant, someone acting on the claimant's behalf, a welfare organisation, the landlord/agent or others may make representations to the authority regarding the problems the claimant is having in managing their financial affairs or the likelihood of them paying the rent. The authority may also take account of information that it already holds or obtains from a home visit without the need for representations (GLHA 5.40-42, 6.40-41).

Sending the claimant a payment for the landlord/agent

16.41 The authority may make the first payment of HB (following a new claim or a supersession) by sending the claimant a cheque or other instrument of payment payable to the landlord/agent for part or all of the amount due. (This also applies in Northern Ireland or in non-LHA cases elsewhere.) The authority may do this if:

- it is of the opinion that the claimant has not already paid the landlord/agent for the period in respect of which any payment is to be made; and
- it would be in the interests of efficient administration of housing benefit.

16.38 HB 96(3B); HB60+ 77(3B);

16.41 HB 96(2); HB60+ 77(2); NIHB 93(2); NIHB60+74(2)

16.42 The DWP advises that this discretion 'is to avoid the possibility of a claimant misusing a first payment covering several weeks' entitlement' (GM A6.163) and advises authorities (GM A6.166) to think about using this power where:

- the amount due is £100 or more; or
- it has reason to think that the claimant might default; or
- there is a rent debt but the case is not appropriate for longer term payments to be made to the landlord/agent.

Is the landlord/agent 'a fit and proper person'?

16.43 Over-riding all other rules, HB must not be paid to the landlord/agent if they are not a 'fit and proper person' – unless it is in the overriding interests of the claimant for payments to be made to the landlord/agent. (This also applies in Northern Ireland and non-LHA cases elsewhere.)

16.44 This rule can be used if the landlord/agent is involved in fraudulent acts related to HB. The DWP suggests (GM A6.199) that the authority might also consider whether the landlord/agent has regularly failed to:

- report changes in tenants' circumstances which he or she might reasonably be expected to know might affect entitlement; or
- repay an overpayment which the authority has decided is recoverable – despite the fact that a proper notice was issued and that the rights of review had been exercised or made available.

16.45 In deciding whether the landlord/agent is 'fit and proper', the authority should not base its judgment on:

- the landlord/agent's undesirable activity in non-HB matters – such as contravention of the Housing Acts (GM A6.196); or
- the fact that the landlord/agent makes use of the right to request a revision or appeal before repaying any recoverable overpayment; or
- the fact that the landlord/agent has made complaints of maladministration to the local government ombudsman.

The DWP also advises that the 'fit and proper' test should only be applied where the authority is 'doubtful about the landlord/agent's honesty in connection with HB' (GM A6.197).

16.46 Even if a landlord/agent is not a 'fit and proper person', HB may be paid to them if it is in the overriding interest of the claimant to pay the landlord/agent – for example where the risk of not paying the landlord/agent outweighs the risk of paying them (GM A6.192).

16.43 HB 95(3), 96(3); HB60+ 76(3), 77(3); NIHB 92(4), 93(3); NIHB 73(4), 74(3)

16.46 HB 96(3)(b); HB60+ 77(3)(b); NIHB 93(3)(b); NIHB60+ 74(3)(b)

Discretionary payment rules in non-LHA cases

16.47 In all rent allowance cases in Northern Ireland, or in England, Scotland and Wales in rent allowance cases which do not fall within the LHA rules (all housing association tenants and a few private tenants), the authority pays HB either to the claimant or the landlord/agent as follows. If one of the mandatory rules applies (paras. 16.30-34), HB must be paid to the landlord/ agent. Otherwise it may be paid to the landlord/agent if:

- the claimant requests, or consents to, such an arrangement;
- the authority considers it to be in the interests of the claimant and family; or
- HB remains due to a claimant who has left a dwelling with rent arrears (in which case payment to the landlord/agent is limited to the amount of rent owing.

In all other cases, the HB is paid to the claimant (or appointee etc: paras. 16.61-63). The rules in paragraphs 16.41-46 apply to non-LHA cases and all cases in Northern Ireland (as well as to LHA cases).

16.48 The above rules mean in practice that the majority of housing association tenants, and many private tenants, have their HB paid to their landlord/agent. What constitutes the 'interests of the claimant and family' is not necessarily the same as the tests used in LHA cases (paras. 16.36-40) but may well come to be regarded as similar.

Other considerations about paying HB

Assisting claimants to manage payments of HB

16.49 As a matter of good practice authorities are expected to provide claimants with details of banks and building societies in their area that offer basic bank accounts. Where necessary – so that claimants can open such accounts – authorities are encouraged to provide a verification letter that financial institutions may be prepared to accept as confirmation of the claimant's identity.

16.50 New claimants who already have bank accounts and overdrafts may face problems when it comes to getting HB payments. The legal theory is that a bank customer can choose how any further money paid into an account is used (this is called the 'first right of appropriation'), but banks can take a great deal of time and persuasion to recognise this.

16.47 HB 95, 96; HB60+76, 77; NIHB 92, 93; NIHB60+ 73, 74

Payment of HB discharges liability for rent

16.51 When an amount of rent allowance is paid to a landlord/agent this discharges the claimant's liability to pay that amount of rent for the relevant period unless the authority recovers any of it as an overpayment from that landlord/agent (table 18.5).

Payment to landlord/agent if HB exceeds the rent

16.52 There is a special rule for LHA cases in which HB is payable to the landlord/agent under any of the earlier rules, but the amount of HB is greater that the rent due to the landlord/agent. In such cases, the excess HB is paid to the claimant (or appointee or nominee if appropriate: paras. 16.61-63) – unless there are rent arrears in which case the excess HB is first paid to the landlord/agent until the arrears are cleared (and then paid to the claimant, appointee or nominee).

16.53 For the above purposes, the term 'rent' includes ineligible service charge payments, e.g. for fuel, that must be paid if the claimant is to occupy the home. The authority should estimate the length of time it will take to clear the arrears and review the case when this should have happened (GLHA 5.86).

Suspending HB while considering who to pay

16.54 When considering whether HB should be paid to the claimant or someone else the authority has the power to suspend payment (para. 17.46-47 and see *CH/1821/2006*) though the DWP encourages authorities not to delay payment when considering the issue (GLHA 5.81).

Information provided to claimants and landlords/agents

16.55 Once the question arises of whether to pay a claimant or landlord/agent, and once a decision is then made, both parties (as a 'person affected') should be notified of that decision within 14 days (para. 16.8) – and this has been confirmed as applying in LHA cases as well as others *(CH/180/2006).*

16.56 If the HB is to be paid to the landlord/agent the notice must inform them of:

- the amount payable and the date from which payments will start;
- their duty to report any change of circumstances which might affect the claimant's amount of, or right to, HB and the kind of change which should be notified;

16.51 HB 95(2), HB60+ 76(2) NIHB 92(2) NIHB60+ 73(2)

16.52 HB 95(2A); HB60+ 76(2A)

16.53 HB 2(1); HB60+ 2(1) def of 'rent'

- that if a recoverable overpayment occurs which is recovered from payments made to that landlord/agent for their other blameless tenants (para. 18.46), then those tenants must be treated as having paid their rent to the value of the amount recovered.

Appeals about who to pay HB to

16.57 Both the landlord/agent and claimant have appeal rights in relation to the decision *(CH/180/2006)*. If one of them appeals the decision both are parties to the appeal. Both should be given notice of the appeal, the opportunity to request an oral hearing and notice of any hearing; and both are entitled to be present and heard *(CH 2986/2005)*.

16.58 The authority should make sure that the Tribunals Service is informed of the claimant's and landlord/agent's addresses and any written submission put to the tribunal by the authority or one of the parties must be copied to the other. The appeal itself should be a full rehearing and is not limited to scrutiny of the authority's decision on judicial review grounds *(R(H) 6/06)*.

When the wrong person has been paid

16.59 If the authority decided to pay HB to the claimant even though it ought to have decided to pay the landlord/agent, the landlord/agent is not entitled to receive HB in respect of the period for which the claimant has already received the benefit *(CH/3629/2006)*. On the other hand, in such circumstances the landlord/agent could seek compensation from the authority (see comments in *CH/3629/2006*).

Can a landlord/agent refuse to accept HB?

16.60 A landlord has the right to refuse to accept payments of rent (e.g. via HB) in respect of anyone who is not a party to the tenancy agreement *(Bessa Plus Plc v Lancaster)*, typically, for example, the tenant's partner or some other person who is not liable to make payments but whom the authority has treated as liable. This may cause problems particularly where the non-tenant member of a couple should be the claimant (e.g. paras. 12.19, 12.24-25, 12.33, 21.24). In such cases the authority should pay the claimant or the claimant may wish to nominate the liable person as the recipient of the payments (para. 16.62) or the authority may identify the payments made to the landlord as made on behalf of the liable person.

16.56 HB sch 9 paras 11-12; HB60+ sch 8 paras 11-12; NIHB sch 10 paras 11-12; NIHB60+ sch 9 paras 11-12

Other people who may receive a rent allowance or CTB

Appointee

16.61 Where an appointee acts for a claimant who is incapable of managing his or her own affairs (para. 5.5) then payment may be made to that person. CTB in most cases, however, is paid by rebating the claimant's tax liability. The authority should also consider whether the claimant's property should be exempt from the council tax (para. 11.11).

Nominee

16.62 In the case of HB, if the claimant requests in writing that the authority makes payment to another person (i.e. a corporate body or an individual aged 18 or more), the authority may make payments to that person. The DWP incorrectly refers to this person as an agent and advises that the claimant must be unable to collect the money himself or herself (GM para. A6.181). This is not the case, however, as the relevant regulation specifically identifies that the claimant may be able to act on their own behalf. The DWP (GLHA paras. 5.100-101) indicates that this power to make payments to a nominated person is subject to the rules governing direct payments to landlords and letting agents. The DWP contends that as a result where a claim has been decided under the LHA rules the authority must not use its discretion to pay a person nominated by the claimant if that person is the claimant's landlord, on the basis that the power to nominate is subject to the rules governing payments to landlords. The specific wording of the regulations does not appear to support this though the existence of the separate rules regarding direct payments to landlords is presumably something the authority may have regard to when considering its discretionary power to pay to a nominee who is also the landlord.

A dead claimant's personal representative or next of kin

16.63 Where the claimant dies any rent allowance (or CTB more than their council tax debt) must be paid to their personal representative or, if there is none, next of kin aged 16 or over, provided a written request is made within the time limit. The next of kin must be aged 16 or over and take priority in the following order: spouse, children and grandchildren, other relatives (parents, brothers, sisters or their children). The time limit is 12 months from the date of the claimant's death or such longer period as the authority allows. But see paragraph 16.34 if the claimant dies with rent arrears.

16.61 HB 94(2); HB60+ 75(2); NIHB 91(2); NIHB60+ 72(2); CTB 78(2); CTB60+ 63(2)

16.62 HB 94(3); HB60+ 75(3); NIHB 91(3); NIHB60+ 72(3)

16.63 HB 97(1)-(3); HB60+ 78(1)-(3); NIHB 94(1)-(3); NIHB60+ 75(1)-(3); CTB 80(1)-(3); CTB60+ 65(1)-(3)

17 Changes to entitlement

17.1 This chapter explains how a claimant's entitlement to HB or CTB can change or end. It covers:

- the reasons why an HB/CTB decision can change;
- what 'revisions' and 'supersessions' are;
- the duty to notify a change of circumstances;
- when changes of circumstances take effect from;
- what happens when changes are notified late;
- the rules about suspending, restoring and terminating HB/CTB; and
- 'extended payments' and 'continuing payments'.

Why decisions can change

17.2 Once an authority has decided a claim (para. 16.2) the decision is changed if:

- the authority reconsiders the decision and 'revises' it – usually because it was wrongly decided in the first place; or
- the authority reconsiders the decision and 'supersedes' it – usually because there has been a change of circumstances; or
- the authority corrects an accidental error in the decision; or
- an first-tier or upper tribunal, or court, alters the decision on appeal.

The first two are described in this chapter. Accidental errors, reconsiderations in connection with disputes, and appeals, are described in chapter 19.

Reconsiderations, revisions and supersessions

17.3 The authority may have to reconsider a decision, and change it if appropriate:

- because a claimant (or other person affected) requests this (para. 19.6); or
- because the authority has the power to do so without such a request (para. 19.13); or
- because the regulations require it.

These are described below (paras. 17.14-41). There are also rules about what factors are taken into account, how to obtain the information and evidence needed, and what details must be notified to the claimant (paras. 17.42-45).

17.2 CPSA sch 7 paras 2,11; NICPSA sch 7 paras 2,11

Table 17.1: Revisions and supersessions: main points

Situation	How it is dealt with
Changes of circumstances	
A change notified more than one month after it occurred (this time limit can be extended) if the claimant qualifies for more HB/CTB	**Supersession:** From the Monday following the day the authority receives the notification
Any other change of circumstances	**Supersession:** From the Monday following the day the change occurs
Overpayments and official errors	
Overpayments, whatever the cause; and underpayments only if caused by official error	**Revision or supersession:** From when the overpayment or underpayment began
Successful requests for a reconsideration, etc	
Reconsiderations requested within one month (which can be extended)	**Revision:** From the date the decision took effect or should have
Reconsiderations requested outside that time limit (sometimes called an 'any time review')	**Supersession:** From the Monday of the week in which the authority received the request
Appeals if the authority is able to revise in the claimant's favour instead	**Revision:** From the date the decision took effect or should have
Rent officer re-determinations (rent referral cases only)	
A rent officer re-determination increases the claimant's HB	**Revision:** From the date the decision took effect or should have
A rent officer re-determination reduces the claimant's HB	**Supersession:** From the Monday following the rent officer re-determination

Note: Only the main points are given. More details are in this chapter and chapter 19.

Examples: Revisions and supersessions

A change resulting in a supersession

A claimant writes to tell the authority that her wages have gone down. Her letter gets to the authority within one month of the change, and she provides acceptable evidence.

The authority should make a superseding decision, so that the increase in her HB/CTB is awarded from the Monday following the date her wages went down.

A late-notified change resulting in a supersession

The same as the above story, except that the claimant took six months to inform the authority (and has no reason for her delay).

The authority should make a superseding decision, so that the increase in her HB/CTB is awarded from the Monday following the date it received the information from her.

A reconsideration resulting in a revision

A claimant has been awarded HB/CTB on the basis that the maximum non-dependant deduction is to apply in respect of her son (because he works full-time but she has been unable to provide evidence of his income). Within one month of notification of the decision on her claim, she writes in with acceptable evidence of his true (low) income.

The authority should revise its decision, so that the lower non-dependant deduction applies from the beginning of her claim.

A reconsideration resulting in a supersession

The same as the last story, except that the claimant took eight months to provide the evidence (and has no reason for her delay).

The authority should make a superseding decision, so that the lower non-dependant deduction applies from the Monday of the benefit week in which it received the evidence from her.

17.4 When a decision is reconsidered, it may or may not need to be changed. If it is changed this is called in the law (but not usually in day-to-day work) a 'revision' or a 'supersession'. Table 17.1 gives a summary of which changes are revisions and which are supersessions. The distinction between them is as follows:

- A 'revision' is typically required when a decision was wrong from the outset. When a decision is revised, the revision goes back to the beginning (to the date of the decision in question).
- A 'supersession' is typically required when there has been a change of circumstances. When a decision is superseded, the supersession does not go right back: there is always a 'before' and an 'after'.

More than one event

17.5 If more than one event occurs in a case (such as two successive changes in circumstances), each is dealt with in turn. However, if a single event apparently requires both a revision and a supersession, it is dealt with as a revision. For example, a claimant may request a reconsideration so late that it can only be dealt with as a supersession (para. 17.37), but the authority realises it has made an official error (paras. 19.16-17) which has to be treated as a revision: the revision 'wins'.

Closed period supersessions

17.6 A 'closed period supersession' is done when someone's HB or CTB is discovered to have reduced to nil for a fixed period in the past (and recommenced at the same or a different rate after that). For example, a claimant has been on JSA(IB) (and HB/CTB) for many years but worked last Christmas for a fixed contract of three weeks for a very high income. He did not declare that fact then, but it is discovered now. A 'closed period supersession' means that the authority (now) reduces his entitlement to nil for that past period (and recovers the overpayment: chapter 18). The advantage (administratively and to the claimant) is that the claimant remains currently entitled to HB/CTB (based on his original claim) without needing to reclaim. There have been doubts about this rule, but it is correct in income support (CIS/2595/203), and the DWP considers it to be correct in HB/CTB (circular HB/CTB A6/2009). The rule can apply to any number of periods in the past, but never applies to current periods of non-entitlement to HB/CTB.

After a revision or supersession

17.7 Once a decision has been revised or superseded (or altered on appeal by a first-tier or upper tribunal), the result is a decision itself, which can in turn be revised or superseded in the same way as an original decision can be.

Duty to notify changes

17.8 The claimant has a duty to notify any 'relevant' change of circumstances (para. 17.12) – though in the case of claimants on pension credit this duty is very limited (tables 17.2, 17.3). The change must be notified to:

- the authority which administers HB/CTB; or
- by telephone to the DWP in the case of some changes relating to JSA or income support (para. 17.9).

17.5 DAR 7(4); NIDAR 7(4)

17.7 CPSA sch 7 paras 1(2),3(1),4(1),(2),(4); NICPSA sch 7 paras 1(2),3(1),4(1),(2),(4); DAR 7(1); NIDAR 7(1)

17.8 HB 88(1),(6); HB60+ 69(1),(9); NIHB 84(1), (Sam?); NIHB60+ 65(1), (Sam?); CTB 74(1),(7); CTB60+ 69(1),(10)

The duty to notify begins on the date the claim is made and continues for as long as the person is in receipt of HB or CTB. If HB/CTB is payable to someone other than the claimant (e.g. a landlord or an appointee), that person is also required to notify relevant changes.

Telephone notifications

17.9 A change of circumstances may be notified by telephone:

- to the authority if it accepts claims made wholly by telephone (para. 5.9). But such an authority may require notification in writing (or some other means) in particular cases or classes of cases;
- to the DWP if it permits this. But this applies only if the claimant or partner is on JSA or income support; and only in the case of starting work; and only if that means that JSA(IB) or JSA(C) will cease, or the amount of JSA(C) will change. The DWP calls this the 'in and out of work process'.

Internet notifications

17.10 An authority may choose to allow changes to be notified wholly by internet – but only with the approval of the authority's Chief Executive (in Northern Ireland, the authority), who must also approve the internet notification form and communication and authentication procedures. Authorities may use an intermediary (e.g. a private firm) for this purpose, and can require internet claims to be made via an intermediary. They may also require claimants to keep written and/or electronic records.

Written notifications

17.11 In all other cases, a change of circumstances must be notified in writing to the authority's 'designated office' (para. 5.12). Authorities often have forms which may optionally be used for this purpose. Other organisations sometimes do too (such as the prison service, which uses forms HCTB6, 7 and 8 to notify authorities of changes relating to its prisoners).

Relevant changes of circumstances

17.12 For the above purposes (para. 17.8) a 'relevant' change is one which the claimant (or other person) could reasonably be expected to know might affect:

- entitlement to HB/CTB; or
- amount of HB/CTB; or
- method of payment (e.g. whether to pay HB to the landlord rather than the claimant or vice versa).

17.9 HB 88(1),(6); HB60+ 69(1),(9); NIHB 84(1), (Sam?); NIHB60+ 65(1), (Sam?); CTB 74(1),(7); CTB60+ 69(1),(10)

17.10 HB 88A, sch 11; HB60+ 69A, sch 10; NIHB 84A, sch 11; NIHB60+ 65A, sch 10; CTB 74A, sch 9; CTB60+ 59A, sch 8

17.11 HB 88(1),(4); HB60+ 69(1),(4); NIHB 84(1),(3); NIHB60+ 65(1),(2); CTB 74(1),(4); CTB60+ 59(1),(4)

Whether a claimant (or other person) could reasonably be expected to know a change might affect HB or CTB, is of importance if failure to notify a change results in an overpayment and the question of recovering the overpayment arises (chapter 18), or results in an underpayment and the question of whether it should be awarded arises (para. 17.37). However, failure to notify a change that does not affect HB or CTB at all is not a criminal offence: *R v Passmore*.

Table 17.2: Changes the claimant must notify*

Claimant and any partner under 60

- The end of his or her (or any partner's) entitlement to JSA(IB), ESA(IR) or IS
- Changes where a child or young person ceases to be a member of the family: for example, when child benefit stops or he or she leaves the household

Claimant or any partner aged 60+

- Changes in the details of their letting (HB rent allowances only)
- Changes affecting the residence or income of any non-dependant
- Absences exceeding or likely to exceed 13 weeks

Additional matters for claimants on savings credit

- Changes affecting any child living with the claimant (other than age) which might affect the amount of HB/CTB
- Changes to capital which take it (or may take it) above £16,000
- Changes to a non-dependant if the non-dependant's income and capital was treated as being the claimant's (para. (d) of table 13.4)
- Changes to a partner who was ignored in assessing savings credit but is taken into account for HB/CTB (para. (d) of table 13.4)

Additional matters for claimants on second adult rebate

- Changes in the number of adults in their home
- Changes in the total gross incomes of the adults in their home
- The date any adult in their home ceases to receive JSA(IB) or IS

* This is a list of the items specifically mentioned in the law. The claimant's duty is wider (paras. 17.12-13).

17.12 HB 88(1); HB60+ 69(1); NIHB 84(1); NIHB60+ 65(1); CTB 74(1); CTB60+ 59(1)

T 17.2 HB 88; HB60+ 69; NIHB 84; NIHB60+ 65; CTB 74; CTB60+ 59

17.13 The law lists certain things which the claimant must inform the authority of (table 17.2) and certain other things which the claimant need not inform the authority of (table 17.3). The claimant should also notify the authority of:

- changes in rent, including changes of address (unless the claimant is a council or NIHE tenant);
- changes in rates in Northern Ireland if they are not collected by the Rating Service;
- changes in the status of non-dependants/second adults;
- changes in family circumstances affecting the applicable amount;
- changes in capital and/or income;
- changes relating to payment of HB to a landlord.

Table 17.3: Changes the claimant need not notify

- Beginnings or ends of awards of pension credit (either kind) or changes in the amount
- Changes which affect JSA(IB), ESA(IR) or IS but do not affect HB/CTB
- Changes in council tax
- Changes in rent if the claimant is a council or NIHE tenant
- Changes in rates in Northern Ireland if they are collected by the Rating Service
- Retrospective changes in social security benefits
- Changes in the age of any member of the family or non-dependant (but see table 17.2)
- Changes in the HB or CTB regulations

Notes

In the first case, it is the DWP's duty (and no-one else's) to notify the authority of the change. In the second, the change has no impact on HB/CTB. In the third, fourth and fifth, the authority itself has made the changes. For the sixth, see paras. 17.23-24. In the last two cases, the authority should implement the change automatically.

T 17.3 HB 88(3),(4); HB60+ 69(3),(4); NIHB 84(2),(3); NIHB60+ 65(2),(3); CTB 74(3),(4); CTB60+ 59(3),(4)

Changes of circumstances which are notified on time or do not require notification

17.14 This section describes how authorities should deal with changes of circumstances which:

- are notified to the authority on time ('on time' means within a month of the occurrence of the change – or longer in special circumstances: para. 17.40); or
- do not require to be notified to the authority (table 17.3).

In each case, the change takes effect from a date at or very near to the occurrence of the change. Late-notified changes are dealt with in the next section (para. 17.36 onwards).

17.15 The authority may alter a decision if there has been a change of circumstances or one is anticipated. As described in the following paragraphs, the effect of this may be to:

- alter the claimant's entitlement to HB/CTB; or
- end the award of HB/CTB.

17.16 All the changes in this section are supersessions (except where mentioned).

The date the change actually occurs

17.17 The date a change actually occurs is an important concept: it affects the date on which the change is implemented in HB/CTB, as described later in this chapter. Generally speaking, the date a change actually occurs is the date something new happens.

17.18 Determining the date a change actually occurs can be straightforward (e.g. in the case of a claimant's birthday) or difficult (e.g. in the case of acquiring a partner). In four cases there are specific rules:

- If entitlement to any social security benefit ends, the date the change actually occurs is defined as being the day after the last day of entitlement to that benefit.
- If there is a change in tax, national insurance or the maximum rate of working tax credit or child tax credit, and this is caused by a change in the law (e.g. the Budget), it may be disregarded (i.e. treated as not occurring) until up to 30 benefit weeks later. This applies to the income of a claimant, partner, non-dependant or second adult.
- If the claimant or partner is aged 65+, changes in non-dependant deductions are delayed for 26 weeks (paras. 6.34-35);
- There are special rules about arrears of income (para. 13.25).

17.18 HB 79(1); HB60+ 59(1); NIHB 77(1); NIHB60+ 57(1); CTB 67(1); CTB60+ 50(1); HB 34; HB60+ 34; NIHB 31; NIHB60+ 32; CTB 24; CTB60+ 24; HB60+ 59(9)-(12); NIHB60+ 57(12)-(14); CTB60+ 50(10)-(13)

Example: A claimant's birthday

A claimant receiving HB and CTB reaches the age of 25 on Wednesday 2nd December 2009. The effect is that her HB and CTB increase.

She has no duty to notify the authority of this. The authority should alter her entitlement to HB and CTB.

The new amounts of HB and CTB are awarded from the Monday following the change, i.e. Monday 7th December.

Implementing changes: the general rule

17.19 The following general rule applies for all changes other than those mentioned in the remainder of this chapter. Typical examples are changes in income, capital, age or household composition.

17.20 So long as the result of a change is that entitlement to HB/CTB continues, the authority alters the claimant's entitlement to HB/CTB. The new amount of HB/CTB is awarded from the Monday after the date the change occurs, even if the change occurs on a Monday. (If the result of the change is that entitlement ends, see paragraph 17.21.)

Changes ending an award of HB/CTB

17.21 If the result of a change of circumstances is that the claimant no longer satisfies all of the basic conditions of benefit (paras. 2.3 and 2.4 – for example, a claimant dies or a claimant not on guarantee credit becomes a millionaire through the lottery), the authority must end the award of HB/CTB. In such cases:

- the last week of HB/CTB entitlement is the benefit week (para. 5.32) in which the claimant's circumstances change; and
- in the last week, the claimant is entitled to a full week's HB/CTB (calculated as if the change had not occurred).

Different rules apply to moves and changes in rent or council tax (paras. 17.29-32).

Changes relating to social security benefits

17.22 When a person's entitlement to a social security benefit starts, changes or ends, the change occurs on the first day of their new, different or nil entitlement (para. 17.18); and takes effect (under the general rule: paras. 17.19-20) on the Monday after that. Further points to note are as follows:

- if the change occurs in the past, the 'relevant benefit rule' may apply (para. 17.23);

17.20 HB 79(1); HB60+ 59(1); NIHB 77(1); NIHB60+ 57(1); CTB 67(1); CTB60+ 50(1); DAR 7(2)(a)(i),8(2); NIDAR 7(2)(a)(i),8(2)

17.21 HB 79(1); HB60+ 59(1); NIHB 77(1); NIHB60+ 57(1); CTB 67(1); CTB60+ 50(1); DAR 8(2); NIDAR 8(2)

- if JSA(IB), ESA or income support (or incapacity benefit or severe disablement allowance) end, the claimant may qualify for a four-week 'extended payment' of HB/CTB (para. 17.54);
- if JSA(IB) or income support end because of the claimant's or partner's age, the claimant may qualify for a four-week 'continuing payment' of HB/CTB (para. 17.61).

Changes relating to tax credits and pension credit are dealt with later (paras. 17.25-26).

Examples: Changes to social security benefits

Going on to disability living allowance (DLA)

A claimant on HB/CTB is awarded DLA from Thursday 20th August 2009.

The date of change is Thursday 20th August 2009. So her entitlement to HB/CTB goes up on the following Monday, 24th August 2009.

Incapacity benefit (IB) goes up

A claimant on HB/CTB is also on IB, which goes up on Monday 7th September 2009.

The date of change is Monday 7th September 2009, so her entitlement to HB/CTB changes on the following Monday, 14th September 2009.

The 'relevant benefit rule'

17.23 The 'relevant benefit rule' applies when a social security benefit (but not a tax credit) is found to have changed in the past in a way which would increase a claimant's HB/CTB. In such cases:

- if a social security benefit, or an increase in a social security benefit, is (or has been) awarded back to a date before the start of an HB/CTB award, HB/CTB is increased from the start of the HB/CTB award (this is a revision);
- if a social security benefit, or an increase in a social security benefit, is (or has been) awarded back to a date after the start of an HB/CTB award, HB/CTB is increased from the date of the award or increase of the social security benefit (this is a supersession);
- if an award of HB/CTB ended due to the end of an award of a social security benefit, but that social security benefit is reinstated, HB/CTB is reinstated (this is a revision of the decision to end HB/CTB).

17.24 The 'relevant benefit rule' reflects the popular belief that the DWP and the authority exchange information and claimants need not do this for them. It applies to awards of, or increases in, benefits awarded to the claimant or any

17.23 HB 77,78(1),79(1); HB60+ 58,59(1); NIHB 75,76(1),77(1); NIHB 56,57(1); CTB 65,66(1),67(1); CTB60+ 49(1),50(1)

member of their family; and over-rides questions of the claimant's lateness (paras. 17.36, 17.39).

Examples: The 'relevant benefit rule'

A claimant is found to have been awarded disability living allowance (DLA) from a date in the past.

No matter how far the DLA goes back, the authority must award the claimant any as-yet-unawarded premium that flows from being on DLA (and remove any non-dependant deductions if appropriate) all the way back to the start of his award of DLA (or the start of his award of HB/CTB if later).

A claimant is found to have been awarded JSA(IB) instead of JSA(Cont) from a date in the past.

No matter how far the JSA(IB) goes back, the council must increase her HB/CTB (unless she was already on full HB/CTB) all the way back to the start of her award of JSA(IB) (or the start of her award of HB/CTB if later).

Changes to tax credits

17.25 When a claimant's entitlement to working tax credit or child tax credit starts, changes or ends, the general rule applies (paras. 17.19-20). But in practice, this causes notorious difficulties. Because of the way tax credits are paid (para. 13.46) it can involve counting backwards or forwards from the pay date to work out when the change actually occurs. Table 17.4 explains this and includes examples. However, the rules are almost impossible to apply when a change in someone's tax credit is followed first by hiccups (such as a number of lump sum payments of that tax credit), and then by a resumption of a fairly regular payment pattern.

Changes to pension credit

17.26 If a change in either guarantee credit or savings credit, whether due to a change in the claimant's circumstances or due to official error (para. 19.16), affects the claimant's entitlement to HB/CTB, this takes effect from the date shown in table 17.5.

Starting and leaving work

17.27 If someone starts work, the change occurs on the first day of the new job, and takes effect (under the general rule: paras. 17.19-20) on the Monday following that. So if someone starts work on a Monday, the change takes effect the following Monday, so the claimant will get HB/CTB in their first week as though their circumstances had not changed – and may also qualify for an extended payment (para. 17.54).

17.26 HB60+ 41(9),60; NIHB60+ 39(11),58; CTB60+ 31(9),51; DAR 8(2),(3); NIDAR 8(2),(3)

17.27 DAR 4(7B),(7C),7(2)(i),8(14); NIDAR 4(6B),(6C),7(2)(h),8(11)

Table 17.4: When a tax credit starts, changes or ends

The table covers four-weekly and weekly instalments of tax credits (other payment cycles are rare: para. 13.46), and assumes there are never any hiccups in payments.

Four-weekly instalments

The pay date is the last day of the 28 days covered by the tax credit instalment.

So if a four-weekly instalment is due on the 30th of the month, it covers the period from 3rd to 30th of that month (both dates included).

For example:

- if that is the first instalment ever of a claimant's tax credit, their HB/CTB changes on the Monday following the 3rd of the month;
- if that is the first instalment of a new rate of a claimant's tax credit, their HB/CTB changes on the Monday following the 3rd of the month;
- if that is the last instalment of a claimant's tax credit, the date the change occurs is the 31st of the month, and their HB/CTB changes on the Monday following the 31st of the month.

Weekly instalments

The pay date is the last day of the 7 days covered by the tax credit instalment.

So if a weekly instalment is due on the 15th of the month, it covers the period from 9th to 15th of that month (both dates included).

For example:

- if that is the first instalment ever of a claimant's tax credit, their HB/CTB changes on the Monday following the 9th of the month;
- if that is the first instalment of a new rate of a claimant's tax credit, their HB/CTB changes on the Monday following the 9th of the month;
- if that is the last instalment of a claimant's tax credit, the date the change occurs is the 16th of the month, and their HB/CTB changes on the Monday following the 16th of the month.

17.28 If someone leaves work, the change occurs on the day after the last day after the job, and takes effect (under the general rule: paras. 17.19-20) on the Monday following that.

T 17.4 HB 77,78; HB60+ 58; NIHB 75,76; NIHB60+ 56,57; CTB 65,66; CTB60+ 49

Examples: starting and leaving work

Starting work

A claimant on HB/CTB starts work on Monday 6th July 2009. He has been on JSA(IB) and that stops the previous day.

The date of change is Monday 6th July 2009. So his entitlement to HB/CTB goes down (or perhaps stops) on the following Monday, 13th July 2009. But if he qualifies for an extended payment, that will cover him for the period Monday 13th July 2009 to Sunday 9th August 2009 (both dates included), so his HB/CTB goes down (or perhaps stops) on Monday 10th August 2009.

Leaving work

A claimant on HB/CTB leaves work. Her last day is Friday 31st July 2009.

The date of change is Saturday 1st August 2009, so her entitlement to HB/CTB goes down the following Monday, 3rd August 2009.

Moves and changes in rent, rates or council tax liability

17.29 The rules about moves and changes in liability are described below. Moves do not require a fresh claim (though some authorities have special forms for moves) unless they are from one authority area to another.

The question of when someone 'moves' from one dwelling to another can be difficult. Misinterpreting it can produce absurd effects. In line with commissioners' decisions in related cases (e.g. *R(H) 9/05:* para. 3.4), the date of the move is the date on which the claimant's normal home changes: this can be slightly different from the date the claimant crosses the threshold of his or her new home (as illustrated in the last but one of the examples).

17.30 The CTB rules for implementing a move, or a change in liability for council tax, are always that the amount of CTB alters on the exact day that the change occurs, and in the benefit week of the change CTB is calculated on a daily basis (the daily amount being one-seventh of the weekly eligible council tax). This is true whether entitlement to CTB continues after the change or reduces to nil.

17.31 The HB rules for implementing a move, or a change in liability for rent or rates, are as follows:

- If a move or change in rent or rates means that entitlement to HB continues, the amount of HB alters on the exact day that the change occurs, and in the benefit week of the change HB is calculated on a daily basis (the daily amount being one-seventh of the weekly eligible rent).

17.30 CTB 57(1),67(2),(3),(5),(6); CTB60+ 40(1),61(2),(3),(5),(6)

17.31 HB 79(2),(2A)(a),(8),80(4)(b),(c),(10); HB60+ 59(2),(2A)(a),(8),61(4)(b),(c),(11); NIHB 77(2),(3)(a),(10),78(4)(b),(c),(9); NIHB60+ 57(2),(3)(a),(14),59(4)(b),(c),(9)

- If a move or change in rent or rates means that entitlement to HB reduces to nil, HB continues until the end of the benefit week (para. 5.32) in which the change occurs, so in the last benefit week, the claimant gets a whole week's HB.
- But in the case of a hostel or certain other accommodation where payments fall due on a daily basis (para. 5.50), a move or a change in rent is always implemented from the exact day of the change (so residents get HB only for the exact days when payments are due).

Table 17.5: When pension credit starts, changes or ends

What the change is	When it takes effect in HB/CTB*
Pension credit starts, increasing entitlement to HB/CTB	The Monday following the first day of entitlement to pension credit
Pension credit starts, reducing entitlement to HB/CTB	The Monday following the date the authority receives notification from the DWP about this (or, if later, the Monday following the first day of entitlement to pension credit)
Pension credit changes or ends, increasing entitlement to HB/CTB	The Monday of the benefit week in which pension credit changes or ends
Pension credit changes or ends, reducing entitlement to HB/CTB:	
◆ if this is due to a delay by the claimant in notifying a change in circumstances to the DWP	The Monday of the benefit week in which pension credit changes or ends
◆ in any other case	The Monday following the date the authority received notification from the DWP about this (or, if later, the Monday following the pension credit change or end)

Note

* If any of the above would take effect during a claimant's 'continuing payment' period (para. 17.62), the change is instead deferred until afterwards.

T 17.5 HB60+ 41(9),60; NIHB60+ 39(11),58; CTB60+ 31(9),51; DAR 8(2),(3); NIDAR 8(2),(3)

Examples: Moves and changes in liability

Moving within an authority's area

A man moves from one address to another within an authority's area on Monday 3rd August 2009. He is liable for rent and council tax at his old address up to and including Sunday 2nd August and at his new address from Monday 3rd August.

- His HB and CTB change on and from Monday 3rd August to take account of his new eligible rent and eligible council tax.

A woman moves from one address to another within an authority's area on Friday 1st May 2009. She is liable for rent and council tax at her old address up to and including Thursday 30th April and at her new address from Friday 1st May.

- Her HB and CTB change on and from Friday 1st May (on a daily basis) to take account of her new eligible rent and eligible council tax.

A hostel resident

A man moves to a hostel for three nights and is liable for rent on a daily basis on Tuesday 1st, Wednesday 2nd and Thursday 3rd December 2009.

- His HB is awarded for those exact three days (on a daily basis).

Moving out of an authority's area

A woman moves out of an authority's area on Saturday 21st February 2009. She is liable for rent and council tax at her old address (which is not a hostel) up to and including Friday 20th February.

- Her HB ends at the end of the benefit week containing her last day of liability for rent, in other words her last day of HB is Sunday 22nd February.
- Her CTB ends on the last day of her liability for council tax. In other words her last day of CTB is Friday 20th February.

Changes in rent and council tax

A woman's rent goes up on Saturday 17th January 2009.

- If her entitlement to HB changes as a result, it changes on and from Saturday 17th January (on a daily basis).

A man's council tax goes down on Tuesday 8th September 2009, because from that day he becomes entitled to a discount.

- If his entitlement to CTB changes as a result, it changes on and from Tuesday 8th September (on a daily basis).

The claimant's normal home changes

A housing association grants a tenancy to a claimant on HB who has been renting from a private landlord. The new tenancy begins on a Monday, but the housing association gives the keys to the tenant on the Friday before, and the claimant first goes in to the property on the Saturday. By the Monday she has completed her move and on that day she hands the keys to her old home to her private landlord (who agrees not to require payment in lieu of notice).

The claimant's HB changes on the date of her move. This is the date her 'normal home' changes, which is the Monday. So HB changes on the Monday, matching the date of the change in her liability for rent.

HB on two homes

A woman flees violence on Wednesday 4th November 2009. She leaves a council tenancy at which the eligible rent is £70 pw. She goes to a hostel where the eligible rent is £140 pw, payable on a daily basis. Her intention to return to the council tenancy means that she is eligible for HB on both homes.

- In benefit week commencing Monday 2nd November her eligible rent is a full week's eligible rent at the council tenancy (£70.00) plus five-sevenths of a week's eligible rent at the hostel (£120), totalling £190.

17.32 The following changes also take effect on a daily basis:

- the beginning or end of a rent-free period;
- starting or stopping being eligible for HB on a former home, or on two homes, including stopping being eligible because the (4 weeks or 52 weeks) time limit runs out. These are described in chapter 3.

And whenever a claimant is eligible for HB on two homes, eligible rent in each benefit week is calculated by adding together the daily eligible rent for the two addresses for the appropriate number of days (as illustrated in the last of the examples).

Errors of law: 'the anti-test case rule'

17.33 The 'anti-test case rule' applies when an upper tribunal or court decides a case (often called a 'lead case') by interpreting the law in a new way. It requires all similar cases (often called 'look-alike cases') to be superseded to follow the new interpretation from the date of the decision on the lead case (not earlier). This does not apply to cases which an authority should have decided before the decision on the lead case; nor to appeals which a first-tier tribunal 'stayed' (put to one side) to await the decision on the lead case; nor to decisions by upper tribunals in any case before them: *CH/532/2006.*

Changes in the regulations and up-ratings

17.34 When regulations relevant to HB/CTB are amended, the authority alters the claimant's entitlement to HB/CTB from the date on which the amendment

---

17.32 HB 79(2A)(b),(2B),80(11),81(2); HB60+ 59(2A)(b),(2B),61(12),62(2); NIHB 77(3),(4),(11),78(10),79(3); NIHB60+ 57(3),(4),(15),59(10),60(2)

takes effect (unless entitlement reduces to nil, in which case para. 17.21 applies). But in HB only, for claimants whose rent is due weekly or in multiples of weeks, the annual HB/CTB up-rating (which for everyone else takes effect on 1st April) takes effect from the first Monday in April (6th April in 2009). These are supersessions. For up-ratings, see also paragraph 13.153.

When there is more than one change

17.35 Each change in circumstances is dealt with separately. But the following rules apply when changes which actually occur in the same benefit week would have an effect (under the earlier rules in this chapter) in different benefit weeks.

- In HB only, if one of the changes is in:
  - the annual up-rating (when it takes effect on the first Monday in April as described in the previous paragraph);
  - the amount of liability for rent on a dwelling;
  - moving into a new dwelling;
  - starting or stopping being eligible for HB on a former home or on two homes, including stopping being eligible because the (4 weeks or 52 weeks) time limit runs out,

  the other changes in entitlement instead apply when that applies. And for this rule, the first item in the above list takes priority over the other three.
- For HB in all other cases, all the changes take effect from the Monday of the benefit week in which the changes actually occur.
- For CTB in all cases, work out the various days on which the changes have an effect (under the earlier rules): all the changes instead apply from the earliest of these dates.

It is fair to add that sometimes the above rules give unworkable results. (It would be highly desirable if all changes to HB/CTB took effect on the date the change occurred. The above and many other rules would thereby be much simplified.)

Changes of circumstances which are notified late

Late notification of changes which reduce entitlement

17.36 If a claimant delays (no matter how long) notifying the authority of a change which would have the effect of reducing his or her entitlement to HB or CTB, the authority must nonetheless implement the change according to the rules in the previous section. This creates an overpayment (which may or may not be recoverable: chapter 18). An example appears below.

17.34 HB 79(3); HB60+ 60(3); NIHB 77(3); NIHB60+ 58(3); CTB 67(4); CTB60+ 50(4); DAR 8(10); NIDAR 8(12)

17.35 HB 79(4),(5); HB60+ 59(4),(5); NIHB 77(6),(7); NIHB60+ 57(6),(7); CTB 67(7); CTB60+ 50(7)

17.36 DAR 8(2); NIDAR 8(2)

Example: Late notified change reducing entitlement

A claimant's wages went up four months ago, but the claimant did not inform the authority until today.

The change is implemented from the Monday following the day the wages went up – thus creating an overpayment (which will very likely be recoverable).

Late notification of changes which increase entitlement

17.37 The rules in the previous section do not, however, apply if the claimant delays notifying the authority of a change which would have the effect of increasing his or her entitlement to HB or CTB – and which he or she had a duty to notify (para. 17.8 and table 17.2). A claimant counts as having delayed notifying a change if his or her written notification is received by the authority more than one month after the change occurred (though this time limit can be extended: para. 17.40).

17.38 In such cases the change is treated as occurring on the date the authority received the written notification – and then the change is taken into account using the rules in the previous section but based on that date. In other words, the claimant loses money (as in the example below).

17.39 The following points are worth noting in connection with this rule:

- the rule applies only to changes which the claimant has a duty to notify (paras. 17.8-12);
- a claimant cannot have a duty to notify something which he or she cannot know;
- the claimant can take longer to provide the notification if the 'relevant benefit rule' applies (para. 17.23);
- the claimant can take longer to provide the notification if the circumstances in the next paragraph apply.

Example: Late notified change increasing entitlement

A claimant's wages went down four months ago, but the claimant did not inform the authority until today. The authority asks why she delayed, but she has no special circumstances.

The change is implemented from the Monday following the day the claimant's written notification of the change was received by the authority. The claimant does not get her arrears. (However, if the claimant has 'special circumstances', she may get her arrears: para. 17.40.)

17.37 DAR 7(2)(a),(3),8(3),(5); NIDAR 7(2)(a),(3),8(3),(5)

Extending the time limit for notifying a change that increases entitlement

17.40 In the case of a change of circumstances which increases entitlement, the one month time limit for notifying it is extended (and the claimant does not lose money) if:

- the notification is received by the authority within 13 months of the date on which the change occurred; and
- the claimant also notifies the authority of his or her reasons for failing to notify the change earlier; and
- the authority is satisfied that there are or were 'special circumstances' as a result of which it was not practicable to notify the change within the one month time limit. The longer the delay (beyond the normal one month), the more compelling those special circumstances need to be; and
- the authority is satisfied that it is reasonable to allow the claimant's late notification of the change. In determining this, the authority may not take account of ignorance of the law (not even ignorance of the time limits) nor of the fact that an upper tribunal or court has taken a different view of the law from that previously understood and applied.

17.41 If the authority refuses the claimant's late notification, the claimant has the right to ask the authority to reconsider or to appeal (chapter 19).

Information, evidence and notifications

What matters are taken into account

17.42 When reconsidering any decision, the authority need not consider any matter which was not raised in the request (if a request was made) or did not cause it to act on its own initiative. It must also ignore subsequent changes of circumstances. (In other words it must focus on the decision being reconsidered.) The authority may ask experts for help with reconsiderations.

Requests for information and evidence

17.43 When reconsidering a decision on its own initiative (for example, in the case of a review or 'intervention'), the authority has the same rights to require information, evidence, documents and certificates as in the case of a claim (para. 5.17).

17.44 When reconsidering a decision because the claimant or other person affected requested this, the authority may request any information or evidence it needs to deal with the person's request – and must take this into account if it is provided within one month, or longer if reasonable.

17.41 DAR 9(6); NIDAR 9(6)

17.42 CPSA sch 7 paras 3(2),4(3),5,16; NICPSA sch 7 paras 3(2),4(2),5,16; DAR 4(10); NIDAR 4(9)

17.43 HB 86(1); HB60+ 67(1); NIHB 82(1); NIHB60+ 63(1); CTB 72(1); CTB60+ 57(1); DAR 13; NIDAR 13

17.44 AA 5(1)(hh),6(1)(hh); NIAA 5(1)(hh); DAR 4(5),7(5),13; NIDAR 4(4),7(5),13

Notifying the outcome

17.45 Whenever the authority changes a decision for any of the reasons in this chapter, the claimant and any other person affected must be notified in writing of the alteration in entitlement (or of the end of the award), within 14 days or as soon as reasonably practicable, including the following matters:

- a statement of what the authority has altered; and
- the person's right to request a written statement of reasons, to request a reconsideration, and to appeal to a first-tier tribunal, and how and when to do these things.

Suspending, restoring and terminating HB/CTB

17.46 This section describes how an authority may suspend, restore and terminate HB/CTB. To suspend means stopping making payments for the time being, usually in order to avoid an overpayment or to seek information or evidence. To restore means starting payments again – either at the same amount as before or at a different amount, depending on the circumstances. To terminate means ending an award of HB/CTB altogether.

Suspending HB/CTB

17.47 The authority may suspend HB/CTB if any of the following circumstances apply:

(a) the authority doubts whether the conditions of entitlement to HB/CTB are fulfilled;

(b) the authority is considering whether to change a decision about HB/CTB;

(c) the authority considers there may be a recoverable overpayment of HB/CTB;

(d) a first-tier or upper tribunal has made a decision (in this or another case) and the authority is awaiting the decision or a statement of reasons, or is considering making a further appeal;

(e) an appeal has been made, or leave to appeal has been sought, against a decision of a first-tier or upper tribunal or court in the case to be suspended;

(f) an appeal has been made, or leave to appeal has been sought, against a decision of an upper tribunal or court in a different HB/CTB case, and this may affect the case to be suspended;

(g) the claimant (or another person affected) has failed to provide information or evidence needed by the authority to consider changing a decision about HB/CTB.

17.45 HB 90(1)(b), sch 9; HB60+ 71(1)(b), sch 8; NIHB 86(1)(b), sch 10; NIHB60+ 67(1)(b), sch 9; CTB 76(1)(b), sch 8; CTB60+ 61(1)(b), sch 7

17.48 In such cases, HB/CTB are usually suspended in full (though the law permits an authority to suspend only part). However, suspending CTB may have no effect on the amount of a claimant's council tax bill because of problems in CTB and council tax law. These problems have been considered by commissioners *(CH/2995/2006, CH/3076/2006);* but the case law appears not to take account of the fact that it is council tax law that requires the authority to assume, for the purposes of issuing a council tax bill, that CTB will stay the same throughout the year (and that such future credits are therefore not in fact CTB).

Restoring HB/CTB

17.49 When payments of HB/CTB have been suspended, they must be restored if:

- in cases (a) to (c) (para. 17.47), the authority is satisfied that HB/CTB is properly payable and no outstanding matters remain to be resolved;
- in case (d), the authority must either make the further appeal, or decide not to, as soon as reasonably practicable;
- in cases (e) and (f), the appeal or request for leave has been determined and HB/CTB remains payable;
- in case (g), the claimant has responded as required (para. 17.50).

In each case, the authority must restore the payments within 14 days or as soon as reasonably practicable.

Information and evidence

17.50 When payments of HB/CTB have been suspended for failure to provide information or evidence (para. 17.47(f)), the authority must notify the claimant of the suspension and of what information and evidence is required. The claimant must then, within one month or such longer period as the authority considers necessary:

- provide the information or evidence required; or
- satisfy the authority that the information or evidence does not exist, or is impossible for them to obtain.

Terminating HB/CTB

17.51 When payments of HB/CTB have been suspended for failure to provide information or evidence (para. 17.47(f)) and the claimant fails to respond as required (para. 17.50) HB/CTB entitlement is terminated from the date on which the payments were suspended (i.e. no further payments are made). In some cases, termination should not be done unless a reminder request has been sent: *CH/1764/2008.* Terminating benefit under this rule is a kind of supersession: *CH/2555/2007.* The rule cannot be used to end HB/CTB from an earlier date: *CH/3736/2006,* so if entitlement did end earlier, this is done as an (ordinary)

17.49 DAR 12(1),(2),13(5); NIDAR 12(1),(2),13(5)

17.50 DAR 13(3),(4); NIDAR 13(3),(4)

Examples: Suspending, restoring and terminating HB/CTB

A change of circumstances

The authority obtains information that a claimant on HB/CTB has changed jobs. It suspends his award immediately, and writes to him allowing him one month to respond.

After two weeks, he sends in the necessary information and evidence, and he remains entitled to HB/CTB.

The authority restores his HB/CTB from the date payments were suspended, making any change in his entitlement from the Monday after the day he got the new job.

Another change of circumstances

A claimant has been on HB for some years. On Wednesday 23rd September 2009 the authority obtains information that he has been doing undeclared work. It suspends his award from the earliest possible date so that the last payment of HB is for week ending Sunday 27th September 2009, and writes to him allowing him one month to respond.

Shortly afterwards he writes in to admit that he has been working since Monday 6th April 2009 and knows that he does not qualify for HB based on those earnings.

The authority terminates his HB/CTB on Sunday 27th September 2009. It also supersedes his HB (at nil) from Monday 3rd April 2009. This creates an overpayment of HB from Monday 13th April to Sunday 27th September inclusive. The overpayment is not due to official error and so is recoverable.

A review

The authority decides to review a claimant's award of HB/CTB and sends her a short form asking her to confirm her circumstances, allowing her one month to reply. Because the claimant does not reply within the month, the authority suspends her HB/CTB and writes to her requesting her to say what her circumstances are, allowing her one further month to respond.

Because the claimant again does not reply within a month, the authority terminates her award of HB/CTB and notifies her of this.

Two weeks later she returns the original short form, declaring that her circumstances have not changed. The authority is satisfied with this and restores her HB/CTB from the date payments were suspended.

supersession from that earlier date. The second of the examples illustrates this. As may be observed, the two concepts (termination as a type of supersession, and ordinary supersession at nil) each have the same effect of stopping someone's HB (though the case law generally disapproves of this being described as 'cancelling' HB/CTB, because that word does not appear in the law: *CH/2555/2007*). If in the above or other circumstances HB/CTB were wrongly terminated, they must be reinstated: *CH/2995/2006.*

17.52 A decision to terminate HB/CTB must be notified to the claimant and any other person affected.

Appeals

17.53 The claimant has a right of appeal to a first-tier tribunal (table 19.2) about a decision to terminate HB/CTB *(CH/402/2007),* or to restore HB/CTB at a different amount or for a different reason; but not about a determination to suspend HB/CTB, or to restore HB/CTB at the same amount for the same reasons.

Extended payments

Entitlement

17.54 Extended payments (EPs) help long-term unemployed people who find work, by giving them four weeks extra HB/CTB. They are also sometimes called HB/CTB 'run-on'. A claimant is entitled to an EP if they meet the conditions in table 17.6.

17.55 No claim is required for an EP. All the matters referred to in table 17.6 are for the authority to determine (not the DWP). The claimant must be notified about their entitlement to an EP (or not).

Period and amount

17.56 An EP is awarded from the Monday following the date the change (getting a job, etc) takes effect, and it last for four weeks (as illustrated in the example). In each of those four weeks, the amount of the EP is the greater of:

(a) the amount awarded in the last full benefit week before the EP started; and

(b) the amount which would be the claimant's entitlement in that particular week if there were no such thing as EPs. For example, a claimant whose non-dependants all left home might qualify for more HB/CTB using the ordinary calculation than she was getting before she started work.

17.51 CPSA sch 7 para 15; NICPSA sch 7 para 15; DAR 14; NIDAR 14

17.54 HB 2(1),72,73; HB60+ 2(1),53; NIHB 2(1),70,71; NIHB60+ 2(1),51; CTB 2(1),60,61; CTB60+ 2(1),44

17.56 HB 72A,72B,73A,73B; HB60+ 53A,53B; NIHB 70A,70B,71A,71B; NIHB60+51A,51B; CTB 60A,60B,61A,61B; CTB60+ 44A,44B

Table 17.6: Entitlement to an extended payment

Claimants who have been on a 'qualifying income-related benefit'

The claimant is entitled to an extended payment if:

- the claimant or any partner starts employment or self-employment, or increases his or her hours or earnings; and
- this is expected to last for at least five weeks; and
- the claimant or partner has been entitled to ESA(IR), JSA(IB), JSA(C) or IS continuously for at least 26 weeks (or any combination of those benefits in that period);
- immediately before starting the job, etc, the claimant or partner was on ESA(IR), JSA(IB) or IS. At this point being on JSA(C) is not enough; and
- entitlement to ESA(IR), JSA(IB) or IS ceases as a result of starting the job, etc.

Claimants who have been on a 'qualifying contributory benefit'

The claimant is entitled to extended payment if:

- the claimant or any partner starts employment or self-employment, or increases his or her hours or earnings; and
- this is expected to last for at least five weeks; and
- the claimant or partner has been entitled to ESA(C), IB or SDA continuously for at least 26 weeks (or any combination of those benefits in that period);
- immediately before starting the job, etc, the claimant or partner was on ESA(C), IB or SDA. And neither of them must be on ESA(IR), JSA(IB) or IS; and
- entitlement to ESA(C), IB or SDA ceases as a result of starting the job, etc.

T 17.6 HB 2(1),72(1),73(1); HB60+ 2(1),53(1); NIHB 2(1),70(1),71(1); NIHB60+ 2(1),51(1); CTB 2(1),60(1),61(1); CTB60+ 2(1),44(1)

17.57 For the above purposes if the claimant or a partner reaches 60 during the EP, the figure used for (b) throughout the EP is whichever would have been higher using their before and after 60 entitlement.

17.58 Throughout the EP, all changes in the claimant's circumstances are ignored – except that:

- if a claimant's entitlement to HB on two homes ceases during the EP, the amount of EP is reduced by the amount of the eligible rent on the home they no longer qualify for HB for; and;
- no EP is awarded for rent/rates/council tax during any period during which the claimant is not liable for rent/rates/council tax.

HB/CTB after an extended payment

17.59 If the claimant qualifies for HB/CTB based on their new income after the end of the EP this is awarded in the normal way. (The requirement to make a fresh HB/CTB claim was abolished on 6th October 2008.).

Variations for movers

17.60 Claimants who are entitled to an EP are entitled to it even if they move home during the EP. In England, Scotland and Wales, if the move is to another authority's area, the determination, notification and award of the EP is done by the authority whose area the claimant is moving out of. That authority may liaise with the authority whose area the claimant is moving into; and may pay the EP to them or to the claimant.

Example: Extended payments

A claimant who meets all the conditions for an extended payment starts work on Monday 12th October 2009.

His award of HB/CTB continues up to and including Sunday 18th October 2009. His extended payment covers the period from Monday 19th October 2009 to Sunday 15th November 2009. If he then continues to qualify for HB/CTB after that, the new amount of HB/CTB is awarded from Monday 16th November 2009.

17.57 HB60+ 52; NIHB60+ 50; CTB60+ 41

17.58 HB 72A,72B,73A,73B; HB60+ 53A,53B; NIHB 70A,70B,71A,71B; NIHB60+ 51A,51B; CTB 60A,60B,61A,61B; CTB60+ 44A,44B

17.59 HB 72D,73D; HB60+ 53D; NIHB 70C,71C; NIHB60+ 51C; CTB 60D,61D; CTB60+ 44D

17.60 HB 72C,73C,115,116; HB60+ 53C,96,97; CTB 60C,61C,96,97; CTB60+ 44C,81,82

Continuing payments

Entitlement

17.61 Continuing payments are awarded automatically to someone on HB/CTB who has been on JSA(IB) or income support and:

- they have reached 60 (or 65 if they stayed on JSA(IB) beyond age 60), or they have a partner and the partner claims pension credit; and
- the DWP informs the authority of these matters.

Continuing payments enable award of HB/CTB to continue without a break while their new entitlement to pension credit (if any) is determined.

Period and amount

17.62 The continuing payment starts immediately after the last day of entitlement to IS/JSA(IB), and lasts for four weeks plus any extra days to make it end on a Sunday. The amount during that period is calculated as follows:

- the claimant is treated as having no income or capital; – and if they move home
- the claimant's eligible rent or council tax or rates are the higher of the amounts at the old and new addresses;
- any non-dependant deductions are done according to the circumstances at the new address.

Example: Continuing payments

A man is on HB/CTB and JSA(IB) when he reaches 65, on Thursday 16th April 2009. The DWP informs the authority that his entitlement to pension credit is being considered.

His continuing payment of HB/CTB is awarded from Thursday 16th April 2009 to Sunday 17th May 2009 – a total of four weeks and four days.

By then the authority knows the claimant's entitlement to HB/CTB based on his new circumstances, and awards this from Monday 18th May 2009.

17.61 HB60+ 54; NIHB60+ 52; CTB60+ 45

18 Overpayments

18.1 This chapter explains:

- what an overpayment is;
- how overpayments are caused;
- which overpayments are recoverable;
- the amount of an overpayment;
- the discretion to recover an overpayment;
- who to recover from;
- the methods of recovery;
- information that must be included in overpayment notices;
- court action to recover an overpayment; and
- administrative penalties.

18.2 In CTB law, an overpayment is called 'excess benefit', but in this guide and in day-to-day work 'overpayment' is used for CTB as well as HB.

What is an overpayment?

18.3 When more HB or CTB is awarded than someone is entitled to, this is an 'overpayment'. It may have been paid (e.g. to a claimant or landlord) or rebated (e.g. to a rent or council tax or rates account).

18.4 Overpayments arise when the authority revises or supersedes an award of HB/CTB (table 17.1). Tribunals and commissioners dealing with appeals about overpayments expect the authority to be able to show which revisions or supersessions established the overpayment *(CH/3439/2004* and *C3/07-08(IS)).*

18.5 As described in this chapter, for every overpayment the authority must:

- establish its cause;
- determine whether or not it is recoverable; – and if it is
- calculate the correct period and the correct amount;
- consider whether or not to recover it;
- determine who to recover it from; and
- notify the claimant and any other person affected, within 14 days.

18.3 AA 75(1),76(1); NIAA 73(1); HB 99; HB60+ 80; NIHB 96; NIHB60+ 77; CTB 82; CTB60+ 67

Example: An overpayment

A claimant under 65 is on HB and CTB. On 8th May 2008 her adult son comes to live with her. The claimant has a duty to inform the authority of this but does not do so until 6th August 2008. The authority determines that a non-dependant deduction should have been made for the son from Monday 12th May 2008: this is a supersession. The claimant has received HB/CTB up to and including Sunday 7th August 2008. An overpayment of HB/CTB has occurred for 14 weeks.

The cause of an overpayment

18.6 The authority must determine the cause of an overpayment in order to:

- determine whether or not it is recoverable;
- notify the right people of the right things;
- claim the correct amount of subsidy; and
- in some cases, determine the method of recovery.

18.7 The main ways in which an overpayment can arise are:

- local authority error, e.g. the authority fails to act on notice of a change of circumstances provided by the claimant;
- DWP error, e.g. a jobcentre plus or pension, disability and carers service makes a mistaken award of JSA(IB), income support or pension credit;
- claimant error, e.g. the claimant fails to inform the authority of a change of circumstances which he or she has a duty to report, such as the end of entitlement to JSA(IB) or income support; or
- third party error, e.g. a landlord in receipt of HB notifies an incorrect rent increase;
- no-one's fault, e.g. the claimant wins a backdated pay award and this affects entitlement to HB/CTB in the past;
- a payment on account turns out to be too great;
- technicalities to do with payment of HB/CTB, e.g. a claimant is awarded a rebate for a future period, and then his or her entitlement changes; or
- other reasons, e.g. the claimant obtains a retrospective award of a council tax discount and this reduces the council tax liability for that period.

How is an overpayment 'caused'?

18.8 For how the authority, the DWP or HM Revenue and Customs can cause an overpayment, see paragraph 18.13. The claimant or a third party can only 'cause' an overpayment if they misrepresent, or fail to disclose, a material fact – whether intentionally or not – and even if that is only one contributing factor *(CSB/64/1986)*. However, someone may not be expected to disclose a fact if they were given clear advice to the contrary by an official of the authority or the DWP *(R(SB) 3/89)*.

More than one cause of an overpayment

18.9 If there is more than one cause of an overpayment, these must be separated out *(CH/2409/2005, CH/858/2006)*. For example, a claimant may fail to notify the authority that their earnings have increased. The authority may then not act on that information quickly enough once it is informed. In such a case the two causes, periods and amounts of the overpayment must be separately identified, and separate determinations must be made about whether the two amounts are recoverable.

Which overpayments are recoverable

Overpayments which cannot be recovered

18.10 An overpayment is not recoverable if:

- it arose because of 'official error' by the relevant authority (para. 18.13); and
- the claimant, someone acting on his or her behalf, or the payee, could not reasonably have been expected to realise it was an overpayment (para. 18.14).

Overpayments which can be recovered

18.11 An overpayment is recoverable if:

- it arose because of 'official error' (para. 18.13) and the claimant, someone acting on his or her behalf, or the payee, could reasonably have been expected to realise it was an overpayment (para. 18.14); or
- it is due to an error (or fraud) of the claimant or a third party; or
- it is no-one's fault.

18.10 HB 100(2); HB60+ 81(2); NIHB 97(2); NIHB60+ 78(2); CTB 83(2); CTB60+ 68(2)

18.11 HB 100(1); HB60+ 81(1); NIHB 97(1); NIHB60+ 78(1); CTB 83(1); CTB60+ 68(1)

18.12 The following overpayments are also recoverable:

- an overpayment of CTB, or HB to a council or NIHE tenant, which was caused by an 'official error' (para. 18.13) but which relates to a period in the future.
- an overpayment of a payment on account of HB (para. 16.16) which is being recovered by deductions from ongoing HB;
- an overpayment of CTB caused by a retrospective reduction in council tax due to capping or to a delayed award of a discount or disability reduction;
- an overpayment of HB for rates in Northern Ireland caused by a retrospective reduction in regional rates.

Meaning of 'official error'

18.13 An official error is a mistake, whether in the form of an act or omission, made by the authority, the DWP or HM Revenue and Customs – or someone on their behalf (such as a contractor or a housing association which verifies HB claims). It does not include cases when the claimant, someone acting on his or her behalf, or the payee, caused or materially contributed to that error. The test is whether the claimant contributed towards the error, not whether they contributed towards the overpayment *(CH/215/08)*. Exactly what is and is not an official error has often been considered by commissioners and courts. The main cases are summarised in table 18.1.

Awareness of being overpaid

18.14 An overpayment which arose due to official error is recoverable only if the claimant, a person acting on his or her behalf, or the payee, could reasonably have been expected to realise that it was an overpayment – either at the time the payment was received, or at the time of any decision notice relating to it. Exactly how this rule should be applied has often been considered by commissioners and courts. The main cases are summarised in table 18.2.

18.12 HB 93(3),100(4); HB60+ 74(3),81(4); NIHB 90(3),97(4); NIHB60+ 71(3),78(4); CTB 83(4),(5); CTB60+ 68(4),(5)

18.13 HB 100(3); HB60+ 81(3); NIHB 97(3); NIHB60+ 78(3); CTB 83(3); CTB60+ 68(3)

18.14 HB 100(2); HB60+ 81(2); NIHB 97(2); NIHB60+ 78(2); CTB 83(2); CTB60+ 68(2)

Table 18.1: Overpayments case law: meaning of 'official error'

- *Terminology:* A 'mistake' is not different from an 'official error' and it is artificial to try and read different meanings into these two terms *(CH/943/2003).*
- *Relevant authority:* In this context includes any part of the authority and is not confined to any department within it *(CH/3586/2007).*
- *Designated office:* The claimant's circumstances had been repeatedly notified to the Housing Department. Not to pass the information on to the benefits service or advise the claimant to do so was an official error which the claimant had not contributed to *(CH/2567/2007).*
- *Whether official bodies talk to each other:* The House of Lords in an income support case established an important principle for DWP benefits, which has a bearing on HB/CTB. The Court of Appeal in the same case had held that one department of the DWP was to be presumed to know what another department of the DWP know. The House of Lords overruled this as unrealistic: 'the claimant's duty is to tell whom she is told to tell' (*Hinchy v Secretary of State for Work and Pensions,* reported as *R(IS)7/05*).
- *Mistake by DWP in assessing benefit:* If the DWP makes a mistake and awards JSA(IB) or income support when it should not have, this is an official error regardless of the reason *(CH/943/2003).*
- *Overpayment caused by DWP benefit being reinstated on appeal:* Where the overpayment is caused by the reinstatement of a DWP benefit following an appeal this does not amount to an official error *(CH/38/2008).*
- *Failure by DWP to pass on information:* The failure of the DWP to notify the authority that JSA(IB) or income support has ceased is not an official error because the claimant has a duty to notify the authority of this *(R v Cambridge CC ex parte Sier).* But this does not apply to pension credit cases because it is the pension, disability and carers service's duty to notify the authority of changes.
- *Failure by DWP to act on a promise:* If the DWP undertook to forward a notice of a change to the authority and then failed to do so, that might amount to official error *(CH/939/2004, CH/3761/2005).*
- *Failure by the authority to cross-check:* The fact that the claimant disclosed income (etc) in a previous claim (which they did not disclose in their current claim) does not mean that the authority's failure to cross-check is official error *(R(H) 1/04, CH/2794/2004).*

- *Failure to recognise relevant information on document provided for a different purpose:* There is no general rule that the failure to recognise information as relevant which was provided for a different purpose cannot be official error: it depends on the particular circumstances *(CH/3925/2006)*.
- *Failure by authority to check potential changes:* Failure by the authority to check up on potential changes in entitlement to a tax credit is not official error *(R(H) 2/04),* nor is failure to check up on a potential increase in incapacity benefit *(CH/687/2006)* or earnings *(CH/3/2008).*
- *Delay by authority in dealing with a notified change:* In a case in which the claimant notified her increased earnings on 19th April, but the authority did not take them into account until 13th May (24 days later), this was quick enough not to constitute official error. In reaching this decision, the commissioner compared the authority's duty to act on a change of circumstances with its duty to act on a claim, where there is a time limit of 14 days (para. 16.2). The 24 days the commissioner allowed in this case was based on its individual circumstances *(CH/858/2006).*
- *Delay in applying to the rent officer:* A delay in applying to the rent officer can be an official error *(CH/361/2006).*
- *Claimant reports wrong amount of benefit due to overpayment deductions:* If the claimant reports the incorrect amount of incapacity benefit because the DWP is making deductions, the fact that the authority does not realise the mistake does not amount to an official error *(CH/56/08).*
- *Claimant's method of notifying changes:* Where a claimant had notified a change by telephone but not in writing, and the council had failed to act on it, this did not necessarily mean that the claimant had materially contributed to the official error *(CH/2409/2005).*

Table 18.2: Overpayments case law: awareness of being overpaid in official error cases

- *Purpose of the rule:* The purpose of the rule is to protect a claimant who has relied on being entitled to the payment so that, having innocently spent it, they do not have to repay money they cannot afford *(CH/1176/2003).*
- *'Was' or 'might be' an overpayment?* The test is whether there was a reasonable expectation that there was an overpayment not whether there might be one *(R v Liverpool CC ex parte Griffiths, CH/2935/2005, CH/858/2006).*
- *Burden of proof:* The burden of proof is on the person stating that they could not reasonably have been expected to realise – not on the authority stating that they could *(CH/4918/2003).* But the question of 'burden of proof' only arises in borderline cases (paras. 1.33-35).
- *What can a person reasonably be expected to realise?* The test of what someone could reasonably have been expected to realise varies according to the person's knowledge, experience and capacity *(R v Liverpool CC ex parte Griffiths).* For example, someone who had needed the authority's help to fill in his application form may be less likely to realise he was overpaid *(CH/2935/2005);* someone from a country where (the equivalent of) tax credits are taken into account in a different way (in the assessment of the equivalent of HB) might not realise that they are taken into account as income in the UK *(CH/858/2006).*
- *An ordinary reasonable claimant:* An 'ordinary reasonable claimant' cannot be expected to go and find out more about the HB/CTB schemes than they are informed of by the authority in the notice of their award *(CH/2554/2002).*

- *Receipt of a notice:* Whether a person could reasonably have been expected to realise at the time of any notice, refers to a notice about the award of HB/CTB, not the overpayment notice – otherwise the rule would be meaningless *(CH/1176/2003).*
- *Comprehensible notice:* If a notice of an award contains the basis of the calculation in a reasonably clear manner, and it is clear that there has been a mistake in the claimant's favour, then the overpayment is recoverable – because the claimant could reasonably have been expected to realise *(CH/2409/2005).*
- *Claimant queries notice but authority continues to pay wrong amount:* Where the claimant queries the decision notice but the authority continues to pay, the comes a point where the claimant is entitled to rely on the notice and accept the authority knows best *(CH/3240/2007).*
- *Reference to wages omitted in notice:* If there was no reference at all to the claimant's wages in the notice, whereas their other income was listed, a 'claimant of normal intelligence' could reasonably be expected to deduce that there had been a mistake and that they were overpaid *(CH/2554/2002).*
- *Reference to state retirement pension omitted in the decision notice:* If there was no reference at all to the claimant's state retirement pension in the notice, the claimant might have concluded that the pension was being ignored (perhaps because it was disregarded or because everybody of his age received one); and 'a typical claimant cannot reasonably be expected to read or understand the calculations' so they could not reasonably be expected to deduce that that they were overpaid *(CH/2554/2002).*
- *A disparity between the claimant's declared earnings and the notified assessment:* Where there is a large disparity between the claimant's declared earnings and the authority's assessment as set out in the decision notice (in this case earnings of £210 assessed and notified as less than £50) then it would be reasonable to expect the claimant to realise that they must be being overpaid *(CH/2943/2007).* For a similar case relating to an incorrect eligible rent, see *CH/1909/2008.*

- *The claimant must have some reason to believe the authority's figures are wrong:* A claimant cannot be expected to seek advice unless he or she has some reason to believe the figures are wrong. A tribunal should ask the claimant how he or she reconciled their own knowledge of their earnings with the figures in the notice, to give them the opportunity to explain why they could not be expected to realise there was an overpayment *(CH/2943/2007).*
- *Claimant telephoned to say they thought there was a mistake:* If there has been an official error, and the claimant alleges they telephoned to say they thought there had been, then the authority should determine whether they in fact did so before going on to consider if this affects whether the overpayment is recoverable *(CH/4065/2001).*
- *Claimant's other actions in relation to the award:* The authority in this case had asked for evidence of earnings for the wrong period. The claimant provided what they asked for, but not other evidence that would have shown his income was higher. His other actions (including telephoning to check things) suggested he was not trying to mislead and there was no reason to suppose he could reasonably have been expected to realise there was an overpayment. *(CH/1780/2005).*
- *Time of receipt of a payment:* The 'time' of a payment by cheque is fairly narrow, but a telephone call from the authority a couple of hours after the claimant received a large HB cheque, advising her it was incorrect, may be soon enough to mean that the claimant was aware at the 'time of receipt' that it was an overpayment *(CH/1176/2003).*
- *When the overpayment is a rebate:* It the overpayment is of a rebate, the authority may need to consider whether the claimant could reasonably have been expected to realise that there was an overpayment 'at the times when credits were applied to his rent and council tax accounts' *(CH/1675/2005).*
- *What a landlord could have realised:* When the question arises of what a landlord company or housing association could have realised, it is what the whole organisation might reasonably have been expected to have realised that is relevant *(CH/4918/2003).*

The amount of a recoverable overpayment

18.15 The amount of a recoverable overpayment is the difference between what was paid or awarded and what the person was entitled to. The following rules can reduce the overpayment.

Underlying entitlement

18.16 When calculating the amount of a recoverable overpayment, any amount 'which should have been determined to be payable' must be deducted. This means whatever would have been awarded if the authority had known the true facts of the case throughout, and all changes of circumstances had been notified on time. It also means that the claimant must be treated, during the overpayment period only, as having reclaimed HB/CTB whenever necessary (*Adan v London Borough of Hounslow and Another,* reported as *R(H)5/04*). HB/CTB kept by a claimant (i.e. not recovered from him or her) under this rule is called 'underlying entitlement' to distinguish it from an actual award of HB/CTB.

Why underlying entitlement can occur

18.17 In the past there were many situations in which underlying entitlement could occur, but nowadays there are three:

- underlying entitlement overrides the rule about late notice of beneficial changes (para. 17.37). See example 1;
- underlying entitlement overrides the rule about late requests for a reconsideration (paras. 19.11 and 19.21); and
- underlying entitlement overrides the need for a fresh claim following a break in entitlement. See example 2.

The stage at which the authority allows underlying entitlement

18.18 When a recoverable overpayment arises, the authority may already have information enabling it to allow underlying entitlement (as in example 1). And in all cases, unless there is no possibility of underlying entitlement (e.g. the claimant had more than £16,000 throughout the overpayment period), the authority should invite the claimant to provide information and evidence to establish underlying entitlement (using the usual rules about obtaining information and evidence: para. 5.17) and the onus is on the claimant to do this *(R(H) 1/05).*

18.19 Once the authority has determined and notified the overpayment, the claimant (or other overpaid person) may ask the authority to reconsider or appeal to a tribunal (chapter 19) – and in doing so may include information which establishes underlying entitlement. As the DWP confirm, once the time limit for appeal has expired (one month which can be increased to 13 months in special

---

18.15 HB 99; HB60+ 80; NIHB 96; NIHB60+ 77; CTB 82; CTB60+ 67

18.16 HB 104(1); HB60+ 85(1); NIHB 101(1); NIHB60+ 82(1); CTB 89(1); CTB60+ 71(1)

circumstances), it is not possible to allow underlying entitlement (OG para. 3.57) – unless there has been an official error (para. 19.16).

Calculation rules for underlying entitlement

18.20 There are two calculation rules. See example 3:

- only underlying entitlement falling within the overpayment period is used to reduce the overpayment;
- underlying entitlement may reduce an overpayment to nil, but it can never be used to actually pay money out.

Examples: Underlying entitlement

1. When there has been late notice of a change

Information: A claimant's non-dependant moved out six months ago, but the claimant did not tell the authority until three months ago (and had no special circumstances for lateness) so the authority removed the non-dependant deduction from three months ago. Today it is discovered that the claimant has been doing undeclared work since nine months ago.

Assessment: Underlying entitlement means the authority must reduce the amount of the overpayment due to the undeclared work by the amount it could not award in relation to the non-dependant moving out. This results in a lower recoverable overpayment; it may even reduce the overpayment to nil; but in no circumstances can it result in the claimant being awarded more benefit.

2. When there has been a break in entitlement

Information: The authority suspends a claimant's award of HB/CTB because it discovers that she did some undeclared work several months ago. The authority seeks evidence of earnings from that work and the claimant sends this in promptly, but the earnings are so high that she does not qualify for any HB/CTB for three weeks.

Assessment: Underlying entitlement means the claimant keeps her HB/CTB for the period after those three weeks up until her award is suspended.

3. Calculation rules

Information: In a particular case, there is a recoverable overpayment of £5 per week for weeks 1 to 20 inclusive (20 x £5 = £100), and underlying entitlement (because the claimant did not notify a beneficial change on time) in weeks 11 to 20 inclusive of £15 per week.

Assessment: The underlying entitlement in weeks 11 to 20 inclusive (10 x £15 = £150) is used to reduce the overpayment (£100). It is enough to reduce the recoverable overpayment to nil. The remainder of the underlying entitlement cannot be awarded.

If a claimant still paid rent to the authority

18.21 During the overpayment period a council tenant claimant may have paid rent above his or her erroneous liability. Those payments may be deducted from the recoverable overpayment. The rule applies equally to payments of rates in Northern Ireland. In theory, it also applies to payments of council tax, but this is rarely done.

The diminishing capital rule

18.22 The 'diminishing capital rule' applies if a recoverable overpayment:

- arose due to capital being wrongly taken into account (for any reason); and
- lasted for more than 13 weeks.

18.23 In such cases, the following steps apply:

- at the end of the first 13 weeks of the overpayment period, the claimant's capital is treated as reduced by the amount overpaid during those 13 weeks. This gives an imaginary capital figure which is used to assess the overpayment after that;
- the same is done again at the end of each 13 weeks until the end of the overpayment period;
- but for calculating HB/CTB after the end of the overpayment period, the claimant's actual capital is used (not the imaginary amount).

This reflects the fact that if the claimant had been awarded less HB/CTB due to the capital being taken into account, they might have used some of their capital to pay their rent or council tax or rates.

18.24 The above is complicated enough, but the law has two further cruel twists:

- the above steps must be gone through separately for HB and CTB if the claimant was on both of these during the overpayment period (so the claimant's imaginary capital is different for the two benefits);
- the above 'diminishing capital rule' is not the same as the 'diminishing notional capital rule' (para. 13.146), and the two are calculated in different ways.

18.21 HB 104(2); HB60+ 85(2); NIHB 101(2); NIHB60+ 82(2); CTB 89(2); CTB60+ 71(2)

18.22 HB 103; HB60+ 84; NIHB 100; NIHB60+ 81; CTB 88; CTB60+ 70

Example: The diminishing capital rule

A claimant failed to declare capital of £16,033. When this is discovered, there has been a recoverable overpayment for 30 weeks. Throughout that time she got CTB of £9 per week (and no HB), she had no other capital at all, and the figure of £16,033 remained the same.

- In the first 13 weeks, she is not entitled to CTB:
  Overpayment: 13 x £9 = £117
- Her capital is then treated as reduced by this amount:
  £16,033 - £117 = £15,916
- In the second 13 weeks, based on this reduced capital,
  she is entitled to CTB of £5 per week,
  so the overpayment is £4 per week:
  Overpayment: 13 x £4 = £52
- Her capital is then treated as further reduced by
  this amount: £15,916 – £52 = £15,864
- In the remaining 4 weeks, based on this further
  reduced capital, she is still entitled to CTB of
  £5 per week,so the overpayment is still £4 per week:
  Overpayment: 4 x £4 = £16

- So the total overpayment of CTB for the 30 weeks is £185

The discretion to recover

18.25 If an overpayment is 'recoverable' (paras. 18.11-12), this means the authority has the discretion to recover it or not recover it (para. 1.40). The question of whether an overpayment is recoverable is therefore separate from the question of whether to recover it. Cases must be looked at on their merits, and the DWP advises that 'due regard' should be had to individual circumstances (OG paras. 2.116-117).

18.26 A claimant can ask the authority not to recover a recoverable overpayment but has no right of appeal to a tribunal about this (chapter 19). In unreasonable or irrational cases the claimant could instead seek judicial review. This was once done in a case where an authority sought to recover an overpayment caused by a war pension awarded for a past period – though the outcome was that the court required the authority to think again and did not ban recovery *(R v South Hams District Council ex p Ash).*

Who to recover from

18.27 The HB and CTB rules about who to recover overpayments from have changed, and are much clearer, with effect from 6th April 2009. The previous rules apply to overpayments from before that date: *CH/4213/2007* (and may be found in the 2008-09 edition of this Guide).

Recovery of overpaid CTB

18.28 A recoverable overpayment of CTB may in all cases be recovered from the person who received the CTB – such as the claimant or an appointee. And if the claimant has a partner, it is also recoverable from their partner – but only by deductions from that partner's DWP benefits (para. 18.44). The general points about who counts as a partner apply to CTB as they do to HB (para. 18.31).

Recovery of overpaid HB

18.29 A recoverable overpayment of HB may be recovered as follows:

- if the overpayment was caused by the claimant or payee, or someone on their behalf (para. 18.8), it is recoverable only from that person (and if there is more than one such person, it is recoverable from any of them); but
- if the overpayment was due to official error, and the claimant or payee, or someone on their behalf, could reasonably have been expected to realise it was an overpayment (para. 18.14), it is recoverable only from that person (and if there is more than one such person, it is recoverable from any of them); but
- in any other case (e.g. if the overpayment was no-one's fault) it is recoverable from the claimant and (if different) the payee (in other words from either of them).

And if, for any of the above reasons, the overpayment is recoverable from the claimant, it is also recoverable from their partner (para. 18.31). In some cases, the effect of the above rules is that there can be a choice about who to recover from (para. 18.34).

Recovery of HB from claimants

18.30 The effect of the above rules (para. 18.29) is that most recoverable overpayments of HB can be recovered from the claimant; and if the claimant has died this means it can be recovered from their estate. In fact, the only cases in which a recoverable overpayment of HB cannot be recovered from the claimant

---

18.27 SI 2008/2824 regs 4-7; NISR 2008/504 Regs 2,3

18.28 AA 76(3); CTB 85,86(3)(b); CTB60+ 70,71(3)(b)

18.29 AA 75(3); NIAA 73(3); HB 101(2),(3A),102(1A); HB60+ 82(2),(3A), 83(1A); NIHB 98(2),(3A),99(1A); NIHB60+ 79(2),(3A),80(1ZA)

(and can only be recovered from the payee, typically a landlord or agent) are:

- when the payee was the cause of the overpayment (and the claimant played no part in causing it); or
- when the payee could reasonably have been expected to realise there was an official error overpayment (and the claimant could not have done so).

Recovery of HB from partners

18.31 Whenever a recoverable overpayment of HB can be recovered from the claimant (for any of the reasons in para. 18.29), it can also be recovered from their partner, if they have one. A former partner (following death or the end of a relationship) is not a partner any more, so a recoverable overpayment of HB can no longer be recovered from them. The law requires them to be a couple both at the time of the overpayment and at the time of its recovery; and limits the methods of recovery from a partner to:

- making deductions from the partner's future HB (para. 18.41); or
- making deductions from the partner's future DWP benefits (para. 18.44).

When recovery is to be made from a partner they must be separately notified and have the same rights of appeal as the claimant: *CH/3622/2006* (para. 18.35).

Recovery of HB from landlords and agents

18.32 The effect of the above rules (para. 18.29) is that a recoverable overpayments of HB can only be recovered from a landlord/agent if it was them (rather than the claimant) who was paid the HB; and one of the following must also apply:

- either the landlord/agent caused the overpayment;
- or (in the case of an official error overpayment) the landlord/agent could reasonably have been expected to realise there was an overpayment;
- or the overpayment was no-one's fault (in which case it is recoverable from either the claimant or the landlord/agent; and the mere fact that the landord/agent knew nothing of the overpayment does not prevent recovery from them: *Warwick DC v Freeman.*

In such cases, HB may be recovered from the landlord if the landlord was paid the HB, but from the agent if the agent was paid the HB (even if the agent has paid it to the landlord: *R(H)10/07*). When recovery is to be made from a landlord/agent they must be separately notified and have the same rights of appeal as the claimant: *CH/3622/2006* (para. 18.35).

18.30 HB 101(2),(3A); HB60+ 82(2),(3A); NIHB 98(2),(3A); NIHB60+ 79(2),(3A)

18.31 HB 102(1ZA); HB60+ 83(1ZA); NIHB 99(1A); NIHB60+ 80(1A)

18.32 AA 75(3); NIAA 73(3); HB 101(2),(3A); HB60+ 82(2),(3A); NIHB 98(2),(3A); NIHB60+ 79(2),(3A)

18.33 However, an authority must not recover HB from a landlord/agent if:

- the landlord/agent notified the authority or the DWP in writing that they suspect there has been an overpayment; and
- it appears to the authority that there are grounds for instituting proceedings for an offence in relation to the overpayment, or that a deliberate failure to report a relevant change of circumstances (other than moving home) caused the overpayment; and
- the authority is satisfied that the landlord/agent did not collude in the overpayment, nor contribute (through action or inaction) to its period or amount.

For example, if a landlord/agent in receipt of HB notifies the authority that the claimant is doing undeclared work, and does so promptly, this prevents the authority from recovering the resulting overpaid HB from the landlord/agent provided that the landlord's warning notice reaches the authority before it discovers the overpayment *(CH/2411/2006).* But if a landlord/agent notifies the authority that a claimant has moved out, the authority may recover the resulting overpaid HB from the landlord/agent.

A choice about who to recover HB from

18.34 When the above rules (para. 18.29) allow an authority to recover an HB overpayment from more than one party (e.g. landlord/agent and claimant), the parties have a joint and several liability to repay *(R(H) 6/06)* and the authority may choose which to recover from. In one case an authority billed two parties at the same time, and a commissioner said this was 'unfortunate' but had no lasting effect on the appeal *(CH/2583/2007).*

Appeals about who to recover HB from

18.35 Once the authority has identified which party or parties it may recover an overpayment from, and notified them (all) of this, each of them is a 'person affected' (para. 16.7) and so may ask the authority to reconsider or appeal to a tribunal (chapter 19).

18.36 A tribunal's jurisdiction is limited to deciding first, the true entitlement for the period in question and second, whether the resultant overpayment is legally recoverable from more than one person. But it does not have the power to decide the third and final stage: how the recovery should be enforced *(CH/2298/2007).* A tribunal has a duty to decide whether the authority's selection of the party or parties was correctly drawn up – but not whether it is fair or appropriate to recover from one party rather than another (*R(H) 6/06* and *CH/4213/2007*). This applies whether the appellant is the landlord/agent or the claimant *(CH/1129/2004).* In unreasonable or irrational cases the appellant could instead seek judicial review.

18.33 AA 75(3); NIAA 73(3); HB 101(1); HB60+ 82(1); NIHB 98(1); NIHB60+ 79(1)

Methods of recovery

18.37 Authorities may recover a recoverable overpayment of HB/CTB by any lawful method, but an overpayment of HB cannot be recovered from an award of CTB or *vice versa*. The following methods are laid down in the law, and are described in this section:

- charging overpaid CTB to the claimant's council tax account;
- deducting overpaid CTB from the claimant's future CTB;
- deducting overpaid HB from the claimant's or partner's future HB;
- deducting overpaid HB/CTB from the claimant's or partner's DWP benefits;
- deducting overpaid HB from a blameless tenant's HB;
- deducting overpaid HB from a guilty landlord/agent's payments;
- deducting overpaid HB from a landlord/agent's own HB or DWP benefits;
- sending a bill for overpaid HB/CTB and if necessary pursuing this through the courts.

Table 18.3: Maximum weekly deductions from HB

• If the claimant has been found guilty of fraud, or admitted fraud after caution, or agreed to pay a penalty (para. 18.63)	£12.80
• In any other case	£9.75

Plus, in each of the above cases, 50% of:

- any £5, £10, £20 or £25 earned income disregard (table 14.1)
- any disregard of regular charitable or voluntary payments (para. 13.125)
- the £10 disregard of war disablement or bereavement pension (para. 13.59)

Charging overpaid CTB to a council tax account

18.38 Any recoverable overpayment of CTB may be recovered by charging the claimant's council tax account – in other words adding the overpayment to that account – and issuing a new bill *(CH/1384/2007)*. This means the overpayment simply becomes council tax arrears recoverable under council tax law.

18.39 There is no equivalent rule for HB for a council or NIHE tenant. Although their rent account can include a record of overpaid HB, the overpayments do not normally constitute rent arrears (table 18.5) – and cannot, for example, lead to eviction (unlike the arrears in para. 18.42).

18.38 AA 76(2),(3); CTB 86(2)(b); CTB60+ 71(2)(b)

Deducting overpaid CTB from future awards of CTB

18.40 A recoverable overpayment of CTB may be deducted from the claimant's future award of CTB, but usually the previous method is used instead.

Deducting overpaid HB from future awards of HB

18.41 A recoverable overpayment of HB may be deducted from the claimant's or partner's future award of HB, but this deduction is limited in three ways:

- the award of HB must not be reduced below 50p a week;
- the amount deducted must not be greater than shown in table 18.3; and
- the authority should consider deducting a lower amount in cases where hardship might otherwise arise.

The first two limits do not apply to deductions from lump sum arrears of HB.

18.42 The deductions leave the claimant with more rent to pay – or rent arrears if they do not (table 18.5). These rent arrears do not have to be separately identified – and can, for example, lead to eviction (unlike the arrears in para. 18.39).

18.43 The deductions count as recovery from the claimant, not the landlord/agent. This is true even when HB is paid to the landlord/agent, and in such cases the landlord/agent has no right to appeal to a tribunal (chapter 19) about the deductions *(R(H) 7/04).*

Deducting overpaid HB/CTB from DWP benefits

18.44 A recoverable overpayment of HB/CTB may be deducted from the claimant's or partner's DWP benefits (table 18.4) – but only if the HB/CTB overpayment was due to misrepresentation of, or failure to disclose, a material fact; and only if the authority is unable to recover overpaid HB from future awards of HB, or overpaid CTB from the council tax account.

Deducting overpaid HB from a blameless tenant's HB

18.45 If a recoverable overpayment of HB was paid to a landlord/agent, it may be deducted from payments to that landlord/agent of another tenant's HB. This is often called 'recovery by schedule' (because it is usually only done in the case of landlords/agents with several tenants on HB) or recovery from a 'blameless tenant' (because the other tenant had nothing to do with the overpayment).

18.46 The authority must notify the landlord/agent which tenant's HB was overpaid and who is the blameless tenant. The blameless tenant is not notified, but the landlord/agent must treat them as having paid rent equal to the amount deducted.

18.40 AA 76(2),(3); CTB 86,90; CTB60+ 71,75

18.41 AA 75(4),(5); NIAA 73(4),(5); HB 102; HB60+ 83; NIHB 99; NIHB60+ 80

18.44 HB 102(1),105,106; HB60+ 83(1),86,87; NIHB 99(1),102,103; NIHB60+ 80(1),83,84; CTB 90,91; CTB60+ 84,85

Table 18.4: Recovering overpayments from DWP benefits

A recoverable overpayment of HB/CTB may be deducted from:

- income support
- jobseeker's allowance
- employment and support allowance
- maternity allowance
- industrial injuries benefits
- widow(er)'s benefits
- bereavement benefits
- retirement pension
- incapacity benefit
- state pension credit
- carer's allowance
- disability living allowance
- attendance allowance
- equivalent EU and Swiss benefits

but not from:

- child benefit
- guardian's allowance
- war pensions
- working tax credit
- child tax credit
- statutory sick, maternity, paternity or adoption pay

Deducting overpaid HB from a guilty landlord/agent's payments

18.47 If a landlord/agent has been convicted of HB fraud or agreed to pay a penalty (para. 18.63), the resulting overpaid HB may (though this is rare) be recovered from any payment of HB due to the landlord/agent. The landlord/agent and the tenant(s) involved must be notified of this.

Deducting overpaid HB from a landlord's own benefits

18.48 If a recoverable overpayment of HB was paid to a landlord/agent, it may (though this is rare) be recovered from the landlord's personal entitlement to:

- HB (in which case the limits in table 18.3 do not apply); or
- DWP benefits (table 18.4) – but only if the overpayment was due to misrepresentation of, or failure to disclose, a material fact.

18.45 AA 75(5),(6); NIAA 73(5),(6); HB sch 9 para 15(2); HB60+ sch 8 para 15(2); NIHB sch 10 para 15(2); NIHB60+ sch 9 para 15(2)

18.47 AA 75(5),(6); NIAA 73(5),(6); HB 106(2); HB60+ 87(2); NIHB 103(2); NIHB60+ 84(2)

18.48 AA 75(5); NIAA 73(5); HB 106(3); HB60+ 87(3); NIHB 103(3); NIHB60+ 84(3)

Table 18.5: When recovered HB overpayments create rent arrears

This table is about whether recovered overpayments of HB turn into rent arrears for the claimant.

Rent rebate (local authority/NIHE tenants)

- *Recovery by deductions from ongoing benefit or arrears of HB* (para. 18.41): Assuming the tenant does not pay any shortfall then this always creates rent arrears (because at no point has the rent due been paid).
- *Recovery by charging the tenant's rent account or by sending the tenant a bill* (paras. 18.39 and 18.49): Recovery by this method does not create rent arrears *(R v Haringey ex p Ayub)* except if:
  (a) the tenancy agreement expressly allows for recovered overpayments of HB to be charged as additional rent; or
  (b) following the recovery the tenant fails to say which debt (rent or overpayment) any payments should be attributed to – in which case any payment will go against the earliest debt first.

Rent allowance

- *Recovery by deductions from ongoing benefit or arrears of HB* (para. 18.41): As for rent rebates above.
- *Recovery from the blameless tenant's HB* (para. 18.46): This never results in rent arrears for the blameless tenant; and does not result in rent arrears for the tenant to whom the overpayment relates except in the same circumstances as in (a) and (b) above.
- *Recovery from the landlord by deductions from the landlord's own benefits or by sending the landlord a bill* (paras 18.48-49): The tenant to whom the overpayment relates is treated as not having paid the amount of rent which has been repaid (as a recoverable overpayment) so this creates rent arrears.
- *By deductions from a guilty landlord's payments* (18.47): The tenant to whom the overpayment relates is treated as having paid the rent to the value of the deduction.

T 18.5 AA 75(5),(6); NIAA 73(5),(6); HB 95(2),107(1),(2); HB60+ 76(2),88(1),(2); NIHB 92(2),104(1),(2); NIHB60+ 73(2),85(1),(2)

Recovering HB/CTB by sending a bill

18.49 Any recoverable overpayment of HB or CTB may be recovered by sending a bill to any person it can be recovered from (paras. 18.27-33). This can be followed up by court action (paras. 18.51-55).

The effect of bankruptcy

18.50 Everything depends on whether the authority makes its decision that an overpayment is recoverable before or after the person who is liable to repay it is adjudged bankrupt. If the decision is made before, then their liability to repay it will be extinguished when their bankruptcy is discharged *(Secretary of State for Work and Pensions v Balding)*. But if the decision is made after, they will remain liable even after their discharge *(Secretary of State for Work and Pensions v Steele)*.

Court action

18.51 Although the DWP advises that 'it is for authorities to decide how far to pursue recovery', they expect a serious attempt at recovery and encourage court action in appropriate cases (OG paras. 7.40, 7.42). This court action can be civil proceedings for debt, but the following procedure is more appropriate.

The simplified debt recovery procedure

18.52 Authorities have the power to recover HB overpayments by execution in the County Court in England and Wales as if under a court order; and in Scotland as if it were an extract registered decree arbitral.

England and Wales

18.53 In England and Wales, this procedure allows an HB overpayment determination to be registered directly as an order of the County Court without the need to bring a separate action. The authority applies to the court on a standard form (form N 322A), enclosing a copy of the overpayment notice and the relevant fee. The notice must include all the matters in paragraph 18.59 (OG para. 5.09). An officer of the court then makes an order and a copy is sent to the authority and the debtor. Once an order has been made, the normal methods of enforcement are available to the authority – attachment of earnings; a garnishee order allowing the authority to obtain money owed to the debtor by a third party; a warrant of execution against goods executed by the county court bailiff; or a charging order, normally against land.

18.49 HB 102(1); HB60+ 83(1); NIHB 99(1); NIHB60+ 80(1); CTB 86(2)(a); CTB60+ 71(2)(a)

18.52 AA 75(7),76(6); NIAA 73(7)

18.54 There is no appeal against the above order, but the claimant or landlord/agent may apply to the court to set it aside if the overpayment notice was defective or the authority has ignored their appeal rights. In the case of other disputes, they should ask the authority to reconsider or appeal to a tribunal (chapter 19).

Table 18.6: Overpayments case law: notices and effect on recovery

- *Failure to give a reason why there is a recoverable overpayment:* At one time this was the most common error in overpayment notices. To say it was due to a 'change of circumstances' is not itself an adequate explanation as it covers a multitude of possibilities and so does not give the person affected sufficient information to be able to judge whether they have grounds for an appeal *(R v Thanet DC ex parte Warren Court Hotels Ltd).*
- *Failure to identify the parties the overpayment is recoverable from:* A notice naming only a landlord as the person from whom the overpayment could be recovered was quashed (and so had no effect), because it should have named both the claimant and the landlord (*CH/3622/2005,* in which the commissioner followed *R(H) 6/06*).
- *Failure to issue a complete overpayment notice:* An authority that issues an incomplete notice may undermine the legal basis of its debt recovery action *(Warwick DC v Freeman).*
- *Impact on power to recover:* There is no legally recoverable debt until the authority makes the appropriate decision and issues the required notice *(R (Godwin) v Rossendale BC).* Decisions must be clear and unambiguous with proper use of statutory language and dates *(C3/07-08(IS)).* But if the defect in a notice is only trivial and no substantial harm is caused as a result, the authority may be entitled to recover the overpaid benefit *(Haringey LBC v Awaritefe).*
- *Recovery taken before notice issued:* If, in a 'blameless tenant' case, an authority recovers HB before issuing a valid notice, the landlord/agent can apply to the court for repayment of the recovered HB *(Waveney DC v Jones).*
- *Recovery volunteered before notice issued:* If a landlord/agent voluntarily pays a bill for overpaid HB before the authority has issued a valid notice, they cannot obtain repayment because (unlike in Jones, above) they could have resisted recovery by requesting the authority to reconsider or appealing to a tribunal *(Norwich CC v Stringer).*

Scotland

18.55 In Scotland, an HB overpayment determination is immediately enforceable as if it were an extract registered decree arbitral. It does not need to be registered with the Sheriff Court. The usual methods of enforcement are available – arrestment of earnings; poinding and warrant sale; arrestment of moveable property and inhibition of heritable property.

Time limits

18.56 The above procedures must be started within six years in England and Wales, five years in Scotland, from the date of the overpayment decision (OG paras. 7.20-21). But this limitation does not apply to any other method of recovery – such as by deductions from future HB (OG para. 7.23).

18.57 This time limit does not affect how far back an overpayment can go. For example, it may be discovered today that someone has been overpaid since the beginning of the HB scheme, and the authority may make a determination to recover it. But the further the overpayment goes back, the more difficult it may be for the authority to obtain the evidence needed to prove the overpayment to the court (OG para. 7.00).

Overpayment decision notices

18.58 For every recoverable overpayment, a decision notice must be sent to every person it can be recovered from (paras. 18.27-33), because each of these is a 'person affected' (para. 16.7) – regardless of which party the authority will actually recover it from *(R(H) 6/06)*. This should be done within 14 days of the determination being made or as soon as reasonably practicable thereafter. There is one exception: notices do not need to be sent in the case of a CTB overpayment caused by a retrospective reduction in council tax due to capping or to a delayed award of a discount or disability reduction.

18.59 Overpayment notices must contain the following information:

- the fact that there is a recoverable overpayment;
- the reason why there is a recoverable overpayment;
- the amount of the recoverable overpayment;
- how that amount was calculated;
- the benefit weeks to which the recoverable overpayment relates;
- the method of recovery of CTB;
- if overpaid HB is to be deducted from future HB, the amount of the deduction;

18.58 HB 90(1)(b); HB60+ 71(1)(b); NIHB 86(1)(b); NIHB60+ 67(1)(b); CTB 76(1)(b); CTB60+ 61(1)(b)

18.59 HB sch 9 para 15; HB60+ sch 8 para 15; NIHB sch 10 para 15; NIHB60+ sch 9 para 15; CTB sch 8 para 16; CTB60+ sch 7 para 16

- any other relevant matters;
- the person's right to request a written statement, to request the authority to reconsider, and to appeal to a tribunal, and the manner and time in which to these things.

18.60 Sometimes overpayment notices are poor or incomplete. How this affects recovering the overpayment has often been considered by commissioners and courts. The main cases are summarised in table 18.6.

18.61 The DWP advises authorities that recovery of HB overpayments by deduction from future HB should not begin until one month after notice (unless the overpayment is small) to allow time for an appeal to be made (but advises that it may issue an invoice); but that no similar delay is needed before charging overpaid CTB to a council tax account, or sending a bill for HB/CTB (OG paras. 4.390, 4.400 and 4.410).

Overpayments and fraud

18.62 This guide does not cover HB/CTB fraud or how authorities deal with it. For a good description, see *Countering housing benefit fraud: a management handbook* (Audit Commission, 1997). Officers working for an authority should also see the DWP's *Local authority fraud investigators manual* and fraud circulars.

Administrative penalties

18.63 An authority may offer someone the chance to pay an 'administrative penalty', rather than face a prosecution for fraud, if:

- the overpayment was caused by an 'act or omission' on their part; and
- there are grounds for bringing a prosecution against them for fraud relating to that overpayment.

The person does not have to agree to a penalty. They can opt for the possibility of prosecution instead.

18.64 The offer of a penalty must be in writing, explain that it is a way of avoiding prosecution, and give various other information – including the fact that the person can change their mind within 28 days, and that the penalty will be repaid if the claimant successfully challenges it by asking for a reconsideration or appeal (OG para. 4.672). Authorities do not normally offer a penalty (but prosecute instead) if an overpayment is substantial or there are other aggravating factors (such as being in a position of trust).

18.65 The amount of the penalty is 30% of the recoverable overpayment (with limitations for periods before 18th December 1997, when administrative penalties were introduced).

18.63 AA 115A; NIAA 109A; SI 1997/2813; NISR 1997/514

19 Disputes and appeals

19.1 This chapter is about the HB/CTB disputes and appeals procedure. It covers:

- getting more information about a decision;
- asking the authority to reconsider a decision;
- how the authority can correct mistakes;
- appeals to a first-tier tribunal;
- appeals to an upper tribunal and beyond;
- the separate system of appeals to a rent officer.

The procedure is summarised in table 19.1 which also gives the main time limits. Before 3rd November 2008, 'first-tier tribunals' were called 'social security appeal tribunals'; and appeals to an 'upper tribunal' were called appeals to a 'commissioner'.

The rights of 'persons affected'

19.2 Any 'person affected' by a decision has all the rights described in this chapter. As defined in paragraph 16.7, a person affected could be a claimant or an appointee acting for a claimant, or in certain circumstances a landlord or a landlord's agent.

19.3 Whenever it makes a decision the authority must notify each person affected of their:

- right to a written statement;
- right to ask the authority to reconsider; and
- right to appeal to a tribunal (unless the decision is one which cannot be appealed: para. 19.30).

Written statement of reasons

19.4 A person affected may request a statement of reasons about anything that was not explained in the notice of an HB/CTB decision. There is no time limit for asking for this. The authority should provide it within 14 days, so far as this is practicable.

19.2 HB 2(1),90; HB60+ 2(1),71; NIHB 2(1),86; NIHB60+ 2(1),67; CTB 2(1),76; CTB60+ 2(1),61; DAR 3; NIDAR 3

19.3 DAR 10; NIDAR 10

19.4 DAR 10(2); NIDAR 10(2)

Reconsideration or appeal?

19.5 A person affected who disagrees with a decision has two options. They can:

- ask the authority to reconsider the decision; or
- appeal against the decision to a tribunal.

If they choose the first option, they can go on to the second option next. If they choose the second option, the authority can treat it as a request for a reconsideration in some circumstances (para. 19.27).

Table 19.1: The HB/CTB disputes and appeals procedure

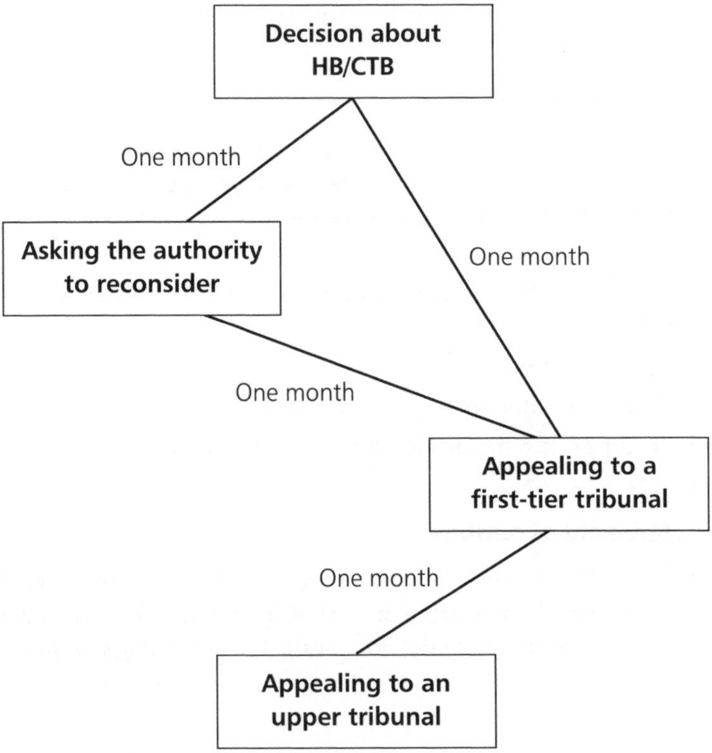

Note

Each of the periods of one month can be extended for special circumstances.

Asking the authority to reconsider

19.6 Any person affected (para. 19.2) can ask the authority to reconsider any decision it has made. They can do this either instead of or before making an appeal to the appeal tribunal. Requests must be in writing and the normal time limit is one month (para. 19.7). The law calls this requesting a revision or supersession, but the person does not have to use these terms, and it is normally called requesting a reconsideration. If the authority needs information or evidence in connection with the person's request, see paragraph 17.44.

Time limit for requests

19.7 If the request for a reconsideration is received:

- within the time limit, the authority must consider revising its decision (para. 19.9);
- outside the time limit, the authority must consider superseding its decision (para. 19.11).

19.8 A request is within the time limit if it is received by the authority within one calendar month of the date the decision was notified. In calculating this time limit:

- any time is ignored from the date the authority received a request for a statement of reasons (para. 19.4) to the date the authority provided the statement (both dates inclusive); and
- any time is ignored before the date on which the authority gave notice of the correction of an accidental error (para. 19.15); and
- the time limit may be extended by the authority as described below (para. 19.10).

Requests received within the time limit

19.9 If the request for reconsideration is received within the time limit, and the authority alters entitlement to HB/CTB, this takes effect from the date of the original decision. The one exception to this rule is where the authority determines that the original decision took effect from a wrong date, in which case it takes effect from the correct date. This is a revision. Whether or not the authority alters entitlement, the outcome must be notified (para. 19.12).

19.6 CPSA sch 7 para 4(1); NICPSA sch 7 para 4(1); DAR 4(1),(8),(9),7(2),(6),(7); NIDAR 4(1),(8),(9),7(2),(6),(7)

19.8 DAR 4(1),(4),10A(3); NIDAR 4(1),(4),10A(3)

19.9 CPSA sch 7 para 3(3); NICPSA sch 7 para 3(3); DAR 6; NIDAR 6

Extending the time limit for requests

19.10 The one-month time limit is extended if:

- the request is received in writing by the authority within 13 months of the date on which the decision was notified; and
- the request says that the person is asking for it to be accepted late, and gives the reasons for his or her failure to request a reconsideration earlier; and
- the person gives sufficient details to identify the disputed decision; and
- the request for revision 'has merit'; and
- the authority is satisfied that there are or were 'special circumstances' as a result of which it was not practicable to request a reconsideration within the one month time limit. The longer the delay (beyond the normal one month), the more compelling those special circumstances need to be; and
- the authority is satisfied that it is reasonable to grant the claimant's request. In determining this, the authority may not take account of ignorance of the law (not even ignorance of the time limits) nor of the fact that a commissioner or tribunal of commissioners or court has taken a different view of the law from that previously understood and applied.

Example: Late request for the authority to reconsider its decision

In May 2009, the authority notified a claimant of its decision on his claim. Amongst other things, the decision depended upon an assessment of the claimant's self-employed income.

In September 2009, the claimant asks the authority to reconsider its decision, as he forgot to tell them about part of his expenditure. He has no special circumstances for his delay. However, the authority accepts that (if it had known) it would have allowed that additional expenditure (and he would therefore have qualified for more HB/CTB).

The change is implemented from the Monday following the day the claimant's written notice of the change is received by the authority. The claimant does not get his arrears. This is a supersession. (However, if the claimant has 'special circumstances', he may get his arrears: para. 19.10).

Requests received outside the time limit

19.11 If the request for reconsideration is received outside the one month time limit, and the authority refuses to extend this limit, the person affected has no right to ask it to accept a further late request to reconsider the same matter.

19.10 DAR 4(8),5(1)-(6); NIDAR 4(7),5(1)-(6)

However, the authority should nonetheless reconsider its decision and should consider making a superseding decision instead: the details are in paragraph 19.21.

Notifying the outcome

19.12 In all the circumstances described in this section, the authority must notify the claimant of the outcome of their request for reconsideration. The decision notice must include the following matters:

- whether it has changed its decision;
- if it has not changed its decision, the reasons why it has refused the claimant's request;
- if it has changed its decision, the same matters as in paragraph 17.45.

The authority's own power or duty to correct mistakes and errors

Correcting mistakes

19.13 This section describes how the authority can correct mistakes in a decision – either because the authority has noticed the mistake itself, or because someone has pointed the mistake out (but is outside the time limits to request a reconsideration or appeal).

19.14 The law uses four different terms for this:

- a 'mistake of fact' means that the decision was based on an incorrect fact (without at this stage saying that it was necessarily anybody's fault);
- a 'mistake of law' means that the decision was based on an incorrect understanding of the law;
- an 'accidental error' is something on the lines of a slip of the pen – a failure by the authority to put into action (or to record) its true intentions;
- an 'official error' is defined independently (para.19.16) and can include one or a combination of the above *(CH/943/2003).*

Correcting accidental errors

19.15 The authority may correct an accidental error in any decision (including a revised or superseding decision), or the record of any decision, at any time. The correction is deemed to be part of the decision or record, and the authority must give written notice of the correction as soon as practicable to the claimant and any other person affected.

19.11 DAR 5(7),7(2)(b); NIDAR 5(7),7(2)(b)

19.12 DAR 10; NIDAR 10; HB sch 9; HB60+ sch 8; NIHB sch 10; NIHB60+ sch 10; CTB sch 8; CTB60+ sch 7

19.15 DAR 10A(1),(2); NIDAR 10A(1),(2)

Example: 'Mistake of fact' and 'mistake of law'

In deciding a claim for HB/CTB, an authority determined that a man and a woman were not a couple.

This would be a mistake of fact if the authority made its decision not knowing that they were actually married (e.g. because the claimant had lied or the authority misread the application form).

It would be a mistake of law if the authority wrongly believed that two unmarried people could never be a couple.

Correcting other official errors

19.16 The authority may revise or supersede a decision at any time if the decision arose from an 'official error'. An 'official error' means an error by an authority, the DWP or HM Revenue and Customs – or someone acting on their behalf (such as a contractor or a housing association which verifies HB claims). However, something does not count as an 'official error' if it was caused wholly or partly by any person or body other than the above, nor if it is an error of law which is shown to have been an error only by a subsequent decision of a commissioner or tribunal of commissioners.

19.17 The effect may be that there has been an underpayment of HB/CTB (in which case the arrears must be awarded – no matter how far back they go) or an overpayment (which may or may not be recoverable: chapter 18).

When an appeal decision applies to a case

19.18 The authority may revise a decision at any time to take account of an appeal decision in the same case (by an appeal tribunal, commissioner, tribunal of commissioners or court) which the authority was not aware of at the time it made the decision.

Mistakes of fact resulting in an overpayment

19.19 The authority may revise or supersede a decision at any time if the decision was made in ignorance of, or was based on a mistake as to, some material fact – and the decision was, as a result, more favourable than it would otherwise have been. This creates an overpayment (which may or may not be recoverable: chapter 18).

19.16 CPSA sch 7 paras 1(1),23(1); NICPSA sch 7 paras 1(1),23(1); DAR 1(2),4(2); NIDAR 1(2),4(2)

19.18 DAR 4(7); NIDAR 4(6)

19.19 DAR 4(2); NIDAR 4(2)

Mistakes of fact discovered within one month

19.20 The authority may revise a decision if, within one month of the date of notifying it, the authority has sufficient information to show that it was made in ignorance of, or was based on a mistake as to, some material fact. This could arise only in the case of increases to entitlement (for decreases see para. 19.19).

Other mistakes of fact – 'any time reviews'

19.21 If none of the previous rules in this section apply, the authority may supersede a decision at any time if the decision was made in ignorance of, or was based on a mistake as to, some material fact. This is sometimes called an 'any time review'. It could arise only in the case of increases to entitlement (for decreases see para. 19.19).

Example: Mistake of fact: 'any time review'

A claimant with a non-dependant in remunerative work was unable to provide the authority with details of the non-dependant's income. So the authority applied the highest level of non-dependant deduction in assessing her HB and CTB (para. 6.30). Now, four months later, the claimant provides evidence which is acceptable to the authority. It means a lower deduction applies.

Because this is outside the time limit for a revision (para. 19.8), the authority alters the amount of the claimant's HB/CTB from the Monday of the benefit week in which it received the evidence. The claimant does not get her arrears.

Note that the outcome would be different if the claimant wrote giving her reasons for the delay and the authority accepted that these amounted to special circumstances (para. 19.10). She would then get her arrears.

19.22 The supersession in such a case takes effect from the Monday at the beginning of the benefit week in which:

- the request was received from the claimant or other person affected (if a request was indeed made); or
- the authority first had information to show that the original decision was made in ignorance or mistake of fact (in any other case).

Other errors of law

19.23 A final rare rule applies if a decision was based on an error of law but was not due to 'official error' (para. 19.16). (This could arise if the commissioners or courts interpret the law in an unexpected way.) The authority may supersede

---

19.20 DAR 4(1),8(4),(5); NIDAR 4(1),8(4),(5)

19.21 CPSA sch 7 para 4(5),(6); NICPSA sch 7 para 4(4),(5); DAR 7(2)(b),8(4)(5); NIDAR 7(2)(b),8(4),(5)

19.23 CPSA sch 7 para 4(5),(6); NICPSA sch 7 para 4(4),(5); DAT 7(2)(b); NIDAR 7(2)(b)

the decision at any time. The supersession takes effect from the date on which it is made (or, if earlier, from the date the person's request was received).

Notifying the outcome

19.24 Whenever the authority alters a decision under the above rules (paras. 19.16-23), it must write notifying the claimant and any other person affected, of the same matters as in paragraph 17.45.

Appeals to a tribunal

19.25 Any person affected (para. 19.2) can appeal about an HB/CTB decision to a first-tier tribunal. They can do this either instead of or after asking the authority to reconsider its decision. If there is more than one person affected by an appeal (for example both the landlord and the claimant in some overpayment cases) each is a party to the proceedings no matter which of them made the appeal.

First-tier tribunals

19.26 First-tier tribunals are independent. They deal with appeals about HB/CTB, other social security benefits, child support, vaccine damage, tax credit and compensation recovery. They are administered by the Tribunals Service which is part of the Ministry of Justice: see *www.appeals-service.gov.uk*. Before 3rd November 2008, they were called 'social security appeal tribunals'.

Revisions prompted by an appeal

19.27 When an appeal is received, the authority may consider whether the decision can be revised. If it can be revised to the advantage of the person affected, the authority should revise the decision and the appeal lapses (does not go ahead). This applies even though the person affected may not receive all that has been asked for in the appeal. Where a decision has been revised to the advantage of the person affected there is then a fresh decision with a fresh dispute period, and fresh rights to apply for a revision or appeal.

19.28 The appeal should automatically proceed to a first-tier tribunal if:

- the decision is not revised by the authority; or
- the decision is revised, but not in favour of the person affected; or
- the decision is superseded by the authority.

19.29 If the authority revises the decision but not in favour of the person affected the appeal is deemed to be against the revised decision and the person affected is given an additional month in which to make further representations.

19.24 DAR 10; NIDAR 10; HB sch 9; HB60+ sch 8; NIHB sch 10; NIHB60+ sch 9; CTB sch 8; CTB60+ sch 7

19.27 CPSA sch 7 para 3(6); NICPSA sch 7 para 3(6); DAR 4(1),(6); NIDAR 4(1),(6)

19.29 DAR 17(3),(4); NIDAR 17(3),(4)

Which decisions can be appealed

19.30 A person affected has a right of appeal to a first-tier tribunal about any decision about HB/CTB (including a revision or a supersession) and about any overpayment. There are however limits. The decisions that are not appealable to a tribunal are mainly to do with claims, payments and certain overpayments matters (table 19.2).

Table 19.2: Appealable and non-appealable decisions

Decisions about claims

Non-appealable

- Which partner in a couple is to be the claimant (para. 5.4)
- Who may claim when someone is unable to act (para. 5.5)

Appealable

- When and how a claim is made (paras. 5.9-14)
- Whether a claim is incomplete (para. 5.28)
- The date of claim (paras. 5.33-47)
- Backdating (paras. 5.53-60)

Decisions about payments

Non-appealable

- When and how benefit is paid (para. 16.12)
- Making a payment on account (para. 16.16)
- The frequency of payment of a rent allowance (paras. 16.21-25)
- Making payment to a person entitled (para. 16.27)
- Paying outstanding benefit after a death (para. 16.63)
- Suspending or restoring benefit (para. 17.46)

19.30 CPSA sch 7 para 1,6(1)(a),(b); NICPSA sch 7 para 1,6(1)(a),(b)

T 19.2 CPSA sch 7 para 6; DAR 16(1) and sch; NICPSA sch 7 para 6 NIDAR 16(1) and sch

Appealable

- Adjusting HB to correct a payment on account (para. 16.20)
- Who HB is to be paid to (e.g. claimant or landlord/agent) (paras. 16.30-48);
- Whether the landlord/agent is a 'fit and proper person' (paras. 16.43-45)
- Terminating benefit (para. 17.51)

Decisions about overpayments

Non-appealable

- What 'an overpayment' (or 'excess benefit') means (para. 18.4)
- The exercise of discretion to recover or not (paras. 18.25-26)
- The method of recovery (para. 18.37)

Appealable

- Whether an overpayment is recoverable (paras. 18.11-14)
- The amount of the overpayment (paras. 18.16-24)
- Who an overpayment can be recovered from (paras. 18.27-36)

Other decisions

Non-appealable

- LHA figures and areas (para. 9.33)
- Rent officer figures in rent referral cases (but see para. 19.102)
- The DWP's assessed income figure or 'AIF' (paras. 13.158-161) – though modifications to it are appealable (para. 13.162 and table 13.4)
- Whether to run a local scheme for pensions for war disablement and war bereavement (para. 22.12)
- A refusal to correct a mistake out-of-time (para. 19.13: *Beltekian v Westminster CC reported as R(H) 8/05*)
- Any figure laid down in the law (e.g. the capital limit)

Appealable

- All other HB/CTB decisions

Appeals against non-appealable decisions

19.31 If an appeal is made against a non-appealable decision (table 19.2), the authority should identify it as 'out of jurisdiction' when forwarding it to the Tribunal Service. It should then be struck out by a tribunal clerk or member so that the appeal does not go ahead. Note, though, that non-appealable matters can be the subject of a request for a reconsideration (para. 19.6).

Making an appeal

How to appeal

19.32 To be properly made an appeal must:

- be in writing;
- be delivered, by whatever means (e.g. post, fax, e-mail) to the authority;
- be signed by the person making the appeal;
- say what is being appealed;
- give their grounds of appeal;
- be within one month or 13 months (paras. 19.36-41).

19.33 An appeal does not have to be on a form, though many authorities do have forms, sometimes based on the DWP's (form GL24). An appeal made in a letter should make it clear that it is an appeal to a first-tier tribunal (not just a request for a reconsideration: para. 19.6).

Appeals that do not meet the conditions

19.34 If an appeal is incomplete, the authority can accept it if it contains enough information. If it does not, the authority must write requesting further details, or return it for completion, and allow the appellant 14 days to reply, or longer if the authority directs.

19.35 If the appellant does not reply within that time, the authority must send the documents to the tribunal (including any other documents it has by now received) for them to determine whether the appeal should go ahead.

The appeal time limit

19.36 The normal limit is that the appeal must be received by the authority within one month of the notice of the decision – or, if later, 14 days after a written statement is provided (in cases where one is requested).

19.32 DAR 20(1); NIDAR 20(1); FTPR 23, sch 1

19.34 DAR 20(2)-(8); NIDAR 20(2)-(8)

19.36 FTPR 23, sch 1; NIDAR 18

19.37 If the authority's decision notice is invalid because it fails to meet the relevant legal requirements (paras.16.9-11, 18.58-61 and table 18.6) the time for appealing does not start until the authority issues a valid notice: *CH/1129/2004*. Disputes about this, or any other question about whether the appeal was within the time limit, are referred to the tribunal.

Requesting a late appeal

19.38 An appellant may, if they are outside the above time limit, write requesting a late appeal, giving their grounds for lateness including details of any special circumstances.

The request must be signed by the person who has the right of appeal and must be received within an absolute time limit of one year after the end of the last 'normal' day for appealing - in other words the absolute maximum time limit is 13 months. An application for a late appeal can only be made once (for that appeal).

Accepting a late appeal

19.39 The authority may grant the request for a late appeal if it is in the interests of justice to do so. If it does not, it must forward the request to the tribunal, which notifies its decision to the principal parties. The tribunal must grant the application for a late appeal if it is in the interests of justice to do so.

'Interests of justice'

19.40 When the authority or tribunal is determining whether to accept a request for a late appeal, only the following count as being in the interests of justice – and only if they meant that it was not practicable to make the appeal within the normal one month:

- the appellant or a partner or dependant of the appellant has died or suffered serious illness; or
- the appellant is not resident in the UK; or
- normal postal services were disrupted; or
- some other special circumstances exist which are wholly exceptional and relevant to the application.

19.41 Ignorance of the law (including the law about time limits) is ignored, as is any change in how the law is interpreted as a result of a decision of a commissioner or court; and the longer the delay (beyond the one month time limit), the more compelling the special circumstances need to be.

19.38 DAR 20(1); NIDAR 20(1); FTPR 23(3)-(5)

19.39 DAR 19(3),(5),(6),(8),(10),(11); NIDAR 19(3),(5),(6),(8),(10),(11)

19.40 DAR 19(5A)-(9); NIDAR 19(6)-(9)

Withdrawing an appeal

19.42 If an appeal has not yet been forwarded to the first-tier tribunal, the appellant or representative may write withdrawing it. The authority may agree or require it to go ahead.

Death of a party to an appeal

19.43 If the appellant dies, the authority may appoint someone to act for them. Grant of probate, letters of administration, etc, have no effect on this appointment. This applies at both levels of appeal.

The authority's duties to deal with an appeal

19.44 When the authority receives an appeal, it should consider revising the decision appealed against (para.19.6). If it revises the decision in a way which is advantageous, the appeal lapses and no further action is taken on it.

19.45 In all other cases, the authority sends the Tribunal Service:

- a notice of appeal completed by the authority (form AT37) along with the appellant's submissions;
- the authority's response to the appeal (in other words its submissions).

The authority also sends its response (with a covering letter) to the appellant and any third party. This should be done as soon as reasonably practicable.

19.46 The authority should tell the Tribunal Service (on form AT37) if eviction proceedings have begun so that the case can be heard urgently, and also if there are special reasons affecting the appellant which may delay their reply (para. 19.48).

The pre-hearing enquiry form

19.47 On receipt of the above, the Tribunal Service sends a pre-hearing enquiry form (TAS1 HB or TAS1 W HB) to the appellant and a similar form (TAS1 HB R) to any third party. This asks the appellant whether they:

- want to withdraw their appeal;
- want an oral hearing (at which they and/or their representative can be present) or paper hearing (which does not require their attendance);
- agree to having less than 14 days notice if they have opted for an oral hearing;
- have an outstanding appeal against another benefit decision; and/or
- need an interpreter or signer.

19.42 FTPR 17(1)(a); NIDAR 20(9)

19.43 DAR 21; NIDR 21

19.45 FTPR 24(1)(b)

19.48 The appellant returns the completed form to the Tribunal Service and should do so within 14 days, a period which the tribunal's clerk can extend for special reasons. Otherwise, the Tribunal Service can strike out the appeal (so it does not go ahead).

The authority's submission

19.49 The law does not say what should go into the submission, but good DWP guidance is in GM C7.260-279.

How quickly should appeals be dealt with?

19.50 The law does not say how quickly the authority should forward appeals to the Tribunal Service. In 2003 the DWP suggested a normal time scale of four weeks except for more complex cases (HB/CTB A20/2003 appendix B, para. A65) and this has not been changed. The law also does not say how soon an appeal should be heard once the Tribunal Service has received the authority's submission and the appellant's response. In 2005-06 their target was a maximum of 11 weeks (Hansard, 24th March 2005: Col. 97WS).

The appeal hearing

Membership of the first-tier tribunal

19.51 All tribunal members are independent of the authority. In the case of an appeal concerning HB/CTB the tribunal normally consists of just one person, a judge, who is legally qualified. In rare instances where financial questions are raised, e.g. regarding a difficult question relating to a self-employed claimant's accounts, there may also be a tribunal member with relevant qualifications. An additional member may also be present to provide that member with experience or to assist with the monitoring of standards.

Venues

19.52 The hearing normally takes place at a tribunal venue near to the appellant. The Tribunal Service has a network of around 140 tribunal venues that it uses to hear cases across England, Wales and Scotland. Information on venue locations in England, Scotland and Wales and available facilities can be found on the web at *www.tribunals.gov.uk/qavenuefinder.aspx.* The Appeal Service (Northern Ireland) currently holds appeal hearings at 19 venues in towns and cities throughout the province.

19.48 DAR99 39(2),(3); NIDAR99 39(2),(3)

19.51 SI 2008/2692; NIDAR 22(1),(2)

Function

19.53 The tribunal's task is to reconsider the specific decision that has been appealed. It does not have to consider any issue that has not been raised in the appeal but is does have the power to do so. The tribunal should not shut its eyes to things where to do so would cause an injustice. It cannot however take into account any circumstances that did not exist at the time the decision appealed against was made.

The judge may also make directions to the parties about their submissions and any hearing.

An oral hearing

Notice

19.54 At least 14 days before the hearing (beginning with the day on which the notice is given and ending on the day before the hearing of the appeal is to take place) notice of the time and place of any oral hearing should be given to every party to the proceedings. If notice has not been given to someone who should have been given it, the hearing may proceed only with the consent of that person.

Postponement

19.55 A tribunal member or the clerk may at any time before the beginning of the hearing postpone the hearing. Where a person affected wishes to request a postponement of the hearing they should do so by writing to the clerk stating the reasons for the request. If it is too late to request a postponement, an adjournment may be requested at the hearing. The clerk or tribunal member may grant or refuse the request as they think fit.

Public or private hearings

19.56 The initial presumption is that a hearing will be in public. In practice, of course, normally only the people involved in the hearing are present. Should there be people in attendance who are not involved in the hearing a (part) private hearing may be held:

- in the interests of national security, morals, public order or children;
- for the protection of the private or family life of one of the parties; or
- in special circumstances, because publicity would prejudice the interests of justice.

19.53 CPSA sch 7 para 6(9); NICPSA sch 7 para 6(9); FTPR 2,5,6

19.54 FTPR 27-29; NIDAR99 49(2)

19.55 FTPR 5; NIDAR99 51(1)

19.56 FTPR 30; NIDAR99 49(6)

19.57 Certain persons such as trainee panel members or trainee clerks are entitled to be present at an oral hearing (whether or not it is otherwise in private). They must not take part in the proceedings.

Deciding to proceed in the absence of a party

19.58 If one of the parties to whom notice has been given fails to appear at the hearing the judge may, having regard to all the circumstances including any explanation offered for the absence:

- proceed with the hearing; or
- give such directions with a view to the determination of the appeal as they think proper.

19.59 If one of the relevant parties has waived the right to be given 14 days notice of the hearing, the judge may proceed with the hearing despite the absence.

The parties' rights at the hearing

19.60 The procedure for an oral hearing is determined by the judge. The parties to the proceedings however have certain rights which the judge must respect. Each party is entitled to:

- be present; and
- be heard at an oral hearing.

19.61 In law, parties entitled to be present at a hearing do not have to be physically present, but can attend by a live television link, e.g. a video conference facility, but only where the judge gives permission. The Tribunal Service is working to extend the use of the video-link in tribunal hearings (Appeal Service *Annual Report and Accounts 2003-2004,* page 17). One of the principal aims is to enable appellants to attend their hearing from remote or rural areas.

19.62 A person who has the right to be heard at a hearing:

- may be accompanied; and
- may be represented by another person whether they have professional qualifications or not.

19.63 For the purposes of the proceedings at the hearing, any representative has all the rights and powers to which the person represented is entitled.

19.58 FTPR 31; NIDAR99 49(4)

19.59 NIDAR99 49(5)

19.60 FTPR 28; NIDAR99 49(1),(7)

19.61 NIDAR99 49(8)

19.63 NIDAR99 49(8)

19.64 Any person entitled to be heard at an oral hearing may:

- address the tribunal;
- give evidence;
- call witnesses; and
- put questions directly to any other person called as a witness.

Order of the hearing

19.65 The procedure for an oral hearing is determined by the judge within the framework set in the regulations, e.g. the need to ensure that the parties have the opportunity to put their case. Failure to observe proper procedures or the rights of the parties may leave the tribunal's decision open to appeal on grounds of natural justice (GM para C7.301) or the right to a fair hearing *(CJSA/5100/2001).*

19.66 The way in which the tribunal actually hears the appeal varies according to the issue that the tribunal has to decide. Each judge has their own way of conducting a hearing. Nevertheless the appellant should expect to have those present in the room introduced and their function explained at the start. The judge should also explain the procedure they wish to follow and seek the agreement of the parties to going ahead in that way. The judge may wish the appellant to start by explaining why they think the decision is wrong. If there is a Presenting Officer for the authority in attendance, they will be asked to explain the basis of the authority's decision. At some point the judge is likely to ask questions of the parties. Usually the appellant is offered the opportunity of having the final word before the tribunal goes on to consider its decision.

Directions

19.67 The judge may at any stage of the proceedings, either of their own motion or on a written application made to the clerk by any party to the proceedings:

- give such directions as they consider necessary or desirable for the just, effective and efficient conduct of the proceedings; and
- direct any party to the proceedings to provide such particulars or to produce such documents as may be reasonably required.

19.64 NIDAR99 49(11)

19.65 FTPR 5,6; NIDAR99 49(1)

19.67 FTPR 5,6; NIDAR 38(2)

Adjournment

19.68 An oral hearing may be adjourned by the judge at any time on the application of any party to the proceedings or of their own motion. This might be, for example, to allow new evidence to be looked at. Where a hearing has been adjourned and it is not practicable, or would cause undue delay, for it to be resumed before a tribunal with the same tribunal member(s) there must be a complete rehearing (DWP A17/2002, para. 33).

Withdrawing an appeal

19.69 An appeal may be withdrawn by the appellant at the oral hearing. If this happens the clerk must send a notice in writing to any party to the proceedings who is not present when the appeal or referral is withdrawn, informing them that the appeal has been withdrawn.

The tribunal's decision

19.70 The tribunal reaches a decision once it has considered all the evidence from an oral or paper hearing. In reaching its decision the tribunal should:

- consider the relevant law applicable to the decision in question;
- identify the relevant facts – and where these are in doubt or dispute find them (if necessary on the balance of probability); and
- apply the law to the relevant facts to arrive at a reasoned decision.

Duty to follow decisions of the courts and upper tribunals

19.71 In its consideration of the legal issues the tribunal has a duty to follow past decisions of the courts and upper tribunals, including their predecessors, commissioners (para. 19.93) unless the case before the tribunal is distinguishable *(R(U)23/59)*. Northern Ireland decisions are of persuasive authority only in England, Wales and Scotland *(R(I) 14/63)* and *vice versa*. Decisions of first-tier tribunals themselves do not set any precedent.

19.72 There is an order of precedence to upper tribunal (including commissioner) decisions *(R(I)12/75(T))*. This is as follows:

- upper tribunal decisions where more than one judge or panel member heard the case are the most authoritative – whether reported or unreported;
- reported decisions (which are given serial numbers by the year and identified by having the prefix 'R', e.g. *R(H)1/02*) come next;
- then come other decisions (which are identified by the file number, e.g. *CH/1502/2004*).

19.68 FTPR 5,6; NIDAR99 51(4)

19.69 FTPR 17; NIDAR99 40(1)(a),(2)

19.73 If there appears to be conflict between two or more upper tribunal or commissioner decisions the above hierarchy should be applied *(R(I)12/75(T))*. If the conflicting decisions are of equal rank, the tribunal is free to choose between them. More recent decisions should be preferred to older decisions. If a more recent unreported decision has fully considered all the earlier authorities, and given reasons for disapproving one or more earlier reported decisions, the tribunal should generally follow the more recent unreported decision *(R(IS) 13/01)*.

19.74 Details regarding the accessing of upper tribunal and commissioner decisions on-line can be found in appendix 2. Reported cases are kept at tribunal venues but unreported cases are not. If an appellant, representative or presenting officer wishes to use an unreported decision in support of their case a copy should, where possible, be sent in advance, otherwise an adjournment may be necessary.

The written decision notice

19.75 If the appellant attends an oral hearing they may be given the decision on the day. It should be confirmed in writing as soon as practicable by the judge. Every decision of an appeal tribunal must be recorded in summary by the judge. The decision notice should be in the approved written form. The judge must sign it. Where there was a legally qualified member and a financially qualified member the decision notice should state if the decision was unanimous or not.

Communicating the decision

19.76 As soon as practicable after an appeal has been decided, a copy of the decision notice must be sent or given to every party to the proceedings. They must also be informed of:

- the right to apply for a statement of reasons; and
- the conditions governing appeals to an upper tribunal.

The Tribunal Service aims to issue a copy of the tribunal's decision to the authority, appellant and appellant's representative, where one exists, within two days of the tribunal hearing (HB/CTB A20/2003, appendix B, para. A59).

Implementing the decision

19.77 The decision notice is the legal document that enables the authority to correct and pay benefit in line with the tribunal's decision. The authority should action the tribunal's decision as soon as practicable. The DWP indicates that the authority should seek to complete the necessary actions within four calendar weeks (HB/CTB A20/2003, appendix B, para. A70).

19.75 FTPR 33; NIDAR99 53(1),(2),(5)

19.76 FTPR 34; NIDAR99 53(3)

A 'statement of reasons'

19.78 A statement of reasons sets out the findings of fact and the reasons for the decision. If an appeal to the upper tribunal is being considered, a statement of reasons must be asked for.

Time limit for application for statement of reasons

19.79 A party to the proceedings may apply to the clerk for a statement of the reasons for the tribunal's decision. A statement of reasons can be asked for at the tribunal. Otherwise the application must normally be made within one month of the date the decision notice was given or sent. If this is not asked for in time the chance of appealing may be lost.

19.80 Late applications for the statement of reasons can only be accepted if the application is made in writing to the clerk within three months of the date the decision note was sent. In calculating this three month period no account should be taken of time that elapses before the day on which notice was given of:

- a correction of a decision or the record of a decision; or
- a decision to refuse to set aside.

Where a correction is made, or where set-aside is refused, the three month period is counted from the day notice of the correction or refusal is given.

19.81 The application must explain why the application is late, including details of any relevant special circumstances. A legally qualified tribunal member considers the application and decides the matter. Similar considerations apply as to those that apply to late appeals.

Requirement to supply written statement of reasons

19.82 Following receipt of an accepted application for a written statement of reasons the tribunal member must:

- record a statement of the reasons; and
- send or give a copy of that statement to every party to the proceedings as soon as practicable.

The Tribunal Service aims to issue a full statement of reasons within four weeks of a request being received (A20/2003, appendix B, para. A61).

19.79 FTPR 34; NIDAR99 53(4)

19.80 NIDAR99 54(1),(12A)

19.81 NIDAR99 54(2)-(5)

19.82 FTPR 34; NIDAR99 54(11)

Record of tribunal proceedings

19.83 A record of the proceedings at an oral hearing, which is sufficient to indicate the evidence taken, must be made by the judge. This record, together with the decision notice, and any statement of the reasons for the tribunal's decision, must be preserved by the Tribunal Service for six months from the date it was created. Any party to the proceedings may within that six month period apply in writing for a copy of the appropriate document, which should be supplied on request.

If a tribunal's decision is wrong

19.84 Once a first-tier tribunal has made and communicated its decision the decision may be:

- altered if the authority supersedes the decision;
- corrected, where there is an accidental error;
- set aside on certain limited grounds;
- appealed to the social security commissioners.

When may the authority supersede the tribunal's decision?

19.85 A decision of a first-tier tribunal may be superseded, either on application or on the authority's own initiative, where:

- the decision was made in ignorance of a material fact; or
- the decision was based on a mistake as to a material fact; or
- there has been a relevant change of circumstances since the decision had effect.

When may a tribunal's decision be corrected?

19.86 The clerk, or a tribunal member, may at any time correct accidental errors such as a typing mistake, misspelling of a name or omission about which both sides agree (*CI/3887/99* para. 8). A correction made to, or to the record of, a decision is deemed part of the decision or record of that decision. Any of the parties to the appeal can ask for a correction to be made. A written notice of the correction must be given as soon as practicable to every party to the proceedings. There is no right of appeal against a correction or a refusal to make a correction.

19.83 NIDAR99 55(1),(2)

19.85 DAR 7(2)(a),(d); NIDAR 7(2)(b),(c)

19.86 FTPR 36; NIDAR99 56(1),(2)

Setting aside decisions

19.87 If a tribunal decision is 'set aside' this means that the decision is cancelled and a new first-tier tribunal must be arranged. Any party to the proceedings may apply for a decision of a first-tier tribunal to be set aside by a legally qualified tribunal member. The member may set the decision aside where it appears just on the ground that:

- a document relating to the proceedings was not sent to, or was not received at an appropriate time by, any of the parties to the proceedings or their representatives or was not received at an appropriate time by the person who made the decision;
- any party to the proceedings or their representative was not present at the hearing.

19.88 In determining whether it is just to set aside a decision on the ground that someone was not present, the tribunal member must consider whether the party making the application gave notice that they wished to have an oral hearing. If not, the decision cannot be set aside unless the tribunal member is satisfied that the interests of justice obviously support acceptance of the set aside application.

19.89 An application for a set aside must:

- be made within one month of the date on which a copy of the decision notice is sent or given to the parties, or the statement of the reasons for the decision is given or sent in, whichever is the later;
- be in writing; and
- be signed by a party to the proceedings or, where the party has provided written authority to a representative to act on their behalf, that representative;
- contain particulars of the grounds on which it is made; and
- be sent to the clerk to the appeal tribunal.

Extending the time limits for applying for a set aside

19.90 A late application for set aside can be made up to one year after the end of the one month time limit (but only one such application can be made per decision). It must give the reasons for the lateness and is determined by a legally qualified panel member. Every party to the proceedings must be sent a copy and given a reasonable opportunity of making representations on it before it is determined. A late application for set aside is accepted if:

- it is in the interests of justice to do so (as described in paras 19.40-41); and
- there are reasonable prospects of success in the application to set aside.

19.87 FTPR 37; NIDAR99 57(1)

19.88 NIDAR99 57(2)

19.90 NIDAR 99(2),(4),(7),(9)-(12)

Notifying the decision on the application to set aside

19.91 Every party to the proceedings must receive a written notice of the decision on an application to set aside as soon as practicable. The notice must contain a statement giving the reasons for the decision.

19.92 There is no right of appeal against the outcome of a set aside request. If the request is refused, however, the time limit for appealing to the commissioner does not start until the notice of the set aside decision has been issued and the application to set aside may be treated as an application for a statement of the reasons for the tribunal's decision, subject to the normal time limits (paras. 19.78-79).

Appeals to upper tribunals

19.93 An appeal against a first-tier tribunal decision can be made to an upper-tier tribunal, but only if:

- the person is entitled to appeal (para. 19.99); and
- their grounds of appeal are that the first-tier tribunal made an error of law (para. 19.98).

19.94 Upper tribunals give interpretations of the law which are binding on all decision makers and first-tier appeal tribunals. Their judges are barristers, solicitors or advocates of not less than ten years' standing who are specialists in social security law, and have a legal status comparable to that of a High Court judge in their specialised area. The DWP gives good guidance on appeals to commissioners (GM paras. C7.550-846). Detailed advice, along with copies of the forms, are at the commissioners' web sites *www.osscsc.gov.uk* and *www.ossc-scotland.org.uk* and for Northern Ireland at *www.courtsni.gov.uk.* Before 3rd November 2008, appeals to an upper tribunal were called appeals to a commissioner.

Leave to appeal and the appeal itself

19.95 Appeals to an upper tribunal should be made on form UT1 (or UT2 for authorities), which has sections for the various stages of seeking leave to appeal and the appeal itself. This should be done within one month of the date the first-tier tribunal's statement of reasons was sent, though this can be extended in special circumstances.

19.91 NIDAR99 57(5)

19.92 NIDAR99 57A(2)

19.93 CPSA sch 7 paras 8(1),(2),(7)(c),(8); NICPSA sch 7 paras 8(1),(2),(7)(c),(8); FTPR 38,39; UTPR 21; NIDAR99 58(1),(3); SSCPR 9,10,12,13; NISSCPR 9,10,12,13

19.96 The appeal goes first to the first-tier tribunal judge who dealt with the case, and if they give leave to appeal, the appeal goes ahead. If they do not, the person can seek leave to appeal from an upper tribunal judge within one month of that refusal (or longer in special circumstances). If the upper tribunal judge gives leave, the appeal goes ahead.

19.97 Most upper tribunal appeals are determined on paper without a hearing. Parties make their submissions in writing. However, parties may ask for an oral hearing. These take place in London, Edinburgh and Belfast and can be arranged elsewhere.

What is an error in a point of law?

19.98 An appeal to an upper tribunal can only be made on an error in a point of law. An error in a point of law is where, for example *(R(IS) 11/99)*, the appeal tribunal:

- failed to apply the correct law;
- wrongly interpreted the relevant Acts or Regulations;
- followed a procedure that breached the rules of natural justice;
- took irrelevant matters into account, or did not consider relevant matters, or did both of these things;
- did not give adequate reasons in the full statement of its decision (para. 19.75);
- gave a decision which was not supported by the evidence;
- decided the facts in such a way that no person properly instructed as to the relevant law, and acting judicially, could have come to the decision made by the tribunal.

Who can apply for leave to appeal?

19.99 Where the disputed decision relates to housing benefit, the following can apply for leave to appeal to an upper tribunal:

- the claimant;
- any other 'person affected' by the decision (para. 19.2) provided that they were the appellant or a party at the first-tier appeal tribunal proceedings;
- the authority against whose decision the appeal to the first-tier tribunal was brought;
- the Secretary of State (the Department for Social Development in Northern Ireland).

19.98 CPSA sch 7 para 8(1); NICPSA sch 7 para 8(1)

19.99 UTPR 2(1); NISSCPR 4(1)

Appeals against an upper tribunal's decision

19.100 There is a right to appeal against an upper tribunal's decision to the Court of Appeal or the Court of Session in Scotland (and after that to the House of Lords). An appeal can only be made on a point of law. Leave to appeal must be obtained from the upper tribunal judge or, if they refuse, from the relevant court. The time limit for applying for leave to appeal to the upper tribunal judge is three months, but they may extend this time limit. If leave to appeal is refused the application may be renewed in the relevant court within six weeks. If the upper tribunal judge grants leave the appeal must be made to the relevant court within six weeks.

19.101 Separately from the above, cases involving European Union law can be referred by upper tribunals direct to the European Court of Justice.

Rent officer appeals

Appeals and errors in Great Britain

19.102 This section deals with appeals to the rent officer in non-LHA cases (chapter 9) in Great Britain. (For Northern Ireland see para. 19.113.) There is no right of appeal to a tribunal against the rent officer's figures. Instead, the following procedures apply. They have been considered by the courts to be sufficiently independent to comply with the Human Rights Act: *R (on the application of Cumpsty) v The Rent Service.*

Appeals by the claimant

19.103 If a claimant makes written representations to the authority relating wholly or partly to any determination by the rent officer (and does so within one month of notification of the HB decision based on that rent officer determination), the authority must, within seven days of receipt, apply to the rent officer for a re-determination for the case in question. The authority must forward the claimant's representations at the same time. This must be done even if the representations are made by a later claimant at the same address. There are however limitations (in the next paragraph).

19.104 For any claimant and any dwelling, only one application to the rent officer may be made in respect of any determination (plus one in respect of any substitute determination: para. 19.110). This is the case regardless of whether the authority itself has previously chosen to make an application for a re-determination.

19.100 UTPR 44; NISSCPR 33

19.103 HB 16; HB60+ 16

19.104 HB 16; HB60+ 16

19.105 However, a claimant who considers that a referral should or should not have been made in the first place has the right to use the ordinary HB appeals procedure to challenge this. This is because the determination whether or not to refer a case to the rent officer is made by the authority.

Appeals by the authority

19.106 The authority may itself choose to apply to the rent officer for a re-determination. For any particular claimant and any particular dwelling, it may do this only once in respect of any particular determination (plus once in respect of any particular substitute determination: para. 19.110); unless a re-determination is subsequently made as a result of an appeal by the claimant (para. 19.103), in which case the authority may do this once more.

Rent officer re-determinations

19.107 In each of the cases described above (paras. 19.103-106), the rent officer must make a complete re-determination. Even if the application for a re-determination relates only to one figure, the rent officer has to reconsider all matters pertaining to the case in question. All the assumptions, etc, applying to determinations (para. 10.27 onwards) apply equally to re-determinations. Re-determinations should be made within 20 working days or as soon as practicable after that. The period begins on the day the rent officer receives the application from the authority or (if he or she has requested this) on the day he or she receives further information needed from the authority.

19.108 The rent officer making the re-determination (called a 're-determination officer') must seek and have regard to the advice of one or two other rent officers. In England, the Rent Service (formerly the rent officer service) has set up independent re-determination units and advises that reasons for their re-determinations are always supplied to the claimant and the authority. Similar arrangements are in place in Wales and Scotland. It would certainly be open to challenge if reasons were not given (as happened fairly frequently in the past).

Rent officer errors

19.109 The rent officer has a duty to notify the authority, as soon as is practicable, upon discovering that he or she has made an error, other than one of professional judgment, in a determination or re-determination (including a substitute determination or substitute re-determination). The authority must then apply to the rent officer for a substitute determination (or substitute re-determination), and the DWP advises (circular HB/CTB G5/2005) that only one such application need be made covering all future cases (rather than the authority applying on a case by case basis).

19.107 HB 15; HB60+ 15; ROO 4, sch 3

19.109 ROO 4A(1),(7)

19.110 The authority must apply, on a case by case basis, to the rent officer for a substitute determination (or substitute re-determination) if it discovers that it made an error in its application to the rent officer as regards the size of the dwelling, the number of occupiers, the composition of the household or the terms of the tenancy. In all such cases, the authority must state the nature of the error and withdraw any outstanding applications for rent officer determinations in that case.

19.111 All the assumptions, etc, applying to determinations (para. 10.27 onwards) also apply to substitute determinations/re-determinations.

The date the re-determination affects HB

19.112 Whenever the rent officer issues a re-determination, substitute determination, or substitute re-determination (for the reasons in paras. 19.107-109), the new rent officer figures apply as follows.

- If the effect of the new figures would be to increase the amount of the claimant's eligible rent, the authority alters its original decision from the date it took effect (or should have). So the claimant gets his or her arrears. This is a revision.
- If the effect of the new figures would be to reduce the amount of the claimant's eligible rent, the authority alters its original decision from the Monday following the date the rent officer made the re-determination, substitute determination or substitute re-determination. So the claimant (if the authority acts promptly) does not suffer from an overpayment. This is a supersession.

Appeals and errors in Northern Ireland

19.113 In Northern Ireland it is the NIHE which sets the figures which may restrict a claimant's eligible rent. Such decisions cannot be appealed to a social security tribunal, but the claimant can ask the NIHE to reconsider in the normal way. The new figures apply as follows:

- If the effect of the new figures would be to increase the amount of the claimant's eligible rent, and the claimant made the request within one month of the original decision (or longer in special circumstances: paras. 19.6 and 19.10), the NIHE alters its original decision from the date it took effect (or should have). So the claimant gets his or her arrears. This is a revision.
- If the effect of the new figures would be to increase the amount of the claimant's eligible rent, and the claimant's request was outside the above

19.110 ROO 4A(1)

19.111 ROO 4A(2)

19.112 DAR 4(3),7(2)(c),8(6),10

19.113 NIDAR 4(1) sch para 1

time limit, the NIHE alters its original decision from the date of the claimant's request (paras. 19.21-22). This is a supersession.

- If the effect of the new figures would be to reduce the amount of the claimant's eligible rent, the NIHE's normal practice (except perhaps in the case of misrepresentation or fraud) is to treat the request as a change of circumstances (i.e. a change in the housing market conditions) and alter its original decision from the date of the request (paras. 19.21-22). This is a supersession.

20 Migrants and recent arrivals

20.1 This chapter describes the rules about people whose rights to enter and remain in the UK are controlled by the immigration authorities and other people who are free enter the UK but who have only recently arrived here. It covers the rules concerning refugees and other people seeking humanitarian protection, British nationals, European Economic Area nationals and other foreign nationals. This chapter contains the rules concerning:

- the three tests that apply to migrants and recent arrivals;
- asylum seekers, refugees and other people seeking permission to enter the UK on humanitarian grounds;
- non-EEA nationals and the immigration control test;
- the right to reside test;
- EEA nationals;
- accession state nationals; and
- the habitual residence test.

The three tests

20.2 There are three separate tests by which a migrant or new arrival can be excluded from HB/CTB. A person will be excluded from HB/CTB if any of the following apply:

- he or she is a person who is 'subject to immigration control' (para. 20.21);
- he or she does not have a right to reside in the UK (para. 20.33-35);
- he or she is a person who is not habitually resident in the British Isles or Ireland (para. 20.75).

A claimant may be subject to one or more of these tests at any one time depending on their nationality, immigration status and any past period of residence in the UK.

20.3 A person who is subject to immigration control will continue to be excluded from benefit indefinitely until their immigration status changes. The right to reside test may also exclude a person from HB/CTB indefinitely, except in the case of EEA nationals who can influence their right to reside by changing their economic status (i.e. by taking up work). The habitual residence test normally only affects those who have only recently entered the UK or who have no previous record of lawful residence. The habitual residence test will normally only disqualify a person from benefit for a limited period and will in any case not normally be applied to a person who has lived in the UK for two years (para. 20.78).

The effect of the three tests on claims by couples

20.4 There is some dispute as to how the immigration status test affects couples. There are two possibilities but it seems likely that the correct approach is that the test applies only to the claimant and not their partner. If this is the case, then where only one member is subject to immigration control the one who is not will be eligible for HB/CTB provided that they make the claim. See paragraph 20.22 for further details.

20.5 Both the right to reside test and the habitual residence test can only disqualify the claimant from benefit. Therefore where only one member of a couple is affected they can often avoid being disqualified by swapping who makes the claim (para. 20.34).

Deciding which of the three tests to apply

20.6 Some claimants are not affected by all three tests because either their immigration status ensures that they pass it or because the HB/CTB rules exempt them from it. Deciding which tests are relevant is not straightforward. Broadly, those who have leave (table 20.1) will also have the right to reside test and all EEA nationals will pass the immigration control test. All claimants are subject to the habitual residence test unless specifically exempted (para. 20.75).

20.7 To assist the reader in determining which of the three tests apply, this chapter has been set out according to the following categories of claimant:

- persons granted leave on humanitarian grounds (e.g. refugees);
- non-EEA foreign nationals;
- EEA nationals (i.e. nationals from member states of the European Economic Area: table 20.2).

Asylum seekers and refugees, etc

20.8 This section sets out the rules for people seeking asylum in the UK or who have applied for the right to remain in the UK for other humanitarian reasons. Most asylum seekers are excluded from HB/CTB (para. 20.9) while their application is processed, and also following a decision if asylum is refused. If asylum is granted or the authorities grant permission to stay in the UK for other reasons then benefit can be awarded (paras. 20.13-17).

Asylum seekers

20.9 An asylum seeker is someone who applies to enter the UK on the grounds that they have a reasonable fear of persecution in their home country. While their asylum application is processed they will be granted 'temporary admission' by the immigration authorities (table 20.1). An asylum seeker who is entitled to

20.9 IAA99 115(1),(3),(9)

JSA(IB)/ESA(IR)/IS or guarantee credit will be entitled to HB/CTB *(CH/2060/2006)* in all other cases, except where identified by paragraphs 20.10-12. A person whose asylum application has not yet been finally determined will be 'subject to immigration control' (para. 20.21) and excluded from HB/CTB. Their only rights to support are through the UK Border Agency asylum support scheme.

Asylum seekers from EEA, ECSMA or CESC states

20.10 Although all EEA nationals are exempt from immigration control, an asylum seeker who is an EEA national will have to show that they have a 'right to reside' (para. 20.35) and pass the habitual residence test (paras. 20.75-95) in the same way as any other EEA national in order to qualify for HB/CTB.

20.11 Asylum seekers from ECSMA or CESC states which are not also EEA states (table 20.2) (i.e. as at 1st April 2009 Turkey, Croatia and Macedonia) will be entitled to HB/CTB if they have a right to reside and are habitually resident (paras. 20.30-31). The ECSMA and CESC treaties do not confer any direct right to reside or right to benefit *(CH/2321/2007)*. Temporary admission (table 20.1) does not qualify as a right to reside (para. 20.31).

Transitionally protected asylum seekers

20.12 If the claim for asylum was made before 3rd April 2000, and the applicant has still not received a decision on their asylum claim, then they may be entitled to HB/CTB: see GM C4.280-331 for details.

Persons granted asylum – refugees

20.13 An asylum seeker whose application for asylum is accepted will receive a 'grant of asylum' and acquire refugee status. All refugees together with their dependants are granted leave (table 20.1) without a public funds restriction and so are not 'subject to immigration control' (para. 20.21). They are also exempt from the habitual residence test and so are entitled to HB/CTB from the date their refugee status is confirmed.

Persons granted humanitarian protection or discretionary leave

20.14 A person whose claim for asylum has been refused (i.e. is not a refugee) may nevertheless be granted 'humanitarian protection' or 'discretionary leave' if there are other humanitarian or exceptional reasons why they should not be returned to their country of origin. Both types of leave are granted at the discretion of the Home Secretary.

20.10 IAA99 115(1),(3),(9); SI 2000 No. 636 sch para 4; NISR 2000 No. 71 sch para 4

20.12 CPR sch 3 para 6(1)-(3); NICPR sch 3 para 6(1)-(2)

20.13 HB 10(1)(3B)(g); HB60+ 10(1)(4A)(g); NIHB 10(1)(5)(g); NIHB60+ 10(1)(5)(g); CTB 7(1)(4A)(g); CTB60+ 7(1)(4A)(g); CPR sch 4 paras 2-4; NICPR sch 4 paras 2-4

20.14 HB 10(3B)(h); HB60+ 10(4A)(h); NIHB 10(5)(h); NIHB60+ 10(5)(h); CTB 7(4A)(h); CTB60+ 7(4A)(h)

20.15 Humanitarian protection is a form of leave granted if there are substantial grounds for believing that the person concerned would face a real risk of serious harm if they return to their country of origin.

20.16 Discretionary leave (table 20.1) is only granted to those who do not fit the criteria for humanitarian protection and in limited circumstances.

20.17 A person granted either form of leave is not 'subject to immigration control' (para. 20.21) and is exempt from the habitual residence test and so will be entitled to HB/CTB from the date their status is confirmed. However, unlike refugees, their status does not confer rights on their family members to come to live with them.

Evacuees (Kosovo, Lebanon, Montserrat, Zimbabwe, etc)

20.18 Occasionally the government will grant 'leave' to persons who are evacuated to the UK to escape a specific humanitarian crisis (e.g. war, famine or natural disaster). Evacuees who are granted discretionary leave or humanitarian protection will be entitled to HB/CTB (para. 20.14). A person granted any other form of leave will be subject to the habitual residence test, except Montserrat evacuees and Zimbabwe nationals who have been offered settlement by the UK government at any time during the period 28/2/2009-17/3/2011, who are exempt from it. For the status of evacuees from the war in the Lebanon in July 2006 and Kosovo in 1999 see circular U10/2006 and GM C4 Annex D.

Non-EEA nationals and immigration control

Who is a non-EEA national?

20.19 This section (paras. 20.20-32) sets out rules for foreign nationals who are not nationals of the common travel area, another EEA member state or Switzerland (table 20.2). In this section these claimants are referred to as non-EEA nationals.

Entitlement to HB/CTB for non-EEA nationals

20.20 A non-EEA national will only be entitled to HB/CTB if they:

- are not 'subject to immigration control'; and
- have a right to reside (para. 20.35); and
- are either habitually resident in the common travel area or exempt from the habitual residence test (paras. 20.75-95).

20.18 IAA99 115(9); HB 10(3B)(h),(j),(jj); HB60+ 10(4A)(h),(j),(jj); NIHB 10(5)(h),(j),(kk); NIHB60+ 10(5)(h),(j),(kk); CTB 7(4A)(h),(j),(jj); CTB60+ 7(4A)(h),(j),(jj); SI 2006 No 1981; NISR 2006 No 320

20.20 IAA99 115(9); HB 10; HB60+ 10; NIHB 10; NIHB60+ 10; CTB 7; CTB60+ 7

Persons who are subject to immigration control

20.21 Except where they are exempted by the regulations (paras. 20.29) a non-EEA national will be subject to immigration control and excluded from HB/CTB if they are a person who:

- requires 'leave' to enter or remain in the UK but does not have it (i.e. an illegal entrant or overstayer) (table 20.1);
- has leave to enter or remain in the UK but on condition that they have 'no recourse to public funds' (e.g. most visitors or students);
- has 'leave' to enter or remain in the UK given as a result of a maintenance undertaking (i.e. a UK resident has formally agreed to sponsor him or her);
- has 'leave' to enter or remain in the UK only while waiting for the outcome of an appeal against a decision to vary, or to refuse to vary, any limited leave.

Couples and the immigration status test

20.22 Where only one member is subject to immigration control, the test only affects the claimant – in which case if the claim is made by the member who is not subject to immigration control then they will be entitled to HB/CTB (GM C4.218). When the claimant is eligible but their partner is an asylum seeker supported by UKBA they should be treated as a couple and the UKBA support should be counted as income (GM C4.128).

Meaning of leave and other immigration terms

20.23 Whether a person requires 'leave' (legal permission) to enter the UK by the immigration authorities is determined by the 'immigration rules' (table 20.1). Nearly all non-EEA nationals will require leave to enter the UK. Leave can be granted for a fixed period or open ended ('indefinite') and with or without a public funds condition (i.e. 'no recourse to public funds'). Most immigrants with limited leave (including those allowed to work) will will be subject to a public funds condition. Table 20.1 describes the meaning of 'leave' and other immigration terminology.

20.24 A person who has leave may apply for its terms to be varied at any time while it is still current. Provided the application is made in the form required and before the leave period expires, the applicant will continue to be treated as having leave until their application has been decided and a further 28 days after any decision to refuse have passed (Section 3, Immigration and Asylum Act 1999). The DWP and authorities often wrongly terminate benefit in these cases.

20.21 IAA99 115(1),(9)

20.25 A person may be granted leave to remain in the UK to join a family member (often referred to as a 'sponsor') on the understanding that their sponsor will provide their maintenance and accommodation. Some applicants are given two years leave, subject to a public funds condition, after which they can apply for indefinite leave to remain (table 20.1). Others, usually elderly dependants, are granted indefinite leave to remain on arrival, but their sponsor has to sign a written agreement (a maintenance 'undertaking') to support them. This excludes them from HB/CTB and other public funds (table 20.1) for five years unless their sponsor dies (paras. 20-28-29).

20.26 For HB/CTB purposes a 'sponsored' immigrant will only be 'subject to immigration control' if their sponsor has signed a formal undertaking to support them. A signed statement will only amount to an 'undertaking' if it is a clear promise to support that person in the future. A statement of ability and willingness to support that person is not sufficient to amount to an undertaking *(R(IS) 8/05)* but a written undertaking not given on an official form my still be a formal undertaking affecting benefit entitlement *(R(IS)11/04).*

Table 20.1 Some immigration terminology

UK Border Agency (UKBA)	The executive agency of the Home Office responsible for immigration, nationality and asylum (including asylum support).
Discretionary leave	A form of exceptional leave reserved for asylum cases (para. 20.16).
Exceptional leave	A form of leave granted by the Home Secretary outside the immigration rules on humanitarian grounds.
Illegal entrant	A person who enters the UK without leave and who has not been granted temporary admission.
Immigration rules	The legal rules which determine entry to the UK, administered by UKBA officers. *(www.ukba.homeoffice.gov.uk/policyandlaw/immigrationlaw/immigrationrules/)*

Leave	Legal permission to be in the UK granted by UKBA officers in accordance with the immigration rules (or in exceptional circumstances outside the immigration rules at the discretion of the Home Secretary). Leave can be for a fixed period (limited leave, e.g. a visa) or open ended (indefinite leave) and with or without a public funds condition (i.e. 'no recourse to public funds'). The length and terms of any leave can be varied if an application is made before it has expired (para. 20.24).
Overstayer	A person whose leave has expired and has not been renewed and for whom no appeal is pending.
Public funds	A claim for any of the following benefits or assistance: ◆ JSA(IB)/ESA(IR)/IS, state pension credit, housing benefit, council tax benefit, child tax credit and working tax credit; ◆ most other non-contributory social security benefits; ◆ housing assistance provided under the homeless persons legislation or the allocation of housing by a local authority.
Right of abode	A person with a right of abode is entirely free from UK immigration control. It applies to all British Citizens but not necessarily other forms of British nationality. Certain citizens of Commonwealth countries also have the right of abode and can apply for a certificate to prove this (a sticker in their passport).
Settled status	Describes a person subject to immigration control who has been granted indefinite leave to remain by the immigration authorities. Their passport may be endorsed as such and accompanied by an authenticating stamp issued by the UKBA, or they may have a letter confirming that indefinite leave to remain has been granted.
Temporary admission	The period of grace allowed a person who has entered the UK while their application for leave or for asylum is determined. Temporary admission is not a form of leave. A person who has been granted it will be 'lawfully present' but will not have a 'right to reside' (para. 20.31).

People who satisfy the immigration control test

20.27 The following people satisfy the immigration control test:

- nationals of an EEA member state (including the accession states);
- non-EEA nationals who are family members of EEA nationals;
- British passport holders who are British citizens or who have 'right of abode' in the UK (table 20.1);
- citizens of countries in the Common Travel Area (table 20.2);
- holders of passports showing them as having the right of abode in the UK (GM C4.33);
- persons who have settled status (table 20.1) (GM C4.33);
- any person who has any form of leave (table 20.1) whether limited or indefinite, provided it is not subject to a public funds condition or a maintenance undertaking (paras. 20.23-26).

All of the above will also have a right to reside in the UK.

People who are exempt from the immigration control test

20.28 For HB/CTB purposes all EEA nationals (table 20.2) are defined as not being subject to immigration control. Certain other categories of claimant who would otherwise be subject to the test are exempted from it by regulations (para. 20.29). Note that where a claimant falls within one of these exempt categories it will override any public funds condition (i.e. 'no recourse to public funds') that would otherwise exclude them from HB/CTB (Rule 6B of the Immigration Rules).

20.29 The exempt groups are:

- ECSMA or CESC nationals who are 'lawfully present' (paras. 20.30-31);
- people admitted to the UK as sponsored immigrants, as a result of a maintenance undertaking, who have been resident for less than five years and whose sponsor (or all of their sponsors if there is more than one) has died;
- people admitted to the UK as sponsored immigrants, as a result of a maintenance undertaking, who have been resident for five years or more;
- people with limited leave whose funds have been temporarily disrupted (para. 20.32).

ECSMA/CESC nationals

20.30 A national of a non-EEA state which has ratified either the European Convention on Social and Medical Assistance (ECSMA) or the Council of Europe Social Charter (CESC) and who is 'lawfully present' in the UK will be exempt from

20.27 IAA99 115(1),(3),(9); SI 2006 No. 1003 Reg 14; SI 2000 No. 636 sch; NISR 2000 No. 71 sch

20.28 IAA99 115(1),(3)(9); SI 2000 No. 636 sch; NISR 2000 No. 71 sch

the immigration control test. ECSMA and CESC member states as at 1st April 2009 are identified in table 20.2. An up-to-date list of countries that have ratified these treaties can be found on-line at *http://conventions.coe.int* (treaties 14 and 35 on the full list).

20.31 A person will be lawfully present in the UK if they have any form of 'leave' or if they have been granted 'temporary admission' (table 20.1): *Szoma (FC) v Secretary of State for Work and Pensions* reported as *R(IS) 2/06.* However, temporary admission (table 20.1) does not amount to a right to reside *(R(IS) 8/07)* and so these claimants will not be entitled to HB/CTB unless they have some other right to reside (para 20.35). The ECSMA/CESC treaties do not confer any direct right to reside or right to benefit *(CH/2321/2007).*

Claimants with limited leave – funds disrupted

20.32 Claimants with limited leave to remain in the UK (and thus normally ineligible for HB/CTB: para. 20.23), but whose funds have been temporarily interrupted, are entitled to HB/CTB for up to 42 days in any one period of leave provided that there is a reasonable expectation that the funds will be resumed. If the disruption of funds has already exceeded 42 days by the time the claim is made, there is no entitlement to HB/CTB *(CH/4248/2006).*

The right to reside

The right to reside test

20.33 In order to qualify for HB/CTB the claimant must have a right to reside in the UK or any other part of the common travel area (table 20.2). The test is intended to prevent someone who has no intention of working from acquiring the right to benefit simply by living in the UK for a reasonably lengthy period. The test applies to all claimants but its main effect is to disqualify economically inactive EEA nationals.

Couples and the right to reside test

20.34 The right to reside test (and the habitual residence test) only applies to the claimant. So where one member of a couple has a right to reside (e.g. as a British citizen) they can normally claim on behalf of their partner and avoid being disqualified from HB/CTB. However, this will not work where the person with the right to reside is not actually liable for rent (e.g. their partner is the sole tenant) (note the rules in paragraph 2.31 do not assist the claim in these cases).

20.30 SI 2000 No. 636 sch para 4; NISR 2000 No. 71 sch para 4

20.32 HB 10(4); HB 10(5); NIHB 10(6); NIHB60+ 10(6); CTB 7(5); CTB60+ 7(5); SI 2000 No. 636 sch para 1; NISR 2000 No. 71 sch para 1

20.33 HB 10(3); HB60+ 10(3); NIHB 10(3); NIHB60+ 10(3); CTB 7(3); CTB60+ 7(3)

20.34 HB 10(1); HB60+ 10(1); NIHB 10(1); NIHB60+ 10(1); CTB 7(1); CTB60+ 7(1)

Who has a right to reside and entitlement to HB/CTB?

20.35 To be entitled to HB/CTB the claimant must have a right to reside and be either habitually resident (paras. 20.75-95) or exempt from the habitual residence test (paras. 20.76-78). The claimant will have a right to reside if they are:

(a) a British citizen or other passport holder with a 'right of abode' (table 20.1) in the UK (para. 20.36);

(b) a citizen of any other common travel area territory (para. 20.36);

(c) a person who has settled status (table 20.1);

(d) a person who has any form of 'leave' (table 20.1) provided it is not subject to a public funds condition or a maintenance undertaking (paras. 20.23-26);

(e) a person who has transitional protection from the right to reside test (para. 20.37);

(f) an EEA national who is a 'qualified person' (para. 20.41) except A8 or A2 nationals who have not yet completed their one year qualifying period in legal work (paras. 20.72-74);

(g) an EEA national with a 'permanent right of residence' (para. 20.54) except A8 or A2 nationals who have not yet completed their one year qualifying period in legal work (paras. 20.72-74);

(h) a 'family member' of a person who satisfies items (f) or (g);

(i) an A8 (table 20.2) self-employed person or a worker who is either registered for work or exempt from the requirement to register (paras. 20.63, 20.65-66);

(j) an A2 (table 20.2) self-employed person or a worker who is either in authorised work or exempt from the requirement to be authorised (paras. 20.63, 20.69-70).

British and Irish citizens and their family members

20.36 All British and Irish citizens have the right to reside in the common travel area (table 20.2). This right applies regardless of economic status or whether they were born or brought up there. These claimants can therefore only be disqualified by the habitual residence test which is only likely if they are visiting the common travel area for the first time (e.g. born abroad to British parents). Note that British citizens cannot normally benefit from EEA 'worker' status (para. 20.51) and therefore a spouse (or other person) cannot acquire a right to reside through them as an EEA family member *(McCarthy v Secretary of State for the Home Department)*. However, a UK national may acquire EEA worker status if they work for a period in another EEA state and then return to the UK (paras. 20.91-95).

20.35 HB 10(3),(3B); HB60+ 10(3),(4A); NIHB 10(3),(5); NIHB60+ 10(3),(5); CTB 7(3),(3B); CTB60+ 7(3),(4A)

Transitional protection from the right to reside test

20.37 A claimant will be transitionally protected from the right to reside test if they were entitled to HB/CTB on 30th April 2004 (including a claim backdated to that date) and have remained entitled without any gaps to at least one of the following benefits since: HB, CTB, IS or any kind of JSA or state pension credit. Note that entitlement to HB or CTB will likewise preserve protection for IS, JSA or pension credit.

EEA nationals

Who is an EEA national?

20.38 This section (paras. 20.38-60) sets out rules for nationals of member states (and their family members) of the European Union (EU) and the other EEA states and Switzerland (table 20.2). The guide refers to all of these claimants as EEA nationals. EEA nationals who have a right to reside, other than those rights set out in paragraph 20.40, will be entitled to HB/CTB provided they are also habitually resident: see paragraph 20.35 for details. Broadly, for an EEA national to have a right to reside they must be a qualified person (para. 20.41) or be the family member of a qualified person (para. 20.58).

20.39 The right of EU nationals to live, work and claim benefits in another member state are set out in EU Directive 2004/38/EC. The Directive is given effect in the UK by the Immigration (European Economic Area) Regulations 2006 ('the EEA regulations'). The rights set out in the EEA regulations apply to nationals of all EEA states and of Switzerland (table 20.2). However, certain restrictions apply to nationals from the eight Eastern European states that became EU members in May 2004 (known as the 'A8 states') and Bulgaria and Romania (known as the 'A2 states') which became EU members in January 2007. These ten states are collectively known as 'accession states'. The rules for accession state nationals are described in paragraphs 20.61-74.

EEA nationals with a right to reside who are not entitled to HB/CTB

20.40 EU directive 2004/38/EC gives a right of residence to all economically inactive EU nationals and their family members for the first three months of their stay in the UK. Article 39 of the EU treaty gives jobseekers the right to reside in a member state while actively seeking work. However, the directive permits member states to exclude the beneficiaries of both these rights from social assistance (i.e. HB/CTB/ESA(IR)/IS/state pension credit), except job-seekers who are entitled to claim JSA(IB) (para. 20.42). These exclusions are given effect in the HB/CTB regulations. Economically inactive EEA nationals who are not workers (or

---

20.37 CPR sch 3 para 6(4); NICPR sch 3 para 6(3)

20.38 EEA 2

20.40 HB 10(3A); HB60+ 10(4); NIHB 10(4); NIHB60+ 10(4); CTB 7(4); CTB60+ 7(4)

treated as workers) or who have not otherwise acquired a permanent right of residence cannot rely on Articles 12 or 18 of the EU to establish a right to HB/CTB *(Abdirahman v Leicester City Council).*

Table 20.2 Member states of certain European treaties

Group	Member States
Common Travel Area	The UK, the Republic of Ireland, the Channel Islands and the Isle of Man.
EEA states (excluding Ireland and the UK)	Austria; Belgium; Cyprus; Denmark; Finland; France; Germany; Greece; Iceland[1]; Italy; Liechtenstein[1 2]; Luxembourg; Malta; Netherlands; Norway[1]; Portugal; Spain; Sweden; Switzerland[3].
A8 accession states	Czech Republic; Estonia; Hungary; Latvia; Lithuania[2]; Poland; Slovakia; Slovenia[2].
A2 accession states	Bulgaria; Romania.
ECSMA or CESC states (excluding EEA states)	As at 1 April 2009 the only states other than the EEA member states that have ratified either of the treaties are: Croatia; Macedonia; Turkey.

1. Indicates not a member of the European Union
2. Indicates has not a ratified either ECSMA or CESC
3. Switzerland is treated as part of the EEA by the EEA-Swiss agreement and EEA regulations (para. 20.39)

Who is a 'qualified person'?

20.41 A 'qualified person' is an EEA national who has a right to reside under the EEA regulations (para. 20.39). An EEA national will be a qualified person if they are:

(a) a self-employed person (para. 20.46);

(b) a worker (para. 20.47), including a person who retains their worker status while temporarily out of work;

(c) a jobseeker (para. 20.42);

(d) a student (para. 20.44); or

(e) a self-sufficient person (para. 20.45).

A self employed person or a worker will be exempt from the habitual residence test (para. 20.77) and so entitled to HB/CTB. Jobseekers, students and self-sufficient persons being economically inactive are only entitled to HB/CTB in certain circumstances: see the relevant paragraph for details. Note that 'jobseeker' has a very limited meaning and does not normally include someone who was previously a worker and who has subsequently become unemployed (para. 20.42).

Jobseekers

20.42 A jobseeker is an EEA national, other than a national from one of the accession states (see para. 20.65 for exceptions) who enters the UK seeking work and who has a genuine chance of being employed. It does not include someone who starts work in the UK and who subsequently becomes unemployed and who retains their worker status (in which case see paragraph 20.52). Jobseekers are excluded from most forms of social assistance but they are entitled to JSA(IB) (or IS provided they are genuinely seeking work (*CH/3314/2005* and *CIS/184/2008*)). Where a jobseeker is entitled to JSA(IB) they will also be entitled to HB/CTB.

20.43 However, where a jobseeker restricts the hours of work they are willing to accept to such an extent that their likely earnings together with any working tax credit would be less than the total of their JSA(IB) applicable amount plus their rent, then they will not be entitled to HB/CTB *(CH/3314/2005)*. In order to qualify, the work being sought must be 'genuine and effective' *(CIS/2364/2006)*.

Students and self-sufficient EEA nationals

20.44 Most students and other economically inactive EEA citizens who are not covered by a right described in paragraphs 20.52-56 below are excluded from HB/CTB. An EEA citizen, or their family member will, however, have the right to reside if they are self sufficient or, in the case of a student, they have provided the Secretary of State with a declaration that they are self-sufficient.

20.45 A person will be considered self-sufficient if they have comprehensive sickness insurance and they have sufficient resources for themselves and their family not to become 'a burden on the social assistance system'. Whether a person is a burden will depend on the personal circumstances of the applicant (GM C4.122). The guidance manual states that a person who has no prospect of finding work or becoming 'self-sufficient' will normally be considered a burden (GM C4.123). DWP guidance also suggests that when a person first claims benefit after having been in the UK for some time, the fact that they have been self-sufficient will be a factor in the decision, as will the length of time they are likely to be claiming benefits (GM C4.123).

20.41 EEA 6(1); HB 10(3),(3B); HB60+ 10(4A); NIHB 10(5); NIHB60+ 10(5); CTB 7(4A); CTB60+ 7(4A)

20.43 EEA 6(1),(4); HB 10(3B)(k); NIHB 10(5)(k)

20.44 EEA 4,6(1),14(1); HB 10(3); HB60+ 10(3); CTB 7(3); CTB60+ 7(3)

20.45 EEA 6(1),(3),14(1); HB 10(3B)(a),(b); HB60+ 10(4A)(a),(b); NIHB 10(5)(a),(b); NIHB60+ 10(5)(a),(b); CTB 7(4A)(a),(b); CTB60+ 7(4A)(a),(b)

Self-employed EEA nationals and EEA workers

20.46 A self-employed person (and members of their family) who is a national of an EEA member state (including the EU accession states) has a right to reside in the UK. Except in the case of A2 nationals, a person does not lose their self employed status while they are temporarily unable to work due to sickness or injury (para. 20.52). A woman will also retain her self-employed status while on maternity leave, provided she intends to return to work afterwards *(CIS/1042/2008).*

20.47 EEA nationals and their family members who are in paid employment, including A8 nationals who are registered and A2 nationals who are authorised, have a right to reside as 'workers'. The definition of 'worker' is exceptionally complex and an area of continually developing case law. The description which follows in paragraphs 20.48-51 can only be regarded as a broad summary. Further, except in the case of an accession national (for which see paras. 20.61-74), in certain circumstances a person who is temporarily out of work will be treated as a worker (para. 20.52).

20.48 To be classed as an 'EEA worker' a person must be currently, or in certain circumstances, previously have been (para. 20.52) engaged in remunerative work in the UK which is:

- 'effective and genuine'; and
- not 'on such a small scale as to be purely marginal and ancillary' *(R(IS) 12/98).*

20.49 No-one should be denied EEA worker status simply because the level of their earnings is insufficient to maintain them without supplementing their income with benefits *(Kempf v Staatssectaris van Justitie).* Mere entitlement to HB/CTB alone while engaged in work would not disqualify a claimant as a worker *(CH/3314/2005).*

20.50 The DWP suggests (GM C4 Annex B para. 6) that a number of factors should be considered before the authority decides whether any work done by the claimant is 'effective and genuine'. These include:

- the period of employment;
- the number of hours worked;
- the level of earnings;
- whether the work is regular or erratic; and
- whether the person has become voluntarily unemployed.

These factors are meant to be considered as a whole. The presence or absence of any one factor is not, by itself, conclusive.

20.51 EEA worker status does not normally include British citizens *(Raulin v Minister van Ondervijsen Wentenschappen)* because they have the right to reside and work in the UK without assistance from European law. However, a British citizen can acquire worker status by living and working in another EEA country (para. 20.92).

Persons who retain their worker status while temporarily out of work

20.52 Except in the case of an accession state national whose right to work is subject to conditions (paras. 20.65 and 20.68), an EEA national who was previously working in the UK but who is temporarily out of work will retain their worker status if they are a person who:

- is temporarily unable to work as a result of illness or accident (but this does not depend on the rules for incapacity benefit or ESA: *CIS/4304/2007*);
- is currently registered as a jobseeker; and who
  - was employed for one year or more before becoming unemployed; or
  - has been unemployed no more than six months; or
  - can provide evidence that they are seeking employment and have a genuine prospect of being engaged;
- is involuntarily unemployed and has started vocational training;
- has voluntarily stopped working and has started vocational training related to their previous employment.

A small gap between a person leaving employment and registering as a jobseeker can be ignored *(CIS/1934/2006)*.

20.53 Whether a person is 'voluntarily unemployed' is established by focusing on the question of whether the claimant is still active in the labour market rather than on the circumstances in which they ceased to be employed, although this may form part of the overall evidence as to their genuine intent *(CH/3314/2005)*. A person will lose their worker status if they withdraw from the labour market voluntarily and remain economically inactive *(CIS/3789/2006)*; a claim for IS is not in itself sufficient to retain worker status *(CIS/3779/2007)*.

Who has a permanent right of residence?

20.54 An EEA national who has lived in the UK for a continuous period of five years under a right to reside as defined by the EEA regulations (whether or not that right to reside allowed them to claim benefit) will acquire a permanent right of residence. Periods of residence as a qualified person count towards the five year period as does the initial three month right of residence (para. 20.41). A non-EEA national who has lived in the UK under their right as a family member for a continuous period of five years will also acquire a permanent right of residence. Certain EEA nationals and their family members who have retired from the UK labour market may also acquire a permanent right of residence (paras. 20.56-58). Once acquired, a permanent right of residence can only be lost through a period of absence from the UK which exceeds two years. A right of residence arising from UK legislation before a state accedes to the EU does not

---

20.51 EEA 6(2); HB 10(3B)(c); HB60+ 10(4A)(c); NIHB 10(5)(c); NIHB60+ 10(5)(c); CTB 7(4A)(c); CTB60+ 7(4A)(c)

20.54 EEA 5,15

count *(CPC/2134/2007)*. But periods of lawful residence under EC law including periods before 2/10/2000 (when the original EEA regulations came into force), or as a jobseeker before 30/04/2006, qualify *(Secretary of State for Work and Pensions v Lassal)*. However, this decision has been referred to the ECJ.

20.55 In calculating the five year qualifying period the following periods of absence from the UK are ignored:

- any periods which do not exceed six months in total in any year;
- any periods due to compulsory military service;
- any single period not exceeding 12 months which is due to an important reason such as pregnancy, childbirth, serious illness, study, vocational training or an overseas posting.

These periods are merely ignored: they do not count towards the five year qualifying period itself *(CIS/2258/2008)*.

Retired workers with a permanent right of residence

20.56 In certain circumstances an EEA national or a member of their family can acquire a right of permanent residence before completing five years employment or other lawful residence in the UK. An EEA national other than an accession state national whose right to work is subject to conditions (paras. 20.65 and 20-68), will acquire a right of permanent residence if they are a person who:

- has retired after working (including self employment) in the UK for at least 12 months prior to reaching age 65 (60 for a woman) and they have lived in the UK for more than three years continuously;
- has taken early retirement as an employee after working in the UK for at least 12 months and they have lived in the UK for more than three years continuously;
- has retired from work (including self employment) after reaching the age of 65 (60 for a woman) and their spouse or civil partner is a UK national;
- has taken early retirement as an employee and their spouse or civil partner is a UK national;
- has ceased working (including self-employment) as a result of permanent incapacity; and either
  - the incapacity is the result of an accident at work or an occupational disease which entitles them to a pension payable by a UK institution (including a pension paid by a private company), or
  - they have continuously resided in the UK for more than two years; or
  - their spouse or a civil partner is a UK national.

20.57 In calculating the length of employment with respect to one of the rights above any period of involuntary unemployment registered with the

20.55 EEA 3

Jobcentre, or period out of work due to illness, accident or some other reason 'not of [their] own making' will be treated as a period of employment.

Family members and the right of residence

20.58 Where an EEA national has a right to reside as a qualified person or as a person with a permanent right of residence then the right to reside will also extend to their family member. In this context member of family means:

(a) their spouse or registered civil partner (note that until a separated spouse is divorced he or she still qualifies as a spouse: *CIS/2431/2006*);

(b) their direct descendants who are aged under 21 (whether or not they are dependent on or live with the qualified person: *CF/1863/2007*);

(c) the dependants of that person or of their spouse or their registered civil partner;

(d) their dependent direct relatives in ascending line (i.e. parents, grandparents, etc) and those of their spouse or their registered civil partner;

(e) any other family member, irrespective of nationality, not included above, who holds a valid EEA family permit, registration certificate or residence card and who:

- in their country of origin is a dependant or member of the household of that EEA citizen;
- is a person whose serious health grounds strictly require personal care by the EEA citizen;
- has a partner with whom the EEA national has a 'durable relationship'.

20.59 A family member will acquire a permanent right of residence if:

- he or she is a family member of a worker or self employed person who has retired (para. 20.56);
- he or she was the family member of a worker or self-employed person who has died provided that they lived with that person immediately and the worker or self-employed person had lived in the UK at least two years before their death or the death resulted from an accident at work or occupational disease.

20.60 In certain circumstances a family member will retain their right of residence following their separation from the person with the right to reside whether that separation is caused by death, a relationship breakdown or the qualified person leaving the UK. A short gap between the qualified person leaving work and leaving the UK can be ignored *(CIS/608/2008).* A family member will retain their right to reside if:

20.58 EEA 7,8,14(2)

20.59 EEA 15(1)(d),(e)

- he or she had lived in the UK for at least a year as a family member immediately before the qualified person died;
- he or she was the spouse or civil partner of the qualified person and was attending an educational course immediately before the qualified person died/left the UK and they continue to attend that course;
- he or she is the direct descendant of a qualified person and was attending an educational course immediately before the qualified person died/left the UK and they continue to attend that course;
- he or she is the parent with custody of a child that satisfies the condition immediately above;
- he or she is a person who, if they were an EEA national, would satisfy item (a), (b) or (e) of paragraph 20.41 and who, while living in the UK, only ceased to be a family member when they divorced the qualified person and either:
  - prior to the legal proceedings to divorce the marriage/civil partnership had lasted for at least three years and both parties had lived in the UK for at least one year during its duration;
  - he or she or a family member was a victim of domestic violence during the relationship;
  - he or she has custody of a child of the qualified person;
  - he or she has a right of access to a child of the qualified person which must take place in the UK.

Accession state nationals

20.61 Rules restricting rights to live, work and claim benefits apply to certain nationals of the states that joined the EU in May 2004 (known as the 'A8') and January 2007 (known as the 'A2') – see table 20.2 for member states.

20.62 All restrictions outlined below that apply to nationals of these states are expected to be lifted after their countries have been members of the EU for seven years.

Accession state nationals who are not subject to restrictions

20.63 Restrictions on accession state nationals do not apply to the following claimants:

- any person who is currently engaged in self-employment in the UK (note the self employed are not required to register or seek authorisation to work). See paragraph 20.64 for those who are temporarily unable to work through sickness or injury);

20.60 EEA 10,14(3)

- certain persons in paid employment who are exempt from the requirement to register or receive authorisation to work (table 20.3);
- a person who would otherwise be required to register or obtain worker authorisation but who has since completed their 12 month qualifying period in registered or authorised work (paras. 20.65 and 20.69);
- students and other persons who are self sufficient (for which see paragraphs. 20.44-45).

All of the above are treated as any other EEA national (i.e. as if they were not from an accession state).

20.64 In addition, nationals from the A8 state who are self-employed but who are temporarily unable to work due to sickness or injury are treated as if they are in self-employment. Except where they are exempt from worker authorisation (table 20.3) there is no equivalent rule for A2 nationals.

Table 20.3: Accession state nationals who are allowed to work without conditions

A8 Nationals who are not subject to worker registration

(a) a person who had leave to enter the UK on the 30/04/04 which was not subject to any condition restricting their employment;

(b) a person who has legally worked in the UK for an uninterrupted period* of 12 months (whether that period started on, before or after 1st May 2004);

(c) a person who is also a national of the UK or another EEA state, other than an A8 or A2 state (i.e. has dual nationality);

(d) a person who is a family member** of an EEA national who has a right to reside in the UK other than an accession national who is subject to worker registration or worker authorisation who has not yet completed their one year qualifying period of work;

(e) a person who has been posted to work in the UK by an organisation that is based in another EEA member state.

20.63 SI 2004 No 1219 Reg 2(3),(4),(8); SI 2006 No 3317 Reg 2(3),(4),(12)

20.64 EEA 6(1),(3); SI 2004 No 1219 Reg 2(6)

T 20.3 SI 2004 No 1219 Reg 2(2)-(8); SI 2006 No 3317 Reg 2(2)-(12); HB 10(3B)(f); HB60+ 10(4A)(f); NIHB 10(5)(f); NIHB60+ 10(5)(f); CTB 7(4A)(f); CTB60+ 7(4A)(f)

A2 Nationals who are not subject to worker authorisation

(a) a person who has leave to enter the UK which is not subject to any condition restricting their employment;

(b) a person who has legally worked in the UK for an uninterrupted period* of 12 months (whether that period started on, before or after 1st January 2007);

(c) a person who is also a national of the UK or another EEA state, other than Bulgaria or Romania (i.e. has dual nationality);

(d) a person whose spouse or civil partner is either a UK national or a person with settled status (table 20.1);

(e) a person who has a permanent right of residence (para. 20.54);

(f) a person who is a family member** of an EEA national who has a right to reside in the UK other than an EEA national who is subject to worker authorisation;

(g) a person who meets the Home Office criteria to enter the UK under the highly skilled migrant programme and who holds a registration certificate that includes a statement that they have unrestricted access to the UK labour market;

(h) a student who does not work for more than 20 hours per week and who holds a registration certificate which allows them access to the UK labour market for up to 20 hours per week;

(i) a person who has been posted to work in the UK by an organisation that is based in another EEA member state.

* any intervening periods within the 12 months in which that person was not in work are ignored provided they do not together exceed 30 days.

** family member includes spouse, civil partner and any direct descendants up the age of 21, and certain other relatives.

A8 nationals required to register for work

20.65 Except as set out in paragraphs 20.63-64, most nationals from the A8 states are required to register with the Home Office for work during their first 12 months employment in the UK. After completing 12 months uninterrupted employment in registered work (paras. 20.72-74) they will be treated as any other EEA national (paras. 20.38-60). Not all A8 nationals are required to be registered for work: see table 20.3 for exceptions.

20.66 A8 nationals who are working while registered or who are working and exempt from worker registration (table 20.3) are entitled to HB/CTB. An A8 worker who is on maternity leave remains a worker while on leave *(CIS/4237/2007)*.

20.65 EEA 6(2); SI 2004 No 1219 Reg 5

20.67 All other A8 nationals who are not working and who would otherwise be required to register for work (i.e. anyone not included in paragraphs 20.63-64 or table 20.3) are not entitled to assistance.

A2 nationals requiring worker authorisation

20.68 Most A2 nationals can only take up work which has been 'authorised' by the Home Office. Authorised work is limited to certain specified occupations and in most cases the applicant must meet other further conditions. Except for applicants who are 'highly skilled', the numbers of applicants in each employment category are also subject to strict quotas.

20.69 Except as set out in paragraphs 20.63-64, most nationals from the A2 states must receive Home Office authorisation to work during their first 12 months employment in the UK. After completing 12 months continuous employment in authorised work (paras. 20.68-70) they will be treated as any other EEA national (paras. 20.38-60). Not all A2 nationals are required to obtain authorisation to work: see table 20.3 for exceptions.

20.70 A2 nationals who are authorised for work and who are working or who are working and exempt from worker authorisation (table 20.3) are entitled to HB/CTB.

20.71 All other A2 nationals who are not working and who would otherwise be required to be authorised for work (i.e. anyone not included in paragraph 20.63 or table 20.3) are not entitled to assistance.

Completing the 12 month qualifying period

20.72 After an accession state national has been legally working in the United Kingdom without interruption for 12 months, they are no longer required to be registered or authorised by the Home Office and acquire the right to be treated as any other (non accession state) EEA national (paras. 20.38-60). Certain accession state nationals are exempt from these requirements (table 20.3).

20.73 During this qualifying period work will count as 'legal' only if they hold the appropriate worker registration or authorisation document and, in the case of an A2 national, they are complying with any conditions set out in it (*CIS/3232/2006* and *CJSA/700/2007*).

20.74 A person will be treated as having completed their 12 month qualifying period if they are legally working at the beginning and end of that period and any intervening periods in which they were not legally working do not in total exceed 30 days.

20.71 SI 2006 No 3317 Reg 6

20.72 SI 2004 No 1219 Reg 2(3),(4),(8); SI 2006 No 3317 Reg 2(3),(4),(12)

The habitual residence test

20.75 Unless they are exempt (paras. 20.76-78) all claimants, irrespective of their nationality, have to satisfy the authority that they are 'habitually resident' in the United Kingdom, the Channel Islands, the Isle of Man or the Republic of Ireland to be entitled to HB/CTB. A person who is not habitually resident is a 'person from abroad' and not entitled to HB/CTB. For the effect of this test on couples, see paragraph 20.34.

Exempt claimants

20.76 The following claimants, whether or not they are EEA nationals, are exempt from the habitual residence test:

- a person in receipt of JSA(IB), ESA(IR), IS or state pension credit (but this does not include any period where the award of that benefit is later revised: *CH/411/2007*);
- a person granted refugee status or humanitarian protection;
- a person granted exceptional leave (including discretionary leave) (paras. 20.14 and table 20.1);
- a person who left the territory of Montserrat after 1st November 1995 because of the volcanic eruption;
- a Zimbabwe national who has been offered settlement by the UK government at any time during the period 28/2/2009-17/3/2011 (para. 20.18);
- a person not subject to immigration control and who is in the UK as a result of their deportation, expulsion or removal by compulsion of law from another country to the UK;
- a person whose funds have been temporarily disrupted (para. 20.32).

20.77 In addition, the following EEA nationals are also exempt:

- a person who is self-employed, a 'worker' (paras. 20.46-47) or a former worker who has retained worker status while temporarily out of work (para. 20.52);
- a person who is a 'family member' (para. 20.58) of a worker or self-employed person;
- a person who has acquired a right of permanent residence (para. 20.54);
- a person who is an A8 national who is working (or was within the last 30 days) and is registered under the Home Office Worker Registration Scheme or who is working and is exempt from the requirement to register;

20.75 HB 10(2); HB60+ 10(2); NIHB 10(2); NIHB60+ 10(2); CTB 7(2); CTB60+ 7(2)

20.76 HB 10(3B)(g)-(k),(4); HB60+ 10(4A)(g)-(k),(5); NIHB 10(5)(g)-(k),(6); NIHB60+ 10(5)(g)-(k),(6); CTB 7(4A)(g)-(k),(5); CTB60+ 7(4A)(g)-(k),(5)

20.77 HB 10(3B)(a)-(f); HB60+ 10(4A)(a)-(f); NIHB 10(5)(a)-(f); NIHB60+ 10(5)(a)-(f); CTB 7(4A)(a)-(f); CTB60+ 7(4A)(a)-(f)

- a person who is an A2 national who is working and who has obtained worker authorisation or who is exempt from the requirement to obtain authorisation.

20.78 DWP guidance suggests that the test should be applied to anyone who has entered the Common Travel Area in the last two years (GM C4.40). However, the guidance also stresses that the two year period is guidance only (given that most people who have been resident two years will satisfy it) and there is no requirement in the rules that a person is resident for a specific length of time (GM C4.42-43).

The meaning of habitual residence

20.79 The term 'habitual residence' is not defined in the regulations but it has been the subject of a substantial body of case law from the Commissioners, the UK courts and the European Court of Justice. The term has been adopted from European legislation, in particular EEC Regulation 1408/71 dealing with social security for migrant workers.

20.80 The test is 'intended to convey a degree of permanence in the [claimant's] residence in the Common Travel Area' (GM C4.80). Its purpose is to prevent the possibility that someone who has not lived in the UK but who has a right of residence could claim benefit immediately on their entry, for example a person born abroad to British parents who has British citizenship.

20.81 An authority must have evidence to support a decision that a claimant is not habitually resident. If there is no evidence then the authority must accept that the claimant is habitually resident *(R(IS) 6/96).*

20.82 Whether a person is habitually resident is a question of fact to be decided by reference to all the circumstances of the case *(Re: J (a minor) (abduction)).* All the facts must be considered and it is not possible to draw up a comprehensive list that can be applied to all cases *(R(IS) 6/96).*

20.83 A person cannot be habitually resident unless they are actually resident; a mere intention to reside is not sufficient *(CIS/15927/1996).* Residence is not the same as physical presence but implies a more settled state in which the person is seeking to make their home here. There is no requirement that it must be their only home, nor that it is permanent, provided it is a genuine home for the time being (R(IS) 6/96).

Acquiring habitual residence

20.84 A person may lose habitual residence in a single day if they leave the UK with the intention not to return and to take up long term residence in another country. However, a person who leaves another country with the intention to settle in the UK will not become habitually resident immediately on arrival; rather, there are two basic requirements which must be satisfied to acquire habitual residence *(R(IS) 6/96):*

- except where paragraph 20.92 applies, the claimant must be resident for an 'appreciable period of time';
- the claimant must have a 'settled intention' to reside in the UK.

20.85 The requirement for an appreciable period of time to have elapsed was confirmed in *Nessa v Chief Adjudication Officer.* There is no fixed period that amounts to an appreciable period of time *(CIS 2326/1995)* but rather it will vary according to the circumstances of the case in which the 'length, continuity and nature' of the residence will be relevant *(R(IS) 6/96).*

20.86 However, in one case a commissioner has held that, in general, the period will lie between one and three months and that a decision maker will need powerful reasons to justify a significantly longer period *(CIS 4474/2003).*

20.87 In determining whether the claimant has a settled intention, a number of factors may be relevant. These include:

- length and continuity of residence;
- future intentions;
- employment prospects;
- reasons for coming to the UK; and
- centre of interest.

20.88 These factors are based on the decision in *Di Paolo v Office National de l'Emploi* and are referred to in DWP guidance (GM para. C4.85). The guidance points out that this should not be seen as a comprehensive list, nor should one aspect be the deciding factor in every case (GM para. C4.86). Further useful guidance on each of these factors is provided (GM paras. C4.87-106).

20.89 In considering a person's employment prospects, their education and qualifications are likely to be significant *(CIS/5136/1995).* An offer of work will also constitute good evidence of an intention to settle. Wherever a worker has stable employment there is a presumption that he or she resides there, even if their family resides in another state (*Di Paolo* case).

20.90 A person's centre of interest is concerned with the claimant's strength of ties to this country and their intention to follow a settled way of life. This might be indicated by the presence of other close relatives, decisions made about the location of their family's personal possessions (e.g. clothing, furniture, transport), substantial purchases made, such as furnishings, which indicate a long term commitment, and the membership of any clubs or organisations in connection with their hobbies or recreations (GM C4.105).

Temporary absence and returning residents

20.91 Habitual residence will resume immediately on return if it is interrupted only by a short period of absence (for example for holidays or to visit relatives) *(R(IS) 6/96).* A returning resident may be absent for a longer period and still resume their habitual residence immediately on their return.

20.92 A UK or EEA national who is returning to the UK to resume their residence after a period of work in another EEA member state may be treated as habitually resident immediately on their arrival in the UK *(Swaddling v Chief Adjudication Officer).*

20.93 However, in order to establish whether a person qualifies as a returning resident the decision maker must consider *(CIS/1304/1997):*

- the circumstances in which habitual residence was lost;
- the claimant's continuing links with the UK while abroad;
- the circumstances of the claimant's return.

20.94 The outcome is likely to be different between a person whose absence was always intended to be temporary (even for long absences) and one in which the claimant never originally had any intention of returning *(CIS/1304/1997).*

20.95 Where the circumstances are such that the claimant's residence is sporadic over a sustained period (for example, a total of 11 months residence over a five year period before the claim) then they will not resume their habitual residence immediately on their return *(CIS/376/2002).* In such cases, habitual residence will only resume after an appreciable period – although what amounts to an appreciable period is likely to be shorter than in the case of a person entering the UK for the first time.

21 Students

21.1 This chapter describes the rules used in assessing HB and CTB for students. It covers:

- who is a 'student';
- which students can get HB and CTB; and
- how their income from loans, grants and other sources is assessed.

Student figures

21.2 The student figures given in this chapter (for loans, grants and disregards) are for the 2008-09 academic year. More details are in circular HB/CTB A14/2008 (revised). Figures for the 2009-10 academic year should be available by May 2009 on the relevant student finance web site:
England: *www.direct.gov.uk/en/EducationAndLearning/UniversityAndHigher Education/StudentFinance/index.htm* **Wales:** *www.studentfinancewales.co.uk*
Northern Ireland: *www.studentfinanceni.co.uk* **Scotland:** *www.saas.gov.uk*

Who is a student?

21.3 For the HB/CTB student rules to apply, the person in question must be a 'student'. The definition is given below. Other important terms are defined after that. Paragraphs 21.20-21 compare these with the definitions used in council tax law, which are different.

Definition of 'student'

21.4 For HB and CTB purposes, a student is defined as any person 'who is attending or undertaking a course of study at an educational establishment'. It also includes someone on a prescribed employment related qualifying course but not someone in receipt of a prescribed training allowance, e.g. the allowances associated with certain government schemes such as Training for Work, Work-Based Learning or Employment Rehabilitation.

21.5 A 'course of study' includes courses for which no grant is awarded and sandwich courses. The term 'educational establishment' is not defined in the regulations. DWP guidance suggests that it should be taken to include not just schools, colleges and universities but also other education establishments 'used for the purposes of training, education or instruction' (DWP GM C2 Annex A para. C2.04).

21.4 HB 2(1),53,54,58; NIHB 2(1),50,51,55; CTB 2(1),43,44

21.5 HB 53(1); NIHB 50(1); CTB 43(1)

Term-times, vacations and breaks in attendance

21.6 Once a course has started, a person carries on counting as a student until their course finishes, or they finally abandon it or are dismissed from it. So they do count as a student during all vacations occurring within the course. But they do not count as a student after the end of a course or between two different courses.

21.7 In sandwich courses (e.g. business studies where students spend time in industry, nursery nursing where students do time with nursery children) it includes the student's periods of work experience as well as their periods of study and holidays.

21.8 A student who takes time out (e.g. for illness or other personal reasons) continues to count as a student if they remain registered with their educational establishment: *O'Connor v Chief Adjudication Officer.*

Students in a couple

21.9 In the case of a couple, the HB and CTB rules vary depending on whether one or both are students and which partner makes the claim. Details are given as each rule is described (and see table 21.2).

'Full-time' versus 'part-time' students

21.10 Some of the HB and CTB rules apply to both full-time and part-time students; some apply only to full-time students. Details are given as each rule is described.

General cases

21.11 There is no all-embracing definition of 'full-time' (or 'part-time'). Certain courses are defined as full-time (see the next few paragraphs). In all other cases authoritities must decide whether a course is full-time by considering relevant factors such as: the nature of the course including the number of hours the student is required to attend, the view of the educational establishment and the amount and nature of any grant or loan received by the student (GM chapter C2, annex A, para. C2.08).

21.6 HB 53(2)(b) CTB 42(2)(b)

21.7 HB 53(1); NIHB 50(1); CTB 43(1)

21.9 HB 54,58; NIHB 51,55; CTB 44

21.11 HB 53(1); NIHB 50(1); CTB 43(1)

Courses funded by the Learning and Skills Council for England or by Welsh Ministers

21.12 In England and Wales a course wholly or partly funded by the Learning and Skills Council or by Welsh Ministers that requires more than 16 guided learning hours per week is a full-time course. This requirement should be stated in the student's learning agreement signed in behalf of the educational establishment in England or in a document signed on behalf of the educational establishment in Wales.

Courses funded by Scottish Ministers at colleges of further education

21.13 In Scotland a course of study at a college of further education that is not higher education and that is wholly or partly funded by the Scottish Ministers counts as a full-time course if it involves more than 16 hours a week of classroom or workshop based programmed learning; or 21 hours a week in total of classroom or workshop based programmed learning plus hours using structured learning packages supported by teaching staff. In either case the requirements should be stated in a document signed on behalf of the college.

Sandwich courses

21.14 All students on sandwich courses count as full-time.

Modular courses

21.15 A modular course is one which contains two or more modules, a number of which have to be completed in order to complete the course. A student on a modular course counts as full-time only during the parts of the course for which he or she is registered as full-time (so a student changing from full-time in her second year to part-time in her third would count for HB/CTB purposes as part-time in her third year).

Retakes on modular courses

21.16 The following applies only to the parts of modular courses that count as full-time for HB/CTB purposes. If someone fails a module or an exam in such a case, he or she continues to count as full-time for any period in which he or she continues to attend or undertake the course for the purposes of retaking the exam or module (including any vacations within that period other than vacations after the end of the course).

21.12 HB 53(1), CTB 43(1)

21.13 HB 53(1), CTB 43(1)

21.14 HB 53(1); NIHB 50(1); CTB 43(1)

21.15 HB 53(2),(4); NIHB 50(2),(4); CTB 43(2),(4)

21.16 HB 53(3); NIHB 50(3); CTB 43(3)

Other definitions

Further education and higher education

21.17 'Further education' means any education after the age of 16, up to and including GCE A Level or BTEC/SVEC National Diploma or National Certificate, whether or not leading to a qualification. 'Higher education' means any education beyond further education, including all the following:

- first degree, postgraduate and higher degree courses;
- teacher training courses and courses for training youth and community workers;
- courses for the BTEC/SVEC Higher National Diploma (HND) or Higher National Certificate (HNC) or the Diploma in Management Studies.

Old system and new system students

21.18 There are two main systems of undergraduate student financing:

- 'new system' students are those who began their course on or after 1st September 2006 (except those who deferred the start of their studies from 2005-06);
- 'old system' students are those who began their course earlier.

Period of study and summer vacation

21.19 Some of the rules refer to a student's 'period of study' or 'summer vacation':

- the period of study for any course requiring more than 45 weeks study in a year (e.g. for many postgraduate courses) runs from the first day of the academic year to the day before the first day of the next academic year (the course is treated as not having a summer vacation);
- for courses of less than one year, the period of study is the whole of the course;
- in all other cases, the period of study runs from the first day of the academic year to the last day before the summer vacation (or in the final year of a course of more than one year, to the last day of the course). This usually means three terms plus the Christmas and Easter vacations;
- subject to the above points, for students on sandwich courses, periods of work experience are included in the period of study.

21.17 HB 53,56; NIHB 50,53; CTB 43,45

21.19 HB 53(1); NIHB 50(1); CTB 43(1)

HB/CTB definitions and council tax definitions

21.20 The definition of a 'student' in council tax law is in category 6 in appendix 6. It can be different from the definitions in this chapter, though this is uncommon.

21.21 Only the (benefit law) definitions in this chapter affect whether a student is eligible for HB or CTB. The council tax law definitions apply to council tax exemptions (para. 11.11) and discounts (para. 11.16). As appendix 6 illustrates (categories 5 and 6), a mixture of the two applies to non-dependant deductions (table 6.2) and second adult rebate (para. 6.36 onwards).

Which students can get HB and CTB?

21.22 To be eligible for HB or main CTB a student must satisfy the following rules. None of the rules prevents eligibility for second adult rebate.

Which students are eligible?

21.23 Students cannot get HB or main CTB unless they fall within certain groups:

- Students who are single claimants are eligible for HB and main CTB only if they are in one (or more) of the groups in table 21.1.
- Students who are lone parents are in all cases eligible for HB and main CTB.
- Couples are eligible for HB and main CTB in all cases unless both are students and neither of them is in any of the groups in table 21.1. (See para. 21.24 for which partner should make the claim.)

Which partner in a couple should claim?

21.24 Table 21.2 explains which partner in a couple is eligible to claim HB and main CTB on behalf of both. In all cases where a claim may be made, it takes into account the income, capital and applicable amount relating to them both.

Students who maintain two homes

21.25 Some students have to maintain two homes, one near their educational establishment and one elsewhere. There are special HB rules for this:

- single claimants in the eligible groups (table 21.1) and lone parents get HB on only one home (para. 3.26);
- for couples, the rules are given in table 21.2 and paragraph 3.28.

The other rules about HB on two homes also apply (para. 3.6).

21.23 HB 8(1)(e),56(2); NIHB 8(1)(e),53(2); CTB 45(2)

21.24 HB 8(1)(e),56(2); NIHB 8(1)(e),53(2); CTB 45(2)

21.25 HB 7(3),(6)(b); NIHB 7(3),(6)(b)

Table 21.1: Eligible student groups

1. Students on JSA(IB), ESA(IR) or income support.
2. Students who counts as part-time rather than full-time (paras. 21.10-16).
3. Students under 21 not in higher education (para. 21.17) (the course must have been started before age 19).
4. Students under 20 on a non-advanced course of full-time education or approved training which they began or were accepted on or enrolled on before the age of 19.
5. Students aged 60+ or whose partners are aged 60+.
6. Student couples where both partners are full-time students or lone parents and in either case responsible for a child or young person.
7. Students who are single claimants responsible for a foster child formerly placed with them by a local authority or a voluntary organisation.
8. Students who qualify for a disability premium or a severe disability premium in the assessment of their applicable amount (para. 12.21 and para. 12.32). This includes for example students who are registered blind, on disability living allowance or on incapacity benefit at the long term rate.
9. Students whose applicable amount would include the disability premium but for the fact that they are disqualified from incapacity benefit (i.e. treated as capable of work).
10. Students who are, or are treated as, incapable of work (as decided by the DWP) and have been so incapable, or have been treated as incapable, for a continuous period of not less than 196 days. Two or more separate periods separated by a break of not more than 56 days should be treated as one continuous period.
11. Students who are, or are treated as having, limited capability for work (as decided by the DWP) and have had, or have been treated as having, limited capability for work for a continuous period of not less than 196 days. Two or more separate periods separated by a break of not more than 84 days should be treated as one continuous period. The claimant should make a claim for ESA to trigger the limited capability for work test.
12. Students who have a UK grant which includes an allowance for deafness (from the date on which the request for the deafness related allowance is made).
13. Students unable to get a grant or student loan following an absence from their studies (with the consent of their educational establishment) due to illness or providing care to another person. This applies only from the date of ceasing to be ill or providing care until the day before resuming the course (or, if earlier, the day their establishment agrees they can resume it) – and only up to a maximum of one year.

Table 21.2: Student rules for couples

An 'eligible group' means one in table 21.1

Partner A	Partner B	Who can claim?	HB on two homes?
Student in an eligible group	Student in an eligible group	Either	Yes, if reasonable, and having two homes is unavoidable
Student in an eligible group	Student not in an eligible group	Partner A only	No, only on A's home
Student in an eligible group	Non-student	Either	Yes, if reasonable, and having two homes is unavoidable
Student not in an eligible group	Student not in an eligible group	Neither	No, not on either
Student not in an eligible group	Non-student	Partner B only	No, only on B's home

Halls of residence, student villages, etc

21.26 In addition to the previous rules the following students cannot get HB on accommodation rented from the educational establishment they attend during the period of study (para. 21.19):

- part-time students – who if they were full-time students would only be exempt from the general student exclusion because they are on IS, JSA(IB) or ESA(IR) (category 1 in table 21.1); or
- full-time students – who are only exempt from the general exclusion because they are waiting to return to the course after a period of illness or caring and are without a loan or grant (category 13 in table 21.1).

This non-entitlement does not apply if the educational establishment itself rents the dwelling from someone other than another educational establishment. It does apply if the educational establishment pays rent for the accommodation to an educational authority which is providing the accommodation in that role or

---

T21.1 HB 56; NIHB 53; CTB 45

12.26 HB 57,58; NIHB 54,55

(in GB only) the accommodation is held by the educational establishment on a long tenancy. Finally, where it appears to the authority that the educational establishment has arranged for the accommodation to be provided by someone other than itself to take advantage of the HB scheme there is no HB entitlement during the period of study. There are no similar rules for CTB (because most such accommodation is exempt from council tax).

Absences during the summer vacation

21.27 In addition to the previous rules, full-time students cannot get HB on term-time accommodation (if it is not their normal home) while they are absent from it during the summer vacation. This rule does not apply to part-time students; nor for absences in hospital. It never applies to CTB.

Assessing student income

21.28 This section describes how student loans, grants and other income are assessed. Table 21.3 summarises the main rules. The main figures for student loans in the 2008-09 academic year are in table 21.4. Other figures and examples are in circular HB/CTB A14/2008 (revised) and GM chapter C2.

Table 21.3: Assessment of student income

Type of student income	Treatment in assessing HB/CTB
New system students (para. 21.18):	
• Maintenance loan ('student loan') The amount is reduced if the student also receives maintenance grant (maximum reduction is £1,260 in 2008-09)	Assessed as income (table 21.4)
◆ Special support grant	Disregarded in full (table 21.5)
◆ Maintenance grant	Assessed as income (table 21.5)
• Fee loan	Disregarded in full (para. 21.31)
• Grants for extra expenses	Mostly disregarded (table 21.5)
Old system students (para. 21.18):	
• Maintenance loan ('student loan')	Assessed as income (table 21.4)
• Fee contribution loan	Disregarded in full (para. 21.31)
• Grants for extra expenses	Mostly disregarded (table 21.5)

21.27 HB 55; NIHB 52

21.29 In the case of a student or partner aged 60+, all student grants and loans are disregarded. For under 60s the rules in the following paragraphs apply.

Income from student loans

Who gets a student loan

21.30 UK students in higher education (para. 21.17) are generally eligible for a student loan. Exceptions include:

- part-time students;
- students on nursing and midwifery diploma courses;
- postgraduate students (unless they are studying for a Postgraduate Certificate of Education); and
- students aged 60+ at the start of the course or, in Scotland, 50+ at the start of the course unless under the age of 55 and intending to enter employment after completion of the course.

21.31 The student loan may include:

- an amount towards living expenses (called a 'maintenance loan'). This is treated as income (para. 21.32);
- an amount towards fees (called a 'fee loan' or 'fee contribution loan'). This is disregarded.

Assessing the maintenance loan

21.32 In assessing HB and main CTB, all students who are eligible for a maintenance loan (including in Scotland any Young Students' bursary and any additional loan) are treated as receiving it at the maximum level applicable to them. This is done regardless of whether they apply for it, so long as they 'could acquire [a maintenance loan] in respect of that year by taking reasonable steps to do so'. The loan is then treated as income as shown in table 21.4, which also gives the main figures for 2008-09. If a condition of entitlement to a loan could not be met by the student taking reasonable steps then the authority should not treat the student as having a loan. In *CH/4422/2006* the fact that a Muslim student considered that they were prohibited from applying for a loan because of religious beliefs was not held to be an impediment to acquiring such a loan by taking reasonable steps.

21.33 If a maintenance loan is assessed on the assumption that the student, or his or her partner, will make a contribution, the amount of that contribution is

---

21.29 HB60+29(1); NIHB60+27(1); CTB60+19(1)

21.31 HB 64, 64A; NIHB 61, 62; CTB 51, 51A

21.32 HB 53,59,64; NIHB 50,56,61; CTB 43,47,51

21.33 HB 66(1),67; NIHB 64(1),65; CTB 53,54

disregarded from the student's or partner's other income. Similarly, a parent who makes a contribution can have that amount disregarded in the assessment of his or her own HB or main CTB (para. 13.131).

21.34 If a student leaves part way through their course and was paid a student maintenance loan – or a grant for a dependant – during the year they leave in, the income continues to be assessed in the same way and for the same period as before for the period to which any instalments of loan received relate. The sole exception is that there is no £10 per week disregard from the loan (but otherwise all the other steps in table 21.4 for loans or table 21.5 for grants for dependants apply). See also DWP HB/CTB A14/2008 (revised) for the treatment of loan income paid other than quarterly when the course is not completed.

Repaying a student loan

21.35 If someone else repays a former student's student loan, that payment is disregarded as that former student's income. This includes government payments under the 'Teacher Repayment Loan Scheme' – and any other such payments. However, when a student himself or herself repays a student loan this is not disregarded from his or her other income for HB/CTB purposes; also, there is no similar rule in Northern Ireland.

Income from student grants

21.36 The rules for assessing grant income apply to the maintenance grants awarded to new system students (table 21.3), and to any other kind of educational grant, award, scholarship, studentship, exhibition, allowance or bursary, whoever they are paid by.

Assessment

21.37 Grant income is assessed for HB and main CTB purposes as shown in table 21.5. If a student leaves part way through their course, see also paragraph 21.34.

21.38 If a student's grant is assessed on the assumption that the student, or his or her partner, will make a contribution, the amount of that contribution is disregarded from the student's or partner's other income. Similarly, a parent who makes a contribution can have that amount disregarded in the assessment of his or her own HB and main CTB (para. 13.131).

21.34 HB 40(7)-(9); NIHB 37(5)-(7); CTB 30(8)-(10)

21.35 HB sch 5 para 12; CTB sch 4 para 13

21.36 HB 59(1); NIHB 56(1); CTB 46(1)

21.37 HB 53,59,63,64; NIHB 50,56,60,61; CTB 43,46,50,51

21.38 HB 66,67; NIHB 64,65; CTB 53,54

Other income

Access funds and learner support funds

21.39 The following rules apply to payments from:

- 'access funds' (sometimes called 'hardship funds') made by educational establishments to students who fall within the student loan scheme (para. 21.30), postgraduates (of all kinds), and students aged 19 or more in further education;
- 'learner support funds' made by educational establishments to students aged 16 or more in further education; and
- financial contingency funds made available by Welsh Ministers.

21.40 These payments are treated as follows:

- single lump sum payments are disregarded as capital for 52 weeks from the date of payment, unless they are for certain necessities (defined below) in which case they are counted in full straight away;
- regular payments are disregarded as income, unless they are for certain necessities (defined below) in which case £20 per week is disregarded (subject to the over-riding £20 limit on certain disregards: para. 13.156). However, even those payments are disregarded in full as income if they are made before the student's course begins or to tide a student over until they receive their student loan.

21.41 The 'certain necessities' mentioned above are food, ordinary clothing and footwear, household fuel, eligible rent (apart from any amount attributable to non-dependant deductions), council tax or water charges – of the claimant or any member of the family.

Other earned and unearned income

21.42 If a full-time or part-time student receives earned or unearned income other than (or as well as) a student loan or grant, the ordinary earned and unearned income disregards apply to it (chapters 13-15).

21.39 HB 53(1); NIHB 50(1); CTB 43(1)

21.40 HB 65,68(2)-(4), sch 5 para 34; NIHB 63,66(2)-(4), sch 6 para 35; CTB 52,55(2)-(4), sch 4 para 35

21.41 HB 65(3)-(4), NIHB 63(3)-(4) CTB 52(3), 2(1)

The extra student income disregard

21.43 There is an extra disregard for student expenditure, which works as follows. If the student has loan or grant income, certain amounts are disregarded from it, as shown in tables 21.4 and 21.5. If the student necessarily spends more on those items than the amounts indicated in the tables, the excess is disregarded from his or her other income (as illustrated in the example). This important disregard is often overlooked: students are advised to check that it has been applied properly.

Example: The extra student income disregard

A student receives a student loan. In the assessment of the loan for HB/CTB purposes, £380 is disregarded towards books and equipment and £295 towards travel (table 21.4). She is not in receipt of any grant for travel, but can satisfy the authority that her actual travel costs for the year will be £720 (£425 more). She uses money from a part-time job to pay for this.

The additional £425 per year for travel is disregarded in assessing her income from her part-time job (as well as any other earned income disregards which may apply: paras. 14.14-15 and 14.24). There is no particular rule for which weeks to allow this in. Since her loan income is averaged over 43 weeks, it may be fair to average this £425 over those 43 weeks.

Table 21.4: Student maintenance loans: 2008-09 academic year

MAXIMUM AMOUNTS	Final year	Other year	Per extra week
English/NI students on courses in London:	£5,895	£6,475	£103
Courses outside London:	£4,280	£4,625	£81
Welsh students on courses in London:	£5,900	£6,480	£103
Courses outside London:	£4,285	£4,625	£81
Scottish students on courses in London:	£4,825	£5,565	£103
Courses outside London:	£3,915	£4,510	£81

21.43 HB 63; NIHB 60; CTB 50

Reductions in main amounts for new scheme students

The maximum amount for a new scheme student (para. 21.18) is reduced by the amount of any maintenance grant they receive, subject to a maximum reduction of £1,260.

Special cases

Lower figures apply to NHS-funded courses and some other courses (see table A1 in DWP HB/CTB A14/2008 (revised)).

Treatment for HB/main CTB purposes

(a) Take the whole amount into account as income (even though it is in fact a loan). Include any amount for extra weeks. Treat any parental or partner's assumed contribution to it as being received (even if not actually paid).

(b) Disregard £675 in all cases. This is a standard amount including £295 towards travel and £380 towards books and equipment.

(c) Average the resulting amount over the period described below.

(d) Then disregard £10 from the weekly figure (in the case of a couple, disregard £10 from each one's weekly figure), subject to the over-riding £20 limit on certain disregards (para. 13.156).

Period over which the loan is averaged

General rule

Average over the period from the first Monday in September to the last Sunday in June. (In 2008-09 this is 43 weeks: 1.9.08 to 28.6.09.)

Exceptions

First years only: If the course begins after the first Monday in September, still average over the period described above, but then ignore it as income for the week(s) before the course begins (CIS/3734/2004).

Final years and one-year courses only: Average over the period from the first Monday in September to the last Sunday in the course.

Courses in Scotland: If any year starts before September, average over the period from the first Monday in the course to the last Sunday in June (or, in final year and one-year courses, the last Sunday in the course).

Courses starting other than in the autumn: From the whole academic year subtract the 'quarter' in which the longest vacation is taken, the 'quarters' (for these purposes) being January to March (3 months), April to June (3 months), July to August (2 months), and September to December (4 months). Average over the period from the first Monday to the last Sunday in the remaining three 'quarters'.

Example: Student income assessment: 2008-09 academic year

Information

A student who rents her home is in the second year of a three-year full-time University course in England (outside London). She is a new system student (table 21.3). She is eligible for HB because she is disabled. No-one lives with her so her home is exempt from council tax.

Student loan and grant

She receives a maintenance loan at the maximum level available to her of £4,625, a special support grant, and a grant for her disability.

Assessment

The special support grant, and the grant for her disability, are wholly disregarded.

From her maintenance loan of £4,625 disregard the standard amount of £675 giving £3,950. Average this over the standard 43 weeks (1.9.08 to 28.6.09) giving £91.86. Then disregard a further £10 giving £81.86.

So her total income during the 43 weeks from Monday 1.9.08 to Sunday 28.6.09 inclusive is £81.86 per week (plus any other income she may have).

Note

Because she is a second year, this income is counted even in weeks when she is not at University (such as the period from 1.9.08 to when the autumn term begins). If she was a first year student, the assessment would be exactly the same giving her a student income of £81.86 per week, but this income would be disregarded until her autumn term began (CIS/3734/2004).

Table 21.5: Student grants: 2008-09 academic year

Treatment for HB/main CTB purposes

(a) Start with the whole amount of the grant (including the maintenance grant: table 21.3) and all allowances for the maintenance of a (child or adult) dependant. Treat any parental or partner's assumed contribution to it as being received (even if not actually paid).

(b) No standard disregard is made for travel or for books and equipment – unless the student neither receives nor is treated as receiving a student loan, in which case disregard £675.

(c) Disregard the following:

- all amounts because the student has a disability;
- all amounts for books and equipment and/or for travel (in addition to the standard £675 if appropriate);
- all amounts for child care (including a parents learning allowance where paid under prescribed legislation, child care grant, etc);
- the special support grant (table 21.3);
- education maintenance awards;
- the higher education grant;
- the higher education bursary for care leavers;
- £675 from the adult learning grant (DWP GM para C2.177);
- the National Assembly for Wales learning grant (but not for 'new style' full-time undergraduates);
- tuition or examination fees;
- expenses for term-time residential study away from the student's educational establishment;
- two homes grant;
- additions for anyone outside the UK so long as the student's applicable amount does not include an amount for that person.

(d) Average the resulting amount over the period described below.

Period over which the grant is averaged

Students who receive or are treated as receiving a student loan

Average over the same period as the student loan (table 21.3: the general rule and exceptions all apply). This is how the new scheme maintenance grant (table 21.3) is treated.

Others

If the grant is attributable to the student's period of study (para. 21.19): Average over the period from the first Monday to the last Sunday in that period of study omitting, for sandwich students, any benefit weeks falling wholly or partly within the period of work experience.

If it is attributable to any other period: Average over the period from the first Monday to the last Sunday in that period.

Exceptions

Nursing and midwifery diploma students: They may get a bursary towards their living expenses (and cannot get a student loan). Their bursary (after any appropriate disregards, including the standard £675) is averaged over the full calendar year (52/53 weeks).

NHS-funded students on degree courses: They may get a bursary towards their living expenses (and can get a student loan at a lower rate than other students). Their bursary (after any appropriate disregards, excluding the standard £675) is averaged over the full calendar year (52/53 weeks) – and their loan is dealt with as in table 21.3.

Care leavers grant: Average this over the period from the first Monday to the last Sunday in the summer vacation.

22 Local variations

22.1 This chapter sets out the local variations to the HB and CTB schemes allowed by the law, including government pilot schemes. It describes:

- discretionary housing payments;
- local schemes to disregard war pensions, etc;
- government powers to vary HB and CTB schemes;
- HB sanctions for anti-social behaviour in pilot authorities.

Discretionary housing payments (DHPs)

22.2 In Great Britain sections 69-70 of the Child Support, Pensions and Social Security Act 2000 give the government the power to make regulations to provide for a scheme of discretionary housing payments (DHPs); pay grants to authorities for the cost of the scheme and impose a limit on the amount of each authority's total payments. The equivalent powers in Northern Ireland are sections 60-61 of the Child Support, Pensions and Social Security (Northern Ireland) Act 2000.

22.3 DHPs are an independent scheme administered by authorities which also administer HB/CTB. They are not a form of HB or CTB, and so the HB/CTB appeals procedure (chapter 19) does not apply but the authority may review any decision it has made.

Circumstances in which DHPs may be made

22.4 DHPs are available to claimants who:

- in Great Britain are entitled to HB or CTB and 'appear to [the] authority to require some further financial assistance... in order to meet housing costs';
- in Northern Ireland are entitled to HB in respect of their rent which has been restricted as a rent referral case or LHA rules and 'appear to [the] authority to require some further financial assistance... in order to meet housing costs'.

22.5 DHPs cannot be awarded towards any of the following:

- service or support charges that are ineligible for HB (para. 8.17 onwards);
- in Great Britain any rent liability if the claimant is entitled to CTB only;

22.2 SI 2001 No. 1167; SI 2001 No. 2340; SI 2008 No. 698; NISR 2001 No. 216; NISR 2001 No. 80; NISR 2008 No. 112

- in Great Britain any council tax liability if the claimant is entitled to HB only or to second adult rebate only;
- in Northern Ireland any liability to meet rates;
- increases to cover rent arrears which are not eligible for HB (para. 8.43);
- reductions in any benefit as a result of Jobseeker's sanctions, Child Support sanctions or sanctions following certain benefit related offences;
- HB/CTB that is suspended (paras. 17.46-53);
- a reduction of HB as the result of an anti-social behaviour sanction (para. 22.18);
- shortfalls caused by overpayment recovery.

Maximum amount of DHP and period of award

22.6 The total weekly amount of the DHP, taken together with the claimant's award of HB or CTB, must not exceed:

- the claimant's eligible rent calculated on a weekly basis as a standard case (paras. 8.5-6);
- the claimant's liability for council tax on a weekly basis.

The Court of Appeal has held that 'the limit placed on DHPs... does not prevent the Council from exercising its discretion to make DHPs for past housing costs (arrears of rent) on the ground that the applicant is currently receiving full housing benefit.' (*Gargett, R (on the application of) v LB Lambeth,* para 32). The authority may award a DHP for any period (i.e. for a fixed period or indefinitely) that it considers appropriate for the circumstances of the case.

Uses

22.7 DHPs are used for such things as:

- making up the shortfall in the eligible rent in a rent allowance case caused by the rent officer's/NIHE figures being used or the local housing allowance;
- in Great Britain only, making up the shortfall in eligible rent in an old case (para. 7.15) where the authority considers there is no other way of doing this;
- making up for the effect of the 65 per cent and 20 per cent tapers used in the calculation of benefit;
- making up for the effect of non-dependant deductions.

Claims, decisions, payments and overpayments

22.8 A DHP may be claimed by the person entitled to HB/CTB or a person acting on their behalf if this appears reasonable. The authority may accept a claim in such form and manner as it approves. Some authorities have a separate DHP claim form. The authority should provide a written notice of its decision on a claim and the reasons for it as soon as is reasonably practicable. DHPs may be paid to the person entitled or to someone else the authority thinks appropriate. A person claiming or receiving DHPs must provide the authority with details of the grounds of claim, information on any changes of circumstance that may be relevant and any other information required by the authority. The authority may stop making payments of DHP when it thinks fit.

22.9 The authority has the discretion to recover DHP payments when it decides that someone has misrepresented, or failed to disclose, a material fact and, as a consequence, a payment was made. DHPs may also be recovered where the authority decides that an error was made in deciding the application and as a consequence payment was made which would not have been made but for that error.

Guidance

22.10 Guidance to local authorities on making DHPs is contained in the DWP's *Discretionary Housing Payments Best Practice Guide* (March 2008) – see *www.dwp.gov.uk/housingbenefit/claims-processing/operational-manuals/dhpguide.pdf.* There is no requirement for the claimant's family circumstances to be 'exceptional', nor does there have to be 'hardship'. The payments are, however, entirely discretionary and authorities vary in their willingness to award them. While it may well be worth asking about and/or claiming DHP, claimants should not rely on an authority actually making an award.

DWP's limits and contribution to DHP expenditure

22.11 The DWP sets an annual limit on each authority's DHP expenditure and partly reimburses this expenditure through a system of grants (separate from the system for HB/CTB described in chapter 23). Since 2007-08 the national annual financial limit on DHP expenditure has been set at £50m of which £20m is made up of the DWP's contribution (S2/2007 para. 37, S1/2008 para. 5 and S1/2009 para. 4). A significant number of authorities spend less on DHPs than even the amount they would be directly reimbursed by the DWP *(www.parliament.uk/deposits/depositedpapers/2008/DEP2008-0069.doc).* Where an authority spends less than its DWP grant allocation, it faces a reduced allocation in the following year (S1/2009 para. 5-6). Authorities must make their grant claim by 31st May each year. Claims for grants do not need to be audited.

22.11 SI 2001 No 2340; SI 2005 No 2052

Local schemes to disregard war pensions, etc

22.12 The HB and CTB schemes described in this guide are those which authorities are required by law to operate. However, authorities in Great Britain (not Northern Ireland) have the power to run an enhanced 'local scheme'. The only enhancements authorities are permitted to make is to disregard prescribed war disablement pensions and prescribed war pensions to surviving spouses or civil partners, in whole or in part, over and above the disregard required by law (usually £10: paras. 13.58-59 but note also the total disregard of the supplementary pension awarded to pre-1973 war widows – para. 13.63 – as well as any mobility supplement or payment of war disablement pension based on a need for attendance – para. 13.52).

22.13 The decision to run, end or vary a local scheme is made by a resolution of the authority. A separate resolution is required for HB and CTB. The question of whether or not an authority should run a local scheme is not open to the appeal procedure. The vast majority, but not all, authorities run a local scheme. In April 2003, 392 of the 408 authorities disregarded war pensions and war bereavement pensions in full and two authorities applied the full disregard to war disablement pensions but not war bereavement pensions. A further 12 authorities applied a partial disregard over the statutory minimum £10 and only two had no local scheme (and so applied only the statutory £10) (Commons *Hansard* 23rd October 2003, col. 723W).

22.14 Before 3rd July 2007 some of the specific war related pensions that could be disregarded under a local scheme were listed in the Social Security Administration Act 1992 and the others were to be found in regulations. Additionally there was no limit on the amount the authority could spend under its local scheme for those pensions listed in the Social Security Administration Act 1992. However, as the result of a legal quirk, the Permitted Totals Orders (SI 1996 No. 677 (HB) or SI 1996 No 687 (CTB)) applied a spending limit to those pensions that were included a local scheme by way of regulations. From 3rd July 2007 Regulations (SI 2007 No. 1619) have listed the specific pensions that may be disregarded under local schemes and no portion of an authority's spending on these schemes is subject to the relevant Permitted Totals Order. Further information on subsidy payments for local schemes can be found in paragraphs 23.41-42 of this guide.

22.12 AA 134(8),(10), 139(6),(8); HB 40(3)-(4A); HB60+ 33(10)-(14); CTB 30(3)-(4A); CTB60+ 23(10)-(14)

Government powers to vary HB and CTB schemes

22.15 The Government possesses powers to vary the HB/CTB schemes to make different rules for different areas. This power has been exercised, for example, to set the rules for the former pathfinder authorities (para. 22.28).

22.16 Powers exist in the Jobseekers Act 1995 (s29) to run local pilot schemes in which the rules for HB/CTB can be varied to test whether the change improves work incentives. These schemes have an initial maximum life of one year and do not permit variation of the maximum eligible rent or council tax. There are no such schemes currently in place.

22.17 From time to time specific legislation is passed to facilitate a new policy initiative. For example, s79 of the Welfare Reform and Pensions Act 1999 allowed payments to be made to HB claimants who traded down if their home was larger than they required. The scheme was wound up after it proved ineffective.

HB sanctions for anti-social behaviour

22.18 This is a pilot scheme that uses reductions in HB entitlement as a sanction for people who are evicted for anti-social behaviour and who then fail to cooperate with rehabilitation services.

Legal framework

22.19 The Welfare Reform Act 2007 added sections 130B-G to the Social Security Contributions and Benefits Act 1992. These sections contain the framework for the HB sanctions scheme. The details are set out in two statutory instruments: the Housing Benefit (Loss of Benefit) (Pilot Scheme) Regulations SI 2007 No 2202 and the Housing Benefit (Loss of Benefit) (Pilot Scheme) (Supplementary) Regulations SI 2007 No 2474. Both statutory instruments came into force from 1st November 2007. The relevant provisions in the Social Security Contributions and Benefits Act 1992 cease to have effect after 31st December 2010. Further primary legislation is required for the scheme to run beyond that date. Also note that the current statutory instruments cease to have effect on 31st October 2009 at the latest.

The pilot authorities

22.20 These sanctions are being piloted in eight authority areas for two years. The pilot authorities are Blackburn and Darwen Borough Council, Blackpool Borough Council, Dover District Council, Manchester City Council, New Forest District Council, Newham London Borough Council, South Gloucestershire Council and Wirral Metropolitan Council.

22.15 CBA 175(6); NICBA 171(6)

22.20 SI 2007 No 2202 3 & sch

Circumstances in which HB may be restricted

22.21 Where an HB claimant has been evicted from their home under a possession order made on grounds of nuisance behaviour their entitlement to HB may be restricted in relation to any new dwelling in the following circumstances:

- the authority has asked the claimant to take certain action with the aim of ending or preventing the repetition of the anti-social behaviour; and
- the claimant fails without good cause to comply with a warning notice requiring that these actions be taken within a certain time.

Where both members of a couple were evicted because of a possession order made on grounds of nuisance a failure by one member of the couple to take the required actions is treated as a failure by the other member to comply.

The warning notice

22.22 A written warning notice requiring the former occupier to take specific action must be served before a housing benefit sanction for anti-social behaviour can be imposed. The warning notice must give the claimant at least 1 week from issue to take the required step.

Good cause for failing to comply with a warning notice

22.23 The matters which must be taken into account when determining whether a claimant has good cause for failure to comply with an action specified in a warning notice are prescribed in great detail in the regulations. They include: any condition or personal circumstance which shows that taking the action would be likely to or did cause significant harm to their health; or subject them to excessive physical or mental stress; caring responsibilities, travel problems, etc.

The reduction

22.24 When a sanction is to be applied HB is reduced in three phases:

- Phase A – a 10% reduction for the first 4 weeks,
- Phase B – a 20% reduction for the second 4 weeks; and
- Phase C – a 100% reduction for the remainder of the restriction period (up to five years),

However if the claimant is a 'person in hardship' (para 22.25) the final stage is a 30% reduction. Where a reduction is also made due to benefit offences the rate of reduction is the greater of the two rates. The claimant can end the sanction if

---

22.21 CBA 130B-G
22.22 SI 2007 No 2474 4, 6
22.23 SI 2007 No 2474 5
22.24 SI 2007 No 2202 4

their household complies with the notice and takes up the offer of support. If the household starts cooperating but then stops, the sanction can be restarted at the rate that applied previously.

Who counts as a 'person in hardship'

22.25 There are three categories of 'persons in hardship':

- the claimant or a family member is pregnant, the claimant is single and under 18 or is a member of a couple and both are under 18;
- the claimant or partner is responsible for a child or young person, or has been awarded an attendance allowance or the care component of disability living allowance at one of the two higher rates, or has claimed an attendance allowance or disability living allowance or devotes a considerable portion of each week to caring for a person who has been awarded or claimed these benefits, or the claimant is aged 60 or more;
- the authority is satisfied in all the circumstances of the case that unless HB is paid the claimant or a family member will suffer hardship, and relevant factors include the resources available to the claimant's family and whether there is a substantial risk that essential items such as food, clothing or heating will stop being available or will only be available at considerably reduced levels.

To be counted as a 'person in hardship' the claimant must provide the authority with a signed statement, on a form approved by the Secretary of State (the DWP), of the circumstances on which they rely to establish their status.

Sharing of information between the courts, DWP and authorities

22.26 For the scheme to work information must be shared between a number of different entities. The court which makes a possession order on grounds of anti-social behaviour in a pilot scheme area must disclose that information to the DWP. The DWP are expected to keep these details on a database and match them against an HB claims database to identify claims by a member of the evicted household. Where a case is identified the DWP should inform the authority which in turn should inform the DWP of action taken in relation to a sanction. If a household moves from one pilot area to another the authorities are expected to share details relating to the application of a sanction.

Decisions, review and appeals

22.27 The rules relating to the notice of HB decisions (chapter 16) also apply to HB sanction decisions. Such decisions also carry the usual rights of review and appeal (Chapter 19).

22.25 SI 2007 No 2202 5

22.26 SI 2007 No 2474 10-13

22.27 SI 2007 No 2474 7-8

LHA – former pathfinder authorities

22.28 The Local Housing Allowance (LHA) arrangements were initially tried out in 18 pilot local authorities prior to the 'national roll-out' on 7th April 2008. LHA rules are slightly different in former pathfinder authorities from those that apply in other authorities. These differences are described in chapter 22 of the 2008-09 edition of this guide.

23 Subsidy

23.1 The DWP pays authorities most of their costs in administering and paying HB and CTB. This is called subsidy. This chapter explains how much subsidy the DWP pays. It applies to Great Britain only, and covers:

- who pays for HB/CTB;
- subsidy for benefit expenditure;
- the areas of expenditure which qualify for lower subsidy; and
- subsidy for benefit administration.

Who pays for HB and CTB

23.2 An authority's expenditure on the HB and CTB schemes includes the following items, and the DWP pays subsidy towards part or all of these:

- benefit expenditure itself, i.e. the money paid out in the form of HB/CTB;
- ongoing administrative costs, e.g. staff salaries, accommodation costs, training, and computer running costs; and
- one-off costs of introducing new schemes (such as, recently, local housing allowances).

23.3 Anything not met by the DWP is paid for by the authority itself, from its general fund, or in Wales from the council fund. For example, part or all of the cost of overpayments of HB/CTB is met by the authority itself (paras. 23.13-30).

Subsidy claims, payments and overpayments

23.4 Subsidy payments make up a large amount of authorities' total income, and also have a big effect on the way they run the HB and CTB schemes. Just as claimants need HB/CTB from the authority, authorities need subsidy from the DWP. Authorities may fail to get their full subsidy entitlement if they:

- fail to claim it, or claim it using the wrong procedures; or
- do not claim it on time (one important deadline being 30th November each year); or
- cannot provide the necessary information and evidence.

23.5 If subsidy is overpaid to an authority, or there is some other breach of subsidy rules, the Secretary of State has the discretion to recover appropriate amounts (circular HB/CTB S1/2002).

23.4 SI 1998/562 art 6

23.5 AA 140C(3)

Subsidy law and guidance

23.6 The Social Security Administration Act 1992 (sections 140A-140G) provides the legal framework for the payment of subsidies to authorities. The detailed legal rules are set out in the Income-related Benefits (Subsidy to Authorities) Order 1998 (SI 1998 No 562) as amended each year. The rules and rates for 2009-10 will be incorporated in an amendment to this Order, made towards the end of the year. However, most of these are known in advance as a result of DWP guidance.

23.7 The DWP gives guidance on subsidy arrangements in a Subsidy Guidance Manual which it reissues each year (see *www.dwp.gov.uk/housingbenefit/performance-value-for-money/subsidy-guidance.asp*). The DWP also issues the 'S' series of circulars to keep authorities up to date (see *www.dwp.gov.uk*).

Benefit expenditure subsidy

23.8 The DWP pays authorities subsidy equal to their 'qualifying expenditure' on HB and CTB. As described below, in practice this means the DWP pays back nearly all of the HB and CTB they pay out.

Qualifying expenditure

23.9 An authority's 'qualifying expenditure' is:

- the total of all HB and CTB lawfully paid (or treated as lawfully paid) by the authority during the relevant year;
- minus part or all of HB and CTB expenditure on certain items – as described in this chapter.

Correctly paid HB/CTB

23.10 Correctly paid HB and CTB qualifies for 100% subsidy. In other words, the DWP meets the whole cost of all correct payments of HB (whether rent rebates or rent allowance) and CTB. Nowadays this includes backdated HB/CTB (para. 5.53), along with retrospective awards of HB/CTB (para. 5.51), extended payments (para. 17.54) and the extra £15 that some people get if they fall within the LHA scheme (para. 9.23). That fact does not necessarily lead to authorities backdating HB/CTB with abandon, because subsidy claims for backdated HB/CTB are subject to the external auditor's certification that good cause has been established (circular HB/CTB S9/2003, para. 13).

23.8 SI 1998/562 art 11(2)

23.9 SI 1998/562 art 13

23.10 SI 1998/562 arts 13,14

Penalised expenditure

23.11 To encourage authorities to monitor and control costs, certain areas of benefit expenditure are penalised. These are summarised in table 23.1, and fuller details follow. As shown in the table, penalised benefit expenditure includes certain overpayments and certain high eligible rents (in other words, the cost of these is not always met in full).

23.12 Authorities must apply the benefit rules fairly, objectively and impartially. They must not allow the subsidy penalties to interfere with this duty; though where the authority has a discretion one factor it may take account of is its own financial position *(R v Brent LBC HBRB ex parte Connery).*

Overpayments

23.13 Subsidy on overpayments of HB and CTB varies depending on the reason for the overpayment (also called 'excess benefit' in the case of CTB: para. 18.2). Table 23.1 gives a summary. The main rules are given in detail below. Other overpayments are covered by the table just mentioned.

Authority error overpayments

23.14 An 'authority error overpayment' means an overpayment caused by a mistake made, whether in the form of an act or omission, by an authority. It does not apply, however, if the claimant, a person acting on the claimant's behalf or any other person to whom the payment is made, caused or materially contributed to that mistake (see also paragraphs 18.11 and 18.13). An authority error overpayment may be caused by the authority making a mistake of fact or law, or it may be caused by its delay in dealing with a change of circumstances. The latter 'administrative delay' overpayments are categorised separately on the authority's subsidy claim form, but nonetheless fall within the rules described here (paras 23.15-18).

23.15 The amount of subsidy an authority receives for authority error overpayments in a year depends on their total of such overpayments in that year, as compared with their total correct payments of HB and CTB (para. 23.10) in that year.

23.16 If in a year the percentage of authority error overpayments (as compared with correct payments) is:

- no more than 0.48%, the authority gets 100% subsidy on all their authority error overpayments;
- 0.48% or more, but no more than 0.54%, the authority gets 40% subsidy on all their authority error overpayments;
- 0.54% or more, the authority gets 0% subsidy on all their authority error overpayments.

23.14-18 SI 1998/562 art 18(1)(e),(6),(6A)

Table 23.1: Summary of benefit expenditure subsidy arrangements 2009-10

Component	Arrangements	Rate
Basic rate	HB/CTB	100%
	In England and Wales the 100% subsidy is subject to HRA rent increases having kept to Government guidelines	See left
LA error overpayments including administrative delay	Where LA error OPs equal to or less than 0.48% of correct payments	100% on all LA error OPs
	Where LA error OPs above 0.48% but equal to or less than 0.54% of correct payments	40% on all LA error OPs
	Where LA error OPs above 0.54% of correct payments	Nil on all LA error OPs
Rebate credited in advance of entitlement	Rent rebate/CTB	Nil
DWP/HMRC error overpayments	HB/CTB	100% Recovered amounts are deducted from subsidy entitlement
Excess CTB due to council tax capping	CTB	Nil
Claimant error/fraud or other overpayments	HB/CTB	40%
Duplicate payments where original alleged to have been lost/stolen/not received and later found to be cashed	Rent allowance	25%

Disproportionate increases in LA rents	Rent rebate Applies in Scotland and Wales only	Nil
Unreasonable rents – deregulated private sector tenancies not subject to a maximum rent calculation	Rent allowance where authority is unable to restrict the eligible rent under 'old' regulation 11 Subsidy on HB attributable to rent above the Rent Officer's determination	60%
	Rent allowance where authority is able to restrict the eligible rent under 'old' regulation 11 Subsidy on HB attributable to rent above the Rent Officer's determination	Nil
Homeless in board and lodging accommodation	Non-HRA rent rebate Subsidy on HB attributable to rent above authority's cap	Nil
	Subsidy on HB attributable to rent above authority's threshold figure up to level of authority's cap	10%
Homeless in accommodation held on licence by LAs	Non-HRA rent rebate Subsidy on HB attributable to rent above authority's cap	Nil
Short term leased accommodation	Rent rebate Subsidy on HB attributable to rent above authority's cap	Nil
Modular Improvement rule	HRA rent rebate rules in England and Wales	Nil
Extended payments	HB/CTB	100%
Discretionary local schemes	HB/CTB	0.2% addition to authority's annual benefit subsidy, capped at 75% of the total benefit cost of the local scheme to the authority

23.17 The percentages (0.48% and 0.54%) are known as the 'lower threshold' and the 'higher threshold'. Reaching either threshold has a big impact on the authority's subsidy, as illustrated in the example. Approaching the lower threshold in a year is a horrible shock for an authority and it will often do all it can to avoid reaching it, let alone getting anywhere near to the higher one – but see paragraphs 23.29-30.

23.18 When an authority error overpayment is recoverable (para. 18.14), the authority keeps any amount actually recovered (and keeps the subsidy too).

Example: Subsidy for authority error overpayments

An authority's annual expenditure on correctly paid HB and CTB is £10,000,000.

So its 'lower threshold' is £48,000 for that year.
And its 'higher threshold' is £54,000 for that year.

If the total authority error overpayments in that year are £45,000, the authority gets subsidy of 100% of £45,000, which is £45,000.

If the total authority error overpayments in that year are £50,000, the authority gets subsidy of 40% of £50,000, which is £20,000.

If the total authority error overpayments in that year are £55,000, the authority gets subsidy of 0% of £55,000, which is NIL.

References in this example to 'authority error overpayments' mean the combined amount of these and 'administrartive delay overpayments (para. 23.14).

Departmental error overpayments

23.19 A 'departmental error overpayment' means an overpayment caused by a mistake made, whether in the form of an act or omission:

- by an officer of the DWP or of HM Revenue and Customs, acting as such, or a person providing services to that department or to HM Revenue and Customs; or
- in a decision of a first-tier tribunal or an upper tribunal.

But an overpayment does not count as a 'departmental error overpayment' in either of the above cases if the claimant, a person acting on the claimant's behalf, or any other person to whom the payment is made, caused or materially contributed to that mistake.

23.20 Although there is no legal requirement to check with the DWP or HM Revenue and Customs that they consider the error is theirs, many authorities consider this is wise except in the most obvious of circumstances.

23.21 The authority receives subsidy equal to 100% of the amount of departmental error overpayments.

23.19-22 SI 1998/562 art 18(4)

23.22 When a departmental error overpayment is recoverable (para. 18.14), the authority keeps any amount actually recovered – but (unlike all other cases) it has to return the subsidy. To put it another way, the authority receives subsidy equal to:

- 100% of the departmental error overpayments it identifies in a year;
- minus 100% of the departmental error overpayments it recovers in a year.

Some authorities might see this as incentive to never attempt to recover such overpayments – but see paragraphs 23.29-30.

Claimant error/fraud overpayments

23.23 A 'claimant error overpayment' means an overpayment caused by the claimant, or someone acting on their behalf, failing to provide information they are required to provide.

23.24 A 'claimant fraud overpayment' means (from April 2009: circular HB/CTB A24/2008) an overpayment where the claimant has:

- been found guilty of an offence, whether under a statute or otherwise; or
- made an admission under caution of deception or fraud for the purpose of onbtaining benefit; or
- agreed to pay a penalty as an alternative to prosecution, and that agreement has not been withdrawn.

23.25 The authority gets 40% of the combined amount of claimant error/fraud overpayments. (In other words, for subsidy purposes, claimant error and claimant fraud are the same.)

23.26 A claimant error/fraud overpayment is recoverable (para. 18.11). The authority keeps any amount actually recovered (and keeps the subsidy too).

Technical overpayments

23.27 Technical overpayments can only occur when:

- CTB is awarded for a future period to a claimant's council tax account; or
- HB is awarded (as a rent rebate) for a future period to a council tenant's rent account.

In those cases, a 'technical overpayment' means an overpayment which arises after that award, because of a change of circumstances or for some other reason. But it only includes the period from the Monday after the change was disclosed to the authority, or after the authority became aware of the overpayment.

23.28 The authority receives no subsidy for technical error overpayments. However, technical overpayments are recoverable (para. 18.12), and the authority keeps any amount it recovers.

23.23-26 SI 1998/562 art 18(4A)-(5)

23.27-28 SI 1998/562 art 18(7)

Overpayments subsidy incentives and audit

23.29 The overpayments subsidy arrangements described above can act, at least in part, as an incentive to authorities – sometimes to recover overpayments they have identified and sometimes not. Also, it has to be said, they could act as an incentive to authorities to close their eyes to having made an overpayment in the first place, or to categorise it in such a way that it receives a more favourable amount of subsidy.

23.30 To counteract this, the authority's external auditors are instructed that 'testing of overpayments needs to provide assurance that overpayments are correctly classified and fairly stated, recognising that there is a subsidy incentive to misclassify overpayments, for example, to code a technical overpayment (nil subsidy) as an eligible overpayment (40% subsidy) or, at or near one of the LA error overpayment thresholds, not to code a local authority error at all' (Audit Commission, Certification Instruction BEN01 (06-07) para. 35).

Limitations on eligible rent

LHA and rent referral cases

23.31 The subsidy rules play no part in limiting eligible rent in these two types of case (described in chapters 9 and 10). Instead, limitations on eligible rent are imposed by a combination of:

- the local housing allowance (LHA) and rent referral schemes themselves; and
- the over-riding power to restrict eligible rents (paras. 9.28 and 10.17).

23.32 However there is a subsidy limitation – for rent referral cases only – which applies if:

- the authority is required to apply for a rent officer determination in a particular case during a year;
- but fails to do so before the date its final subsidy claim has to be submitted for that year.

In that situation, no subsidy is awarded for any of the HB awarded for that case. Several authorities have lost a significant amount of subsidy due to a failure to refer relevant cases to the Rent Service (see *R (Isle of Anglesey County Council) v Secretary of State for Work and Pensions* and *R (London Borough of Lambeth) v Secretary of State for Work and Pensions*).

23.31 SI 1998/562 art 13

23.32 SI 1998/562 sch 4 para 6

Old scheme cases

23.33 The following rule applies when an old scheme case (para. 7.15) has to be referred to the rent officer (para. 7.11). Although in such cases the rent officer's figures are guidance rather than binding in the assessment of eligible rent (para. 8.56), they are nonetheless used in the calculation of subsidy.

23.34 If the authority is:

- obliged by law to set an eligible rent higher than the rent officer's figures (paras. 8.49-66), subsidy at the rate of 60% is payable on any HB attributable to the excess;
- not obliged by law to do so, but chooses to do so, no subsidy is payable on any HB attributable to the excess.

For these purposes, 'the excess' means the excess of the eligible rent over the rent officer's 'significantly high rent' or 'exceptionally high rent' (paras. 10.33, 10.37).

Housing association and other RSL tenants

23.35 Except for old scheme cases (para. 23.33) the subsidy rules do not limit eligible rent for tenants of registered housing associations and other registered social landlords (RSLs). Registered housing associations are subject to their own rent controls.

Council tenants

23.36 The subsidy rules do not limit eligible rent for tenants of the authority itself (rent rebate cases), except that no subsidy is payable on any HB attributable to the following circumstances. For fuller details (and exceptions) see the Subsidy Guidance Manual (para. 23.7).

- The 'rent rebate subsidy limitation scheme' applies in England and Wales only. If an authority increases its tenants' rents by more than its central government guideline rent increase, no subsidy is payable on the HB attributable to the excess (circular HB/CTB S3/2008).
- The 'disproportionate rent increase rule' applies in Wales and Scotland only. If an authority increases rents to its tenants on HB more than it increases its other rents, subsidy on the difference is restricted.
- Limitations on 'modular improvement schemes' apply throughout Great Britain. If an authority offers its tenants the right to select optional services, no subsidy is payable on the amount of HB attributable to these.
- Limitations on 'rent payment incentive schemes' apply throughout Great Britain. If an authority makes payments (in cash or kind) to reward tenants for paying their rent on time, the total value of such payments is deducted from the amount of subsidy paid to the authority.

23.34 SI 1998/562 sch 4 paras 7, 10

23.36 SI 1998/562 art 15, 15A, 19, 20A, sch 4A

Temporary accommodation for homeless people

23.37 The following applies to HB for people whose rent is due to the authority itself (rent rebate cases), who are living in:

- board and lodging (e.g. bed and breakfast) accommodation in which they were placed under homelessness law;
- accommodation held by the authority on licence (e.g. hotel annexes) in which they were placed under homelessness law; and
- accommodation held by the authority on a lease not exceeding ten years, known as short-term leased (STL) accommodation.

The relevant homelessness law in the first two cases is section 206(2)(b) of the Housing Act 1996 (for England and Wales) and section 35(2)(b) of the Housing (Scotland) Act 1987.

23.38 In such cases, the amount of subsidy is based on two figures:

- a lower 'threshold' figure (applicable only to board and lodging accommodation); and
- a higher 'cap' figure (applicable to all three types of case).

These two figures vary from authority to authority and are set by the DWP. The figures for 2009-10 are in circular HB/CTB S5/2008. They have been increased in 2009-10 for all authorities except those in London.

23.39 In the temporary accommodation identified in para 23.37 no subsidy is payable on an HB award which is the same as or less than the amount by which the eligible rent exceeds the cap.

In temporary accommodation except board and lodging accommodation where the HB is greater than the amount by which the eligible rent exceeds the cap:

- no subsidy is payable on the HB equal to the amount by which the eligible rent exceeds the cap;
- 100% subsidy is payable on the remaining amount of HB.

If the eligible rent does not exceed the cap in such accommodation then 100% subsidy is payable on all the HB awarded.

23.40 In board and lodging temporary accommodation where:

- the HB is greater than the amount by which the eligible rent exceeds the cap but not the threshold:
  - no subsidy is payable on the HB equal to the amount by which the eligible rent exceeds the cap;
  - 10% subsidy is payable on the HB equal to the amount by which the eligible rent exceeds the threshold but not the cap;

23.37 SI 1998/562 art 17

- the HB is greater than the amount by which the eligible rent exceeds the cap and the threshold:
  - no subsidy is payable on the HB equal to the amount by which the eligible rent exceeds the cap;
  - 10% subsidy is payable on the HB equal to the amount by which the eligible rent exceeds the threshold but not the cap;
  - 100% subsidy is payable on the remaining amount of HB.

If the eligible rent does not exceed the threshold in such accommodation then 100% subsidy is payable on all the HB awarded.

Example: Reduced subsidy in board and lodging accommodation

Using an illustrative threshold and cap as follows:

Threshold = £100

Cap = £140

(The difference is £40.)

The application of the threshold and cap is as follows:

Weekly eligible rent used to calculate HB is £200. Since the weekly eligible rent exceeds the cap by £60, the first £60 of any HB paid would not attract subsidy. If claimant's HB entitlement were £150 (due to other income, etc), subsidy would be:

- nil on £60;
- 10% on £40; and
- 100% on £50.

If claimant's HB entitlement were £110, subsidy would be:

- nil on £60;
- 10% on £40; and
- 100% on £10

Local schemes for war pensioners

23.41 Local schemes for war disablement and bereavement pensions allow authorities to disregard all of these, or at least more than £10 per week (paras. 13.59 and 22.12).

23.42 Benefit expenditure attributable to a local scheme does not qualify for HB/CTB subsidy (and does not count as part of the HB/CTB correctly paid: para. 23.10). Instead the authority receives an addition of 0.2% to its annual subsidy up to the value of 75% of the cost of the scheme to the authority.

23.42 SI 1998/562 art 11(2)(c)

Discretionary housing payments (DHPs)

23.43 No HB/CTB subsidy is paid towards DHPs because they are not a form of HB/CTB (paras. 22.2-11). Instead authorities receive a separate contribution from the DWP. For 2009-10, the total amount of the contribution for all authorities is £50 million (circular HB/CTB S1/2009).

Benefit administration subsidy

On-going costs

23.44 The DWP pays subsidy to authorities towards their costs in administering the HB and CTB schemes, known as a 'cash-limited specific grant'. For 2009-10 the total amount of administration subsidy allocated for all authorities is £528.3 million (circular HB/CTB S4/2008). The DWP is gradually reducing this subsidy in real terms (circulars HB/CTB S4/2007 and S4/2008) and the figure planned for 2010-11 is £515.4 million (circular HB/CTB S4/2008).

One-off costs

23.45 The DWP also pays subsidy to authorities to help with the introduction of various new schemes and unforeseen events. Recent examples (with totals for all authorities) are:

- £59 million in 2007 towards the cost of introducing local housing allowances (circular HB/CTB S3/2007);
- £20 million in 2008 towards the cost of adapting to employment and support allowance (circular HB/CTB S2/2008); and
- £45 million in 2009 towards the extra HB/CTB administration caused by the economic downturn (circular HB/CTB S2/2009).

23.44 AA s.140B(4A)(a), SI 1998/562 sch 1

Appendix 1: Main legislation affecting HB/CTB and recent changes

Here we list the main primary and secondary legislation for England, Wales and Scotland that contain the detailed rules of the HB and CTB schemes, followed by the amendments made to the secondary legislation that has come into force since 1 April 2008. This is followed by the equivalent list of legislation governing the HB scheme in Northern Ireland.

England, Wales and Scotland

Main primary legislation (Acts)

The Social Security Contributions and Benefits Act 1992
The Social Security Administration Act 1992
The Child Support, Pensions and Social Security Act 2000
The Welfare Reform Act 2007

Main secondary legislation (Regulations and Orders)

SI 2006/213	The Housing Benefit Regulations 2006
SI 2006/214	The Housing Benefit (Persons who have attained the qualifying age for state pension credit) Regulations 2006
SI 2006/215	The Council Tax Benefit Regulations 2006
SI 2006/216	The Council Tax Benefit (Persons who have attained the qualifying age for state pension credit) Regulations 2006
SI 2006/217	The Housing Benefit and Council Tax Benefit (Consequential Provisions) Regulations 2006
SI 1997/1984	The Rent Officers (Housing Benefit Functions) Order
SI 1997/1995	The Rent Officers (Housing Benefit Functions) (Scotland) Order
SI 2001/1002	The Housing Benefit and Council Tax Benefit (Decisions and Appeals) Regulations
SI 2001/1167	The Discretionary Financial Assistance Regulations

The first five in the above list are the main regulations which have governed HB and CTB since 6th March 2006.

Recent secondary legislation (Regulations and Orders)

The following is a list of amendments made (or otherwise relevant) to the main regulations made since 1 April 2008. This list is up to date as at 31 March 2009.

England, Wales and Scotland

Replacement recent secondary legislation

SI 2008/698	The Social Security (Miscellaneous Amendments) Regulations 2008
SI 2008/959	The Housing Benefit and Council Tax Benefit (Extended Payments) Amendment Regulations 2008
SI 2008/1042	The Social Security (Miscellaneous Amendments) (No. 2) Regulations 2008
SI 2008/1082	The Employment and Support Allowance (Consequential Provisions) Regulations 2008
SI 2008/1167	The Discretionary Housing Payments (Grants) Amendment Order 2008
SI 2008/1599	The Social Security (Students and Miscellaneous Amendments) Regulations 2008
SI 2008/1649	The Income-related Benefits (Subsidy to Authorities) Amendment (No. 3) Order 2008
SI 2008/2112	The Social Security (Use of Information for Housing Benefit and Welfare Services Purposes) Regulations 2008
SI 2008/2114	The Welfare Reform Act (Relevant Enactment) Order 2008
SI 2008/2299	The Housing Benefit and Council Tax Benefit (Amendment) Regulations 2008
SI 2008/2424	The Social Security (Miscellaneous Amendments) (No. 4) Regulations 2008
SI 2008/2428	The Employment and Support Allowance (Miscellaneous Amendments) Regulations 2008
SI 2008/2667	The Social Security (Miscellaneous Amendments) (No. 5) Regulations 2008
SI 2008/2683	The Tribunals, Courts and Enforcement Act 2007 (Transitional and Consequential Provisions) Order 2008
SI 2008/2684	The First-tier Tribunal and Upper Tribunal (Chambers) Order 2008
SI 2008/2685	The Tribunal Procedure (First-tier Tribunal) (Social Entitlement Chamber) Rules 2008
SI 2008/2698	The Tribunal Procedure (Upper Tribunal) Rules 2008
SI 2008/2767	The Social Security (Miscellaneous Amendments) (No. 6) Regulations 2008
SI 2008/2824	No. 2824 The Housing Benefit and Council Tax Benefit (Amendment) (No. 2) Regulations 2008
SI 2008/2987	The Housing Benefit and Council Tax Benefit (Amendment) (No. 3) Regulations 2008

SI 2008/3140	The Social Security (Child Benefit Disregard) Regulations 2008
SI 2008/3156	The Rent Officers (Housing Benefit Functions) Amendment (No. 2) Order 2008
SI 2008/3157	The Social Security (Miscellaneous Amendments) (No. 7) Regulations 2008
SI 2009/30	The Income-related Benefits (Subsidy to Authorities) Amendment Order 2009
SI 2009/362	The Social Security (Habitual Residence) (Amendment) Regulations 2009
SI 2009/471	The Social Security (National Insurance Number Information: Exemption) Regulations 2009
SI 2009/480	The Social Security (Flexible New Deal) Regulations 2009
SI 2009/497	The Social Security Benefits Up-rating Order 2009
SI 2009/583	The Social Security (Miscellaneous Amendments) Regulations 2009
SI 2009/614	The Housing Benefit (Amendment) Regulations 2009

Northern Ireland

Main primary legislation (Acts and Acts of Northern Ireland Assembly)

The Social Security Contributions and Benefits (Northern Ireland) Act 1992
The Social Security Administration (Northern Ireland) Act 1992
The Child Support, Pensions and Social Security Act (Northern Ireland) 2000
The Welfare Reform Act (Northern Ireland) 2007

Main secondary legislation (Statutory Rules and Orders)

NISR 2006/405	The Housing Benefit Regulations (Northern Ireland) 2006
NISR 2006/406	The Housing Benefit (Persons who have attained the qualifying age for state pension credit) Regulations (Northern Ireland) 2006
NISR 2006/407	The Housing Benefit (Consequential Provisions) Regulations (Northern Ireland) 2006
NISR 2008/100	The Housing Benefit (Executive Determinations) Regulations (Northern Ireland) 2008
NISR 2001/213	The Housing Benefit (Decisions and Appeals) Regulations (Northern Ireland) 2001
NISR 2001/216	The Discretionary Financial Assistance Regulations (Northern Ireland) 2001

The first three on the list are the main regulations which have governed HB since 19th November 2006.

Recent secondary legislation (Statutory Rules and Orders)

The following is a list of amendments made (or otherwise relevant) to the main regulations made since 1 April 2008. This list is up to date as at 31 March 2009.

Replacement recent secondary legislation

NISR 2008/112	The Social Security (Miscellaneous Amendments) Regulations (Northern Ireland) 2008
NISR 2008/179	The Social Security (Miscellaneous Amendments No. 2) Regulations (Northern Ireland) 2008
NISR 2008/262	The Social Security (Students and Miscellaneous Amendments) Regulations (Northern Ireland) 2008
NISR 2008/285	The Housing Benefit (Extended Payments) (Amendment) Regulations (Northern Ireland) 2008
NISR 2008/342	The Welfare Reform Act (Relevant Statutory Provision) Order (Northern Ireland) 2008
NISR 2008/343	The Social Security (Use of Information for Housing Benefit and Welfare Services Purposes) Regulations (Northern Ireland) 2008
NISR 2008/371	The Housing Benefit (Amendment) Regulations (Northern Ireland) 2008
NISR 2008/378	The Housing Benefit (Employment and Support Allowance Consequential Provisions) Regulations (Northern Ireland) 2008
NISR 2008/410	The Social Security (Miscellaneous Amendments No. 3) Regulations (Northern Ireland) 2008
NISR 2008/417	The Social Security (Miscellaneous Amendments No. 4) Regulations (Northern Ireland) 2008
NISR 2008/428	The Social Security (Miscellaneous Amendments No. 5) Regulations (Northern Ireland) 2008
NISR 2008/497	The Social Security (Child Benefit Disregard) Regulations (Northern Ireland) 2008
NISR 2008/498	The Social Security (Miscellaneous Amendments No. 7) Regulations (Northern Ireland) 2008
NISR 2008/504	The Housing Benefit (Amendment No. 2) Regulations (Northern Ireland) 2008
NISR 2008/506	The Housing Benefit (Executive Determinations) (Amendment) Regulations (Northern Ireland) 2008
NISR 2009/68	The Social Security (Habitual Residence) (Amendment) Regulations (Northern Ireland) 2009
NISR 2009/89	The Social Security Benefits Up-rating Order (Northern Ireland) 2009
NISR 2009/90	The Social Security (National Insurance Number Information: Exemption) Regulations (Northern Ireland) 2009

Appendix 2: Table of cases cited in guide

The following table lists all cases cited in the guide in the order they appear. It does not include cases which are subsequently reported by the social security commissioners. Where possible the table indicates where a free on-line case transcript can be accessed. Where none is available both free and on-line the table provides a reference for a recognised published law report.

Social security commissioners' decisions cited in this guide are not included in this table. For further details on the status of commissioners' decisions and how to access them, see paras. 1.38-39 and 19.71-72.

Para	Case
2.28	*R v Poole BC HBRB ex p Ross* 05/05/95 QBD 28 HLR 351
2.41	*R v Sutton BC HBRB ex p Partridge* 04/11/94 QBD 28 HLR 315
2.41	*R v Sheffield CC HBRB ex p Smith* 08/12/94 QBD 28 HLR 36
2.41	*R v Poole BC HBRB ex p Ross* See 2.28 above
2.45	*R v Solihull MBC HBRB ex p Simpson* 03/12/93 QBD 26 HLR 370
2.45	*R v Sutton LBC ex p Keegan* 15/05/92 QBD 27 HLR 92
2.48	*R v Manchester CC ex p Baragrove Properties* 15/03/91 QBD 23 HLR 337
2.51	*R (Painter) v Carmarthenshire CC HBRB* 04/05/01 HC [2001] EWHC (Admin) 308 Admin *www.bailii.org/ew/cases/EWHC/Admin/2001/308.html 308*
2.53	*Secretary of State for Social Security v Tucker* 08/11/01 CA [2001] EWCA Civ 1646 *www.bailii.org/ew/cases/EWCA/Civ/2001/1646.html*
2.63	*The Governors of Peabody Donation Fund v Higgins* 20/06/83 CA [1983] 1 WLR 1091
3.35	*R v Penwith DC HBRB ex p Burt* 26/02/90 QBD 22 HLR 292
4.17	*Crake and Butterworth v Supplementary Benefit Commission* 21/07/80 QBD [1982] 1 All ER 498
4.35	*R v Swale BC HBRB ex p Marchant* 9/11/99 CA 32 HLR 856 *www.casetrack.com* Subscriber site case reference: QBCOF 1999/0071/C

4.45 *Kadhim v Brent LBC HBRB* 20/12/00 CA [2000] EWCA Civ 344 *www.bailii.org/ew/cases/EWCA/Civ/2000/344.html*

5.17 *R v Liverpool CC ex p Johnson (No 2)* 31/10/94 QBD [1995] COD 200

5.21 *R v Penwith DC ex p Menear* 11/10/91 QBD 24 HLR 115

5.21 *R v South Ribble HBRB ex p Hamilton* 24/01/00 CA [2000] EWCA Civ 518 *www.bailii.org/ew/cases/EWCA/Civ/2000/518.html*

5.22 *R v Winston* 07/07/98 CA [1998] EWCA Crim 2256 *www.bailii.org/ew/cases/EWCA/Crim/1998/2256.html*

8.9 *R (Naghshbandi) v Camden LBC HBRB* 19/07/02 CA [2002] EWCA Civ 1038 *www.bailii.org/ew/cases/EWCA/Civ/2002/1038.html*

8.46 *R (Laali) v Westminster CC HBRB* 08/12/00 QBD *www.casetrack.com* Subscriber site case reference: CO/1845/2000

8.47 *Burton v Camden LBC* 17/12/97 CA 30 HLR 991

8.55 *R v Swale BC HBRB ex p Marchant* See 4.35 above

8.57 *R v Beverley DC HBRB ex p Hare* 21/02/95 QBD 27 HLR 637

8.57 *Malcolm v Tweedale HBRB* 06/08/91 CS 1994 SLT 1212

8.58 *Malcolm v Tweedale HBRB* See 8.57 above

8.61 *R v East Devon DC HBRB ex p Gibson* 10/03/93 CA 25 HLR 487

8.62 *R v Sefton MBC ex p Cunningham* 22/05/91 QBD 23 HLR 534

8.63 *R v Westminster CC HBRB ex p Mehanne* 08/03/01 HL [2001] UKHL 11 33 HLR 46 *www.publications.parliament.uk/pa/ld200001/ldjudgmt/jd010308/mehann-1.htm*

8.63 *R v Beverley DC HBRB ex p Hare* See 8.57 above

8.63 *R v Brent LBC ex p Connery* 20/10/89 QBD 22 HLR 40

8.65 *R v Brent LBC ex p Connery* See 8.63 above

9.36 *R (Heffernan) v the Rent Service* 30/07/08 HL [2008] UKHL 58 *www.publications.parliament.uk/pa/ld200708/ldjudgmt/jd080730/heffer-1.htm*

10.36 *R v Swale BC HBRB ex p Marchant* See 4.35 above

13.127 *R v Doncaster MBC & Another ex p Boulton* 11/12/92 QBD 25 HLR 195

16.5 *R v Liverpool CC ex p Johnson (No 1)* 23/06/94 QBD unreported

16.6 *Waveney DC v Jones* 01/12/99 CA 33 HLR 3 *www.casetrack.com* Subscriber site case reference CCRTF 1998/1488/B2

16.13 *R (Spiropoulos) v Brighton and Hove CC* 06/02/07 QBD [2007] EWHC 342 (Admin) *www.bailii.org/ew/cases/EWHC/Admin/2007/342.html*

16.17 *R v Haringey LBC ex p Ayub* 13/04/92 QBD 25 HLR 566

16.33 *R v Haringey LBC ex p Ayub* See 16.17 above

16.60 *Bessa Plus PLC v Lancaster* 17/03/97 CA *www.bailii.org/ew/cases/EWCA/Civ/1997/1260.html*

17.12 *R v Passmore* 18/06/07 CA [2007] EWCA Crim 2053 *www.bailii.org/ew/cases/EWCA/Crim/2007/2053.html*

T 18.1 *R v Cambridge CC HBRB ex p Sier* 08/10/01 CA [2001] EWCA Civ 1523 *www.bailii.org/ew/cases/EWCA/Civ/2001/1523.html*

T 18.2 *R v Liverpool CC ex p Griffiths* 14/03/90 QBD 22 HLR 312

18.26 *R v South Hams DC ex p Ash* 10/05/99 QBD [1999] EWHC Admin 418 *www.bailii.org/ew/cases/EWHC/Admin/1999/418.html*

18.31 *Warwick DC v Freeman* 31/10/94 CA 27 HLR 616

18.50 *Secretary of State for Work and Pensions v Balding* 13/12/07 CA [2007] EWCA Civ 1327 *www.bailii.org/ew/cases/EWCA/Civ/2007/1327.html*

18.50 *R (Steele) v Secretary of State for Work and Pensions* 16/12/05 CA [2005] EWCA Civ 1824 *www.bailii.org/ew/cases/EWCA/Civ/2005/1824.html*

T 18.5 *R v Haringey LBC ex p Ayub* See 16.17 above

T 18.6 *R v Thanet DC ex p Warren Court Hotels Ltd* 06/04/00 QBD 33 HLR 32 *www.casetrack.com* Subscriber site case reference CO/523/1999

T 18.6 *Warwick DC v Freeman* See 18.30 above

T 18.6 *Godwin v Rossendale Borough Council* 03/05/02 CA [2002] EWCA Civ 726 *www.bailii.org/ew/cases/EWCA/Civ/2002/726.html*

T 18.6 *Haringey LBC v Awaritefe* 26/05/99 CA [1999] EWCA Civ 1491 *www.bailii.org/ew/cases/EWCA/Civ/1999/1491.html*

T 18.6 *Waveney DC v Jones* See 16.6 above

T 18.6 *Norwich CC v Stringer* 03/05/00 CA 33 HLR 15 *www.casetrack.com* Subscriber site case reference FC2 99/7400/B2

19.102 *R (Cumpsty) v The Rent Service* 08/11/02 HC [2002] EWHC 2526 Admin Admin *www.bailii.org/ew/cases/EWHC/Admin/2002/2526.html*

20.49 *Kempf v Staatsscretaris van Justitie* 03/06/86ECJ 139/85 *http://europa.eu.int/smartapi/cgi/sga_doc?smartapi!celexapi!prod!CELEXnumdoc&lg=EN&numdoc=61985J0139&model=guichett*

20.54 *Secretary of State for Work and Pensions v Lassal* 10/03/09 CA [2009] EWCA Civ 157
www.bailii.org/ew/cases/EWCA/Civ/2009/157.htm

20.59 *Raulin v Minister van Ondervijsen Wentenschappen* 26/02/92 ECJ C-357/89
http://europa.eu.int/smartapi/cgi/sga_doc?smartapi!celexapi!prod!CELEXnumdoc&lg=EN&numdoc=61989J0357&model=guichett

20.82 *Re J (A Minor) (Abduction)* 17/05/90 HL [1990] 2 AC 562

20.85 *Nessa v Chief Adjudication Officer* 21/10/99 HL [1999] UKHL 41 *www.publications.parliament.uk/pa/ld199899/ldjudgmt/jd991021/nessa.htm*

20.88 *Di Paolo v Office National de L'Emploi* 17/02/77 ECJ 76/76
http://europa.eu.int/smartapi/cgi/sga_doc?smartapi!celexapi!prod!CELEXnumdoc&lg=EN&numdoc=61976J0076&model=guichett

20.92 *Swaddling v Chief Adjudication Officer* 25/02/99 ECJ C-90/97
http://europa.eu.int/smartapi/cgi/sga_doc?smartapi!celexapi!prod!CELEXnumdoc&lg=EN&numdoc=61997J0090&model=guichett

21.8 *O'Connor v Chief Adjudication Officer* 03/03/99 CA [1999] EWCA Civ 884
www.bailii.org/ew/cases/EWCA/Civ/1999/884.html

22.6 *R (Gargett) v Lambeth LBC* 18/12/2008 CA [2008] EWCA Civ 1450
www.bailii.org/ew/cases/EWCA/Civ/2008/1450.htm

23.27 *R v Brent LBC ex p Connery* See 8.63 above

23.32 *R (Isle of Angelsey County Council) v Secretary of State for Work and Pensions* 30/10/03 QBD [2003] EWHC 2518 Admin
www.bailii.org/ew/cases/EWHC/Admin/2003/2518.html

23.32 *R (Lambeth LBC) v Secretary of State for Work and Pensions* 20/04/05 QBD [2005] EWHC 637 Admin
www.bailii.org/ew/cases/EWHC/Admin/2005/637.html

Abbreviations used in this appendix

AC	Appeal Cases, published by The Incorporated Council of Law Reporting for England and Wales, London
All ER	All England Law Reports, published by Butterworths
BC	Borough Council
CA	Court of Appeal for England and Wales
CC	City Council
ChD	High Court (England and Wales) Chancery Division
COD	Crown Office Digest, published by Sweet & Maxwell
CS	Court of Session, Scotland
DC	District Council
ECJ	European Court of Justice
EWCA Civ	Court of Appeal Civil Division for England & Wales (neutral citation)
EWCA Crim	Court of Appeal Criminal Division for England & Wales (neutral citation)
EWHC Admin	High Court for England & Wales, Administrative Court (neutral citation)
HBRB	Housing Benefit Review Board
HC (Admin)	High Court for England and Wales, Administrative Court
HL	House of Lords
HLR	Housing Law Reports, published by Sweet & Maxwell
LBC	London Borough Council
MBC	Metropolitan Borough Council
QBD	High Court (England and Wales) Queens Bench Division
SLT	Scots Law Times, published by W. Green, Edinburgh
UKHL	House of Lords, UK case (neutral citation)
WLR	Weekly Law Reports, published by The Incorporated Council of Law Reporting for England and Wales, London

Appendix 3: Current and recent HB and CTB circulars

This appendix lists:

- all DWP circulars in the 'A' (adjudication and operations) series issued since 1st April 2008 whether or not they have subsequently been superseded by a later circular or by amendments to the HBGM (up to amendment 18). Circulars that have been superseded are marked *;
- any other A circulars that have remained current since the issue of HBGM amendment 18; and
- all DWP circulars in the 'S' (subsidy) series since 1st April 2008.

Circulars in the 'G' (general), 'U' (urgent) and 'F' (fraud) series are not listed here (but see para. 1.46).

Adjudication and operation circulars

A17/2006 (Revised) November 2006
: Targeting working age cases to reduce fraud and error in HB

A20/2006 December 2006
: Changes to security Performance Measures

HB/CTB A13/2007 (November 2007)
: Funding details for the modernisation of the collection of HB/CTB administrative data

HB/CTB A2/2008 (January 2008)
: HB/CTB Performance indicators from April 2008

HB/CTB A3/2008 (February 2008)
: Recovery of overpayments after discharge of bankruptcy following 'Balding' judgment

HB/CTB A4/2008 (March 2008)
: HB Right Benefit Performance Indicator from April 2008

HB/CTB A5/2008 (March 2008)
: 2008/09 Single HB Extract: Guidance for local authorities

HB/CTB A6/2008 (April 2008)*
: [1] Disregard of payments to persons formerly in care, treatment of public lending right payments and cessation of intensive activity period for 50 Plus [2] In Work Credit

HB/CTB A7/2008 (April 2008)*
: Housing Benefit Matching Service and Data Take-on and Processing Schedule 30

HB/CTB A8/2008 (April 2008)*

[1] The child maintenance disregard

[2] Removal of pensioner premiums from the working age regulations and various other obsolete references

HB/CTB A9/2008 (May 2008)

Housing Benefit Data Service timetable and transfer of the Single HB Extract for 2008/09

HB/CTB A10/2008 (June 2008)

Right Benefit and Right Time Performance Indicators and Comprehensive Performance Assessment 2008

HB/CTB A11/2008 (June 2008)*

[1] Changes to the HB/CTB arising from the introduction of employment and support allowance

[2] Background and ESA policy

[3] How ESA affects HB/CTB

HB/CTB A12/2008 (Revised) (July 2008)*

[1] Changes to the extended payments schemes

[2] Extended payments qualifying income-related benefits scheme

[3] Extended payments qualifying contributory benefits scheme

HB/CTB A13/2008 (September 2008)

Housing Benefit Database and Matching Service timetable and process for 2007/08 returns

HB/CTB A14/2008 (Revised)(September 2008)*

Student support up-rating 2008/2009 (note original A14/2008 contained errors and was reissued in revised version)

HB/CTB A15/2008 (July 2008)*

Valuation of capital assets – new service agreement process changes from September

HB/CTB A16/2008 (September 2008)*

Changes to the backdating rules, including guidance on claims made by men aged 60-64

HB/CTB A17/2008 (October 2008)

Housing Benefit Data Service timetable and transfer of the HB Recoveries and Fraud Return for 2008/09

HB/CTB A18/2008 (October 2008)*

Guidance on the Employment and Support Allowance (Miscellaneous Amendments) Regulations 2008

HB/CTB A19/2008 (November 2008)

Better off in work credit pilot

HB/CTB A20/2008 (November 2008)*

Changes to telephone claims for pension credit cases

HB/CTB A21/2008 (November 2008)
[1] The new appeals system
[2] Appeals to the First-tier Tribunal
[3] Appeals to the Upper Tribunal
[4] Appeals to the higher courts

HB/CTB A22/2008 (November 2008)*
Guidance to local authorities for claimants living in supported accommodation including qualification for the 'old scheme' rules and the definition of 'exempt accommodation'

HB/CTB A23/2008 (November 2008)
[1] Right Time and Right Benefit performance indicators
[2] HB recoveries and fraud

HB/CTB A24/2008 (December 2008)
[1] Amendments to the overpayments regulations, which include changes to the provisions relating to 'recovery from a partner'
[2] Administrative delay
[3] Definition of fraud overpayment

HB/CTB A25/2008 (December 2008)*
Rapid Reclaim: Change to eligibility conditions

HB/CTB A26/2008 (December 2008)
[1] Guidance for local authorities on the in and out of work processes including Jobcentre Plus action
[2] The Housing Benefit and Council Tax Benefit (Amendment)(No. 3) Regulations 2008 which make the changes to support the changes in [1] detailing what information the claimant is required to supply

HB/CTB A27/2008 (December 2008)*
HB/CTB Up-rating from April 2009

HB/CTB A28/2008 (December 2008)
Revised process for the HB Recoveries and Fraud Return from 1 January 2009

HB/CTB A1/2009 (January 2009)
Gypsies and travellers - the Housing Benefit and Council Tax Benefit (Amendment)(No.2) Regulations 2008

HB/CTB A2/2009 (February 2009)
New claim forms for prisoners

HB/CTB A3/2009 (March 2009)
Right Time Performance Indicator and Single HB Extract -update for local authorities

HB/CTB A4/2009 (March 2009)
Change to the requirement for national insurance numbers for partners who are subject to immigration control or who have no right to reside

HB/CTB A5/2009 (March 2009)
Guidance on sale and rent back arrangements for people who used to own their own home

HB/CTB A6/2009 (March 2009)
Guidance on superseding awards to take account of a change of circumstances which has already come to an end (CIS/2595/03)

HB/CTB A7/2009 (March 2009)
Data Take On and Processing Schedule and Single Housing Benefit Extract data for 2009/10

HB/CTB A8/2009 (March 2009)
Right Benefit Performance Indicator: update for local authorities 2009/10

HB/CTB A9/2009 (March 2009)
Further amendments to take account of the introduction of Employment and Support Allowance

A10/2009 April 2009
The Social Security (Use of Information for Housing Benefit and Welfare Services Purposes) Regulations 2008

A11/2009 April 2009
Dealing with changes of circumstance

Subsidy circulars

HB/CTB S1/2008 (March 2008)
Details of the distribution of the government contribution and overall DHPs for 2008/2009

HB/CTB S2/2008 (March 2008)
Details of the allocation of funding for the implementation of Employment and Support Allowance (ESA)

HB/CTB S3/2008 (March 2008)
Rent Rebate Subsidy Limitation for 2008/2009

HB/CTB S4/2008 (September 2008)
subsidy arrangements 2009/10: Details of the specific grant for administration costs, distribution of the government contribution

HB/CTB S5/2008 (November 2008)
Non-Housing Revenue Account (HRA) rent rebate subsidy thresholds and caps 2009/10

HB/CTB S1/2009 (January 2009)
Details of the revised government DHPs contribution for 2009/10 for some local authorities

HB/CTB S2/2009 (January 2009)
Details of additional specific grant for administration costs for 2009/10

Appendix 4: HB and CTB rates and allowances (from April 2009)

Personal allowances

Single claimant		
	aged under 25 – on main phase ESA	£64.30
	aged under 25 – other	£50.95
	aged 25+ but under 60	£64.30
	aged 60+ but under 65	£130.00
	aged 65+	£150.40
Lone parent		
	aged under 18 – on main phase ESA	£64.30
	aged under 18 – other	£50.95
	aged 18+ but under 60	£64.30
	aged 60+ but under 65	£130.00
	aged 65+	£150.40
Couple		
	both under 18 – claimant on main phase ESA	£100.95
	both under 18 – other	£76.90
	at least one aged 18+ but both under 60	£100.95
	at least one aged 60+ but both under 65	£198.45
	at least one aged 65+	£222.50
Child/young person addition		£56.11

Premiums and components

1. 'Any age premiums'

Family	baby rate (at least one child under 1)	£27.80
	normal rate	£17.30
Disabled child	each dependent child	£51.24
Enhanced disability	each dependent child	£20.65
Severe disability	single rate	£52.85
	double rate	£105.70
Carer	claimant or partner or each	£29.50

2. 'Under 60 premiums'

Disability	single claimant/lone parent	£27.50
	couple (one/both qualifying)	£39.15
Enhanced disability	single claimant/lone parent	£13.40
	couple (one/both qualifying)	£19.30

3. ESA components

Work-related activity	£25.50
Support	£30.85

Earned income disregards

Standard disregard (highest one only)

Lone parent,	£25.00
Certain disabled, carers or others in select occupations	£20.00
Couple	£10.00
All others (single)	£5.00

Additional 16/30 hour work disregard

Where conditions are met (para. 14.24)	£16.85

Additional childcare disregard (maximum rate)

Qualifying childcare charges for one child	£175.00
Qualifying childcare charges for two or more children	£300.00

Non-dependant deductions in HB

Age 18 or over and working at least 16 hours

Gross income	
£382.00 or more	£47.75
£306.00 - £381.99	£43.50
£231.00 - £305.99	£38.20
£178.00 - £230.99	£23.35
£120.00 - £177.99	£17.00
Under £120.00	£7.40

Others not in work or working under 16 hours

On pension credit or under 25 on JSA(IB), IS or ESA(IR)	£0.00
Most others	£7.40

Non-dependant deductions in main CTB

Age 18 or over and working at least 16 hours

Gross income	
£382.00 or more	£6.95
£306.00 - £381.99	£5.80
£178.00 - £305.99	£4.60
Under £178.00	£2.30

All others not in work or working under 16 hours

On pension credit, JSA(IB), IS or ESA(IR)	£0.00
Most others	£2.30

Non-dependant deductions in NI rates

Age 18 or over and working at least 16 hours

Gross income	
£382.00 or more	£6.95
£306.00 - £381.99	£5.80
£178.00 - £305.99	£4.60
Under £178.00	£2.30

Others not in work or working under 16 hours

On pension credit, JSA(IB), IS or ESA(IR)	£0.00
Most others	£2.30

Second adult rebate

Circumstances	Amount of rebate
General	
All second adults on JSA(IB), IS or ESA(IR) or pension credit	25% of council tax
Second adults gross income under £169.00	15% of council tax
Second adults gross income £175.00 - £227.99	7.5% of council tax
Second adults gross income £228.00 or more	Nil
Student only	100% of council tax

Appendix 5: Selected benefit rates (from April 2009)

Attendance allowance	
Higher rate	£70.35
Lower rate	£47.10
Bereavement benefits	
Widowed parents allowance standard rate	£95.25
Bereavement allowance standard rate	£95.25
Reduction in standard rate for each year aged under 55 (approx)	£6.66
Child benefit*	
Only or older/oldest child	£20.00
Each other child	£13.20
Carer's allowance	
Claimant	£53.10
Disability living allowance	
Care component	
Highest rate	£70.35
Middle rate	£47.10
Lowest rate	£18.65
Mobility component	
Higher rate	£49.10
Lower rate	£18.65
Employment and support allowance	
Personal allowances	
Under 25/lone parent under 18	£50.95
20 or over/under 25 (main phase)	£64.30
Couple both under 18 with child	£76.90
Couple both over 18	£100.95
Components	
Work-related activity	£25.50
Support	£30.85

* from 5 January 2009

Guardian's allowance	£14.10
Incapacity benefit	
Short-term lower rate (under pension age)	£67.75
Short-term higher rate (under pension age)	£80.15
Long-term rate	£89.80
Spouse or adult dependant (where appropriate)	£53.10
Increase for age higher rate (under 35)	£15.65
Increase for age lower rate (35-44)	£6.55
Industrial disablement pension	
20% disabled	£28.72
For each further 10% disability up to 100%	£14.36
100% disabled	£143.60
Jobseeker's allowance (contribution-based)	
Aged under 18 to 24	£50.95
Aged 25 or more	£64.30
Maternity and paternity benefits	
Statutory maternity, paternity and adoption pay	£123.06
Maternity allowance	£123.06
Retirement pension	
Single person (basic rate)	£95.25
Couple (basic rate)	£152.30
Severe disablement allowance	
Basic rate	£57.45
Age-related addition	
Higher rate	£15.65
Middle rate	£9.10
Lower rate	£5.35
Statutory sick pay	
Standard rate	£79.15

For details of other benefit rates from April 2009 (including means-tested benefits, tax credits and war pensions) see Circular A27/2008.

Appendix 6: Non-dependant categories

For the following categories of non-dependant, this appendix describes:

- whether there is a non-dependant deduction for them in HB and CTB (paras. 6.17-20);
- whether they are a 'disregarded person' for second adult rebate purposes – because a disregarded person cannot be a second adult (para 6.44).

1. People on JSA(IB), ESA(IR) or income support

HB	No non-dependant deduction if aged under 25 – but for ESA(IR) this is true only in their ESA 'assessment phase' (first 13 weeks)
CTB	No non-dependant deduction.
Second adult rebate	Not 'disregarded persons'.

This means anyone receiving JSA(IB), ESA(IR) or income support, including people who would get JSA(IB) or ESA(IR) except that they are currently subject to a sanction or in their 'waiting days' (first three days).

2. People on pension credit

HB and CTB	No non-dependant deduction.
Second adult rebate	Not 'disregarded persons'.

This means anyone receiving guarantee credit or savings credit (or both).

3. People under 18

HB and CTB	No non-dependant deduction.
Second adult rebate	'Disregarded persons'.

This means anyone under 18 whether a member of the claimant's family or not.

4. People under 20 for whom child benefit is payable

HB and CTB	No non-dependant deduction.
Second adult rebate	'Disregarded persons'.

This means anyone under 20 for whom someone receives or could receive child benefit – e.g. at school and shortly after leaving school. See also category 7.

5. Full-time students (benefit law definition)

HB	No non-dependant deduction (with exceptions during the summer holidays: table 6.2)
CTB	No non-dependant deduction
Second adult rebate	'Disregarded persons'.

This means:

- a student in further education (para. 21.16) who is normally expected to undertake more than 16 guided learning hours per week; or
- a student in higher education (para. 21.17) on a course which is regarded as full-time by the academic establishment and/or the local education authority; or
- a student on a sandwich course.

6. Students (council tax law definition)

HB	Whether there is a non-dependant deduction depends on whether they fall within category 5.
CTB	No non-dependant deduction
Second adult rebate	'Disregarded persons'.

This means:

- a student in further or higher education (paras. 21.16-17) – who is on a course of at least one academic or calendar year's duration, and is normally required to study at least 21 hours per week for at least 24 weeks per year; or
- a student under 20 in further education (para. 21.16) – who is on a course of at least three months' duration, and is normally required to study at least 12 hours per week in term times;
- a student nurse studying for a first inclusion in parts 1 to 6 or 8 of the nursing register; or
- a foreign language assistant who is registered with the British Council.

7. Education leavers under 20

HB	A non-dependant deduction applies.
CTB	No non-dependant deduction.
Second adult rebate	'Disregarded persons'.

This only applies from 1st May to 31st October inclusive each year. It means anyone who leaves any of the types of education described in category 6 within that period. It lasts until that person reaches 20 or until 31st October, whichever comes first. See also categories 2 and 3.

8. Youth trainees

HB and CTB	No non-dependant deduction.
Second adult rebate	'Disregarded persons' if aged under 25.

This means people doing youth training funded by the Learning and Skills Council for England or equivalent bodies in Wales and Scotland.

9. Apprentices

HB	A non-dependant deduction applies.
CTB	No non-dependant deduction.
Second adult rebate	'Disregarded persons'.

This means someone who:

- is in employment; and
- is studying for a qualification accredited by the Qualifications and Curriculum Authority (England) or National Assembly (Wales) or Scottish Vocational Education Council (Scotland); and
- is paid no more than £195 per week.

10. Carers for whom the claimant or partner is charged

HB and CTB	No non-dependant deduction.
Second adult rebate	'Disregarded persons' only if they fall within categories 11 or 12.

This means carers caring for the claimant or partner, who are provided by a charitable or voluntary body which charges the claimant or partner for this.

11. Carers of people receiving certain benefits

HB	A non-dependant deduction applies unless they fall within category 10.
CTB	No non-dependant deduction.
Second adult rebate	'Disregarded persons'.

This applies to someone if:

- they are providing care or support for at least 35 hours a week; and
- they reside with the person receiving the care or support; and
- that person is not a child of theirs under 18, nor their partner; and
- that person is entitled to the highest rate of the care component of disability living allowance, or a higher rate attendance allowance, or equivalent additions to industrial injuries and war pensions.

12. Carers introduced by an official or charitable body

HB	A non-dependant deduction applies unless they fall within category 10.
CTB	No non-dependant deduction.
Second adult rebate	'Disregarded persons'.

This means someone who:

- is employed by someone to provide them with care or support for at least 24 hours a week; and
- is paid no more than £44 per week; and
- resides (for the better performance of the work) in premises provided by or on behalf of that person; and
- was introduced to them by a local authority, government department or charitable body.

13. People who are 'severely mentally impaired'

HB	A non-dependant deduction applies.
CTB	No non-dependant deduction.
Second adult rebate	'Disregarded persons'.

This means someone who has 'a severe impairment of intelligence and social functioning (however caused) which appears to be permanent'; and has a medical certificate confirming this; and is receiving one or more of the following (or would do so apart from the fact that he or she has reached pension age):

- the highest or middle rate of the care component of disability living allowance, or attendance allowance or equivalent additions to industrial injuries and war pensions; or
- incapacity benefit, or severe disablement allowance; or
- income support or JSA(IB) (or his or her partner is) – but only if it includes a disability premium awarded because of the person's incapacity for work.

14. Members of religious communities

HB	A non-dependant deduction applies.
CTB	No non-dependant deduction.
Second adult rebate	'Disregarded persons'.

This means someone who:

- is a member of a religious community whose principal occupation is prayer, contemplation, education, the relief of suffering, or any combination of those; and
- has no income (other than an occupational pension) or capital; and
- is dependent on the community for his or her material needs.

15. International bodies and visiting forces

HB	A non-dependant deduction applies.
CTB	No non-dependant deduction.
Second adult rebate	'Disregarded persons'.

This means someone who is a member of certain international headquarters and defence organisations and certain visiting forces (plus in some cases their dependants).

16. Non-British spouses and civil partners

HB	A non-dependant deduction applies.
CTB	No non-dependant deduction.
Second adult rebate	'Disregarded persons'.

This means someone who is not permitted to work or claim and is the husband, wife or civil partner of:

- a student in category 6; or
- an education leaver in category 7; or
- a person in category 15.

17. Long-term hospital patients

HB and CTB	No non-dependant deduction.
Second adult rebate	'Disregarded persons'.

This means someone who has been in an NHS hospital for more than 52 weeks (adding together stays in hospital if the break between them is four weeks or less).

18. People in prison or other forms of detention

HB	No non-dependant deduction.
CTB	No non-dependant deduction unless detained only for non-payment of a fine or (in England and Wales) council tax.
Second adult rebate	'Disregarded persons' unless detained only for non-payment of a fine or (in England and Wales) council tax.

This means someone in any kind of detention (whether on bail, on remand or serving a sentence).

19. Other people not resident in the dwelling

HB and CTB	No non-dependant deduction.
Second adult rebate	'Disregarded persons'.

This means anyone who is not normally resident in the dwelling including, for example, a visitor or to a student returning just for the holidays.

20. Anyone else

HB and CTB	A non-dependant deduction applies.
Second adult rebate	Not 'disregarded persons'.

This means anyone who does not fall into any of the previous categories.

Appendix 7: DWP rent arrears direct scheme

This appendix describes how the DWP can pay part of a claimant's JSA, ESA, IS or pension credit to their landlord towards arrears of their rent. These are called 'direct payments' or officially 'third party payments'. They are additional to the rules about paying HB to a landlord (paras. 16.27-48). Indeed, they are not HB rules at all, but they so often arise in HB cases that they are included here for reference.

The law is in schedule 9 to the Social Security (Claims and Payments) Regulations SI 1987/1968 (as amended) or in Northern Ireland NISR 1987/465 (as amended). For DWP guidance see GM paras. D1.570-689.

Qualifying conditions for direct payments

The power to make direct payments is discretionary even if all the qualifying conditions are met. The qualifying conditions are that the claimant or their partner must be:

- in receipt of a 'qualifying benefit'; and
- in receipt of HB (or claimed HB in the case of a hostel resident); and
- resident in the property for which the direct payments are to be made; and
- either:
  - they have rent arrears and meet one of the rent arrears conditions; or
  - (regardless of whether they have rent arrears or not) they live in a hostel (para. 10.21) for which the overall charge includes payment for one or more of the following services: water; a service charge for fuel; meals; laundry or cleaning (other than communal areas) and the DWP determines that direct payments should be made.

Qualifying benefits for direct payments

The qualifying benefits from which deductions can be made are:

- income support;
- state pension credit (savings credit or guarantee credit or both);
- income-based jobseeker's allowance;
- income-related employment and support allowance;
- contribution-based jobseekers' allowance if there would be entitlement to income-based jobseekers' allowance but for the fact that contribution-based jobseeker's allowance is being paid at the same rate;
- contribution-based employment and support allowance if income-related employment and support allowance would otherwise be payable but for the fact that contribution-based employment and support allowance is being paid at the same rate.

In addition, in the case where any of the first three qualifying benefits are in payment and the amount is insufficient for deductions to be made, deductions can also be made from any contribution-based jobseekers' allowance, incapacity benefit, retirement pension or severe disablement allowance that they also receive (whether or not it is paid in a combined payment with the qualifying benefit).

What are the rent arrears conditions?

There must be 'rent arrears' of at least four times the gross weekly rent and either:

- the rent arrears have accrued or persisted over a period of at least eight weeks and the landlord requests that deductions are made; or
- the rent arrears have accrued or persisted over a period of less than eight weeks but in the opinion of the DWP it is in the overriding interests of the family that payments should be made.

In calculating the four weeks' arrears and any period over which those arrears have accrued, any arrears which have arisen due to the tenant's failure to pay a non-dependant charge must be ignored.

What counts as rent and rent arrears?

For these rules 'rent' and 'rent arrears' includes:

- any charge which is covered by HB;
- any water charges or service charges payable with the rent which are ineligible for HB;
- fuel charges included in the rent provided the charge does not vary more than twice a year;
- any other inclusive charge paid with the rent, whether or not it is eligible for HB, except any unpaid non-dependant charge.

Note that because of the requirement for residence (see qualifying conditions) direct payments cannot be made of former tenant arrears.

Rate of payment

In the case of direct payments for a hostel, the amount of the payment will be the same as whatever amount of the charge is ineligible for HB for water, fuel, etc.

In the case of direct payments for rent arrears the rate of payment will, subject to any maximum amount, be:

- £3.25 per week (the standard amount), plus, if it applies,
- the weekly charge for any fuel or water charged as part of the rent, provided that the qualifying benefit is at least equal to that charge.

When all of the rent arrears have been cleared, weekly payment of the amount for fuel or water can continue if it is in the 'interests of the family'.

Maximum deductions for rent arrears cases

In the case of direct payments for rent arrears, the rate of deduction from any qualifying benefit will be subject to the following rules:

- There must be at least 10 pence of any qualifying benefit(s) remaining after any deduction.
- If the standard amount together with any ongoing fuel/water exceeds 25% of their qualifying benefit applicable amount (or where child tax credit is payable, 25% of their applicable amount plus child tax credit and child benefit) then the deduction cannot be made without the claimant's consent.
- If there are standard deductions for several items such as rent, fuel, water, council tax, child maintenance and fines, the total cannot exceed £9.75.
- If there are deductions for various other debts such that the total would reduce the qualifying benefit to less than 10p, then they are paid in the following order of priority:
  - 1st rent arrears;
  - 2nd fuel;
  - 3rd water;
  - 4th council tax;
  - 5th unpaid fines;
  - 6th child support;
  - 7th repayments of a refugee integration loan
  - 8th loan repayments to certain qualifying affordable credit lenders (e.g. credit unions)

Appendix 8: Overview of welfare benefits

This appendix lists the welfare benefits which have particular relevance in the assessment of HB and CTB. It is for ready reference, uses simplified descriptions, and does not attempt to give all the rules. In this table:

✔ **'Passport benefits'** are the ones which mean the claimant gets maximum ('full') HB/CTB.
'Income-related' means entitlement to the benefit depends on income (as well as other things).
'Contributory' means the person must have paid enough national insurance contributions at some point.

HB: Housing benefit and **CTB:** Council tax benefit
These help lower income people with rent and council tax.
Income-related; non-contributory.

✔ **PC(G):** Pension credit guarantee credit (or just Guarantee credit)
The last resort benefit for 60+s. A passport benefit.
Income-related; non-contributory.

PC(S): Pension credit savings credit (or just Savings credit)
The benefit that says 'thank you' to 65+s who made some provision (not too much) for retirement.
Income-related; contributory.

✔ **JSA(IB):** Income-based jobseeker's allowance
The last resort benefit for people under 60 who are expected to work so have to sign on. A passport benefit.
Income-related; non-contributory.

JSA(C): Contribution-based job-seeker's allowance
The benefit (which lasts for up to 26 weeks) for people who are expected to work so have to sign on.
Contributory; not income-related.

✔ **ESA(IR):** Income-related employment and support allowance
The last resort benefit for people under 60 who cannot work because they have a limited capability to do so. A passport benefit.
Income-related; non-contributory.
Starts with **assessment phase ESA(IR)** for 13 weeks, followed by **main phase ESA(IR).**

ESA(C): Contributory employment and support allowance
The benefit for people who cannot work because they have a limited capability to do so.
Contributory; not income-related.
Starts with **assessment phase ESA(C)** for 13 weeks, followed by **main phase ESA(C).**

✔ **IS:** Income support
The last resort benefit for under 60s who do not qualify for JSA or ESA – for example, lone parents. A passport benefit.
Income-related; non-contributory.

IB: Incapacity benefit
This was replaced by ESA for new claimants from 27th October 2008 (but many still get it). It is for people who cannot work because of incapacity.
Contributory; not income-related.

DLA: Disability living allowance – is in two types, neither of them income-related or contributory:
Care component is for people needing personal care; awarded at a lower, middle or higher rate.
Mobility component is for people with difficulty walking; awarded at a lower or higher rate.

AA: Attendance allowance
The equivalent of DLA care component for 65+s.

WTC: Working tax credit and **CTC:** Child tax credit
The benefits for lower to middle income people who are in work.
Income-related; non-contributory.

CA: Carer's allowance
The benefit for people who are prevented from working by caring responsibilities.
Partly income-related; non-contributory.

Index

References in the index are to paragraph numbers (not page numbers), except that 'A' refers to appendices, 'T' refers to tables in the text and 'Ch' refers to a chapter.

A

B

C

D

E

F

G

H

I

J

L

M

N

O

P

Q

R

S

T

U

V

W

Y